Cyberspace and International Relations

Jan-Frederik Kremer · Benedikt Müller
Editors

Cyberspace and International Relations

Theory, Prospects and Challenges

Springer

Editors
Jan-Frederik Kremer
Center for Global Studies (CGS)
University of Bonn
Bonn
Germany
Friedrich Naumann Foundation
for Freedom
Berlin
Germany

Benedikt Müller
IBM
Düsseldorf
Germany

ISBN 978-3-642-37480-7 ISBN 978-3-642-37481-4 (eBook)
DOI 10.1007/978-3-642-37481-4
Springer Heidelberg New York Dordrecht London

Library of Congress Control Number: 2013950724

Printed on acid-free paper

Springer is part of Springer Science+Business Media (www.springer.com)

Foreword

Today we are on the cusp of a "Cybered Conflict"[1] age in which war as we knew it is likely to be difficult to bound, longer, more covert, more surprising in its scale, targets, and tempo, and ultimately more difficult to discern its beginning, end, adversaries, and motivations. All future conflicts will be 'cybered' in that seminal events will need cyber mechanisms in order to occur. In this emergent form of struggle, 'cybered' adversaries will be using cyberspace to undermine the systemic resilience of a variety of other state and non-state actors long before any overt crisis, public declaration of hostilities, or direct efforts to disable key internal elements of a state. The more open the international cyberspace—best viewed as an increasingly universal 'substrate' to all societies, the more layers of opponents enabled by the global web will be involved in any conflict. It will be difficult to determine who is doing what in the myriad of operations ranging from those directly involved, to fellow travelers and proxies, to those merely opportunistically engaged because they can do so easily in the global digitally connected world. National sovereignty will be routinely challenged along a host of avenues into critical systems, perceptions of reality, and, importantly, economic resources including knowledge processes.

As state leaders respond to the overwhelming insecurities posed by this globally open and unregulated 'substrate,' the international system's topology will be changing as well. A rising "Cyber Westphalian" [2] process likely to take 20 years to solidify will define the accepted characteristics of national jurisdictions in cybered terms. Decisions taken over this transitional generation will establish what is recognized as 'responsible' state cybered behaviors, what constitutes 'cyber power' in terms of institutionalized "systemic resilience and disruption" capabilities of individual states, and where along the 'cybered conflict spectrum' the traditional kinetic war is perceived to initiate. We are at the end of the frontier period in the evolution of cyberspace during which it spread openly and globally as substrate underpinning most critical processes of modern civil society. Now, we are moving into the transitional conflict era in which the nations struggle over control of the

[1] Demchak (2011)

[2] Demchak and Peter (2011)

wealth formed in and through the frontier. At the end of this turbulence, as has always happened, the international system will regularize the rights and holdings of winners and losers. Nations in the coming cyber-bordered international system will have made informed 'systemic' decisions that developed and nurtured their 'security resilience' and wellbeing over this era, or will have poorly perceived the calls to action. Only the former will be considered secure 'cyber powers,' and they will in turn heavily influence what dominates the next 'socio-cyber-economic systems' evolution of our global system [3].

In directly addressing many of these pressing issues, this book contributes to the field of international relations which is currently lagging behind enormous evolutions in the reality of conflict and competitive relations among major actors of the changing international system. Across the policymaking, military, and scholarly communities, only the latter has resisted adapting to the new characteristics of this emergent cybered conflict age. Increasingly, the policymakers and security communities of modern democratic civil societies have recognized and reacted to the global spread of a cyberspace substrate and its changes to the international environment. The militaries of the digitizing democratic and nondemocratic world have already recognized the globally open cyberspace's mutagenic effects on the established forms of conflict. In what many have called the 'cyberization of the military,' we are now seeing the formation of national cyber commands or their equivalents [4]. Policymakers in Europe, North America, and elsewhere have already issued or are writing national cyber security policies and laws. Yet the seminal thinkers of international relations seem bound to their theories developed during a much different, western norms-dominated liberal international system. Such legacy analyses do not capture the emerging world nor adequately explain major events such as the unprecedented rise of China in a single decade given the enormous scale of its poverty. Even the sudden economic collapse of otherwise wealthy western economies due to a cascade across a tightly integrated international financial system in 2008 has not spawned reconsideration of legacy presumptions across the field of international relations.

What this volume offers is a corrective to help the international relations field to recognize the systemic effects of the depth and rapidity of the global and largely unmonitored spread of the cyberspace substrate throughout the critical systems of modern and modernizing nations. It is also a call for more research among scholars who view the world as a system. Cyberizing the thinking of international relations scholars requires published works that challenge them to think beyond state–state conflicts of the past, beyond game or power theories that rest largely on isolating events from the new reality of a host of interrelated and ever more deeply integrated substate systems. The international system now is being shaped by the huge scale of institutional state and non-state players making individual decisions that alter critical oil flows, the magnitude in losses in critical economic knowledge investments from

[3] Demchak (2012)

[4] Demchak (2013)

cybercrime, to tumultuous transnational financial flows driven by computers, and to the slow, steady degradation of future options due to turbulent weather and climate change. The cumulative result is unprecedented for human societies in which distant, unexpected bad outcomes harming one nation or part of the world can ripple through the connections to unrelated communities and harm them. Yet international relations scholars have been slow to widen their view of relevant systems. The lag is in part due to how the civil society democracies emerged within geographic boundaries and were able to move their conflicts largely to outside their own borders. In the pre-cybered eras, largely western communities could establish effective governments able to enforce contracts and ensure value in currency, while disconnecting issues of militaries and war from the normalcy of the rest of the national wellbeing. The vast majority of scholars of international relations in western civil society democracies grew up in this rather well parsed international world. The literature reflects this cognitive habit of speculating profoundly on foreign affairs and war without having to accommodate the rest of their national systems. The field thus became purified and unable to address emergent events with clearly systemic implications. A book such as this is needed to help the willing, but the unwilling, among the field of international relations scholars to see the need to update their worldviews and adopt a more inclusive 'systemic' weltanschauung across the field.

The scope of this foreword does not allow comments on all the authors and their contributions. However, several chapters are worthy of note due to their attempt to contribute terms of art and thus the analytical frameworks useful for scholars and future leaders in evolving the field of international relations for a deeply cybered world. One learns across this book that the global cyberspace substrate has undermined the older distinctions between international and domestic, between peace and war, between state and non-state actors, and between technology, politics, and economics. Today the world is increasingly existentially dependent on the global cyberspace substrate that is beset by actors able to use cyberspace's "connectivity, content, and cognition[5]" against peace, prosperity, and stability. Hanna Kassab ("In Search of Cyber Stability International Relations, Mutually Assured Destruction and the Age of Cyber Warfare") makes an argument similar to John Mallery's "work factors" strategy [6] and my own 'security resilience' strategy as essential elements of deterrence theory. Even what she terms a "virus wall" furthers stability among nations by increasing the costs of successful offense and thereby make defense less expensive for nations effectively defending their emergent cyber jurisdictions. Moving beyond the concrete, Katherina Below ("The Utility of Timeless Thoughts Hannah Arendt's Conceptions of Power and Violence in the Age of Cyberization") argues for consideration of how states conceptualize the threats and their responses. This application of Arendt's allows international scholars to look across fields, and consider domestic decisions with international cybered conflict

[5] Kuehl (2007)

[6] Mallery (2011) published in summary form in Demchak, "Resilience, Disruption, and a 'Cyber Westphalia': Options for National Security in a Cybered Conflict World."

implications. For example, one could consider the evolution and relative successes of a nation's cyber power' expressed in the establishment of national resilience and disruption capabilities across institutions, policies, and strategies in terms of achieving "power to" impede or "power over key elements of the society."

Moving even further into new perspectives on traditional issues, John Karlsrud ("Peacekeeping 4.0 Harnessing the Potential of Big Data, Social Media, and Cyber Technologies") offers one of the more forward looking proposals by engaging the technologically lagging but much loved peacekeeping activities of the collective international community with possible alternative and more effective futures using big data, including social media, and the myriad of other new cybered developments. One can easily foresee a more positive international system in which destructive forces are on the backfoot in many areas due to novel uses of cyberspace. Other international conundrums could benefit from considering his challenge to update such as development studies laud the widespread use of cell phones as bank equivalents in the developing world, but pay little attention to the consequences of loss of security in cell phone companies holding the resources of whole segments of poor populations. One could ask what international disputes may be dampened if environmentalists and the UN worked to use UAVs to conduct real-time protection for the unarmed animals against heavily armed poachers who routinely overwhelm and kill brave park rangers. Peacekeeping in the emergent cybered conflict age has many tools already available for use or repurposing, but so far unexplored fully. Karlsrud has very helpfully opened up a debate that should be critically and immediately engaged.

In one further area of note, this book captures several debates as they stand today, as well as possibly new elements of an emergent lexicon. The chapters with calls for "norms" to be developed and, by inference, imposed by the senior nations of the global deeply cybered community of nations such as the US are part of a widely circulating variety of arguments about how and who might best nurture a less conflictual cybered international system. It is to be expected that this book would reflect those discussions. Several interesting chapters, however, offer new terms useful in decomposing the cognitive and structural complexity of cybered conflict. If the terms capture a complex process in a short form or image such as "lawfare[7]" or "cyber Westphalia,[8]" then a form of 'semantic infiltration' slowly alters the perceptions of scholars and activists alike and open up cognitive opportunities for new theorization and new strategic discussions. In particular, Matthew Crosston ("Phreak the Speak: the Flawed Communications within Cyber Intelligentsia") offers the term, a "Chinese knowledge wall," to capture the enduring dichotomy between the technically literate and the political systems focused scholars and practitioners long noted by the scholars of the large-scale socio-technical systems (LTS) literature such as Mayntz and Hughes, Comfort, and LaPorte, among others[9]. Crosston argues that this dichotomy is particularly influential in an

[7] Dunlap (2003)

[8] Demchak and Dombrowski (2011)

[9] Mayntz and Hughes (2010)

increasingly conflictual cybered international system because the intellectual and cognitive barriers also inhibit progressive cooperation between domestic communities, and inevitably between nations.

In applying her phrase, the "cyberization of global governance," Roxana Radu ("'Power Technology and Powerful Technologies Global Governmentality and Security in the Cyberspace") links the technological choices previously seen as irrelevant to international politics to the topology changing 'glocalization'[10] and 'Westphalian' processes of a cybered world. Radu then makes a solid observation that missing is a robust inclusive and dialectical approach to cyber security within and among nations that could offer ways to shape this process to a less contentious future. Oliver Read ("How the 2010 Attack on Google Changed the US Government's Threat Perception of Economic Cyber Espionage") uses the 2010 STUXNET attack case in order to provide an analytical framework labeled "threat politics." The chapter uses a modern case to capture and update the age-old process by which influential actors in deeply bureaucratic, civil society democracies use 'scare-analytics'[11] to reframe the perceptions of key policymakers and thus their response to threats.

Scholars of both social and technological sciences interested in how their cybered world is likely to evolve over the next 20 years need this volume among others now emerging to update, broaden, or challenge their perspectives and understandings. Practitioners need to consider future counterfactuals raised by the issues discussed here. Will the collective global community be able to use peacekeeping effectively if the theories of conflict, the institutions making decisions and those implementing them, and the tools given to peacekeepers remain mired in a pre-cybered perspective, while adversaries do not? Can the wellbeing of many societies be maintained without breaking into destructive conflict if major state and non-state actors use with impunity the ambiguities of an open cyberspace or the masking benefits of a closed cybered jurisdiction to deprive major populations of their resources, access to knowledge, or future? If major conflicts can occur over years that deliberately degrade the resilience of large populations, slowly denying them services and wellbeing, and yet no action directly triggers the law of armed conflict, how is the international relations theory focused on interstate kinetic war to have meaning for this emergent age of cybered conflict and for the coming cyber Westphalian international system? This book places a marker in dealing with these kinds of critical questions at a pivotal point in time.

Chris C. Demchak
Codirector, Center for Cyber Conflict Studies (C3S)
United States Naval War College
Newport, RI, USA

[10] Robertson (1995)

[11] John Mallery of MIT, Cambridge, MA, is credited with innovating this term in multiple briefings beginning in 2009.

1 References

Comfort, L., Boin, A., & Demchak, C. (2010). *Designing resilience: Preparing for extreme events*. Pittsburgh: University of Pittsburgh Press.

Demchak, C. C. (2011). *Wars of disruption and resilience: Cybered conflict, power, and national security*. Athens, Georgia, USA: University of Georgia Press.

Demchak, C. C. & Dombrowski, P. J. (2011). Rise of a cybered westphalian age. *Strategic Studies Quarterly5*(1), 31–62.

Demchak, C. C. (2012). Resilience, disruption, and a 'cyber westphalia': Options for national security in a cybered conflict world. In N. Burns & J. Price (Eds.),*Securing cyberspace: A new domain for national security* (pp. 59–94). Washington, DC: The Aspen Institute.

Demchak, C. C. (2013). manuscript forthcoming, Cyber Commands: Organizing For Cyber Security and Resilience in the Cybered Conflict Age.

Dunlap Jr, C. J. (2003). It Ain't No Tv Show: Jags and Modern Military Operations. *Chicago Journal of International Law*, *4*, 479.

Kuehl, D. (2007). The information revolution and the transformation of warfare. In Karl. M. M., de Leeuw & J. Bergstra (Eds.), *The History of information security: A comprehensive handbook* (pp. 821–832). Amsterdam, Netherlands: Elsevier Science.

LaPorte, T. R. (1975). *Organized social complexity: Challenge to politics and policy*. Princeton, New Jersey, USA: Princeton University Press.

Mayntz, R. & Hughes, T. (1988). *The Development of Large Technical Systems (Lts)*. Boulder, Colorado: Westview Press.

Mallery, J. C. (2011). *Draft Technical Memo: 'Traffic Tainting at Boundaries: A Thought Experiment in Cyber Defense*'. Cambridge: MIT.

Robertson, R. (1995). Glocalization: Time-Space and Homogeneity-Heterogeneity. *Global modernities*. (pp. 25–44).

Preface

Although the emergence and ever increasing diffusion of the cyberspace have most obviously significant implications for international politics, global economic activity, and transnational social relations, there is still a cloudy spot in research in terms of addressing these implications theoretically and empirically in one comprehensive and wide-ranging volume. Of course there is a vast number of articles and books on security-related issues of the cyberspace (cyber security, cyber warfare, cyber power, and so forth) as well as on the processes and the modalities of what we may call the digital transnationalization of social spaces and relations, but an inclusive volume on the implications of the process of "cyberization" of international relations (IR) has been missing until now. "Cyberization" of IR refers to the ongoing penetration of all different fields of activity of international relations by different mediums of the cyberspace on the one hand, and the growing dependence of actors in IR on infrastructure, instruments, and means offered by the cyberspace on the other hand. Because of the evolution of a "cyberization" of IR and due to the ever-increasing relevance of the cyberspace for contemporary international politics and global economic and social activities, there is profound need for political scientists and scholars of IR to identify, describe, and explain these developments, prospects, and emerging challenges theoretically and empirically in an accurate manner.

Therefore, this book brings together scholars and scientist as well as experts from cyberspace's everyday practice, to provide elaborated and sophisticated answers as well as deep insights about how to cope conceptually, theoretically, and empirically with the relation of *Cyberspace and International Relations*.

Based on the observation that there is not only a considerable deficiency of knowledge on the topic in political science and IR, but also a significant lack of discussion and debate with scholars and experts from other fields of practical and academic work, the idea for a project came up that should tackle this "agonizing lightness" by combining the forces of scholars from different disciplines and practical experts alike. It was obvious from the beginning that a project that should equally address theoretical as well as empirical implications of the cyberspace for international relations would need an editorial team and authors who could rely on academic expertise as well as practical experience in the field. Consequently, the idea was born to invite scholars and practitioners from various fields of activity to join the effort of creating a collective volume that engages the relationship of cyberspace and international relations from as many points of view as possible. The editors hope that this volume is able to contribute to supporting an interdisciplinary and sophisticated debate on the implications of the process of "cyberization" of IR.

To achieve this goal, Part I of the project brings together authors that present their thoughts on how to conceptually and theoretically enlighten the relationship of the cyberspace and international relations, to discuss implications for the discipline of IR and to present fresh and innovative theoretical approaches. By presenting approaches and frameworks that either deal with the general relation of IR and the cyberspace or that develop theoretical approaches to explain the dynamics of this relation in specific fields of activity (like cyber security, cyber warfare, diffusion of information and knowledge through the cyberspace, interconnectedness of economic and social activities through the cyberspace etc.) part I of the project enhances the theoretical and conceptual knowledge on the interaction of the cyberspace and IR. This opening part of the book brings together conceptual and theoretical contributions on the relation of the cyberspace and IR (in terms of actors, spaces, fields of activity etc.), to foster and improve our understanding of the consequences, effects, and implications of the process of "cyberization" for states' security, power positioning, interest achievement, diplomatic activity among others, as well as for economic and civil actors that are likewise affected by the "cyberization" of IR.

The opening chapter of part I, "Power Technology and Powerful Technologies: Global Governmentality and Security in the Cyberspace" by Roxana Radu argues that the best way to grasp the impact of the cyberspace on IR is to study the reconfiguration of global governance techniques brought about by the virtual mediums. By applying the Foucauldian concept of governmentality to investigate the global discourses of security in the cyberspace, this chapter sheds light on a shift in the rationality of governing, and gives empirical evidence of the dominant discourse(s) of security in the cyberspace in the United Nations (UN) ambit. The chapter therefore delivers solid knowledge on how technologies and practices related to the cyberspace shape international politics and IR more generally.

In his chapter "Cyber War and Strategic Thought: Do the Classic Theorists Still Matter?" Craig B. Greathouse tackles the important question of whether or not classical theorist of IR can still be seen as a valuable source of explanation for understanding war, warfare, and conflict in the realm of the cyberspace. With a special emphasis on the strategic options available for states in the field the chapter offers a clear and distinctive typology to view issues of cyber conflict, based on the thoughts of some of our discipline's most influential thinkers. Furthermore, it offers an examination of possible strategic choices for policy makers based on classic strategic thought. The chapter applies the ideas of Clausewitz, Sun Tzu, Jomini, along with more modern theorists such as Douhet and Warden to the idea of cyber war. In doing so the chapter convincingly elaborates the importance of classic and modern thinkers for explaining the implications of cyber warfare and cyber security.

In their contribution, "SAM: A Framework to Understand Emerging Challenges to States in an Interconnected World" Jan-Frederik Kremer, and Benedikt Müller present a new framework to identify and evaluated challenges to states in relation to the cyberspace. Based on the observation, that states and enterprises are increasingly faced with newly emerging threats made possible by interconnected digital infrastructures and that these threats pose different levels of risk to states and their citizens, the chapter identifies the different types of stakeholders, their actions and respective motives in the context of cyber security and introduces the so-called SAM-framework to estimate whether or not a challenge poses a severe risk to the security of the state.

Hanna Samir Kassab ("In Search of Cyber Stability: International Relations, Mutually Assured Destruction and the Age of Cyber Warfare") focuses in his chapter on the possibility of a reliable cyber deterrence option. After a discussion of deterrence theory and the potential of its application for the realm of the cyberspace, Kassab discusses the argument of a virus wall as functional instrument of deterrence. In doing so Kassab's chapter distributes to the theoretical debate on deterrence and its use in the area of cyberspace.

In her chapter "Offense–Defense Balance in Cyber Warfare" Salma Shaheen discusses the possible implication of a proliferation of cyber weapons. She argues that since, until now the cyber weapons are used in an offensive mode; therefore, the probability of more states developing offensive cyber weapons is increasing. The chapter reasons that the offensive nature of cyber weapons without having an adequate defensive character is destabilizing for the international security system. In this regard, her chapter examines the offense–defense balance in the cyber warfare, and how the offensive side does has the advantage in cyber warfare that can destabilize international security.

By linking power relations in the technologically dominated context of cyberspace to Hannah Arendt's theoretical considerations of power and violence the chapter "The Utility of Timeless Thoughts: Hannah Arendt's Conceptions of Power and Violence in the Age of Cyberization" by Katharina C. Below offers fresh perspectives on the importance of power in IR. It is argued that the structure of power and violence in cyberspace can be captured abstractly by dividing cyberspace into two parts that refer to Arendt's conceptions of power as "power to" and violence as "power over". Cyberspace is thus both, a modern space of appearance and political freedom and an unexplored context for Arendt's conception of power as well as an anti-space of appearance, a space filled with Arendt's conception of violence that denies the positive attributes of a space of appearance when filtering and control techniques are implemented. By looking at the cases of the Arab Spring protests, Weibo and the Fifty Cent Party as well as Denial of Service (DoS) attacks during elections or interstate conflicts Below underlines the empirical relevance of her thoughts.

Contributions of the Part II address emerging challenges and prospects for international politics and relations. By highlighting empirical findings in fields like peacekeeping, global governance, diplomacy, economy, cultural activity, transnational communication, cyber espionage, and social media, it explores the process of "cyberization" of IR. The chapters in this part of the book focus on specific empirical phenomena that make the process of "cyberization" of IR comprehensible and visible, while at the same time addressing the implications of their findings on their field of IR.

The first chapter of part II "Clarifying the International Debate on Stuxnet: Arguments for Stuxnet as an Act of War" by Sascha Knoepfel addresses the question whether the use of the Stuxnet computer worm can be seen as an "act of war" in the light of theory on the nature of war and acts of war. By presenting definitional criteria for an act of war in cyberspace the chapter sheds light on the ongoing debate and makes a solid contribution to a discussion on an empirical phenomenon which stands exemplary for a new type of virus worm used by well-equipped actors as instrument to achieve strategic goals.

In his piece of work "A New Way Of Conducting War: Cyberwar, Is That Real?" Hakan Mehmetcik contributes to the more general discussion on both the reality and impact of cyberwar. By discussing the applicability of Clausewitzian and other IR perspectives on war to cyberwarfare, this chapter broadens our understanding of cyberwarfare. Looking into the cases of Estonia and Georgia as defendant of cyberattacks Hakan's contribution will also increase our empirical knowledge on different forms of occurrences of cyberwarfare.

The chapter "Peacekeeping 4.0: Harnessing the Potential of Big Data, Social Media, and Cyber Technologies" by John Karlsrud evaluates, by looking into various cases, the potentials that arise from big data, social media, and other cyber technologies for effective peacekeeping and peacebuilding. The chapter states that actors in the field are still lagging woefully behind when it comes to putting those new technologies and developments to use for peacekeeping and peacebuilding. The chapter shows further, that these tools are already well-known in the areas of humanitarian action, social activism, and development; and that the United Nations, through the Global Pulse initiative, has also begun to discover the potential of "Big Data for Development," which may in time help prevent violent conflict. This chapter details some of the initiatives that can be harnessed and further developed to overcome this shortage, and offers policy recommendations for states, the UN Security Council, and UN peacekeeping at UN headquarters and at field levels. Thereby, the contribution by John Karlsrud delivers not only profound knowledge on the importance of cyber technologies for specific activities of international relations, but also solid and elaborated policy recommendations for future application.

Ryan David Kiggins' chapter "US Leadership in Cyberspace: Transnational Cyber Security and Global Governance" examines US cyber security policy in the light of transnational cyber security, deterrence theory, and hegemonic stability theory. His chapter explores and discusses the problems of deterrence theory, as a state level theory of national security, related to the application on a medium which is per meaning transnational in form and characterized by diffusion of authority, control and leadership—the Internet. The chapter argues for a conceptualization of cyber security as a transnational security issue and that such a framing may assists political leader within the US to develop a comprehensive US cyber security policy that incorporates deterrence and US leadership. Furthermore, the chapter argues that from the standpoint of transnational security, the US should fulfill its role as leader of collective hegemony, by leading cyber space stakeholders to develop norms and rules for global cyber security governance regimes and institutions that will teach states the norms and rules necessary for a stable and secure cyber domain through which global information and economic exchange will continue to flourish. By applying a strong empirical argument, the chapter contributes significantly to the arising debate on the necessity of leadership for a secure and stable Internet.

Starting with the reflection that networked governance is the default modus operandi in Internet governance Andreas Schmidt's contribution "Hierarchies in Networks: Emerging Hybrids of Networks and Hierarchies for Producing Internet Security" analyzes the consequences for Internet security. The chapter argues that Internet security heavily relies on non-hierarchical, networked forms of organization and defines networked governance in this field as "a semi-permanent, voluntary negotiation system that allows interdependent actors to opt for collaboration or unilateral action in the absence of an overarching authority". His chapter analyzes the ability of traditional powerful actors such as state authorities and large enterprises to provide Internet security and exert power in the cyber-domain. The chapter furthermore outlines potential anchor points for traditional powerful actors to introduce more elements of hierarchy and control into Internet security provisioning networks. Empirically, the chapter describes emerging hybrids of networks and hierarchies in Internet security provisioning. In so doing, this contribution not only fosters our empirical knowledge on the importance of networked governance in IR, but also marks out the theoretical implication for IR of such developments.

Oliver Read's part ("How the 2010 Attack on Google Changed the US Government's Threat Perception of Economic Cyber Espionage") shows how the 2010s attack on Google changed the US authorities' perception of cyber threats. Through exploring the evolution of the case and perceptions of the US government and by applying an analytical framework called "threat politics" introduced by the author, this chapter profoundly increases our knowledge on how threat perceptions develop in the realm of cyberspace. The argument is substantiated in two main steps. In step one, it is shown how the American Government conceptualized the threat of economic cyber-espionage before and after the announcement. In step two, we trace how this perception-shift led to a series of countermeasures.

Stephen D. McDowell's, Zoheb Nensey's, and Philip E. Steinberg's chapter entitled "Cooperative International Approaches to Network Security: Understanding and Assessing OECD and ITU Efforts to Promote Shared Cybersecurity" looks into how states have undertaken efforts to increase cybersecurity by promoting network security in international organizations and examines the influence of these institutions in this regard (Organization for Economic Cooperation and Development (OECD), and the International Telecommunications Union (ITU)). The chapter examines existing perspectives on the desirability and feasibility of international cooperation on network security. It further discusses the international efforts to advance cooperative approaches to network security and cybersecurity. Additionally, it assesses these multilateral efforts in the light of states' recent moves to advance more strategic national approaches and thereby delivers profound insights into cyber-security-related bargaining and decision making among international organizations and evaluates the influence of the respective organizations for supporting security in the field.

The contribution of Matthew Crosston entitled "Phreak the Speak: The Flawed Communications within Cyber Intelligentsia" surveys a fundamental dichotomy that has developed within the academic, technical, and policy communities when it comes to understanding, advancing, and communicating work on cyberspace within global affairs. This dichotomy, so Crosston, not only exists as an intellectual barrier between scholars of the hard and social sciences, it impinges on progressive cooperation between the political and technical communities. Consequently, there is a gap weakening the scope and reach of theoretical and empirical work on cyberspace in general. The chapter argues that this problem has the potential to become exponentially larger in the immediate future: not only are real-world professionals and scholars having trouble building bridges between obvious mutual interests, but this 'Chinese knowledge wall' separates each group respectively. Just as phreaking involves a subculture of specialists who experiment and toy with telecommunication systems, the intellectual, technical, and governmental worlds need a new generation of 'phreak-scholars' who are adept at building connections between these diverse, inter-related knowledge bases.

The chapter "Reflections on Virtual to Real: Modern Technique, International Security Studies and Cyber Security Environment" by Marcial A. Garcia Suarez and Igor D. P. Acácio deals with the analysis of the phenomenon of modern technique by Martin Heidegger, especially the issue of information societies and the role that the virtual network has. It gives information about the political behavior of states, which affect the international security environment and estimates implications for IR theory.

The editors would like to express their deepest gratitude to Mrs. Barbara Fess and Mrs. Marion Kreisel (Springer) for their tremendous help and backing throughout the whole project and for their commitment to produce the project true to the editors' visions. Working together with such proficient and pleasant people makes publishing a lot more easy. Furthermore, the editors would like to share their appreciation and admiration for all the participating authors: Without their magnificent chapters, this book would not be such a comprehensive and conclusive contribution to the field. Working together with such highly professional and prudential people makes the editing work most enjoyable. Additionally, the editors wish to express their appreciation to the organizers and respective panel chairs of the ISSS/ISAC Annual Conference 2011, ISA Annual Convention 2012, and the 2012 Joint BISA-ISA Conference for providing an excellent setting to present our ideas and to launch this project.

Jan-Frederik Kremer would like to express his deepest thanks to his friends, family, parents, and to his wonderful wife Katrin for their support and patience not only throughout this project, but throughout difficult times in his life. Without his wife's, parents', familys' and his friends' love and ever ongoing and unconditional support he would not have had the drive or inspiration to complete such a project. He also wants to share his special and deep gratitude for Prof. Dr. Xuewu Gu's ever ongoing backing, mentoring, and his most enjoyable way of (academic) support, which by far exceeded any expectations. Additionally, he would like to thank Prof. Dr. Wilhelm Lowenstein (Ruhr-University) for his personal and professional support throughout the years. Jan-Frederik also owes his gratitude to institutions like the DAAD, DFG, Ruhr-University Bochum Research School, Bonn University, University of Miami (FL), and ISA for grating him numerous grants, scholarships etc., which have made academic networking and project planning possible. Jan-Frederik wish to express his thankfulness also to the Friedrich-Naumann-Foundation for Freedom and especially to Dr. Gerhard Söltenfuß for the confidence and faith he have in me and for his backing and mentoring. Working for the indispensable idea of liberty and freedom is fulfilling and stimulating at the same time. Last but not least, Jan-Frederik would like to thank his co-editor and friend Benedikt Müller for all the enjoyment, support, and professionalism, which has made working together with him at this project truly inspirational.

Benedikt Müller would like to thank his family and friends, especially his wife Lara and his parents for their everlasting love and support. The most powerful force driving him to complete a project like this is having loved ones who believe in him. He is furthermore indebted to IBM and Accenture, two exceptional corporations offering environments full of inspiring people and challenging experiences. Beyond that, he wants to extend his gratitude to his co-editor Jan-Frederik Kremer who, besides being a true friend and his best man, helps a practitioner wander through the world of academics.

Bonn, Germany Jan-Frederik Kremer
Essen, Germany Benedikt Müller

Contents

Contributors

Igor D. Acácio has a B.A. on International Relations (Strategic Studies) at Fluminense Federal University (UFF) and is a Master Candidate in Political Science at the State University Rio de Janeiro State University's Institute of Social and Political Studies (IESP-UERJ). Currently, is also researcher at the Analysis Group on International Politics (UFF) and Research Assistant at Getulio Vargas Foundation (FGV). His current interests of research are related to International Security and International Relations Theory, especially new themes as Cyber Security and his topic of Master's dissertation about regional security and regional powers.

Katharina C. Below is a graduate student at the University of Bonn. Her research interests include Science and Technology Studies, Sociology, and History of Science as well as Knowledge Power.

Matthew Crosston is the Miller Endowed Chair for Industrial and International Security and Founder and Director of the International Security and Intelligence Studies (ISIS) program in the College of Arts and Sciences at Bellevue University. Crosston has authored two well-received books, several book chapters, and nearly a dozen peer-reviewed articles on issues covering counter-terrorism, corruption, democratization, radical Islam, and cyber-deterrence. His research agenda continues in these veins while also focusing on new concepts of future conflict.

Craig B. Greathouse is currently an Associate Professor of Political Science at the University of North Georgia. His research interests include security and defense policy, strategic thought, and strategic culture. He currently is the graduate advisor to the MA in International Affairs and the departmental coordinator of online and distance education.

John Karlsrud is Research Fellow and the Manager of the Training for Peace Programme at the Norwegian Institute of International Affairs (NUPI) and has experience from UN peacekeeping as a Special Assistant to the UN Special Envoy in Chad (2008–2010) and UNDP. He has published numerous articles on peacekeeping and peacebuilding, inter alia in International Peacekeeping, Global Governance, and Global Responsibility to Protect. He is currently doing research on the impact of modern technology and new media on the future of peacekeeping.

Hanna Samir Kassab is an International Studies Doctoral Student at the University of Miami. He specializes in International Relations Theory, National Security, Far Right movements around the world, and acts of political suicide. His dissertation hopes to amend Structural Realism and consider capabilities as an intervening variable.

Ryan David Kiggins completed his Ph.D. in political science at the University of Florida in 2011. His dissertation examined US Internet governance policy from the perspectives of US diplomatic history and US national export strategy, arguing that US policymakers repurposed the Internet, in the post-Cold War era, as a platform for the expansion of American products and political ideals. His current research has examined US cyber security policy and theories of international relations, the international political economy of rare earth elements, and the political economy of US cyber security policy. Most recently, he is Visiting Assistant Professor of Political Science at Williams College during the 2012–2013 academic year.

Sascha Knoepfel is currently a Ph.D. candidate at King's College London. His research interests include a broad range of international security issues, in particular nuclear nonproliferation/disarmament, missile defence, and cyber security.

Jan-Frederik Kremer heads the Regional Office and Program for North Rhine Westphalia of the Friedrich Naumann Foundation for Freedom. Jan-Frederik is Senior Associate Fellow at the Center for Global Studies, Bonn University. Before being appointed his current position Jan-Frederik headed the research Group "Economy and Finance" at the Center for Global Studies, Bonn University where he worked as Research Fellow and Lecturer.

He is (co-)author and (co-)editor of numerous publications on international relations, international political economy, cyber security and international trade, like: "Power in the 21st Century", "Global Power Europe, Vol I and II", "Cyber Space and International Relations", or "Innovative Capabilities and Market Performance: The European Union in International Comparison". He is an expert in international trade (policy), external commercial relations, international political economy and international relations theory.

He is regularly invited to present his work on major international and national conferences and meetings and he has received various scholarships and awards. In August -September 2012 he was invited to stay as visiting researcher/scholar at the University of Miami, FL. Jan-Frederik is also Co-Initiator of cnsltnts and has conducted consultancy projects in South-Africa, the US and Germany.

Stephen D. McDowell is John H. Phipps Professor of Communication at Florida State University. He has co-authored, Managing The Infosphere: Governance, Technology, and Cultural Practice in Motion (Temple), and held fellowships with the Canadian federal Department of Communications, the Shastri Indo-Canadian Institute, and a Congressional Fellowship supported by the American Political Science Association.

Hakan Mehmetcik is a research assistant at the Department of International Relations, Isik University, Turkey. At the same time, he is a Ph.D. candidate at the Department of Politics and International Relations at the Yildiz Technical University.

He has received his MA in Eurasian Studies at Uppsala University, Sweden. His research interests include regional and international security studies, theory of war and conflict, peace building, and comparative politics.

Benedikt Müller is a technical sales professional at IBM with prior work experience as a technology consultant at Accenture. He holds a Bachelor's degree in International Management and a Master's degree in IT Management. His research interests revolve around the business impact of technology and the political and economic impact of cyber security.

Zoheb Nensey is a graduate student in Media and Communication studies at Florida State University. His research interests focus on cybersecurity and government response to cybersecurity leaks. He is also a member of Center for Foreign Policy Studies at Florida State University and the coach of Florida State University's debate team.

Roxana Radu is a research fellow at the Center for Media and Communication Studies (CMCS), Central European University, Budapest (Hungary), and a Ph.D. candidate in International Relations/Political Science at the Graduate Institute of International and Development Studies in Geneva (Switzerland). Prior to starting her Ph.D., she worked as a program coordinator and researcher at CMCS, where she focused on cybersecurity, e-government, and e-participation, and on (new) media regulation in transitional societies. In 2011, Roxana took part of the Next Generation Leadership programme of the Internet Society (ISOC) and in 2012 she was awarded the ISOC Ambassadorship to the Internet Governance Forum. Her publications bridge the academic and policy debates, and her work has been centered on the potential of ICTs for the empowerment of local communities, open knowledge production, and internet governance structures.

Oliver Read is editor at the Global Public Policy Institute in Berlin and a Ph.D. student at Goethe University Frankfurt. From 2007–2010 he worked as Web manager and editor for the Pew Research Center's Forum on Religion & Public Life in Washington, DC. Before Pew, Oliver was an associate editor at the Online NewsHour with Jim Lehrer, also in Washington, DC. He holds master's degrees in journalism from Boston University and international relations from the Free University Berlin.

Andreas Schmidt is a researcher at the Faculty of Technology, Policy and Management at Delft University of Technology. He holds a Master degree in Political Science and Medieval History. He is currently compiling the results of his Ph.D. project on technical communities in Internet security governance. Prior to that, he has worked as an analyst for ICT-focussed business consultancies.

Salma Shaheen is a Ph.D. candidate at the Department of War Studies, King's College London. Her Ph.D. project is related to study the influence of strategic culture on the nuclear command and control system designed for small nuclear forces. Prior to her Ph.D. at King's, she worked as a researcher covering nuclear nonproliferation issues at Strategic Plans Division, Pakistan in the Arms Control and Disarmament Affairs Directorate.

Philip E. Steinberg is Professor of Political Geography at Durham University. He is the author or co-author of several books about political and regulatory issues in spaces that lie partially or wholly outside state borders including The Social Construction of the Ocean (Cambridge), Managing the Infosphere: Governance, Technology, and Cultural Practice in Motion (Temple), and, most recently, Contesting the Arctic: Politics and Imaginaries in the Circumpolar North (I.B. Tauris).

Marcial A. Garcia Suarez is professor of political science and international relations at Fluminense Federal University, Niterói—Rio de Janeiro/Brazil. Developed research on terrorism and the new global threats, like a cyber terrorism, political terrorism, nuclear terrorism, etc. He was a fellow researcher on International Security Program at Harvard University and now coordinates the Analysis Group on International Politics at Fluminense Federal University.

Part I
Cyberspace and International Relations: Theory

Power Technology and Powerful Technologies: Global Governmentality and Security in the Cyberspace

Roxana Radu

Abstract While escaping consistent theoretization so far, the impact of 'cyberization' on the conduct of international relations can be more thoroughly grasped by studying the reconfiguration of global governance techniques brought about by the virtual mediums. The cyberspace remains a highly contested arena for policy-making, and its current institutional architecture is dominated by a multiplicity of tensions over who is entitled to decide on issues that go beyond the traditional functions of the state and what practices of governing are most appropriate in this context. By applying the Foucauldian concept of governmentality to investigate the global discourses of security in the cyberspace, this chapter sheds light on a shift in the rationality of governing, and brings empirical evidence of the dominant discourse(s) of security in the cyberspace in the United Nations (UN) ambit. It reveals that, despite the common acknowledgement of cyber dangers as imminent, transnational and very diffuse, an inclusive and dialectical approach to cybersecurity is not yet in place.

R. Radu (✉)
Graduate Institute of International and Development Studies, Geneva, Switzerland
e-mail: roxana.radu@graduateinstitute.ch

J.-F. Kremer and B. Müller (eds.), *Cyberspace and International Relations*,
DOI: 10.1007/978-3-642-37481-4_1, © Springer-Verlag Berlin Heidelberg 2014

1 Introduction

The increasing societal dependence on information and communication technologies (ICTs) at all levels has changed the way in which individuals interact nowadays, both personally and professionally. But has it done the same for states? Have the traditional power loci been affected by the development of new technologies to such an extent that their modus operandi and their theoretization be challenged? The role of technology in society has long been acknowledged by highly influential thinkers, such as Karl Marx, Max Weber or Talcott Parsons, yet it has remained marginal to their work, being essentially limited to serving economic ends(Shields 1997). By mid-twentieth century, the Frankfurt School placed a central emphasis on the use of technology for the subjugation of the masses by the modern state, and opened the door for critical theories that account for the ICT-driven transformation. The latter has been addressed in different ongoing discussions related to power-embedded entities, however, the current conceptualizations lag behind. This chapter delves into theoretical considerations and brings empirical evidence for the way in which the discourse of security in the cyberspace has evolved within the framework of international organizations, and in particular in the United Nations (UN) system.

The cyberspace has triggered a series of economic, social and political adjustments from the local to the international arenas. Moreover, security has been brought back to the forefront as one of the major concerns affecting the way in which states interact. ICTs have impacted the relations involving international organizations, their constituencies, and other stakeholders of the information society, by fostering the development of horizontal networks (Castells 1996, p. 469), which have supplemented, rather than replaced, the existing hierarchies (Rosenau 2002, p. 281). Presently, the international institutional architecture for the governance of the cyberspace is dominated by a multiplicity of initiatives aimed at increasing cooperation at the international level,[1] as well as by a redefinition of the roles played by existent actors. Such dynamics can be observed in the discourse over security in the cyberspace, as a milestone for the expansion of the information society. So far, states have strongly pushed for empowering existent global institutions to take up new cyber responsibilities and to reshape their agenda accordingly.

Attempts at developing international relations (IR) theories relevant for the information society have remained rather scarce, primarily due to the inner-looking focus of the discipline (Eriksson and Giacomello 2006, p. 222). Different endeavors at framing conceptual frameworks have rarely built on each other for advancing a comprehensive conceptualization or for developing middle-range theories based on interdisciplinary approaches. This chapter is an attempt at filling this gap in the IR literature by analyzing the extent to which the concept of global governmentality could be employed to explain the way in which security in the cyberspace has

[1] See, for example, the NATO cyber defense strategy (2010), ITU resolutions (2007–2010) etc.

been defined so far in the UN ambit. It contends that IR needs to widen its focus in understanding the impact of technology as infused into the fabric of society and in explaining the shift in governmental rationalities with reference to 'cyberization'.

Currently, at the international level, at least 19 global and regional organizations are actively involved in the security and governance of the cyberspace[2] (Government Accountability Office 2010). This growing number reflects a common understanding that the challenges posed by the spread of ICTs cannot be tackled by states in isolation; yet, up to the present, such international engagement was primarily directed towards arms control and cooperation in the cyberspace. The unique governance challenges brought about by the expansion of the internet have also given rise to emerging transnational institutions, such as the Internet Corporation for Assigned Names and Numbers (ICANN) or the Internet Governance Forum (Mueller 2010). At the national level, more and more states re-task existing institutions or establish new ones to oversee the flow of information in computer-mediated environments. While states continue to exert authority and control over both physical infrastructure and over the online content, more and more non-state actors challenge their position (Nye 2011). The cyberspace has become a new domain of power, for which the monopoly is no longer exclusively held by governments (Rosenau and Singh 2002, Radu 2012a).

This chapter begins with a conceptual discussion of governmentality and its applicability to the digital age. The second part delves into an exploration of the evolution of the concept of security in the cyberspace—from a politico-military perspective—in the framework of the UN, the largest and most inclusive international organization. It investigates the resolutions issued by two of the most active UN bodies in this field: the General Assembly (GA), starting in 1998, and the International Telecommunications Union (ITU), starting in 2007, by asking how cybersecurity has been defined and what implications that had for the entitlement to participation in the governance of this new issue domain up to 2011. The third part concludes and points to potential fruitful avenues for further research.

2 The Information Society and Global Governmentality: Contending Perspectives

In spite of the rapid growth of new technologies, access to them remains highly uneven around the globe. The digital gap between 'information rich' and 'poor' persists (Souter 2007, Radu 2012b), and an analog situation can be perceived at the inter-state level, as certain countries appear to be better equipped to take a lead position in negotiating the governance of the internet (Drezner 2007). In scholarly

[2] Apart from the UN system, the most important ones are Shanghai Cooperation Organization, the North Atlantic Treaty Organization (NATO), and the Organization for Economic Co-operation and Development (OECD), Council of Europe (CoE), the Group of 8 (G8), Asia–Pacific Economic Cooperation (APEC).

work, the role of ICTs vis-à-vis society has been primarily assessed in a polarized fashion by two schools of thought: the technical determinists, who have underscored technologies as the fundamental driver of society and cultural values, and the social constructivists, who have seen technology as socially constructed and entirely dependent on the interactions of individuals and groups and their ongoing (re)interpretation. In between these two perspectives, the sociotechnologic approach has highlighted that the dynamics of technological change are potentiated by collective and individual choices and reflect underlying power relations (Law and Bijker 1992, Williams and Edge 1996).

Among such debates, governmentality has permeated the IR field relatively late (Early 2000), yet a substantial body of work emerged under the so-called 'international governmentality studies' (Walters 2012, pp. 82–83), in which the focus of attention has primarily been security and changing forms of surveillance. Shelby notes the tendency 'to selectively appropriate (or misappropriate) social theoretical resources, and apply them a little too unreflectively to the theorisation of world politics' (Shelby 2007, p. 325). The evolution of studies of governmentality has recently incorporated analyses of new territories of power, in particular with reference to the digital age (Flyverbom 2011, Henman 2010).

The past two decades, studies on governmentality, drawing on Foucault's series of lectures from the 1970s at Collège de France, have flourished (Dean 2010, Broekling et al. 2011). Governmentality has been considered a 'somewhat loose set of analytical tools and concepts, rather than a substantive theory about the forces and dynamics of transforming society' (Walters 2012, p. 3), thus accommodating the development and contestation of different theoretical stances. Since the 1990s, governmentality has become 'an independent research field' (Broekling et al. 2011, p. 9) comprising extensive interdisciplinary literature. In his study of 'telegraphic politics', Barry (1996) investigated the link between physical and engineering sciences and their role within liberal government, showing how technology has continuously played a role in governing. In her post-Foucauldian works, Haraway (1991) linked the different concepts attributed to the governmentality sphere and developed new notions such as 'informatics of domination' and 'techno-biopower'.

Governmentality has received many interpretations (Walters 2012, pp. 10–13) as applied to the totality of power relationships (in the family, in society, etc.). Foucault's work on governmentality constitutes primarily analytics of power, rather than a full-fledged theory of power. His genealogical method of selected events has been grounded in shifting the lens of analysis from objects themselves to the practices that produce those objects (Veyne 1997, p. 155). Such an approach can be successfully applied to the analysis of relationships altered by the use of computer-mediated technologies, which represent a non-neutral artifact, designed to serve different purposes. In that sense, ICTs remain biased in the direction of their use, and are deployed in shaping a series of tactics and strategies—or 'power technologies' at different levels. While Foucault referred primarily to the domestic realm, recent analyses have expanded on the concept of governmentality as applied at the global level. Joseph (2009) questions whether states are indeed successful at controlling populations, but contends that there are deliberate interventions of international organizations in conditioning the way in which state power is exercised. For him, 'international organisations are as much a reflection of a particular rationality of governance as they are instigators of one' (Joseph 2009, p. 427). Such interactions between states and international organizations remain understudied, and this chapter aims at bringing more empirical evidence to support an in-depth analysis of current patterns of governing rationalities at the global level.

Foucault defined government as the 'conduct of conduct', for oneself and for the others, individualizing and totalizing at the same time (Gordon 1991, pp. 2–4). In a different lecture, he equated governmentality with liberal governmentality, described as 'the ensemble formed by institutions, procedures, analyses and reflections, calculations, and tactics that allow the exercise of this very specific, albeit very complex, power that has the population as its target, political economy as its major form of knowledge, and apparatuses of security as its essential technical instrument' (Foucault 2007, p. 108). Accordingly, the changes in practices of government represent the very characteristic of government itself, which, Foucault adds, '[…] is a question not of imposing laws on men, but of disposing things: that is to say, of employing tactics rather than law, and even of using laws themselves as tactics—to arrange things in such a way that, through a certain number of means, such and such ends may be achieved' (Foucault 1991, p. 95).

Historically, the development of communication means has been tightly controlled by governments and has supported different technologies of power, either by being directly under state ownership or by abiding by state-imposed regulation (in particular after the liberalization of communication services in the 1980s in the Western world) legitimized in the name of public interest (Irion and Radu 2013). The internet itself developed as a US governmental project in the early 1970s, to overcome the problems posed by the potential disruption of telecommunications infrastructure in the context of the nuclear arms race (Bing 2009). The 1990s have been marked by the so-called 'Internet boom', aided by the quick expansion of the World Wide Web and the fast integration of commerce and politics on electronic platforms; these became accessible to an ever-increasing number of people around the world in a relative short time, but currently exhibit uneven levels of development in different national contexts.

Such modern technological tools did not constitute the focus of Foucault's work, although 'he recognized that the technologies he was interested in were physical in part, for example, the architecture of prisons, schools, the clinic' (Willcocks 2006, p. 275). In an interview from 1984, Foucault asserts: 'What interests me more is to focus on what the Greeks called *techne*, that is to say, a practical rationality governed by a conscious goal… The disadvantage of this word *techne*, I realize is its relation to the word <technology> which has a very specific meaning… One thinks of hard technology, the technology of wood, of fire, of electricity. Whereas government is also a function of technology: the government of individuals, the government of souls, the government of the self by the self, the government of families, the government of children and so on.' (Rabinow 1991, p. 295).

Yet, Foucault's influence on the literature linking technological artifacts with socio-political developments is long-lasting. Opposing perspectives have sometimes stemmed from the dynamic nature of governmentality itself,[3] which has strongly relied on the 'territorialization of national spaces: states, countries, populations, societies' (Rose 1999, p. 34). What emerges is a sort of "electronic governmentality" (Mehta and Darier 1998), or a technique of 'governing from a distance'. In Der Derian's account, virtuality blurs boundaries—not only between online and offline, but also between geographical distance and timing—and affects our perception of the surrounding environment (Der Derian 2000, 2009). With reference to ICTs, Foucault inspired two divergent streams of thought. On the one hand, the Foucauldian idea of knowledge as power gains support in the work of Braman (2002) and Richards (1993), who look at controlling information and diffusion of surveillance in different contexts, including imperial nation-states. On the other hand, there are scholars like Liftin (2002) and Deibert (1997) who support the idea that new technologies may be able to undermine the power of the state and its disciplinary gaze, by contesting the need to centralize surveillance and facilitating a network-like development of power relations.

In line with the second perspective, the expansion of ICTs thus represents a new configuration for governmental rationality, given the role the state is assigned, in light of the "magnitude of information and the multiple entry points that have further exhausted the capabilities of states and their resources to block the penetration of that information" (Eriksson and Giacomello 2007, p. 5). In a similar manner, Singh asserts: 'information technology networks in particular show how the collective social epistemes are shifting away from hierarchical authoritative contexts privileging nation-states. Interconnected networks may flatten hierarchies, or transform them altogether, into new types of spaces where territoriality itself becomes extinct' (Singh 2002, p. 17).

For Nye (2011), the co-existence of private systems and sovereign states in the ICT sector added a new layer to the relations between transnational actors and states, which are no longer submitted to hierarchical control. In his conceptualization, cyberpower appears as "a unique hybrid regime of physical and virtual properties" (Nye 2011, p. 123). Conversely, Drezner (2007) asserts that the power of the state increased in the digital era due to the delegation strategies employed by states—and in particular by great powers—in order to achieve their own interests. He concluded that "states can and will substitute different governance structures within a common regime complex, and they will substitute different policy tools to create those structures, depending on the constellation of great power interests" (Drezner 2007, p. 92).

This tension between ICTs as enabling or disabling certain practices of governmentality is further increased when the level of reference is global. Not only are states themselves applying certain techniques for controlling their populations, but states themselves are subjected to governmentality by international organizations.

3 For a critical analysis of contemporary uses of governmentality, see Walters (201243-81).

As Joseph notes, 'the regulation of states takes place through the targeting of populations. The fact that governmentality is usually unsuccessful at regulating populations does not matter if this can be used as a means to manage states' (Joseph 2009, p. 427). At the global level, institutions themselves are conceived as 'technologies'. Following the analytics of government approach, the focus becomes 'technologies that are materialized and stabilized in institutional settings' (Mitchell 1991, p. 92).

In his genealogical analysis, Foucault identified three major shifts in governmental rationalities and their corresponding technologies. First, the pastoral technique of government was based on the shepherd-flock game. Second, the so-called 'raison d'état', was sustained by a new kind of knowledge: statistics. It relied, on the one hand, on the military-diplomatic technology (system of alliances, balance of power), and on the other, on police as policy (concerned with the internal aspects of state growth). Third, the liberal governmentality as the 'management of freedom' (Foucault 2008, p. 63), operates based on technologies of security (including probability and risk), and this is characteristic of the past decades. Yet, governmentality 'does not exist in a pure form anywhere' (Walters 2012, p. 40), but there are discursive frameworks that constitute and underlie the way in which institutions develop and operate. Modern age power is based on knowledge in the form of discursive practices, which may normalize, evaluate or differentiate behavior.

2.1 *Governmentality and the Modern Risk Society*

Following Foucault, in the modern society, 'we need to see things not in terms of the replacement of a society of sovereignty by a disciplinary society and the subsequent replacement of a disciplinary society by a society of government; in reality one has a triangle, sovereignty—discipline—government, which has as its primary target the population and as its essential mechanism the apparatuses of security' (Foucault 1991, p. 102). In revealing the dynamics of governmentality for the digital era, my exploration here focuses on the evolution of the meaning of security in the cyberspace and the associated risks generated by an omnipresent virtual environment in the framework of the UN, a global organization that has included more and more new issue domains on its agenda.

Looking at the transition from the first to the second modernity, Ulrich Beck introduces the idea that for the latter, risks are predominantly 'human-made', or manufactured, rather than natural. For late (reflexive) modernity, he underscores the global impact of contemporary risk (Beck 1997), understood as "a systematic way of dealing with hazards and insecurities induced and introduced by modernisation itself" (Beck 1992, p. 21). Our societies are constructed around the "perception of threatening risks that determines thought and action" (Beck 2000, p. 213), and policies are framed according to mediated dimensions of risk. In this sense, the discursive representations of security in the cyberspace become instrumental for creating reality, and for determining the risk perception at the global level.

The recognition of dangers and threats with the ensuing classification and prioritization of resources are all part of the usual process through which modern societies develop strategies and forecasts of potential crisis and emergencies. For cybersecurity as a policy space, this happens from the local to the global level. The current risk environment 'transcends the limits of time and space boundaries, and presents a continuous and general challenge. Cyber threats globalize because they universalize and equalize' (Krishna-Hensel 2007, p. x). Drawing on Beck's evolution of modernity, Borne makes a similar observation when he states that 'global risk created a community of nations tied to the same fate" (2010, p. 13). The propagation of cyber threats is also driven by the dual-use nature of ICTs, with applications ranging from cyber peace initiatives to illicit activities (Carr 2012) and cyber warfare applications. The cyberspace is now often referred to as the 'fourth battleground' (Stone 2011). As Lawson (2012) demonstrates in his analysis of the US cybersecurity discourse, the extensive use of the 'war' analogy for the virtual world has given rise to contradictory tendencies: on the one hand, cyber war is seen as an unprecedented military threat; on the other, as similar to the Cold War deterrence strategy. The complexity of the virtual environment plays out in the negotiations for its governance beyond technical aspects, in its global policy dimensions.

The following section unveils how security in the cyberspace is defined in the UN system and what implications that has for shaping the entitlement to participation in its governance for different types of actors and global governmentality dynamics. Given the current stalemate in the UN negotiations concerning the politico-military aspects of cybersecurity, the definition of issues to be covered and of the agents that could or should get involved becomes crucial for understanding the broader roles assigned in the regulation of one of the newest issue domains. My investigation focuses on decision-making bodies for the politico-military aspects of security in the cyberspace, leaving aside the so-called "economic stream" (Maurer 2011), which refers to cyber crime. The underlying premise is that the definition of security concerns, as well as of the roles assigned to different political and non-political bodies in such global deliberation processes represents a discursive practice that may serve for setting precedents and guiding action even in non-binding decision exercises.

3 Negotiating Meanings for Security in the Cyberspace

In the governmentality literature, rationalities are perceived as wide-ranging historically-developed discourses, involving decisions as to who can govern, what and who is to be governed and in what way. At the global level, such rationalities would become visible in the framework of international organizations and institutions, and their daily practices. For the present discussion on the security in the cyberspace, the focus here is on the UN, which represents the world's largest international organization and the most powerful. Its Security Council is the most important decision-making body regarding security issues and international peace.

The UN has contributed to norm creation and norm diffusion in many issues domains, such as human rights and sustainable development (Karns and Mingst 2004). This has been primarily done via resolutions, whose number has exceeded 1,100 for the last two decades (Gruenberg 2009). The protection of the cyberspace has been addressed at different levels within the UN, including the UN Institute for Disarmament Research (UNIDIR), the UN Global Alliance for ICT and Development (UN-GAID), WSIS and the Internet Governance Forum (IGF); beyond deliberation platforms, the most consistent cybersecurity work was done in the framework of the UNGA and the ITU. The Security Council's involvement has been largely limited to the work of the Working Group on Countering the Use of the Internet for Terrorist Purposes, as part of the Counter-Terrorism Implementation Task Force (CTITF). None of the Security Council resolutions have so far mentioned the cyber aspect of security.[4]

While UNGA resolutions remain largely non-binding, they are the only ones voted on by all members of the United Nations, currently comprising 193 states. According to the 1945 Charter of the UN, the UNGA is empowered to consider and make recommendations on the general principles of cooperation for maintaining international peace and security, including disarmament, as well as to "discuss any question relating to international peace and security and, except where a dispute or situation is currently being discussed by the Security Council, make recommendations on it". Hossain refers to it—in a state-centric perspective—as "the only body where global voices of the international community are uttered and heard" (2008, p. 78).

In what concerns security in the cyberspace, three resolutions have been on the agenda. The First Committee of the GA discussed the resolution on "Developments in the field of information and telecommunications in the context of international security" on a yearly basis starting in 1998; the Second Committee of GA discussed the "Creation of a global culture of cybersecurity and the protection of critical information infrastructures", introduced in 2002 and adopted in 2005, and "Creation of a global culture of cybersecurity and taking stock of national efforts to protect critical informational infrastructures",[5] adopted in 2010. The role of the ITU—the UN specialized agency for ICTs—is primarily one of implementation. Since 2003, the ITU has also been actively involved in the cybersecurity, in particular for technical and standardization activities, and is currently in charge of carrying out the WSIS Action Plan C5, "Building confidence and security in the use of ICTs". The ITU comprises 193 UN member states and over 700 private companies and organizations.

The security of the cyberspace appeared on the UNGA agenda in December 1998 with a resolution proposal advanced by Russia on the "Developments in the field of information and telecommunications in the context of international security" (hereafter "Developments in the field…"), which has been discussed every year since, with its most recent iteration in November 2011. In 2002, the US proposed a

---

[4] The cyber aspect has not even been mentioned when cyber attacks occurred at the same time as military operations, as in the case of the 2008 Russian-Georgian war.

[5] UNGA Res 64/211.

complementary resolution (57/239), which primarily called for 'prioritizing cybersecurity planning and management' and for the adoption of nine elements for creating a global culture of cybersecurity. A related resolution was adopted in 2010, whose purpose was to take stock of national efforts to protect critical information infrastructures.

The two types of resolutions differ in both the way in which they refer to protection in the cyberspace and the actors that are identified. To begin with, the 1998 resolution talked about 'information security', whereas the 2002 one referred explicitly to cybersecurity. Notably, neither of them contained a definition of what was to be understood under the labels used (be it "information security" or "cybersecurity"). "Developments in the field…" invited UN member states to express their position on the topic. By 2009, 28 replies were received on behalf of 42 countries. For the first 8 years, the resolution has been sponsored only by Russia, but starting from 2006 other countries joined, including China. The US decided for the first time to enter the group of countries co-sponsoring the resolution in 2010.

The second resolution, proposed by the US in 2002 and adopted without a vote by the General Assembly in January 2005, has aimed at creating a 'culture of cybersecurity' and has proposed a number of baseline principles. Its sponsorship initially included Australia, Japan, and Norway, but later revisions of the draft text added another 36 member states in favor. The most important modification of the text concerns the replacement of "principles" with "elements" for a global culture of cybersecurity. The nine elements it puts forward are: awareness, responsibility, response, ethics, democracy, risk assessment, security design and implementation, security management, reassessment. In a Foucauldian understanding, such initiatives illustrate the struggle over norms that are able to shape all future interactions between states within the ambit of the UN. Following an instance of political contestation, comprise was reached for a wording that is less compelling, and reduces the overall effectiveness of the resolution.

4 Cybersecurity and Cyber Insecurity

Notably, none of the resolutions discussed in the UNGA contained precise reference to what it is to be understood by cybersecurity. Though present in other documents issued by the UNGA or other UN bodies, security in the cyberspace did not come to be defined until the issuing of ITU's "Overview of cybersecurity". One important event preceding this document was the distributed denial of service (DDoS) attacks that paralyzed Estonia for three weeks, between 27 April and 18 May 2007, which may have precipitated the introduction of an operational definition. The "Overview of cybersecurity", which was approved on 18 April 2008 by ITU-T Study Group 17, also contains a taxonomy of the security threats from an organization point of view. Accordingly, cybersecurity was understood as "the collection of tools, policies, security concepts, security safeguards, guidelines, risk management approaches, actions, training, best practices, assurance and technologies that can be used to protect the cyber environment and organization and user's assets",[6] and this was officially acknowledged for further incorporation in activities pertaining to the building of confidence and security in the use of ICTs in the 2010 ITU Resolution 181. This document acknowledges that "the definition of cybersecurity may need to be modified from time to time to reflect changes in policy".

In the absence of a definition, the prescriptions implied in any phasing are many-fold. This can be revealed by investigating the dynamics of "insecurity" connotations and responsibilities assigned to different partakers. As the correlative of security is insecurity (Dillon 1996), scrutinizing the meaning of the latter might explain the scope of power decisions and their actualization in day-to-day practice. Throughout time, multiple important changes occurred in the wording of the UNGA 53/70 Resolution, at several stages. The year after its introduction, in 1999, there is a modification of the phrase "may adversely affect the security of the States" to "may adversely affect the security of States in both civil and military fields". Yet, in 2002, this was replaced with "may adversely affect the integrity of the infrastructure of States to the detriment of their security in both civil and military fields". While these are more refined and precise references to the kind of vulnerabilities entailed by the expanded use of ICTs, the emphasis on "civilian and military" is doubled by their prior mentioning in the first paragraph of the resolution, which reflects a logic pertaining to traditional strategic studies. Following 9/11, a stronger wording towards securitizing cyberspace can be noticed. Further evidence for that comes from the fact that, in the different UNGA resolutions up to 2011, the vulnerabilities and dangers posed by the advent of ICTs are framed as "threats". Notably, resolution 64/211 adopted in 2010 emphasized the "increasingly transnational nature" of cyber threats.

This contrasts sharply with the much more frequent use of "risks" instead of "threats" in the wording of ITU resolutions. The difference between the two implies a differentiated course of action, as threats as understood as direct and imminent, whereas risks are indirect, more distant, unintended (Rasmussen 2001) and, as such, are prone to the elaboration of long-term risk management strategies rather than to the implementation of security measures under extraordinary conditions. The most comprehensive reference to this type of insecurities is to be found in the ITU 181 Resolution cautiously mentioning the "potential emergence of new and unforeseeable risks and vulnerabilities in relation to confidence and security in the use of ICTs". In this direction, it is worth drawing attention to a subsequent modification occurring in 2010 in the wording of the resolution on the "Developments in the field…", namely the phrase "possible measures to limit the

---

[6] The rest of the definition reads as follows: "Organization and user's assets include connected computing devices, personnel, infrastructure, applications, services, telecommunications systems, and the totality of transmitted and/or stored information in the cyber environment. Cybersecurity strives to ensure the attainment and maintenance of the security properties of the organization and user's assets against relevant security risks in the cyber environment. The general security objectives comprise the following: availability; integrity, which may include authenticity and non-repudiation; confidentiality" (ITU-T X.1205, 2008, p. 2).

threats emerging in this field" being changed to "possible strategies to address the threats emerging in this field". This reveals two underlying considerations: first, that limiting threats might not be enough, and a comprehensive approach might be needed instead; second, that strategies would be preferred to measures, which tend to be more punctual and to require less long-term planning.

Apart from "information security" and "cybersecurity", the other type of reference made to protection in the cyberspace comes under the form of securing critical information infrastructures, and it was introduced in the UNGA resolution language in 2003 through the Resolution 58/199 of 23 December, "Creation of a global culture of cybersecurity and the protection of critical information infrastructures", and later on reiterated in resolution 64/211 on "Creation of a global culture of cybersecurity and taking stock of national efforts to protect critical information infrastructures", adopted in 2010. In this context, critical infrastructures are identified as "those used for, inter alia, the generation, transmission and distribution of energy, air and maritime transport, banking and financial services, e-commerce, water supply, food distribution and public health—and the critical information infrastructures that increasingly interconnect and affect their operations". The latter resolution had 40 sponsoring countries under the lead of the US and proposed a voluntary self-assessment tool for national efforts to protect critical information infrastructures.

The technologies used to support cybersecurity present an interesting paradox with regards to the international and national levels that Diebert and Rohozinski (2010) point out. As they show, there are contradictory movements in the actions taken by governments to address these problems: on the one hand, the measures to achieve greater cooperation at the international level for the protection of critical infrastructure underlie the preservation of a free and open internet; on the other hand, increasing divergence can be noticed in the national efforts against risks through cyberspace, as governments tend to impose—within their national boundaries—measures that limit the potential of global connectivity by filtering, blocking, surveilling content, etc. In a Foucauldian understanding, such high-impact technologies may act in a disciplinary way, as they can allow for constant monitoring of individual activities on the internet (Deibert et al. 2008); they may also create incentives for identification of online behavior patterns and may impose a degree of self-restraint on the end-user (Deibert et al. 2011). Such potential has been realized in certain areas around the globe, such as China (McKinnon 2008) or Iran (Sreberny and Khiabany 2010).

5 States, Participants and Stakeholders

A different way in which the definitional aspects of cybersecurity are contested is by defining who the main players are in its governance arrangements. Up to 2000, as depicted in the UNGA resolutions, security in the virtual world was approached primarily from a state-centered perspective. The lack of an official definition of the focal terms employed also had a knock-on effect on the entitlement to participation for the different types of agents. Calling into being constituent parts was done in 2000, when the "need for cooperation between states and private industry to combat misuse of ICTs"[7] is recognized, but without including this in the recommendations made to member states at that point. Two years later, partakers in the cyberspace are explicitly identified and mentioned in the following order: "Governments, businesses, other organizations and individual users who develop, own, provide, manage, service and use information systems and networks ('participants').[8]

Once identified, the partakers are also attributed responsibility; according to the 2002 Resolution, the participants "must assume responsibility for and take steps to enhance the security of these information technologies, in a manner appropriate to their roles". At the same time, each state is empowered to "determine its own critical information infrastructure". In what concerns the phrasing of the "ethics" principle presented in the annex of the same resolution, Yannakogeorgos asserts that it is "founded on utilitarian grounds in that each participant is expected to respect the interests of others and to avoid inaction that will harm others" (Collier 2009, p. 85).

In the UNGA resolution 58/199 of 2003, the term "stakeholders" is used for the first time, implying more leverage for inclusion in the decision-making processes. The ITU Resolution 174 from 2010 extends this further, to "Member States and relevant ICT stakeholders, including geospatial and information service providers". Resolution 64/211 of 2010 acknowledges the mandate of the IGF, 'reiterating that all Governments should have an equal role and responsibility for international Internet governance'. The 2010 Report of the GGE brings up "cooperation between states, and between states, the private sector and civil society", making a first explicit reference to civil society as an equal player in the global governance of security in the cyber environment. The report also talks about "threat actors", pointing out that "of increased concern are individuals, groups or organizations, including criminal organizations, that engage as proxies in disruptive online activities on behalf of others". In that sense, the security concerns are distanced from the logic of linear threats and vulnerabilities originating by default outside the state, as it was the case in the traditional understanding of security (Buzan 1991). Such threats may now emerge from within the state, underlying that the nature of policy responses may have altered.

A reaction to this understanding of threats comes under the form of a letter to the UN Secretary General for the introduction of an "International code of conduct for information security"[9]—a proposal advanced by the representatives of Russia, China, Tajikistan and Uzbekistan in September 2011 to be discussed in the following UNGA meeting(s). The most controversial part of the document states that the signatories of the code "endeavor […] to prevent other States from using their resources, critical infrastructures, core technologies and other advantages to undermine the right of the countries, which accepted this Code of Conduct, to independent

---

[7] UNGA Res. on "Combating the criminal misuse of information technologies" (55/63).

[8] UNGA Res. 57/239 of 20 Dec 2002.

[9] UNGA Res 66/359.

control of information and communications technologies or to threaten the political, economic and social security of other countries". While this resembles a reassessment of the non-interference principle in the cyberspace, by redefining the responsibilities of the international community and individual member states, it can also be perceived as a way to counterbalance the gain of additional powers by ITU,[10] following its attempts at modernizing itself after the 18th Plenipotentiary Conference (Blackman 2011). Such dynamics emphasize the struggle of both specialized agencies and states to retain or accede to a position of power that would allow for their central role in decision-making, while ensuring discretion over the levels of protection of national critical information infrastructures.

6 Conclusions

The present analysis advances the discussion of modern risk societies and governmentality for the digital age by revealing coherent practices that become intelligible in UN-driven discursive exercises over security in the cyberspace. At the outset, governmentality is about different strategies, practices, interactions that amount to forms of control over populations; global governmentality applies the same logic to the exercise of control over states by international organizations. While Foucault explored the unfolding of governmentality within the domestic realm, the understanding of relationships between states and international organizations, and the dynamics of global governmentality appear fundamental in contemporary societies. Many of the current policies in liberal democratic systems—especially with regard to security—are motivated by a perception of risk and threat. At the global level, such concerns may transpire on the agenda of international organizations and the governing mechanisms that states may decide on for the sake of greater protection. This is particularly the case with newer issue domains, such as cybersecurity, which brings forward one aspect of the cyberization of international relations. In that sense, Foucault's 'critical achievement is to help make IR a less disciplined discipline' (Neal 2009, p. 543), by incorporating discursive approaches and genealogical perspectives. His contribution rests with a widening of the spectrum of topics unveiling power relations, and with the methodological approach of key events and documents contextualizing broader shifts of governing strategies.

This chapter drew on empirical analysis to unpack the meanings of security in the cyberspace, by analyzing the working of the UNGA and ITU relevant cybersecurity documents from 1998 to 2011. Starting from the premise that different

---

[10] According to Resolution 136, in spite of the national sovereignty principle, the ITU is empowered to "carrying out its mandate to develop technical recommendations designed to reduce vulnerabilities in the ICT infrastructure, and providing all the assistance that was agreed upon at WTDC-10, including Programme 2 activities such as <assisting Member States, in particular developing countries, in the elaboration of appropriate and workable legal measures relating to protection against cyberthreats>" (ITU Resolution 136 of 2010).

phrasings that act in definitional ways in situations of negotiation over meanings, it revealed a series of dynamics. Firstly, it pointed out that the lack of a clear definition of what is to be understood as "security in the cyberspace" led to a rather long process of 'finding the middle ground', with the main perspectives put forward being those of Russia and the U.S. Up to 2008, when the ITU provided an inclusive definition of cybersecurity, the direction and the positioning of different initiatives regarding the protection of the cyber environment have revealed the differentiated understanding of technologies of power. Secondly, the implied meanings for insecurity have so far structured the dynamics of entitlement to participation at the pace decided on by the UN member states, which have only gradually and indirectly opened up the sphere of tasks and responsibilities to non-state actors, be they for-profit or non-for-profit.

As a new governance field, cybersecurity remains an arena of political contestation, which presently requires a reconceptualization of its definitional matters based on more inclusive participation. The official acknowledgement of cybersecurity as a "high-priority"[11] within the ITU points to the growing importance of creating multilateral instruments for tackling potential risks arising from the virtual space, at the time when cyber dangers are commonly agreed on as imminent, transnational and very diffuse. The predominant use of "threats" in the UNGA resolutions, as opposed to "risks" in the ITU wording, has spread a sense of urgency which can be perceived in the number of changes brought to the 53/70 Resolution of 1998, in spite of the fact that such negotiations did not lead to the conclusion of a treaty for the cyberspace (Mueller et al. 2007, Hughes 2010). With the multi-stakeholder model now dominating the agenda, proposals such as the 2011 one drafted by Russia, China, Tajikistan and Uzbekistan represent an interesting instance of contestation over who is entitled to define actions, their limits and their participants. Its future discussion in the UNGA is likely to reveal underlying patterns of institutionalization and securitization of cyber issues, with the co-sponsorship of smaller states.

These observations suggest that there is still a gap between the increasing diffusion of authority and the growing demand for cybersecurity governance, revealing the need for a dialectic construction of cybersecurity principles and norms at the international level. In that respect, there are two important factors that could further drive the evolution of this new issue domain on the UN agenda: first, a shared understanding of cybersecurity meaning(s) and their implications for global policy processes; second, an enlargement of the debate beyond the traditional stakeholders, towards a more inclusive negotiation process, in which the input from local communities and from the academia would be taken into account more consistently. In making the cyberspace more secure, the benefits of the interaction opportunities brought about by the advent of ICTs could be further explored for enhancing the debate around cybersecurity and its reconceptualization.

[11] ITU Res. 45 (of 2010).

References

Barry, A. (1996). Lines of communication and spaces of rule. In A. Barry, T. Osborne, & N. Rose (Eds.), *Foucault and political reason: Liberalism, neoliberalism, and rationalities of government*. Chicago: University of Chicago Press.

Beck, U. (1997). *The reinvention of politics*. Cambridge, MA: Polity Press.

Beck, U. (1992). *Risk society. Towards a new modernity*. New Delhi: Sage.

Beck, U. (2000). Risk society revisited: Theory, politics and research programmes. In B. Adam, U. Beck, & J. van Loon (Eds.), *The risk society and beyond, critical issues for social theory*. London: Sage.

Bing, J. (2009). Building cyberspace: A brief history of the internet. In L. Bygrave & J. Bing (Eds.), *Internet governance. Infrastructure and institutions* (pp. 8–47). Oxford: Oxford University Press.

Blackman, C. (2011). ITU and the internet: déjà vu all over again. *info, 13* (1).

Borne, G. (2010). *A framework for sustainable global development and the effective governance of risk*. Lampeter, UK: The Elwin Mellen Press.

Braman, S. (2002). Informational meta-technologies, international relations, and genetic power: The case of biotechnologies. In J. Rosenau & J. P. Singh (Eds.), *Information technologies and global politics: The changing scope of power and governance* (pp. 91–112). New York: State University of New York.

Broekling, U., Krasmann, S., & Lemke, T. (2011). *Governmentality: Current issues and future challenges*. New York: Routledge.

Buzan, B. (1991). *People, states, and fear: An agenda for international security in the post-cold war era* (2nd ed.). London: Harvester Wheatsheaf.

Carr, J. (2012). *Inside cyber warfare: Mapping the cyber underworld* (2nd ed.). Sebastopol, CA: O'Reilly.

Castells, M. (1996). *The information age: The rise of the Network Society* (Vol. I). Oxford: Blackwell Publishers.

Collier, S. J. (2009). On vital systems security. International Affairs Working Paper 2009-11.

Dean, M. (2010). *Governmentality: Power and rule in modern society*. Thousand Oaks, CA: Sage.

Deibert, R. (1997). *Parchment, printing, and hypermedia: Communication in world order transformation*. New York: Columbia University Press.

Deibert, R., & Rohozinski, R. (2010). Risking security: Policies and paradoxes of cyberspace security. *International Political Sociology, 4*(1), 15–32.

Deibert, R., Palfrey, J., Rohozinski, R., & Zittrain, J. (Eds.). (2011). *Access contested: Security, identity and resistance in Asian cyberspace*. Cambridge: MIT Press.

Deibert, R., Palfrey, J., Rohozinski, R., & Zittrain, J. (Eds.). (2008). *Access denied. The practice and policy of global internet filtering*. Cambridge: MIT Press.

Der Derian, J. (2009). *Virtuous war. Mapping the military-industrial-media-entertainment network* (2nd ed.). New York: Routledge.

Der Derian, J. (2000). Virtuous war/virtual theory. *International Affairs, 76*(4), 771–788.

Dillon, M. (1996). *Politics of security: Towards a political philosophy of continental thought*. London: Routledge.

Drezner, D. (2007). *All politics is global: Explaining international regulatory regimes*. Princeton: Princeton University Press.

Eriksson, J., & Giacomello, G. (2007). Introduction. Closing the gap between international relations theory and studies of digital-age security. In J. Eriksson & G. Giacomello (Eds.) *International relations and security in the digital age* (pp. 1–28). London: Routledge.

Eriksson, J., & Giacomello, G. (2006). The information revolution, security and international relations: (IR)relevant theory? *International Political Science Review, 27*(3), 221–244.

Flyverbom, M. (2011). *The power of networks: Organizing the global politics of the internet*. Cheltenham: Edward Elgar.

Foucault, M. (2007). *Security, territory, population: Lectures at the College de France 1977–78*. Translated by G. Burchell. New York: Palgrave Macmillan.
Foucault, M. (2008). *The birth of biopolitics: Lectures at the College de France 1975–1976*. Translated by G. Burchell. New York: Palgrave Macmillan.
Foucault, M. (1991). Governmentality. In G. Burchell, C. Gordon, & P. Miller (Eds.), *The Foucault effect: Studies in governmentality* (pp. 87–104). Chicago: University of Chicago Press.
Gordon, C. (1991). Governmental rationality: An introduction. In B. Graham, C. Gordon, & P. Miller (Eds.), *The Foucault effect: Studies in governmentality*. Chicago: University of Chicago Press.
Government Accountability Office (GAO). (2010). *Cyberspace: United States faces challenges in addressing global cybersecurity and governance*. Report to Congressional Requesters, Washington, D.C..
Gruenberg, J. S. (2009). An analysis of the United Nations Security Council Resolutions: Are all countries treated equally? *Case Western Reserve Journal of International Law, 41* (2–3), 469–511.
Haraway, D. (1991). *Cyborgs and women: The reinvention of nature*. New York: Routledge.
Henman, P. (2010). *Governing electronically: E-government and the reconfiguration of public administration, policy and power*. Houndmills, Basingstoke: Palgrave Macmillan.
Hossain, K. (2008). The complementary role of the United Nations General Assembly in peace management. *Uluslararasi Hukuk ve Politika, 4*(13), 77–93.
Hughes, R. (2010). A treaty for cyberspace. *International Affairs, 86*(2), 523–541.
Irion, K., & Radu, R. (2013). Delegation to independent regulatory authorities in the media sector: A paradigm shift through the lens of regulatory theory. In W. Schulz, P. Valcke, & K. Irion (Eds.), *The independence of the media and its regulatory agencies: Shedding new light on formal and actual independence against the national context*. Chicago: University of Chicago Press.
Joseph, J. (2009). Governmentality of what? Populations, states, and international organizations. *Global Society, 23* (4), 413–427.
Karns, M., & Mingst, K. (2004). *International organizations: The politics and processes of global governance*. Boulder, CO: Lynne Rienner Publishers.
Krishna-Hensel, S. F. (2007). Cybersecurity: Perspectives on the challenges of the information revolution. In M. Dunn Cavelty, V. Mauer, & S. F. Krishna-Hensel (Eds.), *Power and security in the information age. Investigating the role of the state in cyberspace*. Burlington: Ashgate.
Law, J., & Bijker, W. E. (1992). Postscript: Technology, stability, and social theory. In W. E. Bijker & J. Law (Eds.), *Shaping technology/building Society: Studies in sociotechnical change* (pp. 290–308). Cambridge, MA: MIT Press.
Lawson, S. (2012). Putting the "war" in cyberwar: Metaphor, analogy, and cybersecurity discourse in the United States. *First Monday, 17* (7).
Liftin, K. (2002). Public eyes: Satellite imagery, the globalization of transparency, and new networks of surveillance. In J. Rosenau & J. P. Singh (Eds.), *Information technologies and global politics: The changing scope of power and governance* (pp. 65–89). New York: State University of New York.
Maurer, T. (2011). *Cyber norm emergence at the United Nations*. Cambridge, MA: Belfer Center for Science and International Affairs.
McKinnon, R. (2008). Flatter world and thicker walls? Blogs, censorship and civic discourse in China. *Public Choice, 134*(1–2), 31–46.
Mehta, M., & Darier, E. (1998). Virtual control and disciplining on the internet: Electronic governmentality in the new wired world. *The Information Society: An International Journal, 14*(2), 107–116.
Mitchell, T. (1991). The limits of the state: Beyond statist approaches and their critics. *American Political Science Review, 85*(1), 77–96.
Mueller, M. (2010). *Networks and states: The global politics of internet governance*. Cambridge: MIT Press.
Mueller, M., Mathiason, J., & Klein, H. (2007). The internet and global governance: Principles and norms for a new regime. *Global Governance, 13*, 237–254.

Neal, A. (2009). Rethinking Foucault in international relations: Promiscuity and unfaithfulness. *Global Society, 23*(4), 539–543.

Nye, J. (2011). Diffusion and cyberpower. In J. Nye (Eds.), *The future of power* (pp. 113–151). New York: Public Affairs.

Rabinow, P. (Ed.). (1991). *The Foucault reader*. London: Penguin.

Radu, R. (2012a). The monopoly of violence in the cyberspace: Challenges of cybersecurity. In E. Fels, J.-F. Kremer & K. Kronenberg (Eds.), *Power in the 21st century. International security and international political economy in a changing world* (pp. 137–150). New York: Springer.

Radu, R. (2012b). From drift to draft: International institutional responses to the global digital divide. In R. Pande & T. van der Weide (Eds.), *Globalization, technology diffusion, and gender disparity: Social impacts of ICTs* (pp. 83–94). Hershey, PA: IGI Global.

Rasmussen, M. V. (2001). Reflexive security: NATO and international risk society. *Millennium: Journal of International Studies, 30* (2), 385–309.

Richards, T. (1993). *The imperial archive: Knowledge and the fantasy of empire*. New York: Verso.

Rose, N. (1999). *Power of freedom*. Cambridge: Cambridge University Press.

Rosenau, J. (2002). Information technologies and the skills, networks, and structures that sustain world affairs. In J. Rosenau & J. P. Singh (Eds.), *Information technologies and global politics: The changing scope of power and governance* (pp. 275–287). New York: State University of New York.

Rosenau, J. & Singh, J. P. (2002). *Information technologies and global politics: The changing scope of power and governance.* New York: State University of New York.

Shelby, J. (2007). Engaging Foucault: Discourse, liberal governance, and the limits of Foucauldian IR. *International Relations, 21*, 324–345.

Shields, M. (1997). Reinventing technology in social theory. In J. Lehmann (Eds.), *Current perspectives in social theory* (Vol. 17, pp. 186–216). Greenwich, CT: JAI Press.

Singh, J. P. (2002). Introduction: Information technologies and the changing scope of global power and governance. In J. Rosenau & J. P. Singh (Eds.), *Information technologies and global politics: The changing scope of power and governance* (pp. 1–38). New York: State University of New York Press.

Souter, D. (2007). Internet governance and development: Another digital divide? *Information Polity, 12*, 29–38.

Sreberny, A., & Khiabany, G. (2010). *Blogistan: The internet and politics in Iran*. London: I. B. Tauris.

Stone, A. (2011). Cyberspace: The next battlefield. *USA Today*, June 19.

Veyne, P. (1997). Foucault revolutionizes history. In A. Davidson (Ed.), *Foucault and his interlocutors*. Chicago: University of Chicago Press.

Walters, W. (2012). *Governmentality: Critical Encounters*. New York: Routledge.

Willcocks, L. (2006). Michel Foucault in the social study of ICTs: Critique and reappraisal. *Social Science Computer Review, 24*(3), 274–295.

Williams, R., & Edge, D. (1996). The social shaping of technology. *Research Policy, 25*, 865–899.

Cyber War and Strategic Thought: Do the Classic Theorists Still Matter?

Craig B. Greathouse

Abstract Warfare in the future will be different from warfare in the past, but are the classic theorists still viable capable of providing insight into the nature of war, conflict, and policy within the realm of cyber war? While a significant amount of work has been directed towards the possibility of cyber war and explaining what it might look like, there is a limited focus on strategic options which states might select in this emerging field. The chapter first offers a typology to view issues of cyber conflict. Second it offers an examination of possible strategic choices for policy makers based on classic strategic thought. The ideas of Clausewitz, Sun Tzu, Jomini, along with more modern theorists such as Douhet and Warden are applied to the ideas of cyber war. The possible ramifications of the application of these strategic options in the cyber realm are then discussed. Classic strategic theorists can provide options for policy makers but significant work still remains to be done.

C. B. Greathouse (✉)
University of North Georgia, Dahlonega, GA, USA
e-mail: craig.greathouse@ung.edu

J.-F. Kremer and B. Müller (eds.), *Cyberspace and International Relations*,
DOI: 10.1007/978-3-642-37481-4_2,

1 Introduction

The impact of the information age on warfare has been a major issue over the last two decades as policy makers, soldiers, strategists, and non-state actors consider how best to use and protect themselves from the threat of cyber war. Unlike weapons of the past, the technology necessary for waging cyber war are not restricted to particular actors within the system. The capacity to assault important systems exists both in state and non-state actors and could possibly cripple whole societies that have become reliant on information. Over the last several years the world has seen examples of cyber war. Attacks include the 2007 cyber attack on Estonia, the 2008 attack on the state of Georgia, the Stuxnet virus from 2009 which attacked the Iranian nuclear program, and the actions by the hacker group "Anonymous" against companies such as Visa, MasterCard, PayPal, and Amazon over the Wikileaks scandal. Each attack illustrates the potential destructiveness of cyber war. "Because cyber warfare is unconventional and asymmetric warfare, nations weak in conventional military power are also likely to invest in it as a way to offset conventional disadvantages" (Geers 2011). Going forward policy makers will be required to develop strategies which address the issues of cyber war. The difficulties of developing effective strategies will be compounded by a multitude of issues including; what qualifies as cyber war, should responses be the same as from attacks by state or non-state actors, does the state respond the same if elements of its civilian sector are attacked rather than the public sector, and whether an offensive or defense stance is necessary? This chapter argues that policy makers do not have to start from scratch in their search for effective strategies. Examining traditional strategic thought will yield possible solutions to the issues of cyber war and state policy.

While a great deal has been written on the topic, there needs to be a stronger examination of how the combination of cyber weapons with traditional strategic approaches might impact strategic choices related to cyber war. Do the past approaches to warfare fit with the evolving world of cyber war or must a new generation of strategists be developed to specifically address the ideas of cyber war within the system? Examining the possible applicability of classic ideas of warfare to cyber war must include possible policy ramifications based on potential outcomes. While "bombs" may not be going off with cyber war, the impact of this type of conflict may in fact be more devastating in terms of disrupting societies. "The more electronically dependent an actor is, the more vulnerable it is" (Liaropoulos 2011, p. 4). In several cases traditional strategies of action will create an impact above and beyond the damage done if that strategy were implemented using conventional weapons.

This chapter is broken up into several parts to logically approach the puzzle raised. First there is a need to address the terms and concepts that exist within the field. As in any developing field there is not a common vocabulary for describing the ideas at use. Second a typology of different types of cyber war will be presented which will show the different levels of action within the cyber realm which are possible and it will briefly discuss the possible weapons of cyber war which can be harnessed within each level. The typology allows for distinctions to be made between cyber war and other forms of action. Not all actions on the internet can or should be considered within the realm of cyber war. The next section examines classic military thinkers and their preferential strategies as applied to cyber war and possible ramifications from their usage. While the weapons of cyber war did not exist when Jomini, Clausewitz, and Sun Tzu put forth their thoughts, their ideas do address conflict between actors and should provide some viable ideas/approaches for how to engage in cyber war. The ramifications of applying these ideas will be addressed. The final section will examine some of the general policy implications of using classic strategic approaches within a new arena of warfare. This section will illuminate areas in which more policy work will need to be done regarding these new capabilities.

2 What is Cyber War?

As with any emerging area of study there no commonality within the field about the correct terms which should be used. Authors can and do create language which they feel best describes the phenomena they are trying to address. However because of the diversity of descriptions offered, the field has quickly become overrun with competing ideas and terms. Concepts such as the revolution in military affairs (RMA), fourth generation warfare, electronic warfare, information warfare, network centric warfare, and cyber war have all been offered to explain the emerging area of conflict. The focus on understanding this new type of conflict matters. Unlike nuclear explosion where millions would die the disruption created within a society or for a group by a major cyber attack or war may be just as serious. As Cetron and Davies observe "major concern is no longer weapons of mass destruction, but weapons of mass disruption" (Cetron and Davies 2009, p. 47). So to understand what these approaches are and how they may work is an important step in developing effective policy. A small sample of definitions is provided to give a taste of the approaches and ideas that have been articulated.

> The Shanghai Cooperation Organization has defined "information war" in part as a "confrontation between two or more states in the information space aimed at… undermining political, economic, and social systems [or] mass psychologic [*sic*] brainwashing to destabilize society and state." (Gjelten 2010, p. 36).

> A cyber attack is "The premeditated use of disruptive activities, or the threat thereof, against computers and/or networks, with the intention to cause harm or to further social, ideological, religious, political or similar objectives. Or to intimidate any person in furtherance of such objectives." (U.S. Army Training & Doctrine Command 2006).

> Cyber power is the ability to obtain preferred outcomes through use of the electronically interconnected information resources of the cyber domain (Nye 2010, pp. 3–4).

> The use of network-based capabilities of one state to disrupt, deny, degrade, manipulate, or destroy information resident in computers and computer networks, or the computers and networks themselves, of another state (Schaap 2009, p. 127).

The Schaap definition works well to describe a range of cyber weapons within the system however there are problems for the definition. It focuses on "of another state" and this assumption/usage fails to take into account the fact that cyber war could be launched against an international organization, supranational actor, non-government organization, or a multinational corporation. The actor which launches the attack may not be a state. Given the low barrier to entrance into this realm of capability, it could be some type of non-state actor. The transformed definition used for this study is that cyber war is the use of network based capabilities of a state or non-state actor to disrupt, deny, degrade, manipulate, or destroy information resident in computers or computer networks or the computers or networks themselves of another actor.

The literature and occurrences in the system show that non-state actors are significantly involved in conducting cyber war (Klimburg 2011 and Manson 2011). The actions of "hacktivists" including the group Anonymous or "patriotic hackers" and actions taken during the 2007 cyber attack on Estonia or the actions of Chinese or Taiwanese hackers (Nye 2010, p. 6) all point to the ease of non-state actors engaging in this form of conflict. The reason for the inclusion of more actors within this emerging realm is that information and the use of information is growing across the globe. But as the use of information grows there is also an increased threat to the control of civilization (Alford 2001). This threat could come in the form of targeting systems which are dependent on software for their operation; Alford (2001) illustrates this point by pointing out aircraft and their move from hardware control to fly by wire/software control. The Stuxnet virus is another example, its focus on disabling safety systems to damage equipment being used in the Iranian nuclear program. Threats to information or the ability to manipulate information could be catastrophic as the world becomes more information reliant.

3 Typology of Cyber Operations

As with traditional forms of war there are different levels of "intensity" of cyber war. Not all of these types of attacks are going to be directed towards destruction of resources or misdirection during an attack. Some will engage in criminal activities while others will engage in intelligence gathering. Due to the nature of the of this evolving realm of conflict they would all fall within cyber operations but an effective typology must be constructed to provide guidance to policy makers and strategic thinkers about how to address certain types of attacks.

Saad et al. (2011) provided a general typology of attacks used between Israel and Hezbollah which provides a starting point for developing a more generalized typology of cyber operations. They argue that there are three dimensions; attacks that focus on strategic objectives, attacks that focus on technical objective, and attacks of a political nature (Saad et al. 2011, p. 1). Attacks with a strategic focus those on include information systems, communications, and civil security; technical targets include weapons control and military communications; while political assaults look to alter the power balance within diplomatic relations (Saad et al.

2011, p. 1). Cyber weapons include viruses, malware, denial of service, spying, along with jamming and blocking (Saad et al. 2011, p. 4). While this typology provides a starting point basing it on objectives limits its usefulness. Following the Clauswitizian definition of war as a political activity all actions will be ultimately directed towards shaping the power relationships between the actors involved (Clausewitz 1984). In addition the separation between strategy and technical objectives does not provide an effective continuum through which cyber war can be analyzed. Nye argues "one should distinguish simple attacks which use inexpensive tool kits which anyone can download from the internet from advanced attacks which identify new vulnerabilities that have not yet been patched, new viruses, and involved "zero day attacks" (first time use)" (Nye 2010, p. 11).

Schmitt's (1999) six criteria could be used to evaluate cyber attacks; these include severity, immediacy, directness, invasiveness, measurability, and presumptive legitimacy (Schmitt 1999, pp. 18–19). These criteria however are focused on international law issues, which while important must be a secondary consideration when building a typology of cyber operations. Liaropoulos (2011) proposes a broad typology including cyber espionage, web vandalism, denial of service, and attacks on critical infrastructure. This provided a more practical approach to defining types of cyber operations but needs to be more fully fleshed out in that denial of service may actually be targeted at critical infrastructure.

3.1 Cyber Espionage and Cyber Crime

Creating a typology of cyber operations is difficult; distinguishing meaningful and separate categories which don't bleed from one area to another may prove to be impossible given the nature of the technology. The typology advocated here attempts to provide distinctive cut points which will then allow for strategy and policy differences based on the severity and intensity of any cyber attack. At the low end of the spectrum exists cyber vandalism, this type of activity is not designed to cause damage but rather to be an annoyance. For example this type of action may entail changing a website to insert text or some other statement which has not been approved by the owners of that site. Within the context articulated here, this would be political statements rather than a singular hacker entertaining themselves. Moving up the spectrum would be cyber espionage, the use of electronic capabilities to gather information from a target. This step in the continuum is an extension of the activities that actors within the system engage in everyday. It simply uses a new means to access different types of data which had previously not been available. The reason cyber espionage is placed so low on the spectrum is that it is an accepted and understood activity within the international system. The next level of the typology is cyber crime. This activity while it may not directly be focused towards a particular state can be targeted towards both public and private actors within the system. The definition of cyber crime used is the use of electronic capabilities to engage in criminal activities by an actor for profit, what distinguishes cyber crime from other cyber activities is the profit motive. The means for many of the previous three elements will be the use of viruses or malware, which are easily created or written to open up vulnerabilities to networks or individual users (Chabinsky 2010). Viruses which have been propagated across the internet have both criminal and espionage motives as they create weaknesses in defenses and allow for information to be transferred outside of the user's control.

3.2 Denial of Service

Within the typology those elements up to and including cyber crime would not fall into the category of cyber war. However beyond cyber crime these categories of the typology could elements of cyber war. While malware may be used to gain information it can also be used to create another effect within the cyberworld, a denial of service attack. Denial of service is the next step up on the spectrum of cyber operations. While denial of service may not be "destructive" it has the potential to prevent actions by the target and cover other types of activity by the attacker. A denial of service attack overwhelms a particular website or network through the use of data overload. This type of attack is designed to crash the system of the targeted actor. Some of the most effective denial of service attacks uses botnets, infected computer networks which are then directed to overloading the targeted site. Recent examples of this type of attack include the assaults on Estonia and Georgia which have been traced to Russia (Klimburg 2011). In both of these instances the denial of service attack was designed to limit the target government's means to communicate and react due to the nature of the attack. In the case of Estonia the attack was limited to creating chaos within the country (Crosston 2011), however in regards to Georgia the attack was meant to assist the actions of Russian troops as they moved into parts of Georgia which had been under dispute (Korns and Kastenberg 2008). The military application of denial of service attacks is visible from these two examples. Anonymous' reaction to the Wikileaks scandal points to the potential of non-state actors using this tactic more in the future. Denial of service does not need the resources of a state within the system. While Anonymous did not completely take down the PayPal, Visa, or MasterCard sites it did cause disruption (BBC December 9, 2010). A more focused and drawn out denial of service attack would have significant potential to disrupt economic activities within an information dependent economy.

3.3 Focused Cyber Attack

The final two categories within the typology are similar but differ in scope. The fifth category in the typology is an attack to destroy or completely disrupt an element of critical infrastructure within the actor. This type of attack would be designed to either destroy the data, software, or hardware which controls a particularly important part of an actor's infrastructure. This might include an electrical grid, water distribution system, banking system data, or any multitude of other systems. These systems need not be government controlled, in the realm of the information society many critical systems are controlled by the private sector. A systematic attack on the New York Stock Exchange or NASDAQ would have significant economic fallout given how connected elements are both within the U.S. and across the globe. A recent example of this type of attack is the Stuxnet worm, designed to attack vital components of the Iranian nuclear program (Farwell and Rohozinski 2011). While the Stuxnet worm was disabled fairly quickly once discovered (Farwell and Rohozinski 2011) the capacity to use the weapons of cyber war to destroy or disable a particular element of infrastructure raises the stakes significantly. Retaliation or escalation due to an attack of this nature may in fact occur. Depending on the critical infrastructure element attacked this could have far reaching consequences for the targeted actor.

3.4 Massive Cyber Assault

The last category in the typology is that of a massive cyber attack designed to destroy network and data systems across the entirety of an actor. What distinguishes this type of attack from the previous one is the scale. Going after one piece of infrastructure could have a negative impact on a society; however at this level of attack the intent is to completely cripple an actor. This attack would not be limited to just military or government assets but would also be directed at civilian networks and assets. The goal would be to destroy or completely degrade the information capabilities of the target and limit their ability to operate. This type of attack would be overwhelming and crippling for actors dependent on information. For example a massive attack across numerous sectors in the United States might have the ability to cripple both the electrical and banking sectors. This type of attack could create a mass disruption scenario within the United States which could provide the attacker with a significant edge in future actions. The question raised by some authors is whether this would in fact be equivalent to an armed attack? (Waxman 2011) One of the weapons which would be at the heart of the final two categories would be the "logic bomb". The logic bomb is a type of program designed to be inserted into a network and when activated destroy data or cause other changes which would cripple the network in question (Klimburg 2011). One example might be attacking the communications points of network within a target which would limit the ability to communicate during times of crisis. In combining a logic bomb with other sorts of cyber attacks like denial of service could possibly create electronic and information mayhem. This type of attack could be further exacerbated with a complimentary physical attack on critical communication nodes. An attack on the Telx facility in Atlanta, GA could cripple the ability of the Southeastern United States to connect to the internet. While cyber war is normally thought of as not directed at physical targets, the operation of the internet and other networks is dependent on power and a physical infrastructure.

Given the possible nature of cyber warfare which has and is emerging there is a significant need for policy makers and military leaders to develop strategies for dealing with these threats and for using the new options that exist. However rather than creating brand new approaches, this study argues that some of the classic and modern military theorists have already provided the basis which can be used and manipulated to address the topic of cyber war. By expanding on the existing ideas strategists can focus on implementation actions rather than spending time on rebuilding a literature.

4 Strategists and Strategies for Cyber War

Historic thinkers in military strategy continue to form the basis for examining how warfare might occur within the international system. The inclusion of forms of cyber war will not stop the applicability of these ideas to how future conflicts may be fought. However the application of these classic ideas to the weapons of cyber war may have ramifications above and beyond the scope they would have in terms of physical conflict. Therefore when examining the baseline strategic suggestions of these thinkers it is imperative to also examine the possible consequences over and above the directed action.

4.1 Jomini

Jomini's strategic ideas were shaped by the Napoleonic period. His main goal within *The Art of War* was to distill for future generals important maxims about war which would hold across time which could then be put to use within any particular situation. At the heart of his argument is that "the art of war consists in bringing into action upon the decisive point of the theater of operations the greatest possible force" (Jomini 2008, p. 85). For Jomini the application of overwhelming force at the most decisive point in the battlefield was a recipe for victory. Decisive points were defined as

1. The features on the ground
2. The relation of the features to the ultimate strategic aim
3. The positions occupied by the respective forces (Jomini 2008, p. 65–66).

Applying this approach to cyber war, one would expect to see attacks such as denial of service or similar actions against particular sensitive elements within a state. The attacks would be designed to cause the target the greatest destruction/confusion and the resulting outcome would limit the ability of the target to respond. This type of cyber attack would not be a limited operation, rather there would be significant resources focused on one point to cause its incapacitation or destruction after a determination was made about the most decisive point a cyber attack could be made. For information dependent societies the vulnerability of being attacked at a decisive point could be crippling. However, a decisive point may not be a military target; it may in fact be civilian with significant ramifications for the entire population.

Using Jomini's approach within the cyber realm is predicated on finding a decisive point within the target's information network on which to launch the assault. If the entirety of the strength of the attacker is directed to destroying one point, a point needs to exist which would cripple the target's ability to react. The diffuse nature of many information networks may mitigate against this approach. However if information nodes or convergence points exist through which the majority of traffic passes, the targeting of this element could be very successful, especially if privately operated. For example in the United States, Telx is a company (telx.com) which provides interconnection between networks. Taking down several of these sites would significantly degrade information transfer in key areas. Any focused attack, as advocated by Jomini, would not be concealed, therefore the knowledge of who launched the cyber attack would be clear to parties within the conflict and those outside of it. This would limit one of the unique features of the current generation of cyber weapons that of being able to disguise who the attackers actually are (Cornish et al. 2010). While the ideas advocated by Jomini may work towards a limited network with one important element, against a more diverse network this approach may not be as effective.

4.2 Clausewitz

Of mid-ninetieth century military theorists there is one name which stands above the rest, Clausewitz. Given the amount of material written about *On War* and some of his baseline ideas of war it is unnecessary to fully delve into those ideas. In examining some of the strategic options proposed by Von Clausewitz the ideas of the center of gravity, the trinity, friction, fog of war, and whether war can be limited come to the fore. One of the biggest misconceptions about Clausewitz is that *On War* advocates total/absolute war. Within Book 1, Clausewitz[1] clearly argues that absolute war can only exist in the world of theory (Clausewitz 1984 Book 1, Chap. 1 pt 6. And pt 10) therefore any cyber war would be of "limited" impact rather than an absolute approach. The nature of any cyber conflict would be "limited" with the other elements becoming more important.

The trinity is "composed of primordial violence, hatred, and enmity…of chance and probability…and its subordination as an instrument of policy" (Clausewitz 1984, p. 89). These three elements balance each other and are elements which must be considered when discussing war. When examining the trinity in the context of

[1] All citations for Von Clausewitz are taken from Michael Howard and Peter Paret Indexed Edition of On War released in 1984.

cyber war some of the ideas of Clausewitz may be limited. The virtual nature of cyber war may limit the impact of violence, hatred, and enmity. By removing some of the physical interaction and issues which can be translated to the people, the nature of war may fundamentally change. In terms of the other elements of the trinity, that of chance and probability and as an instrument of policy there is no doubt both of these elements clearly remain in play. The context of chance and probability and friction due to fog of war could be significantly altered within the context of cyber war. One of the problems Clausewitz articulated was a lack of information is going to limit the ability of commanders and politicians to effectively act. The amount of information that may be gained about how an actor may act due to compromising their protected files may in fact lift the fog of war to a significant extent. However, just as the fog of war may be lifted, the capabilities provided within cyber conflict can actually increase exponentially the ability to increase fog of war.

The cyber attacks on the state of Estonia in 2007 and Georgia during the 2008 conflict with Russia illustrate the capacity of actors that attempt to increase the fog of war by attacking information nodes and important websites to disrupt communications (Ashmore 2009). Clausewitz spent a great deal of time talking about the impact of the fog of war on operations and how it creates friction on the battlefield. The more technologically reliant an actor is, whether at home or abroad, the more susceptible they will be to an effective attack on their information systems. Actors that become reliant on advanced technology may become more vulnerable to issues of friction and fog of war than ever before due to the actions of an enemy using the tactics of cyber war. These issues would not just be related to governments, any cyber operation most likely target civilian networks as well. This will further complicate any actor's capacity to respond and may in fact create more significant problems. Some civilian networks may not be as protected nor have the redundancies built into allow them to be quickly restored. The longer an information based society is limited, the great the damage and confusion will be.

Center of gravity is one of the most debated ideas that come from Clausewitz. Echevarria (2007) shows numerous interpretations about what center of gravity represents. Center of gravity can best be described as a linkage whose loss will have devastating effect on an enemies' capacity to wage war (Echevarria 2007, Chap. 8). By undermining a center of gravity, the ability of an enemy to wage war will be limited or completely impaired. Clausewitz talks about the center of gravity providing unity (Clausewitz 1984, pp. 485–486), which in the information age provides a very different application than Clausewitz's original expectations Echevarria shows that Clausewitz applied the concept of center of gravity to wars where decisions are sought (Echevarria 2007, p. 184) and that the concept does not effectively apply to more limited wars (Echevarria 2007, pp. 183–184). Cyber war can create the ability to target and destroy the connectivity between the operations in the field and the political control. The application of center of gravity taken in the context of cyber war changes the original interpretation of Clausewitz, but the concept still matters. If the center of gravity provides for unity within an actor, destroying or degrading unity will limit or in extreme cases destroy that actor's capacity to engage in effective action within the system.

The previous overview of Clausewitz's ideas show that his theoretical approach to understanding war still holds relevance when examining cyber war. The issues of center of gravity, if understood as unity, and fog of war are incredibly powerful ideas that can be exploited by actors using the tactics of cyber war. The ability to blind information dependent actors through the use of electronic noise, as was attempted in both the situations in Estonia and Georgia, or to neutralize their information unity puts those targets at significant risk. Actors looking to engage in information warfare need to seriously consider creating the ability to blind/jam the information flow within a target to (1) create a fog of war which creates friction for their ability to operate and (2) to effectively break the ability of a targeted actor to act at all. The nature of Clausewitz's work can be applied to cyber war. Fog of war can be seen as coming to play with every denial of service attack that has been launched. In addition specific attacks on communication nodes would be of critical importance in the Clausewitz strategic guide to cyber war.

4.3 Sun Tzu

In contrast to the heft of Clausewitz, the Chinese theorist Sun Tzu provided a series of maxims to shape and guide future military leaders and thinkers. Given the nature of his writings, one of the important advantages is his distillation of fundamental ideas about how to approach conflict. It is easier to apply Sun Tzu to cyber war and in some ways the applicability of Sun Tzu to cyber war is much more effective.

He argues that "all warfare is based on deception" (Tzu 2006, p. 7) and "when able to attack we must seem unable, when using our forces we must seem inactive…" (Tzu 2006, p. 7). These ideas fit perfectly within cyber war. Engaging an enemy through the use of cyber weapons can limit the defender's knowledge of who attacked them and will benefit the attacker. Targets that are attacked without their knowing it will be unable to effective repel the assault and significant damage may be inflicted on them. For example, the Stuxnet virus that was found within the international system in 2009 and 2010 seems to have been designed specifically to cripple elements of Iran's nuclear weapons program (Farwell and Rohozinski 2011; Williams 2011; Broad et al. 2011). This virus would be a clear application of Sun Tzu by attacking an enemy without being visible. The hidden nature of who launched the cyber attacks on Estonia in 2007 (Klimburg 2011) again shows the ability of actors to effectively use these maxims of Sun Tzu to great effect.

Another of Sun Tzu's maxims is "know the enemy and know yourself, you need not fear the result of a hundred battles" (Tzu 2006, p. 15). Through the ability to hack into files, obtain information, and then make use of that information a target is put at risk even prior to their taking action if the instigator is effective in using cyber capabilities to effectively find information about their adversary. Geers (2011) argued that the ability to seize data, attack or defend networks, and shape the digital battlefield are essential elements of information. The Wikileaks case shows the potential vulnerability of actors in the information age. The amount of information obtained could expose critical information and secrets of an actor. This maxim has been has been pursued relentlessly by states in the system during war, most spectacularly during World War II, with the breaking of Ultra by the British and the Japanese JN-25 code by the Americans. This action put the Germans and the Japanese at a significant disadvantage due to their enemies knowing a great deal about their plans. In the modern information age the damage that could be done may be exponentially greater.

"So in war the way is to avoid what is strong and to strike at what is weak" (Tzu 2006, p. 34). Again this element guides potential activity within the course of cyber war. "If he sends reinforcements everywhere, he will everywhere be weak" (Tzu 2006, p. 33) the ability to fully defend all important elements within an information society does not exist. While certain systems may be shielded, other systems may not be so protected, and that vulnerability can be exploited by an effective strike.

Examining Sun Tzu it is clear that the ideas advocated by him matter today as much or more than they did when the ideas were posited. The focus on knowledge is a critical element of the information age. Those actors which can exploit the information aspects of cyber war provide themselves with a much stronger position of power. The use of deception within cyber war is also another critical element that applies; it can exploit knowledge or can be used to prevent the targeted actor from responding to an attack. During the 2007 cyber attack on Estonia it was not clear who the attacker was, (Ashmore 2009). This ability to deceive limits the ability of the targeted state to launch a counter attack. While there was evidence about where the attacks originated there were enough questions to prevent absolute proof from being offered (Ashmore 2009). Lastly Sun Tzu's argument about trying to protect everything will create vulnerabilities in all systems has merit. Actors, especially those that are more dependent on information, will have to pick which systems to most heavily protect; many of those elements will be beyond the scope of state protection and have to be left to civilian means of defense which may not be fully secure. For example is the Telx center at 56 Marietta Street in Atlanta, GA completely secure against a targeted attack? Given the nature of Sun Tzu, his arguments would be an effective guide for action across the entire cyber war spectrum.

4.4 Airpower Theorists

While the aforementioned theorists have a great deal to say about ideas which may be incorporated into the strategic development of cyber war, another set of theorists may be better positioned to draw lessons from are the airpower theorists, who created doctrine for employing the "new" weapons system of the twentieth century, the airplane. Many of the ideas of airpower theory can be directly translated to cyber war in that they contain issues predicated on technology and also the idea of movement that is not limited by geography which is a critical difference between classical military theorists and the issues related to cyber war.

4.4.1 Douhet

The first airpower theorist to be addressed is Guilio Douhet, an Italian artillery officer who wrote during the inter-war period. In *Command of the Air* he articulated his most important ideas related to the use of aircraft in war (Meilinger 2001). One of the core ideas for Douhet was the ability of airpower to attack vital centers for the enemy (Douhet 1983). This idea while on its face similar to those offered by Clausewitz and Jomini was not just directed against armies. Rather a vital center was "the key industries and structures that allowed a state to function" (Meilinger 2001, p. 104). The expansion of war beyond just the armies and/or navies to the civilian sector is an important idea which was enabled by the development of new technology (Douhet 1983, pp. 9–10 and MacIsaac 1986) synthesized Douhet's most important ideas.

1. Modern warfare allows no distinction between combatants and noncombatants
2. Successful offensives by surface forces are not longer possible
3. The advantages of speed and elevation in the three dimensional arena of aerial warfare have made it impossible to take defensive measures against an offensive aerial strategy
4. A nation must be prepared at the outset to launch massive bombing attacks against the enemy centers of population, government and industry—hit first and hit hard to shatter enemy civilian morale leaving the enemy government no option but to sue for peace (MacIsaac 1986, p. 630).

While there are some elements from Douhet which obviously have not proven correct including offensives by surface forces will be limited and that there are limited effective defenses against an offensive aerial attack (Douhet 1983, pp. 15–19) by taking the remaining ideas to the cyber realm a very aggressive approach is developed. The most controversial but also one of the most critical assumptions made by Douhet is that there are no distinctions between combatants and non-combatants (Douhet 1983, p. 20). Within the cyber realm this argument has significant implications. For the United States more than 98 % of government information flows along civilian means of communication (Jensen 2010, p. 1534). The interdependence that has been generated between in the realm of information makes separating government and civilian components almost impossible (Jensen 2010). Just as government and society are inexorably linked together within information societies, targeting for cyber war will be both civilian and military/government oriented. Attacking just government servers/systems will in fact not prevent the target from reacting; only by engaging systems across the entire information spectrum can a fully successful cyber attack occur. This raises the question of what is the state's role in defending private interests and vice versa. While this issue is not the focus of this study, it is an important implication that emerges and must be addressed.

Another element that Douhet (1983) raises is speed of attack. Cyber attacks that can be launched to overwhelm existing defenses quickly will be the most successful attack. Combining this with a broad based attack across both military and civilian sectors could ensure that the target of the attacks be incapacitated. Speed within the information world has always been a hallmark whether processing speed of CPUs, how fast information flows across the internet. To effectively destroy defenses an attacker is going to have to quickly and effectively overwhelm the defenses of those systems to achieve a positive outcome.

The idea of shattering civilian morale has been one of the most criticized elements that Douhet argued (Meilinger 2001). While a massive attack on the information system of a country may not break civilian morale it could in fact bring a country to a halt. Using the ideas advocated by Douhet systems from communication, electric, water, banking, transportation, and other critical elements could all be overwhelmed in the initial attacks. For technologically advanced states this could completely disrupt the way they live and work. For example if a massive cyber attack were to cripple electrical and banking systems, this would create widespread panic within a state. The loss of power would cripple a society like the United States, which would have a massive effect on communication as well; in addition an attack on the banking sector would limit economic markets and basic transactions for a significant amount of time. Disruption of society and the ability to effectively wage war was one of the reasons that Douhet argued for attacking vital centers. This process actually becomes easier to do within the context of cyber war. Disruption may be further exacerbated by the issues of private and public coordination. With neither sector being in control of this realm, an effective response may be limited. Cornish et al. (2010) argued that a major weakness between the private and public is their reluctance to share information. This is further exacerbated by the loyalties of many corporations in the west not to their countries but to their shareholders (Cornish et al. 2010, p. 22).

4.4.2 Mitchell and Trenchard

Following on the heels of Douhet is William "Billy" Mitchell and Sir Hugh Trenchard who both took some of the basic ideas of Douhet and advocated similar but more nuanced strategic approaches. Both agreed that control of the air was a vital component in winning any war, however they did not go to the lengths of Douhet to win (Chun 2001 and Meilinger 2001). One of the important differences between these two and Douhet was their unwillingness to attack civilians directly. Both advocated that airpower should be directed against infrastructure and industrial targets to limit the ability of the target to effectively fight in the war (Chun 2001).

In contrast to Douhet, this differentiation of targeting is morally acceptable but when looking at the application of ideas to the cyber world, this position becomes difficult to address (Swanson 2010). The overlap between information systems and their interconnectedness is a major issue in any technologically advanced country. Therefore being able to only target specific information systems is much more difficult and requires a much more focused approach. Attacking specific systems to disrupt the ability of that target to act can produce the outcome sought by the attacker without imposing a significant cost on the general population. This type of targeted attack could be represented by the Stuxnet virus which was specifically created to target a very specific type of structure in the state of Iran (Williams 2011 and Broad et al. 2011). However the cost of creating a virus or cyber weapon to target each particular type of machine might be beyond an actor's resources. Thus a more general attack to disrupt systems across the country may be a more effective outcome as compared to a focused approach.

4.4.3 Warden

Col. John Warden, whose ideas have been used by the United States Air Force during Operational Iraqi Storm (Chun 2001), brought together some of the strategic threads posited by the classical theorists, earlier airpower thinkers, and combined them with an understanding of modern technological innovation. Warden is a proponent of strategic war, "in strategic war, a clash may well take place, but it is not always necessary, should normally be avoided, and is almost always a means to an end and not an end in itself" (Warden 1995). He argued that any actor must be viewed as a system, and within that larger system there are five subsystems that can be targeted, he phrases his approach as a five ring model. The five subsystems or rings include leadership, organic essentials, infrastructure, population, and fighting mechanism (Warden 1995). These rings should be attacked from inside out with the leadership at the core and then working out to each subsequent ring. At the core of each actor are numerous centers of gravity, these can be located using the five ring model which will then illustrate circles of vulnerability. Targeting the circles of vulnerability from inside out, conflicts can be more effectively ended faster. By destroying the actor's leadership or the ability of the leadership to communicate compromises the ability of the entire system to effectively respond. Likewise the targeting of organic essentials "leads to the collapse of the system" (Warden 1995) and makes it difficult for the actor to engage in action.

An additional element that Warden claims is important in effectively attacking the enemy system is to use the parallel attack. "States have a small number of vital targets at the strategic level…These targets tend to be small, very expensive, have few backups and are hard to repair. If a significant percentage is struck in parallel the damage becomes insuperable" (Warden 1995). The ability to hit multiple strategic targets at once prevents the target from bringing those elements back into good order and respond effectively to future attacks. "The greater the percentage of targets hit in a single blow, the more nearly impossible his response" (Warden 1995).

Bringing together disparate threads Warden generated an approach which proved to have a significant impact on how conventional wars were approached. However the ideas of Warden would be even more devastating if used within the context of a cyber war. The targeting advocated by Warden across the entire system starting at the leadership and then moving to forces in the field would generate a significant number of targets. Using the ring model, communications systems would be the foremost element of any attack. The ability to cut the leadership level from the rest according to the model would create almost catastrophic impact; this would not even include attacks on infrastructure and organic essentials which would only increase the impact. Combining this strategic targeting scheme with parallel attacks through cyber war, a technologically dependent actor could be crippled more quickly than Iraq. If an attacker had the capacity of using parallel attacks, they would strike to bring down whole systems including communications, electrical, and financial to prevent the target from being able to effectively respond due to the massive impact of the initial assault.

5 Cyber Defense

Up to this point strategic approaches which point to offensive types of operations have been examined. The question becomes can defense and deterrence be a viable policy stance for states? Defense is the ability to actively resist if an attack is launched against an actor. Fixed defenses are the classic representation of this type of approach. From castles, forts, coastal and harbor defenses, to the Maginot Line each of these was designed to defend a specific objective from assault. The problem historically is that none of these defensive structures has ever been able to survive changes in technology. Castles became vulnerable to the emergence of gun powder based weapons, air power, or attack based on movement. Some of the strongest defensive positions have fallen as new weapons and tactics have moved the advantage, in some respects, to the offensive side of the ledger. Fixed positions have become vulnerable to the destructive power of precision weapons and the ability to attack the fortification from multiple directions.

If one were to apply only the strategy of defense in the realm of cyber war, this choice is defective from the start. Defending computers and networks has created a massive sector which develops and maintains security, the capacity of this approach is always being threatened. First and foremost the defensive aspects of cyber war are at a disadvantage due to the 'offensive dominance' which has been shown to this point (Cornish et al. 2010). Second these defenses are never going to be perfect either due to programming issues, the need for the system to be connected to the larger internet, or human error. The only way to completely protect a system from external threats would be to full segregate the system from external connection, but even by doing this the system still could be threatened by the human element either intentional or not (Brechbuhl et al. 2010 and Ashmore 2009). However, given the need for interconnectiveness, segregating most systems from the ability to communicate defeats the purpose of connectivity. Some defenses that can be put into place include encryption, firewalls, and automated detection. But as with most defenses these are as good at the updates and operators, and even then can still be penetrated.

Another issue in developing a defensive posture for an actor in the cyber world is what to defend. If a state were only to defend its networks, that may be feasible but that then leaves whole segments of infrastructure which are operated by the private sector open to assault which could have a debilitating impact on society. Even though the private sector does build in defenses against types of cyber threats, an intentional attack is very likely to disrupt their business. Operation "Payback" launched by the hacker group Anonymous against Visa, MasterCard, PayPal, and Amazon.com over their treatment of Wikileaks is but one example. Of those four only Amazon was able to effectively resist the denial of service attack due to the capacity that Amazon has built into its system (BBC 2010). Just taking this simple example and extending it, if three out of four companies could not effectively protect themselves or their capacity the impact by sustained cyber attacks would be devastating to the domestic economic structure of a state. There are arguments that governments are required to help defend private networks and sites due to inter-connectiveness (Brechbuhl et al. 2010 and Jensen 2010). However, in attempting to defend a whole array of elements beyond that of their own sites and capacity would potentially leave the government vulnerable. In many western states, especially within the United States, private industries are essential in protecting important systems from a cyber attack (Klimburg 2011).

6 Cyber Deterrence

A deterrent stance provides another option, but only with a clearly articulated and known capacity to back up the threat of retaliation should any cyber attack be launched. Only with capability and willingness to retaliate can deterrence be achieved (Cornish et al. 2010). In a cyber war situation, deterrence means that a state would have to have an offensive capability which could cause disproportionate harm if it were attacked. Given the problems of finding who is launching an attack, the ability to deter is limited. Deterrence is only effective if the attacker could be clearly identified and punished. In the Estonian cyber attack there was not clear evidence at the time of the attack who was responsible. The state of Georgia also suffered a significant cyber attack, however it appears that this attack was launched via non-state nationalist groups (Ashmore 2009), whether at the behest of the state is still unclear. If a cyber attack's origin can be hidden then the threat of deterrence is lessened. Blank (2001) put forth a compelling argument that deterrence in information war (IW) may not be effective given the nature of the "weapons" at work.

> IW cannot be deterred by another IW force since both sides can easily deceive or cripple their opponent's ability to make the kind of evaluations that deterrence depends on. Pre-emptive IW becomes a viable, almost a necessary, option here. Since everyone has access or will have access to forms of IW and can use commercially available satellites, cell phones, PCs and the like to launch delayed attacks, hack systems, etc., *IW deterrence must be ubiquitous and universal to be effective*. Otherwise the temptation to strike first can be overwhelming. This trend towards defending everything can be seen in the US' accelerated efforts to set up homeland and anti-terrorist defense organizations. But evidence to date suggests that despite our technological superiority we cannot accurately deter or predict what enemy forces will do, especially when they can target our insight

into their thought processes or vice versa. Nor is it clear that we can deter our adversaries if our strategy focuses on destroying their ability to command troops, govern their country, and control their WMD (Blank 2001, p. 133).

7 Policy Ramifications/Conclusion

In looking at strategic choices that are available to states and other actors in the international system to address the issue of cyber war and cyber attacks the need to have clearly articulated policy stances in place is necessary. Without having defined policy stances before a cyber attack occurs, the actor's ability to respond to that attack will be limited and disjointed at best. However in trying to build an effective policy for cyber conflict, states will continually have to reassess the issue given the technological developments that are always occurring and the capacity which actors may be developing. There are three important areas that all actors must clearly lay out in terms of cyber policy; first what are viable targets, second how to deal with non-state actors, finally what offensive/defensive balance will be pursued. The issue of defense capacity is more difficult due to the inclusion of the private sector in the policy discussion and the necessary coordination which must be developed. In examining the issues surrounding the cyber world the situation becomes more complex than threats from physical attacks. "In a networked world, there are no real safe harbors—if you are on the network, you are available to everyone else on the network. A key consequence is that security is not the concern of someone else" (Brechbule et.al. 2010, p. 84).

Through the development of an effective cyber war typology states and other actors may be able to effectively match actions to events in the system. Using the proposed typology of cyber operations and relying on previously developed strategic models would allow states to build strategies and policies to provide a basis for action in this area. The typology also helps to define elements of cyber deterrence given the need for an escalation threat to make deterrence viable. However even with this typology of cyber operations strategic development is still in its infancy. The classical theorists provide a basis but given the nature of cyber war their ideas need to be nuanced into the cyber world.

There are divergent strategy choices that are being put before actors on which they will have to make decisions in the near future. If an actor ignores the evolution of cyber issues it will put them at a significant disadvantage going forward. Ashmore (2009) contends that there needs to be defense in depth created across the society within both the civilian and military networks. The problem of this approach is that in a country like the United States the number of possible actors is massive. Combine this with the need to develop commonality of action across the public and private sectors and the complexity and cost potential for this approach would grow exponentially. Given the speed of advances in cyber capabilities there is no guarantee that complete safety or anything even close would emerge.

Another possible option to explore as the debate occurs is to assess how much of a response to develop within an actor. Does the actor need to develop a counter cyberspace policy or should it focus on offensive action? "Counter cyberspace: a function consisting of operations to attain and maintain a desired degree of cyberspace superiority by the destruction, degradation, or disruption of an enemy's capabilities to use cyberspace" (Trias and Bell 2010, p. 96). But in either developing a counter response or just focusing on offensive cyber war capability an issue will be raised that will require significant thought. "Attacks through cyberspace against cyber assets can also result in cascading collateral damage. The fear of such common side effects had kept American leadership from pulling the trigger of cyber weaponry" (Trias and Bell 2010, p. 97). Given the degree of disruption that could possibly be raised through creating a counter attack or offensive cyber capability policy makers need to very clearly address this issue.

There needs to be significant work done at all levels of the emerging field of cyber war. There is a need for both strategic thought but also tactical innovation but at the same time these two levels must be able and willing to talk to each other. Further complicating this issue going forward will be the need for actors to develop a grand strategic approach to cyber war which will provide the direction necessary for strategic and tactical development. All the while technology will continue to grow and evolve which mean the thinking necessary cannot be static in nature, it must continue to evolve to address new developments both in terms of technical capabilities but strategic situations.

References

Alford, L. D. (2001). Cyber warfare: A new doctrine and taxonomy. *Crosstalk: Journal of Defense Software Engineering, 14*(4), 27–30.

Ashmore, W. C. (2009). Impact of alleged Russian cyber attacks. *Baltic Security & Defence Review, 11*(1), 4–40.

BBC. (2010). Pro-Wikileaks activists abandon Amazon cyber attack. Retrieved December 9, 2010, from http://www.bbc.co.uk/news/technology-11957367.

Blank, S. (2001). Can information warfare be deterred? *Defense Analysis, 17*(2), 121–138.

Brechbühl, H., Bruce, R., Dynes, S., & Johnson, M. E. (2010). Protecting critical information infrastructure: Developing cybersecurity policy. *Information Technology for Development, 16*(1), 83–91.

Broad, W., Markoff, J., & Sanger, D. E. (2011, January 15). Israeli test on worm called crucial in Iran nuclear delay. *The New York Times*. Retrieved October 8, 2011, from http://www.nytimes.com/2011/01/16/world/middleeast/16stuxnet.html?_r=2.

Cetron, M. J., & Davies, O. (2009). Ten critical trends for cyber security. *The Futurist*, 43(5), 40–49.

Chabinsky, S. R. (2010). Cybersecurity strategy: A primer for policy makers and those on the front line. *Journal of National Security Law and Policy, 4*(1), 27–40.

Chun, C. K. S. (2001). Aerospace power in the twenty-first century: A basic primer. USAF Academy in Cooperation with Air University Press: Colorado Springs, CO. Retrieved October 30, 2012, from http://www.dtic.mil/cgi-bin/GetTRDoc?Location=U2&doc=GetTRDoc.pdf&AD=ADA421723.

Cornish, P., Livingstone, D., Clemente, D., & Yorke, C. (2010) On cyber war. Chatham House. Retrieved October 3, 2012, from http://www.chathamhouse.org/publications/papers/view/109508.

Crosston, M. D. (2011). World cyberMAD: How "mutually assured debilitation" is the best hope for cyber deterrence. *Strategic Studies Quarterly, 5*(1), 100–116.

De Jomini, B. (2008). *The art of war* (G. H. Mendell & W. P. Craighill, Tans.). Radford: Wilder Publications.

Douhet, G. (1983). *The command of the air*. Washington, D.C.: Office of Air Force History.

Echevarria, A. J. (2007). *Clausewitz and Contemporary War*. Oxford: Oxford University Press.

Farwell, J. P., & Rohozinski, R. (2011). Stuxnet and the future of cyber war. *Survival, 53*(1), 23–40.

Geers, K. (2011). Sun Tzu and cyber war. Cooperative Cyber Defence Centre of Excellence. Retrieved March 20, 2012, from http://www.ccdcoe.org/articles/2011/Geers_SunTzuandCyberWar.pdf.

Gjelten, T. (2010, November/December). Shadow wars: Debating cyber disarmament. *World Affairs, 173*(4), 33–42.

Jensen, E. T. (2010). Cyber warfare and precautions against the effects of attacks. *Texas Law Review, 88*, 1533–1569.

Klimburg, A. (2011). Mobilising cyber power. *Survival, 53*(1), 41–60.

Korns, S. W., & Kastenberg. J.E. (2008). Georgia's cyber left hook. *Parameters*, 38, 60–76. Retrieved March 22, 2012, from http://www.carlisle.army.mil/usawc/parameters/Articles/08winter/kokor.pdf. (Last accessed March 22, 2012).

Liaropoulos, A. (2011). Cyber-Security and the law of war: The Legal and Ethical Aspects of Cyber-Conflict. GPSC Working Paper # 7. Retrieved March 22, 2012, from http://www.gpsg.org.uk/docs/GPSG_Working_Paper_07.pdf.

MacIsaac, D. (1986). Voices from the Central Blue: The air power theorists'. In P. Paret (Ed.), *Makers of modern strategy*. Princeton: Princeton University Press.

Manson, G. P, I. I. I. (2011). Cyberwar: The United States and China prepare for the next generation of conflict. *Comparative Strategy, 30*(2), 121–133.

Meilinger, P. S. (2001). *Airmen and air theory: A review of the sources*. Maxwell Air Force Base: Air University Press.

NYE, J. S. (2010). *Cyber Power*. Harvard Kennedy School, Belfer Center. Retrieved March 22, 2012, from http://www.dtic.mil/cgi-bin/GetTRDoc?Location=U2&doc=GetTRDoc.pdf&AD=ADA522626.

Saad, S., Bazan, S., & Varin, C. (2011). *Asymmetric cyber-warfare between Israel and Hezbollah: The web as a new strategic battlefield.* Proceedings of the ACM WebSci'11, June 14–17 2011, Koblenz, Germany. Retrieved March 22, 2012, from http://www.websci11.org/fileadmin/websci/Posters/96_paper.pdf.

Schmitt, M. N. (1999). Computer network attack and the use of force in international law: Thoughts on a normative framework. *Columbia Journal of Transnational Law, 37*, 885–937.

Schaap, A. J. (2009). Cyber warfare operations: Development and use under international law. *Air Force Law Review, 64*, 121–174.

Swanson, L. (2010). The era of cyber warfare: Applying international humanitarian law to the 2008 Russian-Georgian cyber conflict. *Loyola of Los Angeles International & Comparative Law Review, 32*(2), 303–333.

Trias, E. D., & Bell B. M. (2010). Cyber this, cyber that… so what?. *Air & Space Power Journal, 24*(1), 90–100.

Tzu, S. (2006). The art of war. London: Filiquarian Publishing LLC.

U.S. Army Training & Doctrine Command. (2006). DCSINT Handbood No. 1.02, Critical Infrastructure Threats and Terrorism. Retrieved October 30, 2012, from http://www.fas.org/irp/threat/terrorism/sup2.pdf.

Von Clausewitz, C. (1984). *On War: Indexed Edition* (M. Howard & P. Paret, Ed. and Trans.). Princeton: Princeton University Press.

Warden, J. A. (1995). The enemy as a system. *Airpower Journal*, 9, 40–55. Retrieved October 8, 2012, from http://www.airpower.au.af.mil/airchronicles/apj/apj95/spr95_files/warden.htm.

Waxman, M. C. (2011). Cyber-attacks and the use of force: Back to the future of article 2(4). *The Yale Journal of International Law, 36*, 420–459.

Williams, C. (2011, January 21). Stuxnet: Cyber attack on Iran 'was carried out by Western powers and Israel'. The Telegraph. Retrieved October 8, 2011, from http://www.telegraph.co.uk/technology/8274009/Stuxnet-Cyber-attack-on-Iran-was-carried-out-by-Western-powers-and-Israel.html.

SAM: A Framework to Understand Emerging Challenges to States in an Interconnected World

Jan-Frederik Kremer and Benedikt Müller

Abstract States and enterprises are increasingly faced with newly emerging threats made possible by interconnected digital infrastructures. These threats pose great risks to states and their populations and can result in shifts in power. The inherent interdependent character of the digital infrastructure and its growing importance for economies, public safety and our society in general make controlling and countering these threats a demanding and critical challenge for both enterprises and governments. This chapter identifies the different types of stakeholders, their actions and respective motives in the context of cyber security and introduces the so called SAM-framework for the analysis of cyber security. Building on that, the implications for governments will be discussed including the resulting threats and responsibilities.

J.-F. Kremer (✉)
Center for Global Studies, University of Bonn, Bonn, Germany
e-mail: jkremer@uni-bonn.de; jan-frederik.kremer@freiheit.org

J.-F. Kremer
Friedrich Naumann Foundation for Freedom, Berlin, Germany

B. Müller
IBM, Düsseldorf, Germany
e-mail: mueller@me.com

J.-F. Kremer and B. Müller (eds.), *Cyberspace and International Relations*,
DOI: 10.1007/978-3-642-37481-4_3, © Springer-Verlag Berlin Heidelberg 2014

1 Introduction[1]

> Cyberspace touches practically everything and everyone. It provides a platform for innovation and prosperity and the means to improve general welfare around the globe. But with the broad reach of a loose and lightly regulated digital infrastructure, great risks threaten nations, private enterprises, and individual rights. The government has a responsibility to address these strategic vulnerabilities to ensure that the United States and its citizens, together with the larger community of nations, can realize the full potential of the information technology revolution. (The White House, Cyberspace Policy Review, Preface)[2]

The cyberspace is everywhere—this saying is no longer just a saying, it is an empirical fact. In today's world nearly everything is connected to the Internet, not only our computers and mobile phones, but also our cars, fridges and other things of everyday use. The world is becoming increasingly interconnected through cyberspace—the Internet has made business and communication a lot easier than they used to be at any other time of human economic activity; it has created new innovative and productive branches of business we don't want to miss today (think about Amazon, Google Mail or Facebook for example). Likewise, cyberspace has not only fostered business around the globe, it has also created the so called "global village"—cyberspace connects people and enterprises and helps us consume or produce information from all over the globe in real-time. Making money and business in our times has become dependent on the interconnectedness made possible by the Internet and the cyberspace. Even elementary things like the supply of water have become more and more dependent on the cyberspace. Given this grade of dependency, it can be argued that the cyberspace[3] has a Janus-faced character: On the one hand it has created immense opportunities for economic activity, communication, etc., but on the other hand, due to fact that an increasing number of processes are dependent on the interconnectedness of today's digital infrastructure, it has also become a serious source of newly emerging threats for national, commercial and private security. In the words of the U.S. government Cyberspace Policy Review:

> The architecture of the Nation's digital infrastructure, based largely upon the Internet, is not secure or resilient. Without major advances in the security of these systems or significant change in how they are constructed or operated, it is doubtful that the United States

---

[1] The authors would like to acknowledge the many valuable suggestions and helpful comments of the chair, discussant, participants and audience of the panel "Cyber security: Emerging Challenges" (at 2011s ISSS/ISAC Annual Conference—Irvine, CA) and of the panel "Cyber security" (2012s Joint BISA-ISA Conference, Edinburgh, UK) on this chapter. Furthermore the authors owe their thankfulness to Maximilian Mayer, Andrej Pustovitovskij, Xuewu Gu and Katrin Kremer for their annotations on the topic and our writings.

[2] See: http://www.whitehouse.gov/assets/documents/Cyberspace_Policy_Review_final.pdf.

[3] In this chapter we will stick to the term "cyberspace" to capture the whole empirical phenomena of interconnected digital infrastructures (mainly the Internet), their occurrence, instruments, mechanisms and modalities.

> can protect itself from the growing threat of cybercrime and state-sponsored intrusions and operations (Ibd.).

Or as pointed out in the Cyber Security Strategy for Germany[4] and the Cyber security Strategy of the European Union[5]

> In recent years attacks against information infrastructures have become ever more frequent and complex, while at the same time perpetrators have become more professional. Further there is a serious risk for companies, because the trend to develop information systems for industry on the basis of standard components and connect them to cyberspace, which is motivated mainly by economic concerns, entails new vulnerabilities (Cyber Security Strategy for Germany: Preface).

> Over the last two decades, the Internet and more broadly cyberspace has had a tremendous impact on all parts of society. Our daily life, fundamental rights, social interactions and economies depend on information and communication technology working seamlessly (Cyber security Strategy of the European Union: 2).

States and enterprises are increasingly faced with newly emerging threats made possible by interconnected digital infrastructures (Dunn Cavelty 2007, 2010; Dunn Cavelty and Kristensen 2008, Geers 2010), threats that governments and enterprises are still looking to find appropriate responses to. Foreign governments and independent groups infiltrate company or state facility networks, hacker groups steal and publish sensitive data and telecommunication infrastructures rely increasingly on technology provided by manufacturers owned or controlled by overseas administrations or military. These threats pose enormous risks to states and their citizens and can result in shifts in power. Like Radu (2012) precisely points out: "The growing dependence of individuals, groups, institutions and organizations—from local to international level—on computer-mediated systems has transformed the types of security threats over the years (…)."

The naturally interdependent character of the digital infrastructure and its growing importance for economies, public safety and our society in general makes controlling and countering these threats a demanding and critical challenge for both enterprises and governments.

In recent years, a vast amount of working papers, studies, journal articles and grey-literature[6] have tried to analyze the consequences and implications of these developments for governments, societies and individual citizens (p.e. Dunn Cavelty 2010; Dunn Cavelty and Kristensen 2008; Manson 2011; Hjortdal 2011; Lawson 2013; Clarke and Knake 2010), to identify the actors and means involved (p.e. Deibert 2003; Earl and Kimport 2011; Manson 2011) and to develop approaches or categorizations

[4] See: Federal Ministry of Interior of the Federal Republic of Germany (2011).

[5] See: http://eeas.europa.eu/policies/eu-cyber-security/cybsec_comm_en.pdf

[6] At this point we will not attempt to discuss the entire body of literature, which has been written on cyber security over the last years, because this task alone would by far exceed the space limitations of one chapter. For this purpose see the CSIS's (2011) Selected Bibliography for Cyber Security, which is updated quite regularly (http://csis.org/publication/selected-bibliography-cyber-security).

for classification (see below). However, due to the fact that most of the approaches rely on frameworks which establish specific (assumed!) links between certain actors, their intentions or motivations and their instruments on an a priori conceptual level, existing approaches rarely offer satisfying classifications.

After discussing existing approaches, this chapter therefore introduces a framework for analyzing cyber security (SAM-framework), which in our understanding is better suited to cope with the conceptual challenges of categorizing the involved stakeholders, actions and motives in the realm of cyber security. Following the outline of this framework, implications for governments will be discussed with regard to the relevance of a cyber incident, its scope and the urgency for governments to take actions/measures.

2 Frameworks for Understanding Cyber Security

2.1 Existing Frameworks

Various frameworks and approaches have been developed to analyze actors, means and threats related to cyber security. In general, when looking at the body of literature on cyber security, we can distinguish between approaches which concentrate either on the means and motivations of the actors involved (Klimburg 2011; Billo and Chang 2004), or on the specific instruments used by the offenders in the specific context of an attack (Farwell and Rohozinski 2011; Hughes 2010, Kshetri 2005). Other frameworks do not make a distinction between different layers and dimensions of threats for categorization (IBM US Federal 2010, p. 16). Cornish et al. for example distinguish between four cyber-threat domains: "state-sponsored cyber attacks; ideological and political extremism; serious and organized crime; and lower-level/individual crime" (Cornish et al. 2009, p. 3). The problem here is that these approaches are neither distinctive nor conclusive, since they mix up different layers of analysis (like actors, motivational/intentional arguments, scope). Furthermore, some of the existing frameworks make assumptions about the relation between the attacking party and the defending party (e.g. by presuming that a state-sponsored cyber attack must be aimed at another state), while empirical evidence hints at the occurrence of all kinds of possible combinations, including for instance state-sponsored attacks on foreign enterprises or terrorist groups.

Some scholars focus on developing taxonomies/offering classifications for specific fields of activity (cyber-warfare, conflict situations, cyber terror, transnational activism etc.) and/or a limited scope of incidents distinguishable by the use of common means/instruments or carried out by relatively homogenous groups (p.e. Ahmad and Yunos 2012; Alford 2001). Another body of literature in (international) law addresses the implications of newly emerging security risks—made possible by the interconnectedness of today's life—and tries to classify them (p.e. Schmitt 2012; Shackelford 2008; Kesley 2008; Farwell and Rohozinski 2012). Although considerably enhancing our knowledge on how to evaluate and classify certain empirical occurrences of cyber threats and incidents, the offered classifications and taxonomies are naturally restricted to limited spheres of applicability, or selective issue areas (international law etc.). Sure, these approaches deliver the benefit of accurateness of classification for their restricted areas of application, but contrariwise have to pay the price of (very) limited general applicability and a lack of generalizability. Solid analysis and acute understanding of empirical phenomena need approaches that offer tools for understanding the very specifics of empirical phenomena as well as approaches that deliver features of generalization in order to be able to fully grasp the whole picture.

These elaborations point to the need for a more holistic framework that does not mix up different dimensions in a single categorization, limit the parties involved to an attacking and a defending one and make a priori assumptions about their respective relations.

2.2 SAM Framework

To extend the understanding of cyber incidents' characteristics, actors involved and implications for authorities in a broader and more general scope of application we have developed the SAM framework, which is based on three dimensions and allows for a classification of cyber threats that is both distinctive and conclusive. It distinguishes between stakeholders, activities, and motives (see Table 1).

2.3 Stakeholders

The first step in making the complex nature of interactions in the cyber domain approachable is clustering the respective stakeholders in this domain.

Based on the observation that "the low price of entry, anonymity, and asymmetries in vulnerability means that smaller actors have more capacity to exercise hard and soft power in cyberspace than in many more traditional domains of world politics" (Nye 2010, p. 19) it becomes even more important to identify the stakeholders involved in cyber incidents.

Nye for example distinguishes three different types of actors which possess specific relative power resources in the cyberspace: governments, Organizations and highly structured networks as well as Individuals and lightly structured networks (Ibd, p. 10). Even though Nye's general considerations on cyber power are conclusive and persuasive, his distinction between different types of actors and their respective power resources is not totally convincing because several of his resources attributed to specific actors are far from being unique to only one category of actor (p.e. "Large budgets and human resources", "Provision of public goods", "Virtual anonymity and ease of exit" etc.).[7]

[7] Nye himself considers his division of actors as insufficient to serve as a conclusive classification, but more as a "rough approximation" (Nye 2010, p. 9).

Table 1 SAM-framework

Stakeholder	Who?	Who is mandating, who is executing and who is affected?
Activities	What?	What activities have been carried out and what are the results in terms of defects?
Motives	Why?	Why have the activities been carried out, what are the underlying motivations and intentions?

Cornish et al. (2009, p. 3) on the other hand distinguish between "four cyber-threat domains: state-sponsored cyber attacks; ideological and political extremism; serious and organized crime; and lower-level/individual crime." The Cyber Security Strategy of the United Kingdom divides actors in Criminals, States and Terrorists (Cyber Security Strategy of the United Kingdom 2009, p. 12f). These classifications already take into account the motivation of the different actors—be it criminal, political or ideological motivation. As these examples show, classifications that attribute an a priori relation between actors and respective motives, actions and/or power resources are ill-suited since the assumption of a general relation between specific actors and respective motives, actions and power resources is at least not always valid. Or as Nye points out: "The diffusion of power in the cyber domain is represented by the vast number of actors, and relative reduction of power differentials among them. Anyone from a teen age hacker to a major modern government can do damage in cyber space" (Nye 2010, p. 9), which means that the ascription of particular actions/power resources to specific classes of actors is at least problematic considering the logic of the cyberspace (diffusion of power and accountability).

Therefore, we propose a classification of actors that is agnos tic with respect to their motivation or choice of instruments. Moreover, the clustering of actors is not limited to the party considered as an offender or aggressor in the area of cyber security, as the classical differentiation between attacker and defender does not seem to be suited to describe these modern types of conflict.

As a first step it seems to be more suitable for the analysis to identify and categorize the stakeholders involved in cyber security.

Therefore, we propose to differentiate between different types of stakeholders involved in cyber security related incidents: Individuals, Collectives/Swarms, Groups, Organizations/Enterprises and States/Intergovernmental and Supranational Organizations (Table 2).

2.3.1 Individuals

Individuals are naturally the smallest unit involved in cyber security issues. This category includes independently operating hackers as attackers as well as private persons as victims, for example when targeted in credit card fraud operations.

Table 2 Stakeholders

Name	Description	Examples
Individuals	Individual people	Comodohacker, Kevin Mitnick
Collectives, swarms	Temporary, cause-related pooling of individuals	4Chan, anonymous
Groups	Structured and perpetual assemblage of individuals	Al-Qaeda, LulzSec
Organizations, enterprises	Constituted legal entities	Cisco, VW, GE, Exxon, Lockheed Martin
States, intergovernmental and supranational organizations		USA, UN, NATO, EU, Germany, China, Iran

2.3.2 Collectives/Swarms

This is the category of actors that could only emerge through the Internet. Informal, loosely coupled groups of people coming together for a certain purpose are often described as swarms. An example is 4Chan, an Internet forum originally created to post and share images, which has become relevant for cyber security in the form of Anonymous, a hacker movement originating from this very forum (Maslin 2012).

2.3.3 Groups

This category encompasses both organized groups that have existed independently from the Internet and are adapting new technologies to support their existing agenda as well as organized groups that were formed over the Internet and are specifically pursuing objectives related to the cyber space.

The category includes, but is not limited to, international insurgents, jihadists, and terrorist organizations using the internet "as a tool for radicalization and recruitment, a method of propaganda distribution, a means of communication, and ground for training" (Theohary and Rollins 2011; Weimann 2011).

2.3.4 Organizations/Enterprises

Enterprises as well as other organizations such as non-governmental organizations, research organizations or think tanks rely increasingly on information and communications technology (ICT). The emergence of new business models based on the Internet as well as the enhancement or transformation of existing business models on the one hand and the rising dependence of business processes on ICT on the other hand contribute to an interlock between a successful business and a reliable IT infrastructure.

2.3.5 States/Intergovernmental Organizations

States and intergovernmental organizations are affected by questions of cyber security on different levels. They might be the source of or subject to malicious activities themselves (e.g. in regard to the communication infrastructure of the government or by engaging in cyber warfare activities), but they also represent the interests of their population and economy, respectively the interests of their members.

Examples in this category include states like the United States, Germany, France, China, Russia as well as intergovernmental organizations like the United Nations, NATO or the European Union. A prominent cyber security incident involving state actors happened in 2008, when "a series of sophisticated cyber assaults" preceded "Russian conventional air and ground attacks on Georgia" (IBM 2011, p. 8).

Regarding these different classes of stakeholders it is important to note that in an incident all possible constellations are imaginable (individuals attacking organizations, organizations attacking states, swarms attacking individuals, and so forth) and that theoretically their potential power of impact is equally high, although the realization of this potential is of course linked to the amount of resources available (e.g. funding, manpower). Furthermore it is important to note that there are targeted activities in cyberspace (purposely executing an action for achieving defined goals) but that there are also "opportunistic" activities, happening more or less incidentally and target/goal-insensitive. This can for example be observed when viruses or worms are spread Internet-wide, aimed for example at collecting credit card data or stealing identities but also causing collateral damage like traffic congestions impacting network connections. The spread of digital weapons like Stuxnet, which are developed with very specific intentions in mind (e.g. politically motivated) but are later used for secondary purposes (e.g. criminal activities) by additional parties is also included in this scenario. In our understanding, "actions" always refer to targeted activities carried out purposely by specific stakeholders to achieve defined goals.

2.4 Actions

Due to the complex nature of ICT, a wide variety of malicious activities can be observed in the cyberspace. Although there are attempts of classifications on a technical level, the focus of this chapter on regulatory and political implications calls for a taxonomy that is focused on the designated outcome of a certain activity rather than the actual technical implementation. Table 3 provides such a taxonomy, listing actions graded from mainly non-disruptive activities to mainly destructive activities along with their respective form of potential physical/kinetic impact.

2.4.1 Stealing

The most non-disruptive and least aggressive malicious action in the cyberspace is to steal or intercept information. In 2010 for example, the Trojan Hydraq was

Table 3 Actions

		Example	Physical impact
Non-disruptive	To steal, to intercept	Stealing of trade secrets	Indirect
	To influence	Influencing public opinion	Indirect
	To manipulate, to control	Manipulation of financial services	Indirect, direct
Destructive	To disrupt, to destroy	Disruption of power supply	Direct

released in an attempt to steal intellectual property from enterprises (Symantec Internet Security Threat Report: 4).

Another example is the penetration of the U.S. electrical grid by foreign spies in order to map the U.S.'s infrastructure (Gorman 2009), although this might also be a preparation for other actions such as the disruption of the system. Data theft is probably the most common type of attack, 75 % of global energy organizations for example reported at least one data breach in a period of 12 months when surveyed in 2011 (Davies 2011, p. 60). Another case in this category is the recently discovered systematic cyber espionage by a Chinese Army unit targeting western businesses (Ewalt 2013; Sanger et al. 2013).

2.4.2 Influencing

Besides espionage/stealing, influencing is one of the less destructive/disruptive malicious activities (cf. Cyber Security Strategy of the United Kingdom 2009, p. 12) that can be observed in the cyberspace. Influencing refers to the direction of (public) opinion by either providing, shaping or withholding information. As Dartnell (2003, p. 477) points out, ICT provides "enormous opportunities for non-state actors and enhances the global profile of previously marginalised issues and movements".

Terrorist groups for example may use the cyberspace for propaganda, training and instruction purposes (Denning 2001). An example of this is the spreading of propaganda by terrorists as well as the counter-propaganda campaigns carried out by State Department officials on al-Quaeda websites in Yemen (DeYoung and Nakashima 2012). Influencing can also come in the form of blocking access to information, for example in the case of the Chinese government censoring critical websites in China (Hughes 2010) or the blocking of access to social networks like Twitter and Facebook by authoritarian governments during the Arab Spring (Howard and Hussain 2011). The systematic release of confidential information, as done by Wikileaks (Cull 2011), also falls into this category, because it can have a serious negative effect on an actor's soft power and credibility and undermine his diplomatic standing. Similarly the growing importance of influencing the public option of target states' populations to gain/increase soft power through public/digital diplomacy can be considered here.

2.4.3 Manipulating

In contrast to the category described above, the term manipulating is used in this chapter to address the direct modification of electronic data, in order to affect the functioning of a system (e.g. change the target of a drone or let a machine produce altered or defect parts) or to have people act on the basis of wrong information (e.g. display altered stock prices to change buying behavior). Some of the activities described by Denning as "Hacktivism" ("convergence of hacking with activism") also fall into this category (2010, p. 263).

2.4.4 Disrupting

Disrupting refers to the most destructive actions, which encompasses cyber attacks aimed at disrupting a service or destroying virtual or real assets. This includes for example attacks on systems used to manage and operate water, power or oil and gas utilities—attacks that are most likely to inflict physical damage (IBM 2011). A recent example for an incident in this category is the case of the Stuxnet worm which destroyed centrifuges in the Iranian nuclear program (Farwell and Rohozinski 2011) and which may actually be classified as a weapon (Davies 2011; Knoepfel 2013).

2.5 Motives

Although this framework includes motives as an important dimension to understand cyber security incidents, it does not provide a conclusive list of categorizations. Due to the fact that motives are very versatile and not mutually exclusive, Table 4 can only provide a starting point and first approximation for trying to determine the motives behind an incident.

The table lists five common classes of motives: economic, ideological, political, psychological and power-related motives. It is important to note that there is no direct association between certain types of motives and classes of stakeholders or categories of actions, although it can be anticipated that certain combinations have a higher correlation than others. The combination of states as attackers with political and power-driven motives would for example be expected to be significantly correlated. Furthermore it should be noted that multiple motives can be combined or that motives can act as a proxy for other motives, for example in the case of extremist groups that carry out cyber attacks with an economic motive, but

Table 4 Motives

Economic	Ideological	Political
Psychological	Power-related	…

are ultimately driven by an ideological or political agenda which they are seeking to finance through these attacks (Rollins and Wilson 2007).

3 Implications for Governments

> Networks and control systems are under repeated cyberattack, often from high-level adversaries like foreign nation-states. (Baker et al. 2010, p. 3)
>
> Cyberspace provides the ultimate environment for asymmetric warfare. Determined individuals or small groups are attracted to the extremely low costs and the relatively low levels of technical expertise needed to conduct offensive operations against important government, military and economic assets. (IBM US Federal 2010, p. 8)

Now that we have introduced a framework that makes it possible to categorize cyberspace threats much more precisely, we turn to the question which implications for governments result from our observations. We have seen that there are different stakeholders within the realm of cyber security who take different actions in order to achieve their goals. Within this context it is important to point out that only a small number of cyberspace actions are carried out by or against states. For a large number of the daily-occurring cyberspace threats non-governmental actors (individuals, groups, swarms etc.) can be identified as stakeholders and most of the actions are also not directed against governments or other national institutions (e.g. credit card fraud against individuals, industrial espionage, identity theft, etc., cf. Luiijf 2012; Alperovitch 2010; Grow et al. 2008).

3.1 Direct Versus Indirect Threats

Depending on the threat a government is faced with, different measures or actions are called for. It is therefore important to differentiate the direction as well as the relevance of a threat. In a first step the difference between "direct" and "indirect" threats has to be defined. Apart from the obvious direct threats, which are aimed directly at a state's government, there are a significant number of scenarios in which governments and other national institutions are threatened indirectly. Table 5 shows the distinction between direct and indirect threats to authorities:

Direct threats to authorities can be defined as:

> *All kinds of direct attacks against the IT-infrastructure of a government/national institution.*

Table 5 Threats for governments

Direct threats to authorities	Indirect threats
Government is directly affected	State (population, economy,...) is affected, government might be responsible for protection
Disruption of government communications, stealing of state secrets, influencing of government decisions, attack of military infrastructure, ...	Attacks on power grid, water supply, industrial espionage, disruption of major production facilities and communication networks, manipulation or disruption of financial transactions, ...

Direct attacks might for example be aimed at the disruption of military infrastructure, theft of sensitive information/secrets, as well as the manipulation of public opinion within a state in case this is perceived as a threat by the regime in charge (e.g. totalitarian regimes and autocracies). A prime example of a direct threat is for example an attack on the IT-infrastructure by a foreign country, as explained by Inkster:

> In 2003 the Pentagon began to register a series of cyber attacks against US government and contractor sites which have collectively been referred to as Titan Rain. In 2006–07, a number of Western European governments, including Germany and the UK, publicised the extent to which they too had suffered attacks, with the director-general of the British Security Service taking the unusual step of writing a letter to 300 chief executives and security advisers alerting them to the threat from China (Inkster 2010, p. 55).

If the attack is directed against the IT-infrastructure of a private company, this might constitute an indirect threat to authorities, as opposed to a direct threat. An indirect threat is perceived as an action directed against the general public, the private industry or non-governmental actors located within the state, which for example includes attacks on the power grid or water supply, industrial espionage, disruption of major production facilities and communication networks, manipulation or disruption of financial transactions, and many more.

All those actions do not target the authorities directly, but may still pose a significant threat to the state.

Thus, indirect threats are defined as:

Threats that are not targeted at authorities (*and therefore do not fall in the aforementioned category*) *but that pose a certain risk to the state in form of state security, public safety, economic stability, and so on.*

These threats have to be separated from direct threats to authorities and have to be graded according to their relevance and urgency in regard to matters of state (e.g. individual credit card fraud vs. disruption of stock market).

> The Federal government has the responsibility to protect and defend the country, and all levels of government have the responsibility to ensure the safety and wellbeing of citizens. The private sector, however, designs, builds, owns, and operates most of the digital

infrastructures that support government and private users alike. (The White House 2011, p. iv)

3.2 Relevance of Threats

At this point another crucial factor becomes very clear: Apart from differentiating between direct and indirect threats to authorities, it is just as important to include the relevance the incidents have for the state in the analysis. There are direct, as well as indirect threats which are highly relevant for the security of a state (attacks on military IT-infrastructure, private power supply, the stock market) and others which are less important (individual credit card fraud, low scale industry espionage, hacking of email accounts of a junior official, etc.).

It cannot be the aim of this chapter to offer a general model for the identification of the relevance of certain incidents. Since the relevance of an incident always depends on its case-specific effect (so to say the 'total damage' to the state), it is only logical that it has to be estimated on a case-by-case basis.

Finally, let us have a look at the correlation between relevance and competence. Competences for authorities in this context are defined as:

The authorities being legally competent or qualified to either conduct procedures to impose counter-measures against security sensitive cyber incidents, or to implement laws and/or directives which are suitable to effectively coerce non-state actors to impose counter measures.

Table 6 Relevance of threats: illustrative examples

Low relevance for authorities (examples)	High relevance for authorities (examples)
Individual credit card fraud, hacking of an individual mail account, very limited stealing of insensitive corporate data, limited influencing attempts	Cyber-attack on government/military IT, disruption of stock-market communication etc., attack on power grid, coordinated hacking of senior officials mail accounts, systematic and wide range stealing of sensitive industrial secrets

If these conditions are not or only partly fulfilled (either because the authorities cannot impose counter measures by themselves, e.g. in the case of an attack on the power grid in the hand of a private company, or because the authorities have no or only insufficient constitutional/legal competences to coerce non-sate actors to impose such measures, e.g. in the case of constitutional constraints, or in the case that laws/directives cannot be executed properly), we must speak of the authorities having no competencies or indirect competences.

Consequently, we can formulate the following thesis:

The greater the relevance of a cyber security related incident (see above) and the lesser the competences of the authorities in regard to react to this incident, the greater is the overall threat for the state and the greater is the need for action (see Table 6).

This taxonomy enables us to work out the status of a threat to a state by using the case-by-case analysis of relevance and competences. Furthermore, and maybe even more importantly, this classification makes it possible to identify in which areas there is a need for action, due to the possibility of determining where the relevance is high while at the time the competences are insufficient (Table 7).

The following examples will illustrate the functioning of the taxonomy:

- Low Relevance, Indirect/No Competences:
  Hackers target Lloyd Blankfein (CEO Goldman Sachs)[8,9]
  In this case, in which the CEO of the American bank Goldman Sachs fell victim to a hacker attack, we cannot speak of a high relevance for the security of the state since only private data was stolen and apart from the personal embarrassment no consequences could be noted. The competences of the authorities were also low, because an individual (here: Blankfein) can obviously not be bound by law to protect his PC, Smartphone, etc. against possible attacks and even if that was possible, this requirement could realistically not be implemented.
- High Relevance, Direct Competences:
  Israel used electronic attack in air strike against Syrian mystery target [10]
  The case shows a state's direct attack on another state's military IT-infrastructure. The high relevance of this incident is obvious, since sensitive military infrastructure was specifically targeted. The competence here is also direct, because the Syrian authorities are directly responsible for the choice and implementation of measures (firewalls, protection of servers) that can be considered as counter-measures against the incident. The state's need for action thus lies within the implementation of suitable measures.
- High Relevance, Indirect/No Competences:
  Electricity grid in U.S. penetrated by spies[11]
  This last case serves as an example of high relevance as well, because a highly sensitive network, the functioning of which is crucial to the smooth running of the economy, as well as the country's national security, were spied on. However, in this case we are dealing with an indirect competence of the authorities because they can only indirectly influence the implementation of suitable protective measures. The effectiveness of such directives and laws, meant to force private actors to take more suitable protective measures, seems also highly questionable since a complete control of the execution would not be possible. Here, the authorities are dependent on the sometimes difficult cooperation with

---

8 http://dealbook.nytimes.com/2011/09/28/hackers-target-lloyd-blankfein/

9 http://news.cnet.com/8301-27080_3-20112400-245/hackers-leak-data-of-goldman-sachs-ceo/.

10 http://abcnews.go.com/Technology/story?id=3702807.

11 http://online.wsj.com/article/SB123914805204099085.html.

Table 7 Competence versus relevance

	Low relevance	High relevance
Direct competences	Low threat level, low need for action by authorities, authorities are able to react—*non-critical situation*	High threat level, high need for actions by authorities, authorities are able to react—*critical, but solvable situation*
Indirect/no competences	Low threat level, low need for action by authorities, authorities are poorly to react—*partly critical situation*	High threat level, high need for action by authorities, authorities are poorly to react—*critical situation*

commercial actors, who will always try to implement costly measures as slowly as possible. The constellation of high relevance and indirect competences calls for immediate action.

Concluding it has to be pointed out that in cases like the one mentioned last, as well as in all the other cases in which the authorities hold only indirect competences and are thus dependent on a cooperation with non-governmental actors, the need for action is the most urgent and none of the actors is able to meet the challenge on his own.

In cases as critical as this it is necessary to define common responsibilities and *modi operandi* between the representatives of the authorities and the other actors involved, which increases the efficiency of the implemented measures sufficiently. It goes without saying that this problem also applies to those cases in which the federal government has no direct authority over the subordinate administration levels (that is only indirect competences) and these subordinate levels are responsible for the security of sensitive areas (such as local water supply, etc.). Here, the need for action is also significant.

4 Conclusion

Emphasizing the relevance of cyber security in today's world, this chapter provides an introduction to different approaches of understanding cyber incidents from a non-technical point of view. Having pointed out deficiencies of existing categorizations, a new framework encompassing the three dimensions of stakeholders, actions and motives has been proposed. The chapter has further discussed potential implications of threats for governments, pointing out that there are threats with direct effects on authorities and threats that indirectly pertain to the government.

Finally, it has been suggested to differentiate between threats that target areas where the government has direct competences (like state or military infrastructure) and areas where the government has only indirect or even no competences (like privately run infrastructure). In combining this distinction with the differentiation of high or low relevance of threats from the perspective of a government, the situation of highly relevant threats in an area of indirect or no government competence has been identified as the most critical situation. This is also the area where the greatest necessity for further research has been identified.

Thus, the framework presented above can be considered a useful tool for a holistic categorization of cyber incidents as well as the assessment of the potential risk and relevance of cyber threats.

References

Ahmad, R., & Yunos, Z. (2012). A dynamic cyber terrorism framework. *International Journal of Computer Science and Information Security, 10*(2), 149–158.

Alford, L. D. (2001). Cyber warfare: A new doctrine and taxonomy. *Journal of Defense Software Engineering, 14*(4), 27–30.

Alperovitch, D. (2010). Revealed: Operation shady RAT. An investigation of targeted intrusions into 70+ global companies, governments and non-profit organizations during the last 5 years. McAfee White Paper.

Baker, S., et al. (2010). In the crossfire. Critical infrastructure in the age of cyber war. McAfee Report.

Billo, C., Chang, W. (2004). Cyber warfare. An analysis of the means and motivations of selected nation states. Institute for Security Technology Studies at Dartmouth College.

Cabinet Office of the United Kingdom. (2011). Cyber Security Strategy of the United Kingdom.

Clarke, R., & Knake, R. (2010). *Cyber War: The next threat to national security and what to do about it*. New York: HarperCollins.

Cornish, et al. (2009). Cyberspace and the national security of the United Kingdom. Threats and responses. London: Chatham House Report.

CSIS. (2011). Selected bibliography for cyber security. http://csis.org/publication/selected-bibliography-cyber-security

Cull, N. J. (2011). WikiLeaks, public diplomacy 2.0 and the state of digital public diplomacy. *Place Branding and Public Diplomacy*, *7*(1), 1–8.

Dartnell, M. (2003). Weapons of mass instruction: Web activism and the transformation of global security. *Millennium, 32*(3), 477–499.

Davies, S. (2011). Infrastructure cyber attack threat grows. *Engineering and Technology Magazine,* 6(6). Retrieved June 2012 from http://eandt.theiet.org/magazine/2011/06/out-of-control.cfm

Deibert, R. J. (2003). Black code: Censorship, surveillance, and the militarization of cyberspace. *Millennium, 32*(3), 501–530.

DeYoung, K., Ellen N. (2012). U.S. uses Yemeni Web sites to counter al-Qaeda propaganda. *The Washington Post*, May 24, 2012. Retrieved June 2012 from http://www.washingtonpost.com/world/national-security/us-hacks-web-sites-of-al-qaeda-affiliate-in-yemen/2012/05/23/gJQAGnOxlU_story.html.

Denning, D. (2000). Hacktivism: an emerging threat to diplomacy. American Foreign Service Association. Retrieved from http://www.fsjournal.org/sept00/Denning.cfm

Denning, D. (2001). Activism, hacktivism, and cyberterrorism: The internet as a tool for influencing foreign policy. In J. Arquilla, D. Ronfeldt (Eds.), *Networks and netwars: The future of terror, crime, and militancy* (pp. 239–288). Santa Monica, CA: Rand Corporation

Dunn C, Myriam. (2007). Critical information infrastructure: Vulnerabilities, threats and responses. *UNIDIR Disarmament Forum*, 2007(3), 15–22.

Dunn, C. (2010). Cyber-threats. In C. Dunn, Myriam & V. Mauer (Eds.), *The routledge handbook of security studies*. London: Routledge.

Dunn, C., Myriam, Kristensen, K. S. (2008). Securing the homeland: critical infrastructure, risk and (in)security. In C. Dunn, Myriam & K. S. Kristensen (Eds.), *Securing 'the Homeland': critical infrastructure, risk and (in)security*. London: Routledge.

Earl, J., & Kimport, K. (2011). *Digitally enabled social change: Activism in the internet age*. Cambridge: MIT Press.

Ewalt, D. M. (2013). Chinese army directing cyber espionage against western businesses. Forbes online. Retrieved February 19, 2013 from http://www.forbes.com/sites/davidewalt/2013/02/19/chinese-army-directing-cyber-espionage-against-western-businesses/

Federal. (2011). Cyber security strategy for Germany. Retrieved from http://www.bmi.bund.de/SharedDocs/Downloads/DE/Themen/OED_Verwaltung/Informationsgesellschaft/cyber_eng.pdf;jsessionid=2095EA88BC38F69CD38133AECEE4E192.2_cid295?__blob=publicationFile

Farwell, J. P., & Rohozinski, R. (2011). Stuxnet and the future of cyber war. *Survival, 53*(1), 23–40.

Farwell, J. P., & Rohozinski, R. (2012). The new reality of cyber war. *Survival: Global Politics and Strategy, 54*(4), 107–120.

Geers, K. (2010). A brief introduction to cyber warfare. *Common Defense Quarterly*, Spring, 16–17.

Gorman, S. (2009). Electricity grid penetrated by spies. *The Wall Street Journal*, April 9, 2009. Retrieved June 2012 from http://online.wsj.com/article/SB123914805204099085.html

Grow, B. et al. (2008). The new E-spionage Threat, *Business Week*, April 10, 2008. Retrieved from http://www.businessweek.com/magazine/content/08_16/b4080032218430.htm

Howard, P. N., & Muzammil, M. H. (2011). The role of digital media. *Journal of Democracy, 22*(3), 35–48.

Hughes, C. R. (2010). Google and the great firewall. *Survival, 52*(2), 19–26.

IBM, US Federal. (2010). Meeting the cybersecurity challenge: Empowering stakeholders and ensuring coordination. White Paper, February 2010.

IBM X-Force®.(2011)Mid-year Trend and Risk Report. September 2011, IBM Corporation.

Inkster, N. (2010). China in cyberspace. *Survival, 52*(4), 55–66.

Kelsey, J. T. G. (2008). Hacking into international humanitarian law: The principles of distinction and neutrality in the age of cyber warfare. *Michigan Law Review, 106*(7), 1427–1451.

Knoepfel, S. (2013). Clarifying the international debate on Stuxnet—arguments for Stuxnet as an act of war. this volume.

Kshetri, N. (2005). Pattern of global cyber war and crime: a conceptual framework. *Journal of International Management, 11*, 541–562.

Klimburg, A. (2011). Mobilising cyber power. *Survival, 53*(1), 41–60.

Lawson, S. (2013). Motivating cybersecurity: Assessing the status of critical infrastructure as an object of cyber threats. In: A. Badii, & C. Laing (Eds.), *Securing critical infrastructures and industrial control systems: Approaches for threat protection* (pp. 168–189). Hershey, PA: IGI Global.

Luiijf, E. (2012). Understanding cyber threats and vulnerabilities. *Lecture Notes in Computer Science, 2012*(7130), 52–67.

Manson, G. P., III (2011). Cyberwar: The United States and China prepare for the next generation of conflict. *Comparative Strategy, 30*(2), 121–133.

Maslin, J. (2012). The secret lives of dangerous hackers. *New York Times,* May 31, 2012. Retrieved June 2012 from http://www.nytimes.com/2012/06/01/books/we-are-anonymous-by-parmy-olson.html?_r=1&ref=anonymousinternetgroup

Nye, J. S. (2010). Cyber power. Belfer center for science and international affairs paper series. Harvard Kennedy School. Retrieved from http://belfercenter.ksg.harvard.edu/files/cyber-power.pdf

Radu, R. G. (2012). The monopoly of violence in the cyber space: Challenges of cyber security. In E. Fels, J. Kremer, & K. Kronenberg (Eds.), *Power in the 21st century—international security and international political economy in a changing world* (pp. 137–149). Heidelberg: Springer.

Rollins, J., Wilson, C. (2007). Terrorist capabilities for cyberattack: Overview and policy issues. CRS Report for Congress, RL33123.

Sanger, et al. (2013). Chinese army unit is seen as tied to hacking against U.S. *The New York Times online.* Retrieved February 18, 2013 from http://www.nytimes.com/2013/02/19/technology/chinas-army-is-seen-as-tied-to-hacking-against-us.html?hp&_r=1&

Shackelford, S. J. (2008). From nuclear war to net war: Analogizing cyber attacks in international law. In ExpressO. Retrieved from http://works.bepress.com/scott_shackelford/5

Schmitt, M. (2012). Classification of cyber conflict. *Journal of Conflict and Security Law, 17*(2), 245.

Theohary, C. A., Rollins J. (2011). *Terrorist Use of the Internet: Information Operations in Cyberspace.* CRS Report for Congress, R41674.

Weimann, G. (2011). Cyber fatwas and terrorism. *Studies in Conflict and Terrorism, 34*(10), 765–783.

The White House. (2011). Cyberspace policy review. Retrieved from http://www.whitehouse.gov/assets/documents/Cyberspace_Policy_Review_final.pdf.

In Search of Cyber Stability: International Relations, Mutually Assured Destruction and the Age of Cyber Warfare

Hanna Samir Kassab

The characteristic vice of the utopian is naivety; of the realist, sterility.

EH Carr

Abstract Deterrence theory states that world stability can be maintained if the costs of war far out-weigh its benefits. Weapons and strategies that make defense cheaper and offense more costly decrease the likelihood of conflict. Nuclear weapons may have thereby helped create the stability of the Cold War via the costs associated with launching first; according to this argument, war between the US and USSR never occurred because the price of war (i.e. mutual destruction) was too high. This theoretical paper will extend this argument to cyber-attacks and suggest that in order to maintain the security of a nation's information technology, cyber-defense systems that correspond with Deterrence theory must be introduced. Cyber-attacks can be deterred if the proper system, a virus wall, is in place to counter any infiltration of a nation's defense systems. This proposed virus wall would be a way to achieve stability from nation state cyber-attacks. Theoretical advancements of International Relations will also be proposed, specifically considering the area of Security Studies.

H. S. Kassab (✉)
Department of International Studies, University of Miami, Miami, FL, USA
e-mail: h.kassab@umiami.edu

J.-F. Kremer and B. Müller (eds.), *Cyberspace and International Relations*,
DOI: 10.1007/978-3-642-37481-4_4,

1 Introduction

Deterrence theory states that world stability can be maintained if the costs of war far out-weigh its benefits. Weapons and strategies that make defense cheaper and offense more expensive decrease the likelihood of conflict. Nuclear weapons may have thereby helped create Cold War stability via the costs associated with launching first; according to this argument, war between the United States and Soviet Union never occurred because the price of war (i.e. mutual destruction) was too high.

This theoretical paper will extend this argument to cyber-attacks and suggest that in order to maintain the security of a state's information technology, cyber-defense systems that correspond with Deterrence theory must be introduced. Cyber-attacks are on the rise because it is cheap, easy and hard to detect. Attackers do not need to spend much time or money learning how to break into computer (Cheswick et al. 2003, p. 259). As such, the difficulty entails discouraging such behavior.

This chapter will specifically discuss cyber-attacks as infiltrations. One way to counter infiltration and deter cyber-attack is to introduce proper defense systems such as the virus wall. A virus wall would operate like a defense shield; if an attacker attempts to penetrate a system, then, it would bring about the complete destruction of the attacker's own system through a sudden onslaught of highly sophisticated computer viruses. Since the exact nature of the viruses that compose any given retaliatory attack would be unknowable in advance, attackers would be unprepared to develop their defenses and therefore, rational actors would be discouraged from such engagements. This proposed virus wall would be a way to achieve stability from state cyber-attacks via infiltration, eliminating the benefits of cyber-attack by making it harder, more expensive and easier to detect. Current strategies are inadequate and self-perpetuating, centreing around offensive behavior. This proposed strategy seeks to stabilize cyberspace now vital to national security.

This chapter will be broken up into five main sections. It is first necessary to apply cyber-warfare to the theory of Structural Realism. Cyberspace is the new anarchy, a new battle ground with no overarching authority to place limits on an actor's behavior. Within this new anarchy, new forms of capabilities can be found, but not as we expect. Cyber-warriors, state sponsored hackers, can now break into state institutions and compromise the national security of that state. Structural Realism, with all its elegance, will be applied to these new features of the international system. The second part of this essay will dwell on a reformulation of power. Power can no longer be the inflexible definition formulated by Waltz so many years ago. Rather, I recommend a more elastic concept of power borrowed from the Classical Realist, Hans Morgenthau. Power cannot be considered as a laundry list of state led formulations. Instead, power can be everything and anything: the control of man over man (Morgenthau 1985, p. 11). The third part of this essay aims to focus on more theoretical issues: how best to conceptualize (or re–re-conceptualize) security considering the introduction of cyber-warfare in the international system. I will consider broadened notions of security such as the Copenhagen school of Security Studies. Fourthly, I will discuss the unsustainability and the danger of continuing cyber-attacks in the long-term. Fifthly, I will delve into the task at hand: formulating a system to protect states and more importantly humanity, from the volatility of the international system. I will conceptualize the virus-wall as a way to confront cyber-infiltration. This will be done by borrowing from the lessons of Mutually Assured Destruction and Offense-Defense theory. I will then conclude by discussing the theoretical tradition within International Relations, defining its tradition since its inception: to theorize stability and peace within a system of anarchy.

2 The Trojan War and the Growing Importance of Cyber-Security

Globalization has been hailed as the way to world peace. According to Giddens in his book "Runaway World," the forces of globalization grates against the sovereignty of states and its ability to regulate and govern domestic international affairs, while trying to create one sovereign: the market (Giddens 2003, p. 31). Globalization was brought about by increased modes of communication that destroys time and space (Ibid, 10). This makes state borders more porous and changing. Rapid technological innovation facilitated this transformation, reducing costs of transport and communication and supposedly making the world a better place (Ibid, 28). The globe is interconnected and this has made all nations more prone to shock.

The problem with cyberspace, like any international problem today (the financial and monetary systems for example, another paper perhaps), is the lack of governance to manage this new fast paced world (Mathiason 2009, p. xiv). Governance is needed to ensure the smooth running of the system by solving market failures and cyber-warfare. There has been attempts to raise the issue, but disagreements as to who is to govern and how has delayed progress. There are five competitors in the race to control the internet; states are not the only contenders. International organizations, the private sector, non-governmental organizations and lastly, academics are those seen as stakeholders in the race to regulate the internet (Ibid, 23). There are no established rules or norms to monitor behavior in cyberspace, not to mention a lack of institutions to define expectations and make states accountable for their actions.

A good way to understand cyber-attacks is to use a metaphor: the Trojan horse. Mentioned in Homer's Odyssey, the Trojan horse, a hallowed out wooden statue, was used by the Greeks during the Trojan War to infiltrate the impenetrable walls of the city of Troy. The horse is considered divine by the Trojans who took it as a sign of victory against the Greeks and as a gift from the gods. Many said to burn it, but they eventually welcomed it into the city and celebrated their perceived triumph. However, as the story goes, the Greeks filled the empty replica with soldiers who took the city as the Trojans slept. This metaphor is integral to appreciate the necessity for cyber-security; a cyber-attack may very well

Table 1 Watershed moments in history

Year	Type of attack[a]	Summary of Cyber-attack[b]
2007	Denial of service	Estonian ministries, banks and media attacked by Russia
2008	Hacking/infiltration/denial of service	Russia, South Ossetian, Georgian and Azeri websites attacked during Russia/Georgia war
2010	Hacking/infiltration/denial of service	Between Pakistan and India: an extension of their state of war
2010	Viral attack	Iranian nuclear facilities attacked by two intricate worm, Stuxnet and Flame which targeted and destroyed 58 % of all hardware
2000s	Infiltration/spear-phishing/theft/espionage	People's Republic of China attack on US government, Chinese activists, business and citizens
2011	Hijacking	Iran brings down US drone
2000s	Hacking and hactivism	Breaking into systems for pleasure, criminal and political purposes

[a]From: Cheswik et al. 2003, p. 105
[b]From BBC News 2012a, b, c

destroy a state's ability to survive within the anarchical international system. States have already broken into sensitive databases. The armies of cyber-warfare are its hackers. Their weapons: ingenuity, dexterity and intelligence. They use these skills to infiltrate, steal and destroy, using programs such as viruses and techniques like phishing to accomplish their goals. These attacks can be for espionage, sabotage and destructive purposes. They can shut off power grids, siphon money, disrupt communication, cut off shipping, transport, fuel and water, disrupt the stock market and even hijack drones. This ultimately destroys the domestic stability of a state and creates chaos. Even more pertinent is cutting off state communication resulting in decapitation to gain strategic and tactical advantage prior to full scale invasion (Table 1).

Furthermore, cyber-warfare is a continuation of past strategies that destroy the state from within. In the past, kingdoms during war, sent spies to infiltrate the walls of other kingdoms to destroy or infect the water supply. Attackers threw dead bodies over citadel walls and made life difficult for those protected inside. These offensive measures are similar to cyber-attacks: they desire to weaken the state from inside. Again, the Trojan horse is a related strategy inherent to the strategy of cyber warfare and so, cyber-warfare is not anything new, but an extension, a new episode, an innovative technique that seeks to weaken the state from its interior, rather than through symmetrical means.

Considering this, cyber warfare is something to be expected considering the anarchical structure of the world; it is not entirely a new phenomenon. Rather, it is simply another arena of world politics that has been militarized to ensure security while limiting the security of others. It presents an opportunity to destroy a state's national security and autonomy and create a vulnerability that is so precarious, that its very survival, and that of its people, is at stake.

3 Revisiting Theory, Reconsidering Power

In order to relate to cyber-warfare theoretically and in terms of the Cold War, Structural Realism will be used. In the field of International Relations, Structural Realism was developed primarily as a reaction to Social Science's challenge for a more rigorous and scientific method. Structural Realists, like Kenneth Waltz, take on this challenge. This theory looks at the structure of the world system and the way it shapes the behavior of states. States rationally pursue their interests through a self-help system, without an overarching orderer. Therefore, the primary aim of all states, regardless of size and strength, is survival.

This world system of anarchy is permanent unless the structure changes. No state, or unit of that structure, can alter this framework. This, according to the theory, is the cause of war (Waltz 1979, p. 118). Structural Realism posits that states and state interaction is governed within this structure. To Waltz, a system is defined as a set of interacting units. A system consists of a structure, and "... the structure is the systems-level component that makes it possible to think of the units as forming a set as distinct from a mere collection" (Ibid, 40). The structure is defined by three factors. First, by anarchy, that is the absence of an overarching authority. Second, by the functions and then the capabilities of interacting units, more specifically, states (Ibid, 88). In this environment states seek to survive by any means, either through war or isolation. Nothing can alter the state's behavior unless the system itself transforms. Thus, Waltz sees the world as afflicted by the overwhelming structure of anarchy that cannot be mitigated. Structural Realists like Waltz see power as "...defined in terms of the distribution of capabilities" (Ibid, 192). For Waltz, the distribution of capabilities makes up the third pillar that forms the structure of the international system. The structure deviates with fluctuations in the distribution of capabilities among nations (Ibid, 97). Power "...is estimated by comparing the capabilities of a number of units" (Ibid, 98). Structural Realism claims that these capabilities can be economic, military and other factors like: size of population and territory, political stability and competence. States must use this capability in order to ensure their survival (Ibid, 131).

Considering the theory of Structural Realism, are cyber-attacks worth studying? Yes, they affect the distribution of capabilities, the relative power, and thus survival of states in the international system. As said in the previous section, cyber-warfare is not novel but just another arena in which states, and state interests, will collide. It only seems new because Waltz's definition of power, does not take into consideration new forms of power. For the purpose of this paper, I will reconceptualize power to take into consideration cyber warfare as a new plateau states upon which states will fight. I will adopt Morgenthau's conception of power defined in his magnum opus "Politics Among Nations." For Morgenthau, power "...may comprise anything that establishes and maintains the control of man...power covers all social relationships which serve that end, from physical violence to the most subtle psychological ties by which one mind controls another" (Morgenthau 1985, p. 11). The techniques of cyber-war desire to limit one's autonomy and control. Consider the weapons of cyber-war (Table 2).

Table 2 Some weapons of Cyber-warfare that redefines power (Cheswick et al. 2003, pp. 95–118)

Theft	Passwords, sensitive data through guessing, theft or compromised computer system
Bugs/back doors	Incorrect coding, difficult to find in prog ram resulting in system failure.
Authentication failure	Sign-in mechanism failure due to interference, server compromised
Protocol failures	Denial of use of application due to faulty protocol
Information leakage	Computer espionage
Exponential attacks	Use of Viruses and Worms that rapidly spread and cause harm to computer systems
Denial of service attacks	Overuse and straining of hardware to shut down or degrade service
Botnets	Espionage, Trojan horses and worms
Active attacks	Intruder who modifies, deletes and sends own data

These weapons not only decrease the power of the state, but render it under the control of another actor. Considering this, the problem is that we do not know where control begins, and where it ends. In this arena, power is no more state centric or real, it can be technological and can manifest itself through binary code. Power, especially considering cyber-warfare, must always be conceptualized holistically, and, as a result, an integral part of national and human security. The United States Department of Defense sees this new realm as integral to their national security. The Navy and Airforce now have cyber bureaus. The army, for example, has developed US Army Cyber Command (USCYBERCOM) which: "…plans, coordinates, integrates, synchronizes and conducts activities to: direct the operations and defense of specified Department of Defense information networks and; prepare to, and when directed, conduct full spectrum military cyberspace operations in order to enable actions in all domains, ensure US/Allied freedom of action in cyberspace and deny the same to our adversaries" (US Army Cyber Command). The aim of this bureau is to ensure that the United States and its allies are guaranteed free access to internet facilities and not to be controlled as such. Also, they desire to control the internet for their adversaries as identified. Thus, for the purpose of this chapter, cyber-warfare, and other arenas of warfare that defy the state, the concept of power must be redefined as Morgenthau distinguished so many years ago. The concept of power must be kept fluid and flexible, so that students of international relations can readily recognize new arenas of warfare and identify new generations of threats to ensure stability and security in the international system.

4 Re–re-Conceptualizing Security?

While this paper uses Structural Realism to analyze cyber-warfare, I must first address the diverse theoretical perceptions of what constitutes security. With all that is happening, scholars must finally decide to agree on this concept.

Cyber-security fits well with broadened notions of security and the Copenhagen Sectorial Approach of Security Studies. We must briefly integrate cyber-warfare into these perspectives. Traditional notions of state centered security still dominate today's discourse, and much of this chapter. I would like to discuss these matters to fully understand and acknowledge threats to the well-being of the state and humanity.

Traditional notions of security have centered mostly on the state. Realists argue that since the beginning of organized units of people, their primary concern has been survival and autonomy from outsiders. To Waltz, security is main function of the unit of analysis, the state. Anarchy is the main causal mechanism for this push for security. Arms races, alliances and concerts have existed to try to guarantee survival from threats to a state's security.

By the early eighties, the concept of security began to be contested. Richard Ullman, in his piece on "Redefining Security" 83' does not agree with such a "narrow" definition of security. He argues that security cannot simply be with the state and achieved through military. He defines national security as anything that interferes with the autonomy of states and the degradation of human life (Ullman 1983, p. 133). There are two main tradeoffs to any formulation of security: the first is liberty and security and the second, costs verses prevention (Ibid, 131). On many occasions, security curtails individual liberties and destroys the security and autonomy of the individual. This stems from the Hobbesian notion of security as one that sacrifices liberties for security. For Ullman, security cannot be defined by the state, but rather by what the state is supposed to protect: the human inside and the prevention of violent death. Violent death can be brought on by a bullet from a foreign soldier or from a violent person ostracized from society. The second is the costs verses prevention (Ibid). Looking at economic security, Ullman argues that it may be more efficient to invest in Green technology and energy alternatives than to build up military strength in the Persian Gulf. Military buildup may lead to the security dilemma which is essentially a negative sum game: in an attempt to become secure through military buildup, others perceive you as a threat and will balance against you. Thus, everyone is made more insecure (Ibid, 140).

To Ullman, security should be redefined by looking at the object of security rather than the means to security: a bullet in the head results in death; where it came from, whether from a looter or a neighboring state, is irrelevant. Integrally, security according to Ullman can no longer be considered state centric, but human centric. Thus, insecurity can be defined as anything that degrades human life and reduces state autonomy. Cyber-security fits in well with this analysis. As discussed prior, cyber-attacks have the potential to degrade human life and reduce state autonomy. National security can no longer be considered as military threats to the state, but rather, must focus on these aspects, even if we have to sacrifice an analytical concept. Furthermore, I would imagine he would agree with this chapter's proposition. Cyber-deterrence considers the long-term costs of cyber-warfare and chooses to prevent conflict for the sake of human enjoyment.

The next innovation of Security Studies is the Copenhagen school developed soon after the fall of the Soviet Union. This approach absorbs both traditional and broadened notions of security using referent objects and levels of analysis. Barry Buzan, along with Ole Waever and Jaap de Wilde developed the theory of Securitization in "Security: A new framework of analysis" 98'. Securitization literature uses discourse analysis, speech acts, to understand how referent objects are securitized, moved from normal politics, or standard procedures within set laws and institutions, to an area of exceptional urgency. This is done through a speech act by someone with significant agency to shape structures and an accepting audience: a statesman, someone from an epistemic community, etc. (Buzan et al. 1998, p. 23).

The authors' use levels of analysis to see how each sector (military, economic, environmental, political and societal) can impact, influence and affect one another. These levels are systemic, subsystemic, regional and local (Ibid, 6). From this, the Copenhagen school presents a very convincing and practical answer to the traditional challenge for an elegant definition of security. It takes seriously the traditionalist challenge for coherence, but rejects their focus on solely military matters (Ibid, 4). Rather the Copenhagen school prefers to explore the logic of security itself to discover what distinguishes security and the process of securitization from other less pertinent matters (Ibid, 5).

Considering levels and sectors, levels are the ontological objects where events occur (Ibid). Buzan et al. cite four: local, regional, non-regional/subsystemic and global. Sectors serve as referent objects to disaggregate the clutter of the world's insecurity for the purposes of analysis by removing the irrelevant factors or variables (Ibid, 8). Security is divided into five distinct sectors: military, economic, environment, political and societal. These five sectors are referent objects that overlap and influence another (Ibid, 7). However, they are divided in order to explain just now they can create insecurity. The levels of analysis are used to see how sectors compare with one another and affect different referent objects. Thus, in a very scientific way, Buzan et al. disaggregate the different sectors of society to simplify and then, put them all back together again (Ibid, 167). This creates a formidable innovation to security studies.

To update this theory, cyberspace is simultaneously a level of analysis, and a sector. Cyber-space should be considered a level of analysis because it is a place where things happen (Ibid, 5). It is an ontological object that this chapter (and entire book) seeks to analyze.

5 New Copenhagen School

Six sector approach	Levels of analysis
(1) Military	(1) Global
(2) Political	(2) Non-regional—sub-systemic
(3) Societal	(3)Regional
(4) Economic	(4) Local
(5) Environment	(5) Cyberspace
(6) Cyberspace	

Table 3 Securitization at different levels of analysis (Ibid, 165)

Dynamics/ sectors	Military	Environment	Economic	Societal	Political	Cyber
Global	**	****	****	**	***	****
Non-regional/subsystemic	**	**	**	**	*	****
Regional	****	***	***	****	****	****
Local	***	****	**	***	**	****
Cyber	****	***	****	***	**	****

****- dominant securitization, ***- subdominant securitization, **- minor securitization, *- no securitization

Cyberspace is also a sector as it is currently being securitized by state and non-state actors; it is a site of contention. The act of securitization can move issues/referent objects from normal politics and bracket it to take extra-ordinary measures, above politics, to a more extreme form of politicization (Ibid, 24). There are two stages of securitization: the first is the portrayal of event/issue/person as a threat to the referent object. The second is the need for the public to consent, to successfully convince the audience. We see this happening. First, states perceive that their security as under attack and are doing what they can to exert control. The kill-switch is a firm example of this (to be discussed in the following section). Non-state actors see the internet as being attacked. They are doing their part to securitizing cyber-space as well. For example, hacktivists like Anonymous and Lolzsec see their freedom of speech and expression on the internet under threat. Their activities are a response to what they perceive as an attempt by states and corporations to annex the internet for their purposes.

The purpose of the Copenhagen school is to see what sector matters most at what level, and how easily a referent objects are securitized. For this reason, I have updated Buzan et al's chart that analyzes securitization at different levels of analysis.

As one can see, I have ranked the cyber sector as a high priority. As Buzan et al. says "the relative weight of sectors should depend primarily upon the degree of securitization but should also consider the relative importance of types of issues when sectoral concerns clash" (Ibid, 165) (Table 3). This is because information, especially military, economic and political sectors all are highly dependent on the integrity of electronic information systems. Worms and viruses have the ability to spread across borders, regions to even cover the globe, affecting all levels of analysis. With sectors, a successful large-scale cyber-attack could collapse the entire world economy. There could be military reprisals as well; political and societal cohesion would be torn asunder, resulting in anarchy and environmental destruction. All aspects of life would be disturbed; the acquisition of food clothing and shelter would be the only things that matter. Here, we see that Morgenthau's conception of power fits in better than Waltz's, as cyber-attacks are an extension of an actor's power that desires to control and supplant.

6 Dangerous Reactions to Cyber-Warfare and the Unsustainability of the Obama Doctrine

Thus far, there are no adequate plans for dealing with cyber-attacks. Although the Pentagon and the Executive branch of the United States as well as academics of International Relations and Foreign Policy have contemplated a handful of ideas, none have proved robust and viable. This is because the threat has not been adequately identified. This of course stems from the improper use of power as an analytical concept as well as the neglect of Structural Realism and the lessons of the Cold War.

The first, and most erroneous, is the military option. In the future, a US president could consider economic sanctions, cyber-retaliation or a military strike if key computer systems were attacked. According to Pentagon spokesman Colonel Dave Lapan, "A response to a cyber-incident or attack on the US would not necessarily be a cyber-response. All appropriate options would be on the table" (BBC News 2011a, b). As such, the United States will respond in ways that would bring further reprisals and military responses.

This of has not been an effective deterrent to stop cyber-attacks. Rather, there have been more: the United States and its allies continue to be victims of these attacks, not only from states, but by hackers and hactivists alike. More importantly, the credibility of the United States can potentially be called into question for failing to respond to cyber-attacks in military fashion. This goes against the doctrine of Mutually Assured Doctrine (discussed later), in that states should remain not only capable, but credible, when it comes to promises of reprisal. In this regard, the United States has been irresponsible in its behavior, not only to the American people, but to global stability and peace.

Another idea that has been toyed with is the Kill Switch. The Kill Switch is effectively a "a device…or…a typed code…that can bring the World Wide Web to a sudden halt against an impenetrable wall of 404 Error codes" (Radford 2012, DiscoveryNews.com). There many issues with this. Electric grids, water, security systems, the bar code readers at supermarkets, international commerce and trade, would be immobilized. Production would come to a sudden halt, businesses will close. Our entire contemporary way of life will be held hostage. How will persons live? How will the government keep power and prevent theft and anarchy? This option will do more harm than good: it should not be on the table. The ability of governments to do this is also in question, especially because the internet is a decentralized apparatus of communication. As of today, there are no borders on the internet; states have sought to control the internet, but face competition with private enterprise and other non-state actors for ownership (Mathiason 2009, p. xiv).

Academics have also suggested policy to engage cyber-warfare. Most are adequate, but not enough. Clark and Levin "Securing the Information Highway" in 2009 suggests ways to enhance electronic defenses against cyber-attacks by state and non-state actors. They argue that while cyber-attacks are hard to trace, cheap, effective and on the rise, there are procedures to defend against them. He employs risk management and develops strategies that address everything from communication networks to chips inside computers, through diversity. His most effective suggestion is the use of multiple systems. If one system is lost in a cyber-attack due to viral or worm infection, then there would be two or three other identical systems waiting to replace it. This minimizes the cost of attack for a while. There is of course the possibility for a second or third strike to take out these replacement systems. Another useful suggestion by Clark and Levin is to become self-sufficient in the manufacture and consumption of significant national security computer hardware. Outside hardware systems from the People's Republic of China and the use of other imported technologies could have monitoring bugs in place for espionage purposes. There is much to be done on the defense side of cyber-security. The offense-side of these matters has been developed over the years, especially during the Obama Administration. This, even though it presents important strategic advantages, can lead to dangerous and deadly reprisals.

The Obama Doctrine has been defined by many scholars, but has been discussed most succinctly by Charles A. Kupchan in his article "Enemies into Friends" in 2010. The Obama Doctrine formulates a foreign policy of engagement with those previously considered enemies: Iran and North Korea. As said, Obama is willing to "extend a hand" to those "who cling to power through corruption and deceit" if they "are willing to unclench" their fists (Obama, Inaugural Address). Obama is known for using soft power over hard. He takes credit for rebuilding alliances and won the Nobel Peace Prize for his example. He is also known for other activities. The Obama Doctrine uses other forms of power other forms that extend the influence of the United States. The Obama Doctrine combines diplomacy with a new form of high-tech, low-budget and politically astute intervention, one that maximizes America's influence while minimizing costs for a cash-strapped government. James M. Linsday also discusses this in his article "George W. Bush and Barack Obama: the future of US leadership." He argues that the change of leadership brought about a more multilateral rather than unilateral approach to defending similar goals. Both leaders want to maintain US security and global leadership, but go about it in fundamentally different ways. Rather than the "shock and awe" of the Bush Doctrine, the Obama Doctrine uses diplomacy and inexpensive, yet effective technological weaponry, like drones, viruses and covert operations (Osama bin Ladin assassination). It is suspected that the United States, in conjunction with Israel, developed the Stuxnet and Flame worms that destroyed much of the Iranian nuclear facilities in Natanz, Iran (BBCNews 2012). These worms are said to be the most complex and advanced pieces of malware ever to be created. Many doubt that this was created by a non-state actor. Instead, many point to the mentioned states as the perpetrators. This act significantly increases the profile and popularity of cyber-warfare as method of advancing state interests.

Attacks such as this are an integral extension of the Obama Doctrine and possess many advantages, especially in the respect to the growing debt. The United States cannot afford another war and must seriously consider retrenchment in a conventional sense (Parent and Macdonald 2012). It is a cost effective way of neutralizing the enemy, more specifically, delaying Iranian nuclear capability and preventing all-out war in the Middle East. This, in conjunction with assassination of nuclear scientists, presents a seductive argument in favor of cyber-warfare. However, in many respects, I think this policy is not only unsustainable, but counter-productive and a product of short term thinking. That which we have done can also be done to us. The Iranians, with their own allies and invent, can also develop capabilities to respond to these attacks. Costs have nothing to do with these endeavors; any nation or non-state actor can create or duplicate a worm just as sophisticated as Stuxnet and Flame. The United States with its allies must prepare for this eventuality; Pandora's Box has been opened, and once open, it will be difficult, almost impossible to close. Like the atomic bomb of 1945, the United States must consider that belligerent nations may also be developing their own Stuxnet and Flame worms; duplication is far easier than innovation. Considering this, the right policies must be developed to dissuade. The Cold War and Deterrence theory presents an opportunity to devise ways to do so. In this respect, Cyber-deterrence must be considered as an automatic response to cyber-attacks for the preservation of national autonomy and human enjoyment.

7 Revisiting the Cold War

After World War II, scholars and statesmen came up with the traditional, state-centric definition of security which still dominates today. This conception advocates that one's autonomy and the ability to deter an enemy, enables a nation's security. This gave rise to deterrence theory. Thomas C. Schelling in "The strategy of Conflict" outlines Deterrence theory as the ability to absorb a sudden nuclear attack from the Soviet Union and counter attack. This was referred to as Mutually Assured Destruction (Schelling 1960, p. 207). Deterrence theory argues that international political stability can be upheld if the costs of attack are greater than its rewards. Tactics and armaments that make defense easier and offense more difficult are integral to achieve such balance. Conversely, if offense is easier and cheaper, then war is more likely. For example, World War I began because offense was easier than defense; it was easier to attack first than to try to absorb an attack. It is argued that during the Cold War, nuclear weapons achieved such equilibrium. Through second strike capability, ensuring Mutually Assured Destruction, the US would be able to successfully deter the Soviet Union by absorbing their first strike, reorganizing, and launching a devastating second strike to neutralize the Soviets. This of course may cause a nuclear winter, destroying much of the world, but the very thought of being annihilated would successfully deter both parties (Waltz 1989, p. 626). For this to work, actors must be always credible and capable to maintain a balance.

Mutually Assured Destruction also forms the foundations of Offense-Defense Theory, an integral part of Defensive Realist theory (van Evera 1998, p. 6). Defensive Realism argues that states pursue power optimization rather than power maximization. States look at the costs and benefits of war before embarking on military adventures: the costs of attack must be more than the cost of defense.

In sum, Deterrence theory suggests that in order to guarantee stability, one must make the costs of war much greater than the benefits for the other party (Ibid, 7). Once an aggressor understands that the costs of war would be far greater than the benefits of war, his actions would be curtailed. In essence, the purpose of this work is to extend this argument to cyber-security: to maintain the security of a nation's information technology, cyber-defense systems and policies must be formulated with Deterrence theory in mind.

8 MAD, the Viruswall and Cyber-Stability

As said, contemporary efforts to create cyber-security are not sustainable and will do more harm than good in the near future. As argued, scholars must look to Cold War and learn innovative ways to counter cyber-attacks. This is my attempt.[1]

The idea of the virus-wall comes from the combination of a firewall and a virus. As will be discussed firewalls fail as a way to protect a sensitive databases. Instead of a simple firewall, I would like to imagine a firewall that has the ability to infect infiltrators with a virus that is so powerful, contagious and unstoppable, it would be designed to destroy the attacker's computer system and those in its proximity. This is to make the costs of cyber-attack more costly and create some stability in cyber-space.

First, firewalls are defined as "…any device, software or arrangement or equipment that limits network access" (Cheswick et al. 2003, p. 175). It acts as a barrier to deny access to the unwanted and unauthorized. The firewall must remain full-bodied and impenetrable to deflect attacks. Firewalls can be found inside hardware such as routers, modems and so on (Ibid). There are four main categories of firewall: packet filtering, circuit gateways, application gateways and dynamic packet filters. Without going into much detail, each type attempts to block unwanted users. These function in similar ways, using their source and destination address to identify users (Ibid, 176). In this way, it is a passive way to deny access to the unauthorized.

Secondly, viruses are exponential attacks that use programs to spread themselves quickly. Worms follow the same logic, except are programs that travel by themselves. They operate the same way as biological weapons, their effects being felt in a matter of hours (Ibid, 106). They work best within weak and unprotected systems, those prone to bugs and users that practice irresponsible behavior. Viruses and worms can cause economies to slowdown and stop, and sometimes result in loss of life (Ibid, 17). They usually infect "targets of opportunity" or weak security systems, but can also be sophisticated enough to destroy political targets.

Firewalls do help keep access out and can defend against viral and worm attacks, but the fact remains, break-ins do occur. Failures can be a result of poor

[1] I am in no way a computer expert, but I am attempting to create a new way to protect data. In this sense, this part presented some difficulty, but the idea behind, deterrence, is solid. Hopefully, this idea will be picked up by an agency or computer security company.

design as well as conscious efforts to undermine security, i.e., cyber-attacks. There are many ways to get past a firewall. One of the most malevolent ways to tunnel in, which is "an architectural concept in which one or more protocol layers are repeated so that a virtual topology is created on top of a physical topology" (Ibid, 223). In other words, unauthorized users can encapsulate data from one area of a database to another using the faculties of the firewall. Once inside, the message is inserted into the network and tucks itself inside the database rendering it undetectable. This way, unauthorized actors can infiltrate, steal or control the database that is supposedly protected by this firewall.

What can be done to avoid this type of infiltration? It is here that I will discuss the proposed virus-wall system. If an attacker infiltrates a database's virus-wall by tunneling through it, a virus should attach itself onto the attacker, that is, use the tunnel that was created to seek out and destroy the source of the attack. To recall, a virus attaches itself through contact with an uninfected user. If there is no communication, then there is no transmission. There will be no infection if there are no attackers making contact with the infected database (Ibid, 106). The problem with firewalls is that it is a passive means of defense; after all, the walls of Troy were penetrated by enemy forces. The scheme is to infect the database with the virus without harming the database.

Furthermore, the virus should be so aggressive to knock out all the computers within its vicinity. This way, the cost of attack would be so outrageous, no further attacks would be launched. Staying true to Defensive Realism and the assumptions of Mutually Assured Destruction, such a system would minimize the occurrence of cyber-warfare as the benefits of carrying out such activities would be cancelled out by its enormous and unreasonable costs (van Evera 1998, p. 8).

To understand this further, consider this analogy. Let us imagine a much sought after database as a sick person. If one willfully touches the infected person with a very infectious virus, for example, to steal their wallet, one will become ill. This would be enough to insure that that person's wallet will remain safe. The key to this is communication: the potential crook must know that the wallet is infected. In this sense, like Mutually Assured Destruction, actors must always remain credible and capable: they must maintain such a system and follow through, and communicate this strategy to any potential attackers. Once attackers know and understand the repercussions of attack, then there would be no attack.

There are, of course, moral and ethical issues that must be discussed. Like Mutually Assured Destruction of the Cold War, cyber-deterrence disturbs the lives of many innocent people. I am arguing for a system that seeks to destroy the computers in proximity to the attacker's. An entire state's economic growth and development can be hindered by this proposed system. Is it fair? Of course not, but like the logic of sanctions (the way they are supposed to work) the citizens must confront the initial attacker to prevent any further cyber-attacks. However, there must be an antidote available to the attackers after some time. The antidote would effectively remove the virus from infected computer systems. Before the antidote is given, a second virus-wall will replace the first to continue cyber-deterrence. In this sense, cyber-warfare can be effectively stopped bringing balance to cyberspace.

Fortunately, there is a similar system to this already in existence. Overwatch Textron Systems, a cyber-security company, is proud to demonstrate the abilities of their capabilities which,

> Through our breakthrough CogDat® technology, users can track and visualize every action performed on all of the files in their control. This unprecedented situational awareness at the file level-of-detail allows users to understand how their data is handled. Multi-source data access and correlation extends this situational awareness to other environments such as access controls (who is in your facility and when), network account log monitoring, traffic monitoring, and other inputs (overwatchsys.com 2012).

This means total transparency; one would be able to identify and monitor those accessing the program, identifying the perpetrator before the infiltration is committed. This would dramatically cut down espionage and crime as this system presents the perfect deterrent. States and non-state actors would thus be discouraged from conducting illegal activities.

However, this may not stop cyber-attack. Rather, this system is a soft version and differs to what I recommend. Currently, there are no laws to punish states who conduct cyber-attacks; there is a definite lack of governance over cyber-space and the internet. As said, states operate within an international system as described by Structural Realism: it is one of the self-help comprising of an anarchical structure. Even with the perpetrators properly identified, it would be very difficult to bring offenders to justice. They would be protected by their state's borders. Thus, actors may continue their attacks with no fear; only of reprisal. There would be no stability as described by the idea of Mutually Assured Destruction. There should be a mechanism in place to disrupt these activities by making punishment for such indiscretion a reality.

Fundamentally, any system is better than the non-system in place. It places a check on states who seek to ruin the quality of life of others in order to raise their own relative power. The cat is already out of the bag, and once states begin attacking one another's electrical grids and defense secrets, there is a very good chance war could break out. To recall, a military response is an option as a response to cyber-attack, according to the United States government. While the benefits of cyber-attack are great, so are the costs to those attacked; a response to attack should be expected and this makes for a very dangerous world. In the long-run, cyber-warfare can only become more costly with reprisals. Once this happens, all-out war becomes more and more attractive. This paper tries to solve this by imagining a system where the tactic of cyber-attack becomes more and more expensive and less and less likely.

9 Defining and Continuing the International Relations Tradition

I began with E.H. Carr's quote "The characteristic vice of the utopian is naivety; of the realist, sterility" (Carr 1978, p. 12) to stir up the issue of this work's scholarly contribution. In doing so, I define academia's raison d'être in terms of his theoretical tradition. Carr is known as the founder of modern International Relations. He begins his classic "The Twenty Years' Crisis by identifying the duty of academics: "Our [political scientists] first business…is to collect, classify and analyze our facts and draw our inferences…" (Carr 1978, p. 2). He continues: "The passionate desire to prevent war determined the whole course and direction of this study" (Ibid, 8). Further, that "Political Science is the science not only of what is, but of what ought to be" (Ibid, 5), that a good mix of the two antithetical forces of utopianism and realism will result in coherent and productive foreign policy (Ibid, 222).

Following Carr, the Realisms of International Relations have a normative aspect which inherently defines them as well as the field. For example, Classical Realism through Morgenthau argues that "…it shares with all social theory the need, for the sake of theoretical understanding, to stress the rational elements of political reality; for it is these rational elements that make reality intelligible for theory" (Morgenthau 1948, p 10). Neoliberal Institutionalism also has its own normative roots, i.e. world peace through cooperation. Keohane expounds: "although it would be naïve to believe that increased cooperation…will necessarily foster humane values in world politics, it seems clear that more effective coordination policy among governments would often help" (Keohane 1984, p 11). Even Structural Realism, with its purposive theory serves a normative function: to explain and predict. More so, the need take international politics and forcibly divorce variables from one another needs normative faith. Thus, our honored tradition includes the search for something good: world peace and stability.

Furthermore, the Realisms dictates that states must be made to behave well through power, whether through Carr's appeasement (1978), Morgenthau's Diplomacy (1948), Waltz's Balance of Power (1948, 1979), Schelling Deterrence theory, (1977), Keohane's Regimes (1984), and of course, Offense-Defense theory (van Evera 1998). This world is undeniably anarchical. Stability must be brought to it with the strategic use of power. Power is common to all forms of the political and the Realisms deem power as a dualist force that simultaneously prevents and enhances peace.

This chapter continues the tradition of Realism, in that it desires to see a stable world through the use of power. As said, cyber-warfare is nothing novel, only a part of the structure of the international system and its distribution of capabilities, or power. Like other capabilities such as conventional and nuclear weapons, the use of weapons of cyber-warfare, viruses and worms, can be checked through strategies borrowing from Offense-Defense theory: if the costs of war outweigh the benefits, then states would not go to war. States must make cyber-attacks more expensive than advantageous, and thus, impossible. Currently, states are attacking one another through the cyber realm because it is cheap, easy and hard to detect. My argument, the use of cyber-deterrence, hopes to end cyber-warfare by making it too expensive and difficult, not to mention easier to detect as a nation's cyber infrastructure would be knocked out. In such a way, I, as an inheritor of this discipline, engage with those who went on before, as we continue to comprehend the complexities of war and peace.

10 Conclusion

The search for cyber-security in a realm of anarchy is not an elusive one. Using the tools of International Relations, Structural Realism and Offense-Defense theory, we are more able to suggest ways to counter cyber-attacks. States now rely on cyber-space for defense and internal cohesion. Coherent cyber-security policy must be in place to defend the nation and its people against attack. Contemporary responses are not enough; computer engineers must think up new ways to counter new threats, and defend the security of the nation and the citizen.

This chapter searches for such a solution. It suggests that cyber-attacks can be deterred if there was a system in place to make any infiltration costly. Borrowing from Mutually Assured Destruction, if a nation's security is at risk due to infiltration, then the response should be an overwhelming, resulting in the destruction of the attack's computer systems. In this way any act of aggression, and any perceived advantage of carrying out such an attack, would result in instant defeat.

Ultimately, my conclusion remains: cyber-warfare presents a new chapter in international politics while continuing business as usual. While there are many benefits to conducting cyber-warfare, the costs to the citizen is simply too great. States can achieve their goals through diplomacy, not espionage. The international system is anarchic volatile enough. A stabilizer must be introduced to force states to be good. This can be done with the introduction of a system borrowed from the Cold War: the cyber-deterrent.

This chapter also discussed the field of International Relations. Cyber-warfare tests the theories of Structural Realism and its concept of power. Structural Realism passes in its explanation of cyber-warfare as an extension of the world's structure. As a theory, it possesses great explanatory powers that elucidate, and, in this case, predict international events and outcomes. However, its rigid concept of power fails in its flexibility to take into account change: new fronts and methods of conflict. It must be substituted for that of the Classical Realist. The purpose of cyber-warfare is to control and avoid control: in essence, it is a way that states can blackmail and alter one another's behavior. In order to adapt to changing environments, a flexible theory of power must be considered to predict new methods and techniques of control. States cannot afford to be caught by surprise. This is the purpose of theory, to make sense of a confusing and cluttered world. In writing this chapter, I proudly continue the tradition International Relations was founded on: to discover ways to secure some stability in a world forever ignorant of it.

References

Buzan, B., Waever, O., & de Wilde, J. (1998). *Security: A new framework for analysis*. Colorado: Lyne Rienner.

Carr, E. H. (1978). The twenty years crisis, 1919–1939: An introduction to the study of international relations. London: Macmillan.

Cheswik, W., Bellowin, S., & Rubin, A. (2003). *Firewalls and internet security: Repelling the wily hacker*. Boston: Pearson Education, Inc.

Clark, W. K., & Levin, P. L. (2009, November 1). Securing the information highway. *Foreign affairs*. Retrieved September 12, 2012, from http://www.foreignaffairs.com/articles/65499/wesley-k-clark-and-peter-l-levin/securing-the-information-highway.

US Army Cyber Command (2012). Retrieved September 12, 2012 from http://www.arcyber.army.mil/.

Giddens, J. (2003). *Runaway world: How globalization is reshaping our lives*. New York: Routledge.

Keohane, R. (1984). *After hegemony: Cooperation and discord in the world political economy*. Princeton, NJ: Princeton University Press.

Krasner, S. (1983). *International regimes*. Cambridge: Cornell University Press.

Kupchan, C. A. (2010, March 1). Enemies into friends. *Foreign affairs*. Retrieved September 12, 2012, from http://www.foreignaffairs.com/articles/65986/charles-a-kupchan/enemies-into-friends.

Linday, J. (2012). George W. Bush and Barack Obama: The future of US leadership. *International Affairs, 87*(4), 765–779.

Mathiason, J. (2009). *Internet governance: The new frontiers of global institutions*. New York: Routledge.

Morgenthau, H. (1985). *Politics among nations: The struggle for power and peace*. New York: Alfred A. Knopf.

BBC News, (2012a).US Pentagon to treat cyber-attacks as 'acts of war'. Last modified June 1, 2011. Retrieved September, 2012 from http://www.bbc.co.uk/news/world-us-canada-13614125.

BBC News, (2012b). Internet based attacks on critical systems rise. Last modified April 18, 2011. Retrieved September 12, 2012 from http://www.bbc.com/news/technology-13122339.

BBC News (2012c). Flame: Massive Cyber-attack discovered, researchers say. Retrieved September 12, 2012 from http://www.bbc.com/news/technology-18238326.

Obama, B. (2009). Inaugural Address. Retrieved September 2012 from http://www.presidency.ucsb.edu/ws/index.php?pid=44&st=&st1=#axzz1cX85656y.

Parent, J. M., & MacDonald, P. K. (2011, October 14). The wisdom of retrenchment. *Foreign affairs*. Retrieved September 12, 2012, from http://www.foreignaffairs.com/articles/136510/joseph-m-parent-and-paul-k-macdonald/the-wisdom-of-retrenchment.

Radford, B. (2012) Does the internet have a 'kill-switch'? in Discovery News. Retrieved September 12, 2012 from http://news.discovery.com/tech/does-the-internet-have-a-kill-switch-120907.html.

Schelling, T. (1960). *The strategy of conflict*. London: Oxford University Press.

Ullman, R. (1983). Redefining security. *International Security, 8*(1), 129–153.

van Evera, S. (1998). Offense, defense and the causes of war. *International Security, 22*(4), 5–43.

Waltz, K. (1979). *Theory of international relations*. New York: Columbia University Press.

Waltz, K. (1989). Origins of War in Neorealist theory. *Journal of Interdisciplinary History, 18*(4), 615–628.

Overwatch Textron Systems. (2012). September 14, 2012 from http://www.overwatchsys.com/.

Offense–Defense Balance in Cyber Warfare

Salma Shaheen

Abstract The revelation of Stuxnet in 2010 as the world's first cyber weapon of its own kind that attacked Iranian enrichment facility has led to an extensive debate on the issue of cyber security. In every cyber attack, the attacker may risk of handing over the ammunition to the enemy as a blueprint for the latter to develop a cyber weapon of its own. In cyber warfare, there is possibility that victims of cyber attack develop their own cyber weapon resulting into proliferation of cyber weapons, which is going to be awfully perilous for the security of international system given the complex interconnectivity of computer networks and internet across the world. Since, until now the cyber weapons are used in an offensive mode; therefore, the probability of more states developing offensive cyber weapons is increasing. The chapter argues that the offensive nature of cyber weapons without having an adequate defensive character is destabilizing for the international security system. In this regard, this chapter examines the offense-defense balance in the cyber warfare, and how does offense has the advantage in the cyber warfare that can destabilize the security.

S. Shaheen (✉)
Department of War Studies, King's College London, London, UK
e-mail: salma.shaheen@kcl.ac.uk

J.-F. Kremer and B. Müller (eds.), *Cyberspace and International Relations*,
DOI: 10.1007/978-3-642-37481-4_5, © Springer-Verlag Berlin Heidelberg 2014

1 Introduction

The revelation of Stuxnet in 2010 as the world's first cyber weapon of its own kind that attacked Iranian enrichment facility has raised the concern that whether computer worms can act as a weapon to halt nuclear proliferation. This computer worm has unleashed the vulnerabilities of the industrial structures across the world that alerted the governments, industrialists, and academicians to position the cyberspace within the international political system and explore ways to deal with its associated challenges. It is true that Stuxnet has led to an extensive debate on the issue of cyber security (Farwell and Rohozinski 2011; Ball 2011; Carr 2012); however, in every cyber attack the attacker may risk of handing over the ammunition to the enemy as a blueprint for the latter to develop a cyber weapon of its own. Although, in case of Stuxnet, there is no public evidence available that Iranians are preparing such a computer worm attack against US who is being purported to have planned the Stuxnet attack against Iran, but one cannot deny such possibility.

In cyber warfare, there is possibility that victims of cyber attack develop their own cyber weapon resulting into proliferation of cyber weapons, which is going to be awfully perilous for the security of international system given the complex interconnectivity of computer networks and internet across the world. Significantly, until now, the cyber weapons are used in an offensive mode, as it is difficult to defend against such weapons. Given the complex interconnectivity in the cyberspace, the chapter argues that the offensive nature of cyber weapons without having an adequate defensive character is destabilizing for the international security system. In this regard, this chapter examines the offense-defense balance in the cyber warfare and how does offense has the advantage in the cyber warfare. The understanding of the offense in the cyber warfare is important in order to build defense against cyber offenses.

The impact of offense-defense balance on the international system and the likelihood of war among adversaries is discussed in offense-defense theory (ODT). The ODT postulates that there exists an offense-defense balance among adversaries, which determines the relative effectiveness of offensive and defensive strategies (Van Evera 1998, pp. 5–15; Jervis 1978, pp. 66–80; Quester 1977, pp. 207–208; Glaser 1992, pp. 497–501). The variations in this balance are likely to affect the patterns of international politics. The theory argues that if the offense-defense balance shifts towards an offense then the conquest becomes easier and the likelihood of war increases. The international politics will exhibit more competition and less peace. When the balance shifts towards defense then cooperation among adversaries becomes easier.

Notwithstanding the assumptions put forth by ODT, critics have argued that the debate in the ODT literature largely revolves around the states' (mis) perceptions about the offensive and defensive capabilities that may not be based on an objective analysis. States perceive offensive or defensive advantage in a certain situation based on what is apparent, not what is real (Schweller 1996, 2011). In a related account, Wilcox (2009) highlight the gendered perceptions of military technology and security, and gendered discourse on nationalism as an important constitutive factor in theorizing the offensive and defensive balance. This gendered analysis brings into the debate another dimension of social entities that are constructed and characterized within social structures. The estimation of influence of social structures or gender in particular on the cyber warfare is out of the scope of this paper. The relevant claim here is about the subjective and objective analysis of the offense-defense balance; however, it is important to analysis the fixed concepts of realist paradigm such as offense-defense balance in the changing reality of the international system and threats, for instance, cyber warfare.

Weighing the general assumptions laid out by the ODT in the context of cyber warfare, the competition in the international system to control the cyberspace is likely to be fierce in future because of the use of cyber weapons in an offensive mode. In order to create balance in cyber warfare, it is important to develop a defensive mechanism against the cyber offense. Therefore, in cyberspace states can only maximize their security by minimizing the probability of the cyber attacks on their critical infrastructures. The disturbing feature is the rapid development in the cyber world so is the design of cyber offensive weapons against which defense is difficult to design. However, the vulnerabilities that an offensive cyber weapon exposes are finite and cyber experts promptly react to address these vulnerabilities once exposed. The finite number of vulnerabilities in the network systems is an optimist feature but several of the vulnerabilities have become known to the world after being exploited. For instance, Stuxnet exploited four zero-day vulnerabilities in Microsoft and Siemens' designed supervisory control and data acquisition (SCADA) system, which manufacturers did not know earlier (Bradbury 2012, p. 13; Nicholson et al. 2012, pp. 421–422). This affects the potential victim's capability to defend itself.

In order to apply the ODT the critical point is to ascertain the balance between offense and defense, which could be real or perceived. According to ODT, the offense-defense balance is the amount of resources that a state invest into offensive capabilities to offset the adversary's investment in defense. This balance is affected by the actual amount of investment in offensive or defensive capabilities and the nature of technology. Currently, a number of states notably US, France, China, United Kingdom, and Israel have embarked upon their cyber programs in order to explore the potential of warfare in cyberspace (McAfee 2009; Marquand 2007; Broad et al. 2011; Ball 2011). For instance, the establishment of a Cyber Security Operations Centre (CSOC) and an Office of Cyber Security within the United Kingdom Cabinet Office and the formation of Bill S3480 on "Protecting cyberspace as a national asset act of 2010" in US highlight the growing awareness and interests of state actors in exploring the cyberspace.

In case of Stuxnet, experts suspect the involvement of state actor given the sophisticated and distinct design of Stuxnet that must have required massive resources, which a state could afford (Matsubara 2012). Moreover, it is difficult to ascertain offense-defense balance in the cyber warfare because identifying clearly and timely the attacker is difficult. An attacker can be a state or non-state actor and the attack can be launched from anywhere to mislead the victim. Stuxnet like cyber weapon aside that depicts huge investment in their creation and execution, non-state actors such as hackers can initiate a cyber attack against state's infrastructure with their expertise and limited resources, or a state actor can support hackers. This creates a stark asymmetry between the capabilities of an attacker and victim. Therefore, the continuous development in cyberspace, the attribution problem and asymmetry in attacker-defender capabilities are the factors that debilitate victim's/defender's timely response and defense.

In order to comprehend the offense-defense balance in cyber warfare, the paper in section one explains the distinct nature of cyberspace as a medium for cyber warfare. The second section, based on the debate on ODT, helps in understanding the offense-defense balance in cyber warfare and highlights the offensive and defensive capabilities of cyber weapons with examples. The conclusion of the paper endeavors to place cyber warfare within the international political system based on the argument drawn from earlier sections. The argument is that in many aspects the cyber warfare is related to either conventional or non-conventional warfare; however, it requires the re-definition of warfare nomenclature and mindsets of the states based on an extensive cooperation and partnership between government and private sectors, and state and non-state actors.

2 Dynamic Nature of Cyber Warfare

The landscape of warfare in the twenty-first century is changing so is the strategic thinking required to change accordingly. The catalyst of this change is the cyber warfare, which is consistently being explored with the development of latest and novel cyber weapons such as Stuxnet; thereby increasing the states' concerns to ensure security in the cyberspace. The consensus on the definition of the cyber warfare among the states has not reached yet but the 2001 US Congressional Research Report provides a comprehensive definition. According to this report, the cyber warfare "can be used for the various aspects of attacking and defending information and computer networks in cyberspace" (Hildreth 2001, p. 1). This definition highlights the significance of securing the information loss through computer systems and network. Cyber attacks are the "deliberate action to alter, disrupt, deceive, degrade, or destroy computer systems or networks or the information and/or programs resident in or training these systems or networks" (Lin 2010, p. 63).

States are required to maintain the integrity of their computer and system networks not by the means of physical defenses such as armed forces, armaments and barracks but through the reduction of vulnerabilities into their systems to guard their data. Cyber espionage is different from the cyber attacks as it involves the penetration into the adversary's computers or network through a worm or malware to monitor and obtain information for intelligence purposes (Bajaj 2010, p. 2). It does not involve destruction of data or network but the information processed from cyber espionage can be used for the destructive activity caused by cyber weapons in a cyber attack.

States have to devise international norms to govern the cyberspace in a way in which all states can access the space for peaceful purposes with the condition that the available technology in that space should not be used for malicious purposes. However, there are several ‘ifs’ and ‘buts’ to be resolved and to define the cyber warfare, cyber weapon, malicious purposes and importantly to devise methods for attribution. Such management of cyberspace at international level seems difficult given the complex intricate nature of computer networks across the world and the way designs and functions of cyber weapons are developing. For instance, Stuxnet has unveiled a new level within the cyber warfare.

The growing population in the borderless digital world in terms of digital machines and their users has rendered cyber warriors, either in the shape of state’s force or non-state actors, capable of reaching through and controlling the millions or perhaps tens of millions digital machines (Libicki 2009, p. 4). Similarly, according to the McAfee and Pacific Northwest National Laboratory March 2012 report, the vulnerability of power grids has increased due to their common computing technologies, increase in the exposure of these grids to the cyberspace, and growing automation and interconnectivity (Craig and McKenna 2012, pp. 17–20). In words of Dawson (2003), the “attack surface” for hackers in shape of growing technological convergence is expanding. This intense interconnectivity between the attacker and target within the cyber space provides more advantage towards the attacker’s offensive capabilities as compared to the target’s defense.

The cyber threat is existential. The US President Barack Obama also acknowledged and warned about the unique character of the risk posed by cyber attacks in his July 2012 op-ed in the Wall Street Journal (Obama 2012). He stressed upon the potential of cyber attacks to compromise the contemporary world’s increasingly networked lifestyle. More so, the recent report published by the Georgia Tech Information Security Center (GTISC) and the Georgia Tech Research Institute (GTRI) has predicted specific cyber threats for 2013 including cloud-based Botnets, search history poisoning which targets search engines algorithms, mobile browser and mobile wallet vulnerabilities, and malware counteroffensive in which malicious software will hinder the malware detection techniques (George Tech 2012). The design of cyber weapon is significant in this regard because it prescribes the function that the weapon has to serve as well as the vulnerabilities in the software that it has to exploit. Every new cyber attack uniquely exposes the target’s vulnerable area and enhances its sense of vulnerability by decreasing target’s confidence over its systems.

3 Cyber Attacks

There have been several cyber attacks of varied nature in the past; however, the 2007 cyber attack on Estonian civilian and government systems was a wakeup call that compelled states to think about cyber warfare strategically. During this anonymous and surprise cyber attack, the websites of ministries, banks, broadcasters and newspapers were indiscriminately hit (Kremer and Müller 2007a, b). The attack had adversely affected the Estonian population by causing inconvenience for about an hour to dial emergency numbers and call emergency services such as ambulances and fire brigades. Neither state nor any non-state actor claimed the responsibility of this surprise attack; however, experts' opinion in the light of complex and delicate design of cyber attack indicate towards the involvement of state actor behind this operation (Kremer and Müller 2007a). The impact on civilian's infrastructure and especially the inconvenience caused to population raised the concern about cyber weapons because such a tendency highlights the potential of these weapons to engage countervalue targets. Importantly, it was the first ever cyber attack against the national security of a country (Davis 2009).

Following are some notable cyber attacks:

1. In 1998, cyber weapon with codename "Moonlight Maze" attacked US Pentagon's confidential files about the military hardware designs. The suspected attacker was from Soviet Union but Russia denied any involvement in this attack (Loeb 2001).
2. In 2004, a cyber weapon with a codename "Titan Rain" attacked US government websites and systems. The Chinese sponsored hackers reportedly launched this attack (Kremer and Müller 2005; Scissors and Bucci 2012).
3. In 2009, with a codename "Ghostnet" a cyber weapon attacked to steal confidential information of more than 100 different government and private organizations in several states. This attack had Chinese origin (World Economic Forum 2012, p. 25).

These attacks highlight the power and penetration level of the cyber weapons that these weapons can penetrate into the governmental secured systems and steal or monitor state's confidential information. Moreover, the attacker in these cases is a non-state actor against which defense or deterrence is hard to establish. This further highlights the vulnerabilities of the cyberspace. Besides these real time attacks (Kelsey 2008, pp. 1434–1436), discusses few possible scenarios for the cyber attack that include:

1. An attacker can launch a cyber attack against the enemy's air defense for a particular length of time by introducing some computer virus or a malicious code into latter's defense station or beam a weapon to station from an aircraft that would disable the air defense operation. Such an attack can be carried out without any physical damage to the infrastructure and people (military or civilian). This highlights the extent of precision that cyber weapons can bring to the warfare by only acting as a force multiplier for engaging counter force targets.
2. An attacker can infiltrate into enemy's military centralized defense network in order to disrupt the communication or commands emanating from the center. However, such a target can have adverse effects on the civilian population in case center send out false messages to the air defense. NATO devised such cyber attack during the 1990s Kosovo campaign to induce wrong messages and alerts into the Serbian military's centralized air-defense command network in order to limit Serbian ability to target NATO warplanes accurately during bombing. NATO did not launch this attack but the possibility of such an attack in future remains.

3. Similarly, a cyber attack can disrupt the power grid in the country, transport infrastructure and other critical industrial infrastructure during peacetime or war/crisis time that will affect civilian population. Some observe this kind of adverse impact on civilian population as relatively less damaging in comparison to a conventional attack. Steed (2011, pp. 21–24) also highlights the military applications of cyber weapons that such weapons can neither cause direct physical harm to human beings and the infrastructure nor occupy territory. However, the immediate effects may appear less damaging but, if seen in terms of exposed vulnerability of the target's systems and the after effects of such an attack in terms of monetary and psychological then the cyber attack can be equally damaging or may be more than a conventional attack. The strategic implications are grave.
4. A cyber attack on broadcasting or media network of an enemy can prove highly effective for the attacker because in that case the latter can try to control its enemy's communication with the outside world and can broadcast false or misleading information about the ground hostilities and aggressive maneuvers. This may generate confusion into the minds of international community; therefore, is likely to hamper the international community's effective response towards the aggressor.

The actual and possible scenarios for the cyber attacks highlight certain overwhelming advantages that cyber weapons provide to their possessor. These are as follows (Matsubara 2012):

1. cyber weapons can attack the target in a stealth manner from multiple platforms simultaneously and raise the problem of attribution for the victim,
2. these weapons carries the element of surprise and can give blow to the target when it was not expecting such an attack,
3. these weapons can also act as force multipliers—for instance, an attack on enemy's command, control, communication, intelligence, surveillance and reconnaissance (C3ISR) by cyber weapon can possible degrade or delay the enemy's response during war; thereby, making attacker's forces time and space to carry out their operations.

The existing limitations of the international law regarding conflict and war that does not adequately cover the cyber warfare and the absence of a regulatory mechanism for the cyberspace render the cyber weapon the most attractive and usable weapon for states or non-state actors to develop and use.

4 Stuxnet Attack

The Stuxnet attack was revealed in 2010 when it reportedly destroyed 1,000 out of 9,000 centrifuges at the Iranian Natanz facility (Albright et al. 2011). Iran is the well-documented target of Stuxnet and the Iranian uranium-enrichment plant at Natanz in particular. Microsoft reported that the Stuxnet infected about

45,000 computers out of which 60 % of the infected machines, as Symentac a computer firm reported, found in Iran, 18 % in Indonesia and 8 % in India (Clayton 2010). The countries that were infected by the Stuxnet including Iran, Indonesia and India indicate towards the limited geographical area that was specified for this worm. Or may the target be only Iran and other countries are infected because few SCADA engineers travelled in these countries infected the machines there accidently (Adhikari 2010). The worm spread across by using infected USB stick.

Stuxnet is designed to target a specific process or plant and executes its attack until its finds this specificity (Kremer and Müller 2010). It first exploited the two zero-day vulnerabilities in the Microsoft operating system in order to gain access to the Siemens' programmable Logic Controllers (PLC) and take control of the computers that operate centrifuges. At this point, it displayed decoy signals that indicated normal operation to the operator whereas the Stuxnet followed the instructions that were meant to break these centrifuges. The main target for Stuxnet was the SCADA system manufactured by Siemens that is widely used by Iran in different infrastructures (Beaumont 2010). The novelty of this weapon is that it exploits zero-day vulnerabilities, which was not a usual feature of viruses earlier. A weapon being capable of exploiting four zero-day vulnerabilities means to enhance the probability of its attack (Kremer and Müller 2010). One can regard Stuxnet high with respect to its precision but such cyber weapons are difficult to control within the cyberspace. The possibility of them going out of control and infect other systems generating collateral damage always remains. For instance, the Stuxnet was supposed to remain confined to the Iran's Natanz enrichment facility but it spread out and infected other computers across the world that led to revelation about the existence of Stuxnet (Glenny 2012).

Stuxnet introduced a comprehensive cyber offensive package in the cyber warfare with an ability of attacking the target with high precision. It is likely to induce significant amount of confidence among states to invest in developing cyber offensive weapons; however, it has also unraveled the impotency of defense in cyber warfare. The development of cyber weapons having sophistication and precision that of Stuxnet's require extensive resources in terms of monetary as well as human expertise. According to an estimate of F-Secure Lab, a computer security company, more than ten man-years utilized for the development of Stuxnet that incorporated intensive exploration, research and elaborate testing of this weapon in mirrored environment (Hypponen 2012). It was estimated that countries with highly developed technological infrastructure and extensive funding could develop and launch such weapons (Matsubara 2012). Interestingly, David Sanger's book *Confront and Conceal: Obama's Secret Wars and Surprising Use of American Power* reveals that President Obama after coming to office started several cyber initiatives under the codename "Olympic Games" (Sanger 2012). In addition, the Stuxnet was part of these initiatives. As reported in the New York Times, a special Israeli unit collaborated with US to launch cyber attack on Iranian enrichment facility (Sanger 2012). The governments of both these states have not confirmed neither their involvement nor collaboration in this operation but the development of such operations by the US is an open secret. The development of cyberspace for military purposes is disturbing. Chinese government has also alarmed by saying that "the U.S. military is hastening to seize the commanding military heights on the Internet" (Reisinger 2012).

Regarding the impact, experts from the Institute of Science and International Security believe that Stuxnet probably had negatively affected the Iranian morale significantly not only because of the number of destroyed centrifuges but also because of the uncertainties associated with the Stuxnet attack (Albright et al. 2011). The attack has also shaken the confidence of the SCADA users. More so, such cyber attack has further augmented the Iranian sense of vulnerability as it has not depicted only the extent of Tehran's exposure to the threat, that is, its centrifuges but the exposure of its critical industrial infrastructure to a known-unknown enemy in a vicious cyberspace. Libicki (2011, p. 133), a cyber expert, has suggested two fundamentals for an effective cyber attack including the exposure of the target's systems and the flaws or vulnerabilities in these systems that are exploited.

Besides Stuxnet, other worms have been detected since 2010 that attacked the different systems across the Middle East. These include Duqu, Flame, Gauss, and miniFlame. Iran has been the central target of these worms but reportedly, Flame also infected systems in Syria, other Middle Eastern states and Sudan (McElroy 2012). Commenting on the characteristics of new discovered cyber weapons, Eugene Kaspersky, a computer expert at the cyber security firm Kaspersky Labs said, "That was a shock to us because we didn't expect to find such a serious, very professional, huge project. The typical criminal malware, that's a bicycle. Stuxnet is a car. Flame, it's a space shuttle" (Mitchell 2012). According to Roel Schouwenberg who is a senior researcher at Kaspersky Lab, the aim of Flame was espionage and the Stuxnet's was sabotage (Constantin 2012a). So both these weapons were required to work together in order to achieve their intended aim. In this way, the cyber espionage, which inherently is not a destructive activity, facilitates a cyber attack to destroy the machines. The experts also believe that the Flame was probably created in the first half of the year 2008 and the first variant of Stuxnet was created in June 2009, however, Stuxnet was discovered in June 2010 (Constantin 2012a).

Among these malwares, the Flame and Gauss are the instruments used for cyber espionage as they are designed to steal data and information. The distinctive aspect about miniFlame is that it "serves as a backdoor which gives the operator direct access to an infected machine" (Constantin 2012b), therefore, the function that miniFlame serves makes it different from Flame and Gauss. However, this distinction also indicates towards the intent behind the design of miniFlame, which possibly makes it as an offensive cyber weapon. Experts have found the linkage between the codes of Flame, Gauss and miniFLame indicating that three malwares are part of single operation that works in steps. First step is to "infect as many potentially interesting victims as possible. Secondly, data is collected from the victims, allowing the attackers to profile them and find the most interesting targets. Finally, for these 'select' targets, a specialized spy tool such as

SPE/miniFlame is deployed to conduct surveillance/monitoring" (Constantin 2012b). About Duqu that was discovered in September 2011, security researchers view that its architecture and code resemble to that of Stuxnet, and probably both have been created on similar development platform. The design and functions of these malwares effectively augment the offensive character of cyber weapons.

5 Offense-Defense Balance in Cyber Warfare

The debate about the offense-defense balance largely focuses upon the consequences of this balance on the likelihood of war within the international system. One of the distinctions made between the consequences of offensive and defensive capabilities argues that offense, if in superiority, can increase the probability of war, expand political and territorial pursuits, concentrate power among few within the international system, and can shorten the duration and costs of war (Quester 1977, p. 208; Gilpin 1981, pp. 61–64). Offensive superiority considerably increases the benefits of striking first so is the likelihood of initiating war, and increases the cost of the adversary/target to strike first (Quester 1977, p. 208). Offensive superiority also increases the alliance formation in advance that generates polarization within the international system and heightened tensions, thus leading to the war (Jervis 1978, pp. 66–67).

On the other hand, if defense is superior then the local areas will be strengthened that can lead to revolt, empires will be disintegrated and number of states will increase, wars will become indecisive, and protracted conflicts and wars of attrition will increase leading to much more destruction (Levy 1984, pp. 220–222; Quester 1977, p. 208; Bean 1973, p. 207). The defensive superiority reduces the benefits to the attacker of first strike and the cost of adversary/target to wait and absorb the attacker's first strike; thereby, decreases the incentives of first strike and likelihood of war (Jervis 1978, pp. 212, 313–314, 574; Gilpin 1981, pp. 61–64).

The option of maintaining offensive superiority appears favorable in terms of generating decisive outcome of war quickly as well as making war less costly and less destructive. Hence, in the cyber warfare, developing offensive cyber weapons such as Stuxnet could be an attractive option given its distinct character that cannot be imitated widely and, at the moment, it is not confronted with any defensive mechanism. More so, few states are mastering the cyberspace that makes the concentration of cyber power among the few within the international system. These states may agree to maintain the status quo because with the increase in number of players in the cyberspace the superiority will not remain with the cyber offensive. The increase in number of states in the cyberspace would lead the drive to mend defenses against potential offensives, which is likely to make the cyberspace more competitive as well as exhibit tendency for prolonged conflict.

The advantages associated with the offensive superiority of first strike and seizing the initiative make states to indulge into an arms race to acquire such superiority over their adversaries. However, the defensive superiority enhances deterrence and does not require adversaries to match arm for arm (Levy 1984, p. 221). But it is possible that states in order to enhance deterrence through defensive superior weapons acquire these weapons to further consolidate their deterrence. The Stuxnet attack against Iranian enrichment facility, putting within the context, signifies a preemptive attack in order to achieve the objective of discouraging Tehran's enrichment development. The attack exhibits that offensive superiority in cyberspace is likely to put enormous pressure on the attacker to carry out such attacks because of the mobility advantage of cyber weapons that compels attacker towards first strike. The nature of this offense-defense balance has transformed in the nuclear age where the incentive to strike first has greatly reduced because of the deterrent effect of nuclear weapons and their potential of targeting countervalue targets. However, the offense-defense balance in cyber warfare significantly resembles the one in conventional warfare largely because the defensive side of the balance is weak, which in turn provides superiority to the offense.

In order to define the offense-defense balance of the military technology, four aspects are important to consider. These include the aim of territorial conquest, the characteristics of weapons, the resources required for the offense and the incentive for first strike (Levy 1984, pp. 223–230). Likewise, Van Evera (1998, pp. 5–20) suggests four determinants of the offense-defense balance including military technology and doctrine, geography, social and political order, and diplomatic arrangements. The discussion in this paper about the cyber warfare focuses on the general attributes of offensive cyber weapons in terms of the mobility, penetration, striking power and the manner in which these weapons are used.

The ability of a weapon to acquire enemy's territory and defend one's territory is important to draw distinction between offense and defense. Any state with offensive advantage can easily attack enemy's forces and take its territory; whereas, state with defensive advantage is in good position to keep the attacker outside its territory (Jervis 1978, p. 187). Offensive superiority makes penetration easier and defensive superiority makes penetration difficult. In cyber warfare, the penetration into other's system is easier because of the intense interconnectivity among the systems in a borderless space. The Stuxnet has penetrated into the Iranian systems with much ease in comparison to the armed forces attacking and crossing the Iranian territory. Similarly, the cyber attacks on the civilian infrastructure such as banking system and industrial structures are bound to have huge adverse impact on target country's economy and population. In this way, such a cyber attack can operate against countervalue targets, thus, making it difficult to protect one's infrastructure and people in the cyberspace.

This highlights the problem of defining territory, in conventional sense, in cyberspace because in cyber warfare the aim is to protect the military as well as civilian infrastructures against any foreign penetration by the cyber weapon. Therefore, it is difficult to discuss offense-defense balance in terms of conventional understanding of territory because the cyberspace does not define borders for every state. Consequently, it seems more appropriate to consider the value of protection of infrastructure in the offense-defense balance estimation in cyber warfare. For this reason, it is plausible to postulate that the likelihood of cyber war increases with the increased vulnerability of state's infrastructure within the cyber space and increased cyber offensive superiority. The increased vulnerability will make costly for the target state to engage with and defend its system from the attack, which will make easier for the attacker to initiate cyber offensive against vulnerable state's infrastructure within the cyber space. More so, looking at the Stuxnet attack as a tactical offense in order to prevent nuclear proliferation, the maxim that the best defense is a good offense makes sense. However, this attack has unleashed a new domain or dimension of warfare because of which analyzing Stuxnet attack at the tactical level will overlook the strategic implications of cyber offensive.

States can use weapons for offensive as well as defensive purposes but relevant to the offense-defense balance is the proportion that each weapon contributes to each of the purpose. The character of offensive weapons depends on their mobility, striking power and protection (Levy 1984, p. 225). Together these characteristics serve the offensive purpose of a weapon as mobility provides a particular weapon an ease with which it can penetrate into the enemy's defenses but the weapon should have significant striking power to ensure that penetration. The weapon itself needs to be protected by enemy's attack in order to carry out an offense; therefore, being mobile a weapon can enhance its own protection as compared to an immobile weapon system. The mobility will help a weapon to cover distances easily to execute an attack against enemy without being detected by the enemy.

The issue of mobility in order to bolster the offensive character of a weapon is greatly reduced in the cyber warfare in comparison to the conventional and nuclear war. The cyberspace does not only provide a medium conducive for the rapid mobility of the cyber weapon but the structure of cyberspace in terms of interconnectivity within the global web also helps cyber weapons to move across the web. A USB stick can transfer these weapons. The striking power of the cyber weapons depends on their design that enables them to exploit the existing vulnerabilities in the systems. In the conventional warfare, the offensive weapons are likely to face the challenge of attacking the enemy in its territory because the defender is more familiar with its terrain, defending positions and vulnerabilities as compared to an outside attacker. In case of cyber warfare, target only becomes acquainted about its vulnerability when a cyber weapon exploits it. Therefore, an attacker is more familiar and knowledgeable about the target's systems as compared to the target itself. However, once the vulnerability is exposed the programmers or software engineers address it accordingly and then that vulnerability ceases to exist for any cyber weapon in future. This finite number of vulnerabilities in the cyberspace can exhaust the offensive thrust of cyber weapons.

Likewise, it is observed that Stuxnet exploited zero-day vulnerabilities that exist finite in number and are fixed once discovered. Therefore, any cyber attack exploiting unknown vulnerabilities are eventually going to deplete these vulnerabilities (Milevski 2011, p. 68). This depletion of vulnerabilities may benefit the defense against the cyber attacks but as long as these vulnerabilities exist, no matter finitely, the attack would be intensely dependent on its design. Therefore, the software engineers are significant in this case in order to fix discovered vulnerabilities and the unknown ones as well. Stuxnet attack has considerably increased the importance of software programmers who can balance against the offensive capabilities of cyber weapons by strengthening the defense mechanisms within the softwares and machines.

Despite the offensive attributes of cyber weapons, the conduct of successful cyber offensive is still difficult. The design of Stuxnet type malwares are for specific system configurations in order to exploit specific vulnerabilities of target system; however, such malwares would not operate if there occurs any change in the target system's vulnerabilities. Meanwhile, if the target detects malware is then it can probably reverse engineer the cyber weapon to develop retaliatory mechanism against the attacker in future (Rid 2012). Regarding the expert opinion of leaving the armament with the enemy in any cyber attack, the idea of using cyber weapons by the victim as a blueprint to develop a weapon of its own may be an attractive option. However, if the programmers fix the vulnerabilities that a cyber weapon was designed to exploit after they have been discovered, than the idea of that weapon being a blueprint in victim's hands will become futile. Nevertheless, the design philosophy could be a useful tool such as Stuxnet's.

Another advantage that offensive cyber weapons enjoy is the problem of attribution that the victim faces once attacked. It is difficult for the victim to clearly categorize that who executed the cyber offensive against its systems—whether it is a state actor or a non-state actor, which makes the defense in the offense-defense balance weak. For instance, the design of Stuxnet was to prohibit the attribution. The view about this weapon suggests that the "Stuxnet's core capabilities and tradecraft, including the use of multiple zero-day exploits, render it more of a Frankenstein patchwork of existing tradecraft, code, and best practices drawn from the global cyber-crime community than the likely product of a dedicated, autonomous, advanced research programme or 'skunk works'" (Farwell and Rohozinski 2011, p. 24).

Due to the attribution problem, the victim will not have sufficient information about the attacker's cyber capabilities that, in turn, will affect the victim's timely response. The difficulty of identification of enemy or attacker in the cyber warfare makes the warfare more complicated. States can only ensure defense in the cyber warfare with the further technological progression in developing invulnerable softwares and system programs; however, such a defense will not be directed against any particular attacker instead it will be a defense against any outsider. Defense in cyber warfare is difficult. Deterrence may be possible if states embark upon different offensive cyber weapons program to strike back from a different path or code but the problem here arises is again the issue of attribution, that is, against whom a victim should launch a cyber attack. Geers (2011, pp. 111–121) discusses the deterrence in cyberspace from the concept of nuclear deterrence and finds out that deterrence either by denial or punishment lacks credibility in cyberspace.

The development in the cyberspace regarding the codes, designs and programs is a continuous and rigorous process. At times, a published code for an operative system becomes difficult for experts to analyze and it becomes harder to detect or define a malicious code because a hacker can make use of a legitimate path for system administration to steal data (Cole 2002, p. 727). The hackers can further make it hard for the target to detect by routing their malicious codes or viruses through different computers to reach their target and can route through different countries involving countries that do not enjoy good relations with the target country. Under such circumstances, it becomes difficult for the victim to attribute the attack with some actor—state or non-state and it takes quite long even for speculation. Another problem is that even if victim identifies the attacker than how should it retaliate to such an attack. It is also possible that the continuous development of cyber warfare will make almost impossible for the victim or defender to face with the same cyber weapon attack again.

The perception of offensive advantage is also important because any error in such perception may lead to war. In cyber warfare, given the advantages of mobility, surprise, penetration and precision that cyber weapons offer to an attacker and the underdeveloped defensive side of this warfare, the attacker will develop strong perception about its offensive advantage. Again, the probability of error in building such perception depends upon the extent of defense mechanism of networked systems. The extensive resources dedicated to the cyber offense are likely to strengthen attacker's perception about the offensive advantage. It is also probable that the number of pathways to enter target's computer network is more than the target's system administrators can possible protect. This, in turn, indicates towards the high return on the investment made by the attacker. This further highlights the limitation of the cyber defense against the range of cyber offense. More so, it is not difficult to hide a cyber weapon program because viruses, malicious codes and malwares can be tested in laboratories or on internet anonymously Geers (2011, p. 114). Therefore, it is easy to transfer such programs to other interested parties—state or non-state actors.

6 Conclusion

The imperative of ensuring cyber security in the international system is beyond any debate but the issue is how to ensure that. The ODT suggests that states in order to maximize their security by decreasing the probability of being conquered or destroyed by the other states. For this, states develop and strengthen their defenses against the offensive power of other states. In the presence of strong defense, states tend towards actions that are more cooperative, thus, peace will prevail. In the light of this argument, the paper highlights that the cyber warfare enjoys offensive superiority of cyber weapons that is likely to generate intense competition among states and threaten peace and security within the borderless cyberspace. Therefore, states need to focus on developing strong defense against the cyber offense.

The benefits, however, associated with the intense connectivity across the cyberspace generally overshadow the disadvantages of the network systems. It is difficult to tradeoff openness for security within the cyberspace. Therefore, the challenge for states is to secure their systems, networks and machines when they are placed outside the fence. At some point in future, states may agree to an arrangement advocating arms control within the cyberspace because the cyber threat is existential. Geers (2011, pp. 124–130) considers the Chemical Weapons Convention (CWC) as a model because this convention has vast majority of states as its members and has significantly reduced the threat of chemical warfare by delegitimizing and destruction of the chemical weapons. The success of CWC, according to him, depends on five principles including political will, universality, assistance, prohibition and inspection. Based on the model of CWC, Author proposes a Cyber Weapons Convention or Internet Security Convention in general and argues that first three principles are applicable to the cyberspace, which can provide states to take a step forward. The principles of prohibition and inspection are difficult to apply under current state of affairs because of the lack of understanding about what to prohibit and what to inspect. This proposed model to ensure security in cyberspace appears to be a useful idea but the baseline issue is to have widely agreed framework for the cyberspace.

Within the cyberspace, states need to adopt a cooperative approach towards security along with the need to develop an agreed nomenclature for the cyber warfare such an accepted definition of cyber warfare. In order to devise any defense strategy for cyber warfare, it is essential that both government and private sector should cooperate and work together. It is also possible that few private organizations such as banks will feel difficulty in sharing the information about any successful cyber attacks against them because of the fear of losing good reputation. The information sharing between government and private about cyber attacks will be a critical issue then. However, necessary confidence among the public and private organizations can address the information-sharing problem.

References

Adhikari, R. (2010). Stuxnet: Dissecting the worm. *Tech News World*. Retrieved September September 30, 2012 http://www.technewsworld.com/story/70622.html

Albright, D., Brannan, P., & Walrond, C. (2011). *Stuxnet malware and Nntanz: Update of ISIS December 22, 2010 Report*. Institute for Science and International Security. Retrieved September 30, 2012 from http://isis-online.org/uploads/isis-reports/documents/stuxnet_update_15Feb2011.pdf

Bajaj, K. (2010). The Cybersecurity agenda: Mobilizing for international action. *EastWest Institute Report*. Retrieved October 20, 2012 from http://www.ewi.info/system/files/Bajaj_Web.pdf

Ball, D. (2011). China's cyber warfare capabilities. *Security Challenges, 7*(2), 81–103.

Bean, R. (1973). War and the birth of the nation state. *Journal of Economic History*, (33)

Beaumont, P. (2010). Stuxnet worm heralds new era of global cyberwar. *The Guardian*. Retrieved October 21, 2011 from http://www.guardian.co.uk/technology/2010/sep/30/stuxnet-worm-new-era-global-cyberwar

Bradbury, D. (2012). SCADA: A critical vulnerability. *Computer Fraud and Security*, (*4*).

Broad, W. J. et. al. (2011). Israel test on worm called crucial in Iran nuclear delay. *The New York Times*.

Carr, J. (2012). *Inside cyber warfare: Mapping the cyber underworld.* : O'Reilly Media, Inc.
Clayton, M. (2010). Stuxnet Malware is 'Weapon' Out To Destroy ... Iran's Bushehr Nuclear Plant? *The Christian Science Monitor*. Retrieved October 10, 2012 from http://www.colorado.edu/physics/phys3000/phys3000_fa10/articles-f10/0606.pdf
Cole, E. (2002). Hackers Beware. (London: New Riders) quoted in Geers, Kenneth. 2011. *Strategic cyber security*. Estonia: CCD COE Publication.
Constantin, L. (2012). Report: Flame part of US-Israel cyber attack campaign against Iran. *InfoWorld*. Retrieved October 20, 2012 from http://www.infoworld.com/d/security/report-flame-part-of-us-israeli-cyber-attack-campaign-against-iran-195994
Constantin, L. (2012a). Kaspersky discovers miniflame cyberespionage malware directly linked to flame and gauss. *ComputerWorld.* Retrieved October 20, 2012 from http://www.computerworld.com/s/article/9232367/Kaspersky_discovers_miniFlame_cyberespionage_malware_directly_linked_to_Flame_and_Gauss
Craig, P. A. Jr., & McKenna, T. P Jr. (2012). Technology security assessment for capabilities and applicability in energy sector industrial control systems. *McAfee*. Retrieved October 10, 2012 from http://www.mcafee.com/us/resources/reports/rp-energy-sector-industrial-control.pdf
Davis, J. (2009). Hackers take down the most wired country in Europe. *Wired Magazine*, (15).
Dawson, R. (2003). *Living Networks: Leading your company, customers, and partners in the hyper-connected economy*. New Jersey: Pearson Education, Inc.
Farwell, J. P., & Rohozinski, R. (2011). Stuxnet and the Future of Cyber War. *Survival, 53*(1), 23–40.
Geers, K. (2011). *Strategic cyber security*. Estonia: CCD COE Publication.
Kremer, J. F. & Müller, B. (2005). *The lesson of titan rain: Articulate the dangers of cyber attack to upper management. Homeland Security News Wire*. Retrieved November 1, 2012 from http://www.homelandsecuritynewswire.com/lesson-titan-rain-articulate-dangers-cyber-attack-upper-management
Kremer, J. F. & Müller, B. (2007a). A cyber-riot. *The economist*. Retrieved September 23, 2012 from http://www.economist.com/node/9163598
Kremer, J. F. & Müller, B. (2007b). Newly nasty. *The economist*. Retrieved September 23, 2012 from http://www.economist.com/node/9228757
Kremer, J. F. & Müller, B. (2010). A worm in the centrifuge. *The economist*. Retrieved October 15, 2012 from http://www.economist.com/node/17147818
George Tech. (2012). Emerging cyber threats report 2013. *Report of the Georgia Tech Information Security Summit.* Retrieved November 15, 2012 from http://www.gtsecuritysummit.com/report.html
Gilpin, R. (1981). *War and change in world politics*. Cambridge: Cambridge University Press.
Glaser, C. (1992). The political consequences of military strategy: Expanding and refining the spiral and deterrence models. *World Politics, 44*(4), 497–501.
Glenny, M. (2012). We will ruse stuxnet's cavalier deployment. *The Financial Times*. Retrieved October 10, 2012 from http://www.ft.com/cms/s/0/6b674600-afc7-11e1-a025-00144feabdc0.html#axzz2CitmOS74
Hildreth, S. A. (2001). Cyberwarfare. *Congressional Research Services Report*. Retrieved October 10, 2012 from http://www.fas.org/irp/crs/RL30735.pdf
Hypponen, M. (2012). Stuxnet shifts the cyber arms race up a gear. *BBC news*. Retrieved October 10, 2012 from http://www.bbc.co.uk/news/technology-18825742
Jervis, R. (1978). Cooperation under the security dilemma. *World Politics*, *30*(2), 66–80.
Kelsey. J. T. G. (2008). Hacking into international humanitarian law: The principles of distinction and neutrality in the age of cyber warfare. *The Michigan Law Review*, *106*(7), 1434–1436.
Levy, J. S. (1984). The offensive/defensive balance of military technology: A theoretical and historical analysis. International studies quarterly, (28), 220–222.
Libicki, M. C. (2009). Cyberdeterrence and cyberwar. *RAND Monograph*. Retrieved October 20, 2012 from http://www.rand.org/pubs/monographs/2009/RAND_MG877.pdf
Libicki, M. C. (2011). Cyberwar as a confidence game. *Strategic Studies Quarterly, 5*(1), p. 133.

Lin, H. S. (2010). Offensive cyber operations and the use of force. *Journal of National Security Law and Policy, 4*(63), p. 63.

Loeb, V. (2001). NSA adviser says cyber-assaults on pentagon persist with few clues. *The Washington Post*. REtrieved October 30, 2012 from http://www.washingtonpost.com/ac2/wp-dyn?pagename=article&node=&contentId=A51965-2001May6&notFound=true

Marquand, R. (2007). China emerges as leader in cyberwarfare. *The Christian Science Monitor*. Retrieved January 20, 2013 from http://www.csmonitor.com/2007/0914/p01s01-woap.html

Matsubara, M. (2012). A stuxnet future? Yes, offensive cyber-warfare is already here. *International Relations and Security Network (ISN)*. Retrieved September 20, 2012 from http://www.isn.ethz.ch/isn/Digital-Library/Special-Feature/Detail?lng=en&id=154095&contextid774=154095&contextid775=154091&tabid=1453372088

McAfee. (2009). In the crossfire—critical infrastructure in the age of cyber war. Retrieved September 10, 2012 from http://resources.mcafee.com/content/NACIPReport

McElroy, D. (2012). Flame virus 'has infected 189 systems in Iran'. *The Telegraph*. Retrieved January 20, 2013 from http://www.telegraph.co.uk/news/worldnews/middleeast/iran/9297703/Flame-virus-has-infected-189-systems-in-Iran.html

Milevski, L. (2011). Stuxnet and strategy: A space operation in cyberspace. *JFQ*. (Issue 63). Retrieved September 20, 2012 from http://www.ndu.edu/press/lib/images/jfq-63/JFQ63_64-69_Milevski.pdf

Mitchell, C. (2012). Stuxnet, flame foretell age of cyber warfare. *CBN News*. Retrieved September 30, 2012 from http://www.cbn.com/cbnnews/insideisrael/2012/June/Stuxnet-Flame-Foretell-Age-of-Cyber-Warfare-/

Nicholson, A. et al. (2012). SCADA security in the light of cyber warfare. *Computers and Security*, (31), 421–422.

Obama, B. (2012). Taking the cyberattack threat seriously. *The Wall Street Journal*. Retrieved September 15,2012 from http://online.wsj.com/article/SB10000872396390444330904577535492693044650.html

Quester, G. (1977). *Offense and defense in the international system*. New York: Wiley.

Reisinger, D. (2012). Obama takes cyberwarfare to new level, report says. *CNET News*. Retrieved September 20, 2012 from http://news.cnet.com/8301-1009_3-57445275-83/obama-takes-cyberwarfare-to-new-level-report-says/

Rid. T. (2012). Think again: Cyberwar. *Foreign Policy*. Retrieved September 20, 2012 from http://www.foreignpolicy.com/articles/2012/02/27/cyberwar?page=0,4

Sanger, D. (2012). Obama order sped up wave of cyberattacks against Iran. *The New York Times*. Retrieved September 20, 2012 from http://www.nytimes.com/2012/06/01/world/middleeast/obama-ordered-wave-of-cyberattacks-against-iran.html?pagewanted=all

Schweller, R. (1996). Neorealism's status-quo bias: What security dilemma? *Security Studies, 5*(3), 90–121.

Schweller, R. (2011). Rational theory for a bygone era. *Security Studies, 20*, 460–468.

Scissors, D. & Bucci, S. P. (2012). China cyber threat: Huawei and American policy toward Chinese companies. *The Heritage Foundation,* (3761). Retrieved November 1, 2012 from http://www.heritage.org/research/reports/2012/10/china-cyber-threat-huawei-and-american-policy-toward-chinese-companies

Steed, D. (2011). Cyber power and strategy: So what? *Infinity Journal, 1*(2), 21–24.

Van Evera, S. (1998). Offense, defense, and the causes of war. *International Security, 22*, 5–15.

Wilcox, L. (2009). Gendering the cult of the offensive. *Security Studies, 18*(2), 214–240.

World Economic Forum. (2012). *Global risks 2012* (7th edn.). Retrieved November 5, 2012 from http://www3.weforum.org/docs/WEF_GlobalRisks_Report_2012.pdf

The Utility of Timeless Thoughts: Hannah Arendt's Conceptions of Power and Violence in the Age of Cyberization

Katharina C. Below

Abstract This chapter links power relations in the technologically dominated context of cyberspace to Hannah Arendt's theoretical considerations of power and violence. Even if her work is often marked by skepticism on the technological domination of the human world, some of Arendt's most important works provide a surprisingly rich framework to conceptualize the structure and character of cyberspace. It is argued here that the structure of power and violence in cyberspace can abstractly be captured by dividing cyberspace into two parts that refer to Arendt's conceptions of power as *power to* and violence as *power over*. Cyberspace is thus both, a modern space of appearance and political freedom and an unexplored context for Arendt's conception of power as well as an anti-space of appearance, a space filled with Arendt's conception of violence that denies the positive attributes of a space of appearance when filtering and control techniques are implemented. The empirical cases of the Arab Spring protests, Weibo and the Fifty Cent Party as well as Denial of Service (DoS) attacks during elections or inter-state conflicts will underline this argumentation.

K. C. Below (✉)
Center for Global Studies, University of Bonn, Bonn, Germany
e-mail: katharina.below@uni-bonn.de

J.-F. Kremer and B. Müller (eds.), *Cyberspace and International Relations*,
DOI: 10.1007/978-3-642-37481-4_6,

1 Between Past and Present

Linking Hannah Arendt's conceptions of power and violence with the digital environment of cyberspace seems risky, but nothing ventured, nothing gained. Cyberspace as an operational environment framed by the use of electronics emerged in the 1960s when the Defense Department of the United States started to connect a few computers within the ARPANET. The beginning of the Internet can be dated back to the end of the 1980s, [1]. The two most popular and powerful resources in cyberspace—Google and Wikipedia—were created at the turn of the millennium (Starr 2009). The end-to-end architecture made the Internet resistant to centralized control in its early years, because the complexity of this network is implemented at the end nodes. The core nodes only perform simple data transfer. Control over the Internet is thus not possible through the control of a small number of core nodes, but it can only be exerted at the ends of the several networks (Boas 2004, pp. 438–439). But because the Internet's central mechanism simply transfers data, "the characteristics of the Internet as a whole can be altered by adding new protocols that will help the technology meet the needs of operating in new environments" (Boas 2004, pp. 438–439) and this is the point why governments today are able to decide which information they do let in and which they screen out (Drezner 2010, p. 31).

It is true that during the last years, the man-made environment of cyberspace changed some of the existing power relations among actors. Joseph Nye points out that while traditional large powers are unable to dominate this new context as much as they have dominated sea or air, emerging small actors have more and more capacities to exercise power in cyberspace (Nye 2010, 2011). Nye and others here discuss the creation of a new form of power called cyberpower (Kuehl 2009; Nye 2010, 2011). Some scholars argue that this power shift seems to diminish the capacities of the sovereign state to exercise power. It replaces governments as the most powerful actors in the world and the meaning of geographical space for the current system of sovereign states (Tofler and Tofler 1995; Dyson 1998). Daniel Drezner state that the Internet has probably empowered non-state actors more than states, but the effect of this empowerment is not consistent across all types of political environments. While in open societies the Internet has enhanced the power of civil society, this is not the case for societies under authoritarian governments (Drezner 2010, p. 32). Another argument is made by scholars who point out that cyberspace as a new public sphere has revived democratic discussion. A growing body of literature deals with public opinion and democratic progress in cyberspace (Abramson et al. 1988; Sachs 1995; Papacharissi 2002, 2004; Lee and Liu 2012) as well as the role of civil society in international negotiations by acting together in cyberspace (Kobrin 1998, 2002; Deibert 2000).

But apart from Joseph Nye's conception of cyberpower that is related to his fundamental approach of hard and soft power, little is said about existing

[1] developed by Tim Berners-Lee to share information between scientists around the globe

conceptions of power and violence already excogitated in the last centuries and their relationship to cyberspace. Hannah Arendt's conceptions of power and violence and their relation to cyberspace as a modern emerging space of appearance even seem to be a new research topic. The following chapter therefore links the definition of power and violence in the technologically dominated context of cyberspace to Hannah Arendt's theoretical considerations. This choice is not obvious since Hannah Arendt's work often features skepticism on the triumph of science over nature and the technological domination of the human's world (Arendt 1958); and the topic of cyberspace seems to be the material expression par excellence of the technological domination of men's everyday life. Moreover Arendt's critics always pointed to her conceptions of power or politics that had "little to say about politics here and now" (Canovan 1992, p. 1) and that do not seem to be applicable on human's complex world. But the structures of cyberspace do not have any direct analogy to this known world (Lemley 2012); the novelty of cyberspace offers thus the possibility to rethink and re-contextualize Arendt's conceptions of power and violence.

Some of Hannah Arendt's most important works, *The Human Condition* (1958), *On Revolution* (1965) or *On Violence* (1970), therefore provide a surprisingly rich framework to conceptualize the structure and the character of cyberspace. Arendt's theoretical considerations are influenced by her biographical background and the most crucial events of her lifetime in the first half of the twentieth century in Europe and the United States. The uniqueness of Arendt's thoughts can be seen in the importance of the plurality and equality of men and the analysis of the most elementary articulations of the human condition. Her conceptions are extremely sensitive to men's life on earth and the fundamental human activities are labor, work and action. "Each corresponds to one of the basic conditions under which life on earth is given to man" (Arendt 1958, p. 7). "Action, the only activity that goes on directly between men without the intermediary of things or matter, corresponds to the human condition of plurality, to the fact that men, not Man, live on the earth and inhabit the world" (Arendt 1958, p. 7). This is the very element of power relations in cyberspace. Moreover, the characteristics of the early Internet derived from the norms of its designers: they trusted each other and worked trough consensus rather than hierarchy (Boas 2004, p. 439).

Because the architecture of cyberspace here is not thought in terms of digital devices and its structure is not defined along technological processes that are far from human actions, Hannah Arendt's conceptions of power and violence offer fruitful approaches to analyze power relations in cyberspace. As a side-effect the argumentation of this chapter encourages to rethink the reasonability of the unique characteristics that are attributed to cyberspace. The structure of power and violence in cyberspace can be abstractly captured by dividing cyberspace into two parts that refer to Arendt's conceptions of power as *power to* and violence as *power over*. Cyberspace is thus a modern space of appearance and political freedom and an unexplored context for Arendt's conception of power as well as an anti-space of appearance, a space filled with Arendt's conception of violence that denies the positive attributes of a space of appearance when filtering and control techniques are implemented.

2 Cyberspace: A new context in world politics

"Power depends upon context" (Nye 2010, p. 1) and in the universe of Political Theory context always serves as a fixed star. These important reference points define and limit actors, resources, intentions and options of action, as well as they draw the network of power relations between different domains of power. Consequently, cyberspace is also an important new context in world politics and according to the argumentation of Joseph S. Nye or Dan Kuehl it leads to the creation of a new domain of power, called cyberpower (Nye 2010; Kramer et al. 2009; Kuehl 2009). But cyberspace is more than one emerging power context among others. The illustrated idea of black-boxing different power relations in the context of cyberspace under the homogeneous label of cyberpower is too simple to be true.

> Societies around the world (…) are heavily dependent on globally networked technologies. They have been locked in and interpenetrated by a digital web of their own spinning (Deibert and Rohozinski 2010, p. 12).

Cyber, as a prefix for electronic and computer related activities, does not say much about the environment of cyberspace (Nye 2011, p. 3), but it depends heavily on its resources: information access and exchange through Internet facilities such as hardware routers and software layers. These will be powerful instruments in the near future and as cyberspace will be the most important information hub, it introduces a new era of power diffusion. Cyberspace will be the center of gravity for the power domains of governance, communication, diplomacy and military. A few years from now, it will be an overarching context for different traditional domains and a relevant context for states, citizens and all forms of organizations to act. Despite these primarily overarching characteristics, the inner cyberspace is nevertheless shaped by two antagonistic conceptions of power that had been already formulated and recently reformulated throughout the history of Political Science and Political Philosophy: Hannah Arendt's conceptions of power and violence.

2.1 Contextualizing power: Arendt's space of appearance

According to Hannah Arendt, power is contextualized in a space of appearance.[2] It was initially achieved in ancient Greek polis as a "political space of public freedom in which people, as free and equal citizens, would take their common concerns into their own hands" (Wellmer 2006, p. 220). This space is created by the sharing of words and deeds and opens up the possibility of speech and action (Arendt 1958, p. 200). Within Arendt's space of political freedom rule and coercion were unknown, but political relations were conducted through persuasion (Villa 1998, pp. 149, Arendt 1958, p. 26). Arendt's space of appearance can thus

[2] The notions of space of appearance and space of political/public freedom are used as equivalents here.

be understood "in the widest sense of the word, namely, the space where I appear to others as others appear to me, where men exist not merely like other living or inanimate things but make their appearance explicitly" (Arendt 1958, pp. 198).

In *On Revolution* Hannah Arendt develops her basic argumentation of a space of appearance by tracing back the history of modern revolutions in the United States, France and Russia (Arendt 1965, p. 267f.). She brings forward the argument that liberal-democratic as well as Marxist traditions have both misunderstood the tragedy of modern revolutions. For them, the final goal of revolution as well as of politics is beyond politics, like social justice or the rule of law (Wellmer 2006, p. 220f.). For Arendt, in contrast, participants of modern revolutions attempt to establish a space of appearance by acting together and "relying on nothing more than the power implicit in their own mutual promises and agreements" (Villa 2006, p. 13). The space of appearance was not initially designed to be a political space of freedom, but it was declared and kept open by sharing words and deeds and rendering politics dependent on the existence of a space of political freedom (Arendt 1958, p. 198ff.). Thus, the break with liberal-democratic traditions does not mean, for example, to question the rule of human rights or law, but "in contrast to the liberal tradition, Arendt considers such rights not as the substance, but only as a necessary precondition of political freedom" (Wellmer 2006, p. 222).

According to Arendt's history of modern revolutions, the American Revolution represents the ideal of revolutions by establishing a political space of freedom, not only in the negative sense of a constitutional guarantee of equal and human rights, but also in the positive sense by creating a self-government by the people (Wellmer 2006, p. 219f.). Thus the ancient Greek polis as well as modern revolutions serve as reference points to define and outline the characteristics of the space of appearance. With the modern example of American Revolution Arendt seems to develop her further argument of council democracy. It replaces the complex institutions of modern states by a political system based on councils (Wellmer 2006, p. 224). The Paris Commune that tried to establish such a system in the early 1870s was a model for the conception of council democracy. The most important example for a political system based on councils has been Russia between 1905 and 1936. Arendt believed this form of democracy, as an opposition between direct and representative democracy, to be able to constitute a space of appearance and to contextualize her conception of power. Within this argumentation of council democracy lies the most important point to understand Hannah Arendt's special relationship to liberal-democratic traditions: "[S]he recommends councils as an alternative *to* party systems *for* representative government, not an alternative to representative government per se" (Disch 2011, p. 352). Her argumentation of council democracy thus cannot be understood literally, it rather has to be understood as "a metaphor for a network of autonomous (…) associations, in each of which something like the self-government of free and equal participants takes place" (Wellmer 2006, p. 224). Councils make it "possible to preserve the revolutionary spirit by enabling the 'institutionalization of the constituent power' from extraordinary acts of founding into ordinary politics" (Disch 2011, p. 352). Arendt argues "that no one could be called either happy or free without participating, and having a share, in public power" (Arendt 1965, p. 255). This idea of participation is also closely connected to her conceptions of action and power as well as the share of different opinions. But "representative democracy cannot provide the experience of a plurality of perspectives for the majority of its citizens" (Sitton 1994, p. 310). Representative democracy even disrupts the formation of different opinions on political topics. Therefore, the council system thought by Hannah Arendt is a dualism of the political institutions of a federal political system and a network of organizations of civil society. It is a new type of republican government, enabling participation and the creation of a plurality of opinions.

Even if Arendt's interpretation of revolutions and the political space give the impression that political action as power is a phenomenon of the distant past, the interpretation of political space and council democracy as a metaphor for a network turns out to be a contemporary interpretation that can be applied to the modern times of cyberization (Villa 2006, p. 12ff.). Regarding council democracy as a metaphor, cyberspace is nothing else than a new emerging and networked space of political freedom. In times of cyberization "people will live by multiple voluntary contracts and drop in and out of communities at the click of a mouse" (Nye 2010, p. 1). This interpretation of cyberspace opens up the possibility to re-contextualize Arendt's conception of power and violence in cyberspace.

2.2 *Contextualizing Power Again: Cyberspace as Space of Appearance*

The last section has raised the ideas that cyberspace is an emerging power context in world politics as well as that Arendt's conception of council democracy as a space of appearance can be understood as a metaphor. This argument will be developed and extended in the following section in order to claim cyberspace as a space of appearance.

Putting the argumentation line of Arendt's conception of council democracy in the context of the history of political thought, it becomes clear that Arendt's conception is mostly about the ideas of civic participation and engagement instead of replacing the established administrative institutions by a system of councils as an alternative of representative government (Disch 2011, p. 352). Even though her conception of council democracy seems to break on the first sight with the liberal-democratic tradition, the proper content of Arendt's political thought can be placed within the classical republican tradition. Important thinkers like Aristotle, Machiavelli or Montesquieu put the emphasis on active citizenship, civic virtue, the rule of law and political equality (Villa 2006, p. 15; Canovan 1992, p. 202f.). In this tradition, Arendt agrees most with Aristotle's identification of citizenship with participation in judgment and authority, "Montesquieu's insistence that the laws of a republic establish not just boundaries between public and private (and thus limits to action), but relations (rapports) between citizens as well" (Villa 2006, p. 15) as well as Machiavelli's conception of "islands of freedom" that people establish through acting in concert, but which are surrounded by a sea of different hostile forces.

In Hannah Arendt's world, the greatest emphasis is put on "the sharing of diverse opinions as the sine qua non of any politics worthy of the name" (Villa 2006, p. 15). Persuasion and debating do not necessarily create solidarity, but thoughtfulness and a meaningful life. It enables the individual to accept the plurality of the world as well as to develop the essential faculty of moral judgment (Villa 1998, pp. 148–151). Putting this argumentation in the biographical background of Hannah Arendt, who as a Jewish intellectual suffered under the terror of the National Socialists, her main argumentation can be based on the implementation of fundamental characteristics and structural ideas of active citizenship and civic engagement. Arendt pushes this argument forward when the example of European working classes which created revolutionary councils (Arendt 1958, p. 215f, Arendt 1965, pp. 258–266) is given.

> She makes it clear that what she has in mind is not the contribution of such councils to the betterment of economic conditions (…), but the ability of working men and women to think of something other than their interest. They discovered for themselves both the nature of directly democratic political participation and its advantages in experience rather than in economic gains (Katep 2006, p. 134).

The space of appearance does not need institutional structures to be established, but it needs the fundamental idea of Arendt's conception of power; an autonomous, networking association of people, in which something like the self-government of free and equal participants with a variety of opinions takes place by the means of speech. The space of political freedom is therefore a potential space.

> Wherever people gather together, it is potentially there, but only potentially, not necessarily and not forever (Arendt 1958, p. 199).

When Robert O. Keohane and Joseph S. Nye argued in the late 1990s that "one reason that the information revolution [had] not transformed world politics to a new politics of complete complex interdependence is that information does not flow in a vacuum but in political space that is already occupied" (Keohane and Nye 1998, p. 84), they could not foresee that access to the Internet would become a global norm in the early 2000s. The Internet made communication and business easier than it had been at any other time of human economic activity. Countries even start to govern through the Internet. In France, Greece and Estonia as well as some other European countries, Internet access is guaranteed by law. Since 2005 even Internet based elections are possible in Estonia (Runnel et al. 2009). The worldwide access to Internet has increased not only in the traditional industrialized countries, but also in the heavily indebted poor countries (HIPC) and the low-income countries (Worldbank 2012a).[3] The digital divide still creates a gap between the quantitative access to Internet as well as the quality of Internet

[3] The Worldbank classifies countries according to 2011 GNI per capita, calculated using the World Bank Atlas method. Low income countries have a GNI per capita of $1.025 or less. In contrast, high income countries have a GNI per capita of $12.476 or more. The World Bank also holds a list of the Heavily Indebted Poor Countries (HIPC). The HIPC Initiative currently identifies 39 countries, most of them in Sub-Saharan Africa, as potentially eligible to receive debt relief (Worldbank 2012b, c).

infrastructure in these countries and the industrialized countries. But the final statements of the Special Rapporteur on the Promotion and Protection of the Right to Freedom of Opinion and Expression on a report to the Human Rights Council of the United Nations General Assembly encouraged a debate about whether Internet access should be recognized as a human right.

> Given that the Internet has become an indispensable tool for realizing a range of human rights, combating inequality, and accelerating development and human progress, ensuring universal access to the Internet should be a priority for all States (Special Rapporteur to the Commission on Human Rights and Human Rights Council 2011, p. 22).

In the past, flows of goods and information were controlled by multinational corporations, bureaucracies or even the Catholic Church. But the loosely structured network of cyberspace and its cheap access opens the space for all people to debate on their preferred agenda (Keohane and Nye 1998, p. 83). Because of modern data storage possibilities, members of digital communities can debate about political affairs whenever they want. They can also enter and leave these communities by a mouse click wherever they are, because cyberspace enables the discussion between people on far sides of the globe (Parachissi 2002). Moreover, the Internet and cyberspace have unleashed a wide ranging and globally significant shift in communication (Deibert and Rohozinski 2010, p. 3) and political discussions are shifted to the cyberspace-based networks as newsgroups or mailing lists (Levine 2000). Speech is no longer the means of political action, but digital discussion statements at Google+ or identi.ca, Twitter hashtags or Facebook status updates are transforming the spoken words into written binary codes. Thus "[i]nformation does not just exist, it is created" (Keohane and Nye 1998, p. 84). And Internet users create information by connecting each other in cyberspace, which can be seen as a political space appearance as far as affairs of political purpose are discussed.

3 Breaking up and Assembling Hannah Arendt‘s Conception of Power and Violence

To refine the argument about cyberspace as a space of appearance, political action and thus the content of political speech will be discussed in the following section after having finally outlined Hannah Arendt's conceptions of power, violence, politics and action. Hannah Arendt was one of the most important and influential philosophers of the twentieth century. She discussed a wide range of different political terms—like force, domination, authority or work—in her studies and essays. In order to distinguish them and develop clear theoretical foundations for the following argumentation, her conceptions of power, violence and (political) action are the most important ones. These four are heavily interconnected with the conception of the space of appearance, because the case of power illustrates that "power springs up whenever people get together and act together" (Arendt 1970, p. 52) and then create a space of appearance.

3.1 Power, Politics and so on

Individuals acting in concert on political affairs through speech represents Arendt's conception of power in contrast to violence—the conception of power in a Weberian tradition. This definition already includes the important terms of power, politics and action. Action itself is what Arendt calls essentially human, because "[a]ction alone is the exclusive prerogative of man; neither a beast nor a god is capable of it, and only action is entirely dependent upon the constant presence of others" (Arendt 1958, p. 23). The term of acting in concert is borrowed from Edmund Burke (Arendt 1975, p. 474). It strongly relies on Arendt's fundamental differentiation between man in the singular and men in the plural as well as her assumption that a meaningful life is only possible in awareness of human plurality.

> Plurality is the condition of human action because we are all the same, that is, human, in such a way that nobody is ever the same as anyone else who ever lived, lives or will live (Arendt 1958, p. 8)

For Hannah Arendt, action and speech are constitutive for the world we live in and plurality is the condition and consequence *per quam* of human action, because men in the plural can only experience the meaningfulness of life by talking and using words and only men in the plural are able to act in concert. Speech is therefore what makes men political beings and constitutes political action (Arendt 1958, p. 4). Arendt outlines that in the original Greek understanding "most political action, in so far as it remains outside the sphere of violence, is indeed transacted in words" (Arendt 1958, p. 26). Scientific discovery and progress cannot be the basis for human's future life, because in the world of science and technology, words and speech have lost their power. Speech, as authentic political action, does not need to be formal; talk or persuasion is the means for deciding about issues of public welfare (Arendt 1958, pp. 3–4, 7). It is therefore one of the most fundamental elements of Hannah Arendt's conception of power and action. She uses the instrument of speech for the sake of acting together and creating power. In past times the means of speech always came along with a get-together of people, while the use of script always implied a delay in time and space. But the digital environment of cyberspace is able to connect and mobilize people otherwise separated in time and space both by the means of script and speech. Putting Arendt's argument thus in the modern context of cyberization, script and speech both become means of action. However you express yourself, it is speech and this coincidence of script and speech is more evident than ever in the digital environment of cyberspace.

Power is expressed through political action and the rule of law, but does not only represent the capacity, but also the empowerment of people to act. Arendt's conception here encourages civil behavior to enhance democratic conversation as well as to regain support for subjects of political purpose among equal men. For her, "politics takes place in a public realm free of force and coercion, a 'stage' suitable for the expression of human plurality and civic equality" (Villa 1998, p. 148). Individuals learn to think of themselves as members of a society that transcends the individual and supports the political purpose. Support requires group participants to be viewed not only as targets and recipients but also as sources and providers of various types of support (Tichon and Shapiro 2003).

For Max Weber, in contrast, politics is about the idea of leadership: deciding for others and affecting the course of events. Here, politics is "essentially what some do to others, rather than—as with Arendt—what all do together" (Katep 2006, p. 132). Max Weber defines politics by the power of imposing one's will to others. This kind of power requires the will to power as well as the passion to rule "for power's (and not for law's) sake" (Arendt 1975, p. 137). This is redefined as violence by Arendt and it is not political at all, but seen in a radically negative way, because violence left to itself turns into a destructive principle (Arendt 1965, p. 276, 1975; Katep 2006, p. 136). In her theoretical conceptions, Arendt always tries to distinguish power from violence. For her, these two terms are even opposites in the sense that power decreases when violence increases. The best example of violence is war, because violence is always instrumental and in need of guidance and justification through the end it pursues (Arendt 1970, pp. 51–56). And even if the war against Nazism had been for the people suffering under the regime an "unusual unequivocal example of just war" (Canovan 1992, p. 186), the advent of nuclear weapons put a different view upon this matter.

Arendt argues that "[t]o be political, to live in a polis, meant that everything was decided through words and persuasion and not through force and violence" (Arendt 1958, p. 26). She stresses the special dangers when political violence is used for political intentions. Violence is used to monopolize the public sphere, to control what is seen and heard in it (Villa 1999, p. 135). "[T]o force people by violence, to command rather than persuade, were prepolitical ways to deal with people characteristic of life outside the *polis*, of home and family life, where the household head ruled with uncontested, despotic powers" (Arendt 1958, p. 27). And even if Arendt agreed with Machiavelli concerning the "islands of freedom", his justification of violence in the sense that it is justified by a good cause was an anathema for her (Canovan 1992, p. 167f.). Political violence can destroy power by isolating people that want to exercise power as well as the support of one group of people by the government can enable it to rule by violence (Canovan 1992, p. 210). But her theoretical distinctions of power and violence are not as clear as the example given above: in government, they are often combined. This combination is common and it is less frequent to find them in their pure and extreme form (Arendt 1970, p. 47). To better understand the combination of power and violence, Arendt connects these two conceptions to the terms of legitimacy and justification. The use of power and violence within political communities thus becomes clear:

> Power needs no justification, being inherent in the very existence of political communities; what it does need is legitimacy. (...) Power springs up whenever people get together and act together, but it derives its legitimacy from the initial getting together rather than from any action that then may follow. Legitimacy, when challenged, bases itself on an appeal to the past, while justification relates to an end that lies in the future. Violence can be justifiable, but it will never be legitimate (Arendt 1970, p. 52).

3.2 The Power of Virtual Communities

After having distinguished power from violence and having outlined the fundamental characteristics of Arendt's conception of power, the question as how cyberspace serves as a context for the content of political action has to be answered. The last sections have shown that cyberspace can be seen as a space of appearance in so far as affairs of political purpose are discussed in cyberspace. When political action is carried out by the public and takes place within cyberspace as space of appearance, what *should* the content of political affairs and actions be about? And what is the cyberspace content *really* about? The following section tries to answer these questions.

For Hannah Arendt, spaces of appearance are needed where disputes of political relevance are solved by the means of discussion instead of violent action. Politics is thus the canvas for the exercise of a creative will without the will to govern and dominate (Canovan 1992, pp. 276–278). Therefore, political speech carried out in the political space of freedom can neither be of social or economic policies, nor is extensive or technical knowledge directly relevant. In contrast, authentic political speech is all about citizens, who have to interpret their situation in a way which renders it appropriate for being passed on in the form of stories and the teaching of history.

> The content of authentic politics is therefore deliberation and dispute about what policies are needed to preserve and keep in good repair a political body, a form of government that has been designed to carry on its business by free deliberation, discussion, and dispute; or in an insurgent situation, about the creation of a government that institutionalizes the spontaneous deliberation and discussion that are now trying to bring it into being (Katep 2006, p. 134)

Due to data storage and retrieval facilities, the infrastructure of cyberspace opens up the possibility of using rare information in web-based discussions. Moreover, cyberspace enables the discussion between people on far sides of the globe and is able to carry out political action as well as to exercise Arendt's conception of power (Papacharissi 2002). But it is true that the overall content of cyberspace activities is definitely not only about affairs of political purpose, since affairs of political purpose have been ruled down in cyberspace in recent years when cyberspace became a fundamental part of the nowadays called information society.

In the very beginning of the age of cyberization, in the late 1980s and early 1990s, some interactive digital projects were already established to fulfill political needs: The Public Electronic Network (PEN) in 1989, the Blacksburg Electronic Village in 1993 and the La Plaza Telecommunity in Taos in 1995 (Rogers and Malhotra 2000). Another network, PeaceNet, was established in 1985 to discuss issues of peace and democracy. John D. H. Downing and H. Sachs both traced the development of this Internet based computer network. While Downing found that it fostered democratic discourse in 50 states and over 70 countries (Downing 1989), Sachs pointed to the "cooperation among participants, the non-linearity of discussion, the reflection that users invest in their responses, and the gratifications"

(Papacharissi 2004, p. 268). They concluded that such computer networks enabled the mobilizing of a constituency otherwise separated in time and space. They may function as forums for developing the requisite language and agendas for political action and may serve as an alternative for individuals who want to express their views and opinions while influencing mainstream politics (Papacharissi 2004, p. 267f., Downing 1989; Sachs 1995). Despite these early examples of cyberspace as a space of appearance, some scholars argue that "the Internet is sacred *and* profane" (Hill and Hughes 1998, p. 185) as well as that "online communication is about venting emotion and expressing what Abramson et al. (1988) refer to as 'hasty opinions', rather than rational and focused discourse" (Papacharissi 2004, p. 270; Abramson et al. 1988). A content analysis of a random sample of postings to Usenet newsgroups—self-identified as being political—was conducted by Wilhelm at the end of 1990s. He found out that these digital newsgroups showed short-lived conversations, but that sustained deliberation was rare in these forums (Wilhelm 1998).

The contemporary example of the Arab Spring as pro-democracy protest in 2011 has shown how cyberspace today builds a space of appearance and encourages people to exercise power. Concerning the recent revolutions in Egypt and Tunisia, which led to the demission of President Mubarak in Egypt as well as President Ben Ali in Tunisia, the Internet has enabled people to push their democratic will forward as well as to organize parts of their protests. Protesters who flooded the streets of Cairo in 2011 used digital media to organize and coordinate their protest and the opposition used Twitter and other blogs to express their opinion against the repressive government (Kyriakopoulou 2011, p. 21f.). Pictures and news on Tunisian and Egyptian blogs informed the foreign media and press in order to encourage their support for this democratic movement. "It seems that, in the case of Egypt, the social media are recognized as having played a significant role in supporting and triggering the offline protest that put an end to a 30 years authoritarian rule" (Kyriakopoulou 2011, p. 22). These events dominated the media and news during the first months of 2011. People used digital sources like Twitter or blogs as their stage "suitable for the expression of human plurality and civic equality" (Villa 1998, p. 148). When these people came together, a space of appearance was created by organizing public demonstrations and exchanging information in cyberspace. As the space of appearance and political freedom "finds its actualisation in the actions and speeches of individuals who have come together to undertake some common project" (d'Entrèves 1994, p. 77), it emerges in the moment when words and opinions are spread by Twitter or other social media platforms. Cyberspace as space of appearance is declared and kept open by protesters even against the will of the officials as it was the case for the Arab Spring.

But this is only one side of the story. Arab Spring protests were not only based on political discussion and the exchange of ideas, but street protests seemed to be the main driver for change. Organized protests that materialized in the streets of Cairo often turned out to be violent acts. People, which first organized their actions within cyberspace as a space of appearance, were then confronted to government's violence, confronted "not by men but by men's artifacts, whose inhumanity and destructive effectiveness increase" (Arendt 1970, p. 53). The outcome of this head-on clash between violence and power is hardly in doubt and the resulting impotence of the people led to their violent acts in the end. Loss of power became a temptation to substitute violence for power and that is what happened during the street protests in Cairo when powerful organized protests turned out to be violent acts. While power is never the property of an individual, violence is. This is why protests in cyberspace could only be organized by people acting together, but violent acts could be done by individuals. This brought victory to the people in the end with the demission of President Mubarak and President Ben Ali, but the price for this victory has to be paid in terms of the people's own power (Arendt 1970, pp. 53–54).

> Where violence is no longer backed and restrained by power, the well-known reversal in reckoning with means and ends has taken place. The means, the means of destruction, now determine the end with the consequence that the end will be the destruction of all power (Arendt 1970, p. 54).

Violence, in the end, thus destroyed power and "what can never grow out of it is power" (Arendt 1970, p. 53). This lack of power that occurred during the street protests might thus serve as a first approach to understand the ongoing difficulties in these countries in establishing democratic institutions.

3.3 The Violence of Filtering and Control Techniques

Even if Arendt's conceptions of power and political action can be applied to the context of cyberspace, it does not only exist for citizens carrying out political action and constituting cyberspace in the sense of a space of a political freedom. People's everyday life is dispersed through clouds of digital-electronic telecommunications that are owned by private companies and that also establish spaces of private authority in cyberspace (Deibert and Rohozinski 2010, p. 11). When Arendt opposes power to violence—and to put it in Machiavelli's words: islands of freedom that people establish trough acting in concert are surrounded by a sea of different hostile forces—these hostile forces seem to also exist in the context of cyberspace. "[M]anaging cyberspace has shifted subtly from policies and practices aimed at denying access to content to methods that seek to *normalize* control and the exercise of power through a variety of means" (Deibert and Rohozinksi 2010, p. 6). States do much more than enforcing order in cyberspace. Through filtering and control techniques, they minimize the capability of Internet users to establish and use cyberspace as a space of appearance: "Governments are not neutral parties, despite the growing degree to which the autonomous and uncontrolled nature of the Internet is celebrated" (Papacharissi 2004, p. 269; Sassi 2000). As Arendt has demonstrated, power and violence are always combined within governments; even the governments in democratic states try to control and filter web content. This emerges "from a desire to shape and influence as much as tightly control national and global populations that are increasingly reliant on cyberspace as their main source of information" (Deibert and Rohozinski 2010, p. 7). This new form of power emerging in cyberspace by governments as well as by outsourced third parties is violence according to Hannah Arendt. It monopolizes the public sphere and controls what is seen and written in it.

Information control within cyberspace also occurs beyond these filtering techniques. Even if blockages of web content are not always distinguishable from technical problems, these blockages often have occurred during political events in the countries. Denial of Service (DoS) attacks has been observed during the Kyrgyzstan parliamentary elections in 2005 when websites of opposition newspapers shut down, as well as during the dispute between Russia and Estonia in 2007 and the conflict between Russia and Georgia in 2008 (Deibert and Rohozinski 2010, pp. 4–8). The so-called just-in-time-blocking occurs when states disrupt communication networks for political purposes around elections or demonstrations to avoid social unrest (ONI 2010a).

The political violence used here destroys power by isolating people who want to exercise power (Canovan 1992, p. 210). During the 2005 Kyrgyzstan parliamentary elections, a shutdown of the opposition's websites banned their ability to participate in the election process: "Attacks included flooding journalist e-mail accounts with large amounts of spam, and spoofing of e-mail from Kyrgyz websites located in the US" (ONI 2005). A similar situation emerged in 2008 during the Russia-Georgia War. Georgian Internet providers filtered Russian websites to prevent inaccurate reports about the situation and the political events (ONI 2010b, p. 179). The opposition was not able to exercise power and to come together and engage in a discussion of freedom and democratic politics (ONI 2005, Bowe et al. 2012), because power is not only about persuading and discussing, but also about being aware of its own situation. And this awareness requires the freedom of expression as well as the freedom of information and thus the access to media websites with even opposite opinions. Hannah Arendt characterized power and violence as two parts of a zero-sum game: Power increases, when violence decreases. Thus when the possibility to discuss and persuade is restricted by the limited access to websites with dissent opinions, violence increases by monopolizing the public sphere with one single opinion.

3.4 Caught in the Middle: Weibo and the Great Firewall of China

The People's Republic of China was among the first to adopt a national filtering system that became known under the name of the Great Firewall of China. One technical filtering option used by Chinese officials is the Transmission Control Protocol (TCP) reset (Wang and Faris 2008). Sensitive information that could have impact on the Communist Party's control over public life and order is targeted. This concerns not only content about sensitive events in history like the June 1989 military crackdown or the Tibetan rights movement, but also content about more common subjects like human rights, sovereignty issues or independent media (ONI 2010a, p. 468). Another filter technique is related to the control of Chinese Blogs. Service providers have to install filters that do not allow the posting of a huge number of keywords and keyword combinations as well as to flag posts to review as far as they contain sensitive information (ONI 2010a, p. 460, Wang and Faris 2008, p. 107). Aside from technical filtering, China has implemented a wide range of other methods to control public opinion and discourse. The so-called *Fifty Cent Party* refers to about 300,000 nationwide commentators that earn 50 cents per post and are engaged by the government to "guide online public opinion" (ONI 2010a, p. 454). By supporting the group of commentators by offering them special trainings and certificates, the government enabled them to rule by violence over others. Especially the service of Weibo, the Chinese version of Facebook, is concerned by Internet censorship. Surprisingly, Weibo was initially born out of the Communist Party's desire to control social media. It is for this reason that Weibo officially has never been a threat to the regime (Mackinnon 2012).

Weibo is therefore caught in the middle, between violence and power, freedom of expression and governmental censorship. The various filter and control techniques as well as human censors that guide public discussion seem to bolster Communist rule through the wide spread use of Weibo. The content oriented filtering techniques at Weibo present a case of political violence Hannah Arendt warned of. Commentators that guide public opinion within digital communities and forums are trying to monopolize the public sphere as well as to control what is written. They force people to adopt a coordinated opinion instead of persuading them by words and deeds (Arendt 1958, p. 27). Even if the Communist Party legitimated this control technique by a good cause, this argumentation had always been an anathema for Hannah Arendt. For her, violence can never be justified by a good cause (Canovan 1992, pp. 167–168). But "despite the filtering, Weibo is changing China" (Mackinnon 2012) in a more positive sense. The automated censorship that dominates Weibo in large parts opens up new spaces for clever users to avoid filtering techniques: Even if the date of the Tiananmen Square crackdown was blocked, the discussions used the code of May 35th instead of the real date of June 4th 1989 (Mackinnon 2012). Moreover a variety of topics has been discussed at Weibo: The discussions about the Wenzhou train disaster in 2011, where 40 people were killed and the officials tried to hide the disaster or the forced abortions after 7 months of pregnancy because of the one-child-policy are among the public taboos that have been discussed digitally on Weibo. Because power is never the property of an individual, but belongs to a group and is only in existence as long as the group keeps together (Arendt 1970, p. 44), discussions of Weibo users create rare spaces of appearance in Chinese cyberspace by debating about previously off-limits topics (Mackinnon 2012).

Even though power and violence appear in this context side by side, this is not a head-on clash, but rather a constant struggle with an unpredictable end. Distribution of power in cyberspace has less to do with the power of information technology itself, but rather with the power of norms (Drezner 2010, p. 38).

The distribution of power therefore does not depend upon the mastering of technological aspects such as the implementation of filtering techniques through governments or the knowledge of avoiding theses filtering techniques through users in cyberspace. It is about the power of imposing and control norms: "Even if the internet empowers global civil society, the question is whether governments are willing to tolerate more vocal citizen activists or not" (Drezner 2010, p. 38).

Thus, it seems that the creation of power within the Chinese cyberspace in the future heavily depends on the willingness of the government to tolerate citizen's voices. But the situation is even more asymmetric as it seems. Even if the authoritarian government in China might decide to not tolerate the emerging voice of its citizens in cyberspace, it will nevertheless be in a weak position. The government's actions are merely based on violence and violence is never legitimate and always instrumental. It is the *ultima ratio* of a government when all power is nearly lost. Power can never grow out of violence, only terror can in the end. But no government exclusively based on violence has ever existed, even the totalitarian ruler had a certain kind of power base with the secret police and its net of informers. Violence and terror would only remain in durable existence if robot soldiers eliminated the human factor completely and conceivably (Arendt 1970, p. 50). And only such a situation "could change this fundamental ascendancy of power over violence" (Arendt 1970, p. 50). Therefore power is always existent and it is the "very condition enabling a group of people to think and act in terms of the means-end category" (Arendt 1970, p. 51). And these means-end categories do include all means that at the very essence and absolute like peace, government and power and not in the need of guidance and justification like war, terror or violence (Arendt 1970, p. 51). It is thus likely that the Chinese government will and has to tolerate its citizens' voice in cyberspace to a certain extent in order to maintain the state apparatus as such. But it is unpredictable how it will turn out in the end when citizens use their small spaces of appearance within cyberspace to create power and act in terms of means-end categories.

4 The Condition of Cyberspace

Utopian views of cyberspace as a space of appearance would illustrate a polis-like world where equal citizens act together in order to discuss and debate affairs of political purpose, thus enhancing democracy and bringing people across the world closer together. But analyzing power relations in cyberspace through rose-colored glasses is not the goal of this chapter. Even if the preceding sections have shown that empirical evidences theoretically match Hannah Arendt's conception of power and (political) action, the example of Arab Spring has also shown that power relations, created in cyberspace, might turn out into violent actions in the non-digital world. The practical potential of cyberspace to create stable power relations thus remains rather fragile and questionable.

Access to the Internet is a necessary precondition in order to use cyberspace as a space of appearance, to exercise power and to engage in political action. But unfortunately, Internet access does not necessarily guarantee the use of cyberspace to exercise power. In 2010, Chinese officials formulated the policy goal that "every village had access to the telephone and every township had access to the Internet" (ONI 2010a, p. 453). In 2010 China was also the world leading country with 300mio Internet users (Worldbank 2012a). But despite these efforts in terms of Internet access, China is also the world leading country in implementing filtering and control techniques in cyberspace. It is therefore that empirical evidence has shown that cyberspace is both, a space of political freedom and power as well as a space of censorship and violence. Especially the example of Weibo illustrates that power and violence do not emerge separately, but that they are always side by side. In a political space of appearance where power is created, there are always areas of violence, by governmental censorship or the individual spread of rumors. Thus, power that is created in cyberspace as political space of appearance had, has and will ever have its enemies.

Analyzing this topic in the context of International Relations, it becomes clear that the distribution of power in cyberspace affects foremost the level of state-society relations. According to Daniel Drezner the Internet has probably empowered non-state actors more than states, but the effect of this empowerment is not consistent across all types of political environments (Drezner 2010, p. 32). The absolute ascendancy of power over violence in cyberspace merely occurs in states where the rule of law is the very essence of the government. But there is no government which is exclusively based on violence and even in authoritarian states only rare spaces of appearance in the cyberspace exist. Activities in cyberspace do not only concern national politics, but the global system of states and nations is heavily dependent on the global network of cyberspace. Global economic, social and diplomatic independencies are also created and maintained through cyberspace. Power will hardly win over violence in authoritarian states, but violence will do even less. Thus, even if power in cyberspace is constantly threatened by violence, the absolute victory of violence over power in cyberspace would not only mean to silent the people's voice, but also to give up the integration in the global system and its benefits. And this seems hard to believe.

The argumentation of this chapter does not necessarily mean a complete revival of Hannah Arendt's thoughts for the modern times of cyberization, but it has shown that Hannah Arendt still has something to say about politics here and today. This chapter encourages to rethink the reasonability of the epochal and unique characteristics that are often attributed to cyberspace as well as the need to re-conceptualize power relations in cyberspace again and again.

Acknowledgments I am grateful to Gaye Ilhan Demiryol, Maximilian Mayer and Jan Christoph Suntrup for their useful critiques, constructive suggestions and references that enriched this chapter. I also wish to thank Paula Küppers who never tired of correcting my English.

References

Abramson, J., Arterton, F., & Orren, G. (1988). *The electronic commonwealth: The impact of new media technologies on democratic politics*. New York: Basic Books.
Arendt, H. (1958). *The human condition* (2nd ed.). Chicago: University of Chicago Press.
Arendt, H. (1965). *On revolution* (2nd ed.). New York: Viking.
Arendt, H. (1970). *On violence*. New York: Harcourt Brace Javanovich.
Arendt, H. (1975). *The origins of totalitarianism: New edition with added prefaces*. San Diego: Harcourt Brace and Company.
Bandurski, D. (2008). China's guerilla war for the web. *Far Eastern Economic Review*, http://feer.com/essays/2008/august/chinas-guerrilla-war-for-the-web (Accessed 28 Aug 2012).
Boas, T. C. (2004). Weaving the authoritarian web. *Current History, 102*(677), 438–443.
Bowe, B., Blom, R., & Freedman, E. (2012). Cyber-dissent and power: Negotiating online boundaries in repressitarian regimes. *International Journal of Information Communication Technologies and Human Development, 4*(2), 1–19.
Canovan, M. (1992). *Hannah Arendt: A reinterpretation of her political thought*. Cambridge: Cambridge University Press.
Connery, B. A. (1997). MHO: Authority and egalitarian rhetoric in the virtual coffeehouse. In D. Porter (Eds.), *Internet culture* (pp. 161–180). New York: Routledge.
Deibert, Ronald. (2000). International plug'n play? Citizen activism, the internet, and global public policy. *International Studies Perspectives, 1*, 255–272.
Deibert, R., & Rohozinski, R. (2010). Beyond denial: Introducing next-generation information access controls. In R. Deibert, J. Palfrey, R. Rohozinski, J. Zittrain (Eds.), *Access controlled. The shaping of power, rights, and rule in cyberspace* (pp. 3–14). Cambridge: MIT Press.
d'Entrèves, M. (1994). *The political philosophy of Hannah Arendt*. London and New York: Routledge.
Disch, Lisa. (2011). How could Hannah Arendt glorify the american revolution and revile the French? Placing on revolution in the historiography of the French and American Revolutions. *European Journal of Political Theory, 10*(3), 350–371.
Downing, J. D. H. (1989). Computers for political change: PeaceNet and public data access. *Journal of Communication, 39*(3), 154–162.
Drezner, D. W. (2010). Weighing the scales. The internet's effect on state-society relations. *Brown Journal of World Affairs, 16*(2), 31–44.
Dyson, E. (1998). *Release 2.1: A design for living in the digital age*. New York: Broadway.
Hill, K., & Hughes, J. (1998). *Cyberpolitics: Citizen activism in the age of the internet*. New York: Rowman and Littlefield Publishers.
Katep, G. (2006). Political action: Its nature and advantages. In D. R. Villa (Ed.), *The Cambridge companion to Hannah Arendt* (pp. 130–148). Cambridge, HA: Cambridge University Press.
Keohane, R. O., & Nye, J. S, Jr. (1998). Power and interdependence in the information age. *Foreign Affairs, 77*(5), 81–94.
Stephen, K. (1998). The MAI and the Clash of Globalization. *Foreign Policy*, (112), 110-122.
Stephen, K. (2002). Economic governance in an electronically networked society. In: B. H. Rodney, & T. J. Biersteker (Eds.), *The emergence of private authority in global governance* (pp. 43-75). Cambridge: Cambridge University Press.
Kramer, F., Starr, S., & Wentz, L. (2009). *Cyberpower and national security*. Washington D.C.: Potomac Books Inc.
Kuehl, D. (2009). From cyberspace to cyberpower: Defining the Problem. In F. Kramer, H. Starr, & L. Wentz (Eds.), *Cyberpower and national security* (pp. 24–42). Washington D.C.: Potomac Books Inc.
Kyriakopoulou, K. (2011). Authoritarian states and internet social media: Instruments of democratisation or instruments of control? *Human Affairs, 21*(1), 18–26.
Lee, J.-A., & Liu, C.-Y. (2012). Forbidden city enclosed by the great firewall: The law and power of internet filtering in China. *Minnesota Journal of Law, Science, and Technology, 13*(1), 125–150.

Lemley, M. (2012). The dubious autonomy of virtual worlds, stanford public law working paper No. 2021521, http://ssrn.com/abstract=2021521 (Accessed 24 October 2012).

Mackinnon, M. (2012). Do China's bloggers threaten or bolster communist rule? The globe and mail, 9 September 2012, www.theglobeandmail.com/news/world/does-chinas-sina-weibo-threaten-or-help-to-entrench-communist-rule/article4528701/?service=mobile (Accessed 10 October 2012).

Nye, J. (2010). Cyber power. Belfer Center for Science and International Affairs, Harvard Kennedy School, http://belfercenter.ksg.harvard.edu/files/cyber-power.pdf (Accessed 30 August 2012).

Nye, J. (2011). *The future of power*. New York: Public Affairs.

OpenNet Initiative (ONI 2005). *Special Report: Kyrgyzstan. Election monitoring in Kyrgyzstan*, http://www.opennetinitiative.net/special/kg/ (Accessed 28 August 2012).

OpenNet Initiative (ONI 2010). China. In R. Deibert, J. Palfrey, R. Rohozinski, & J. Zittrain (Eds.), *Access controlled. The shaping of power, rights, and rule in cyberspace* (pp. 449–488). Boston: MIT Press.

OpenNet Initiative (ONI 2012). *Global internet filtering in 2012 at a lance*, http://opennet.net/blog/2012/04/global-internet-filtering-2012-glance (Accessed 30 August 2012).

Papacharissi, Z. (2002). The virtual sphere. The internet as a public sphere. *New Media and Society, 4*(1), 9–27.

Papacharissi, Z. (2004). Democracy online: Civility, politeness, and the democratic potential of online political discussion groups. *New Media and Society, 6*(2), 259–283.

Rogers, E., & Malhotra, S. (2000). Computers as communication: the rise of digital democracy. In K. L. Hacker, & J. van Dijk (Eds.), *Digital democracy: Issues of theory and practice* (pp. 10–29). London: Sage.

Runnel, P., Pruulmann-Vengerfeldt, P., & Reinsalu; K. (2009). The Estonian Tiger leap from post-communism to the information society: From policy to practice. *Journal of Baltic Studies, 40*(1), 29–51.

Sachs, H. (1995). Computer networks and the formation of public opinion: An ethnographic study. *Media, Culture and Society, 17*(1), 81–99.

Sassi, S. (2000). The controversies of the internet and the revitalization of local political life. In K. Hacker, & D. Dijk (Eds.) *Digital democracy: Issues of theory and practice* (pp. 90–104). London: Sage.

Sitton, J. F. (1994). Hannah Arendt's argument for council democracy. In L. Hinchman, & S. Hinchman (Eds.), *Hannah Arendt: Critical essays* (pp. 307–330). Albany: State University of New York Press.

Special Rapporteur to the Commission on Human Rights and Human Rights Council (2011). *Report of the Special Rapporteur on the promotion and protection of the right to freedom of opinion and expression*, http://www.ohchr.org/Documents/Issues/Opinion/A.66.290.pdf (Accessed 28 August 2012).

Starr, S. (2009). Toward a preliminary theory of cyberpower. In F. Kramer, H. Starr, & L. Wentz (Eds.). *Cyberpower and national security* (pp. 43–89). Washington D.C.: Potomac Books Inc.

Tichon, J. G., & Shapiro, M. (2003). The process of sharing social support in cyberspace. *CyberPsychology and Behavior, 6*(2), 161–170.

Toffler, A., & Toffler, H. (1995). The *politics of the third wave*. Kansas City: Turner Pub.

Villa, D. R. (1998). The philosopher versus the citizen: Arendt, Strauss, and Socrates. *Political Theory, 26*(2), 147–172.

Villa, D. R. (1999). *Politics, philosophy, terror: Essays on the thought of Hannah Arendt*. Princeton: Princeton University Press.

Villa, D. R. (2006). Introduction: The development of Arendt's political thought. In D. R. Villa (Ed.). *The Cambridge companion to Hannah Arendt* (pp. 1–22). Cambridge: Cambridge University Press.

Wang, S., & Faris, R. (2008). Welcome to the machine. *Index on Censorship, 37*(2), 106–113.

Wellmer, A. (2006). Arendt. On revolution. In D. R. Villa (Ed.). *The Cambridge companion to Hannah Arendt* (pp. 220–241). Cambridge: Cambridge University Press.

Wilhelm, A. (1998). Virtual sounding boards: How deliberative is online political discussion? *Information, Communication and Society, 1*(3), 313–338.

Worldbank (2012a). Internet users, http://data.worldbank.org/indicator/IT.NET.USER (Accessed 28 August 2012).

Worldbank (2012b). *Heavily indebted poor countries*, http://go.worldbank.org/TQUQE8C1M0 (Accessed 28 August 2012).

Worldbank (2012c). *How we classify countries*, http://data.worldbank.org/about/country-classifications (Accessed 28 August 2012).

Zheng, Y., Chen, G., & Lye, L. F. (2012). China's politics: Preparing for leadership reshuffling and maintaining status quo. *East Asian Policy, 4*(1), 5–13.

Part II
Cyberspace and International Relations: Prospects and Challenges

Clarifying the International Debate on Stuxnet: Arguments for Stuxnet as an Act of War

Sascha Knoepfel

Abstract Discovery of the Stuxnet computer worm has brought to the fore ongoing discussions concerning the classification of cyber attacks as "acts of war". In the aftermath of its detection, experts and media personnel alike were quick in putting the implicative tag 'act of war' onto the use of the malicious program, although no competent justification for such labelling was offered. The following chapter aims to clarify the international debate by presenting definitional criteria for an act of war in cyberspace and applying it to the empirical case of Stuxnet.

S. Knoepfel (✉)
King's College London, London, UK
e-mail: sascha.knoepfel@kcl.ac.uk

J.-F. Kremer and B. Müller (eds.), *Cyberspace and International Relations*,
DOI: 10.1007/978-3-642-37481-4_7, © Springer-Verlag Berlin Heidelberg 2014

1 Introduction

Stuxnet, a complex piece of malware discovered in June 2009, gained great attention from IT-Experts, security researchers and national officials in 2010.[1] Terms like "warfare" (e.g., Infosecurity 2010) and "war" (e.g., Mehr News Agency 2010) were and still are frequently used to describe the malicious software in the heated international debate. The declaration of Stuxnet as an act of war,[2] however, seems to be superficial. Indeed, no competent and comprehensive justification for describing the piece of code in such a way—and not as an act of criminality or delinquency—is available. Among other consequences, this use of the term warfare based on vague arguments creates a potentially dangerous situation by inciting victims to take tougher actions against any potential attacker.

Recognising the significance of defining the malware, this chapter sets out to contribute to a clearer international debate regarding Stuxnet. It does so by examining whether and on which definitional bases Stuxnet might be classified as an act of war. I argue that given the absence of a widely accepted definition of an act of war in cyber space,[3] Clausewitz's political definition of war is adequately suitable in providing a foundation for the characterization of Stuxnet. After illustrating this definition and its elements, I apply it to the empirical case of Stuxnet and find that the use of the code fulfils all listed definitional criteria. On this basis, I argue that Stuxnet can be reasonably classified as an act of war. The conclusion states the findings and some of its limitations.

2 Definition of an Act of War

According to Martin Libicki, a recognised cyber warfare expert at RAND Corporation, there are three ways to define what constitutes an act of war in cyber space: universally, multilaterally and unilaterally (Libicki 2009, pp. 179–180). As close to a universal definition as possible comes an official statement by the United Nations or the adoption of a widely signed international treaty or law. As neither such a statement nor treaty currently exists, alternative forms of agreement need to be considered. The most obvious organisation with the capacity to develop a multilaterally acceptable definition of cyber warfare would be the North Atlantic Treaty Organisation (NATO). However, when Estonia, a member of NATO, fell

[1] This text was compiled in 2011 (not updated since) and similar versions have been released in *ADLAS Magazin für Außen—und Sicherheitspolitik* (Issue 2/2011) and on the blog of *Young Initiative on Foreign Affairs and International Relations* (11, August 2011). The opinion express in the chapter is solely that of the author.

[2] The term *act of war* is used in this chapter synonymously with *warfare*.

[3] The prefix *cyber* refers to the use of information and communication technologies as target and/or means.

victim to a range of cyber attacks in 2007, NATO refused to activate its collective defence clause by defining the actions as warfare. Given NATO's silence on this issue to date, the onus of supplying a definition of cyber warfare falls on the individual state. A range of nations have established such definitions individually, and have changed and adjusted them over time (Ventre 2009). However, such a definition, whose validity of which reaches hardly beyond state borders, is not able to provide a basis for an investigation motivated by the task to establish clarity for the international debate.

Due to the non-existence of a suitable—that is agreed by a good portion of states worldwide—definition for an act of war in cyber space, the first task ahead is establishing a working definition that satisfies two primary conditions. Firstly, it needs to be applicable to the realm of cyber space and secondly, it has to be acceptable to as many nations as possible as a definition of cyber war, at least potentially.

One such alternative is the definition proposed by Carl von Clausewitz' in his treatise *On War*.[4] Even though there is no explicit link to cyber space, his definition of an act of war can be applied to this dimension and could potentially be acceptable to many nations for the following reasons. It is applicable, because Clausewitz aims to define the nature of war itself and not a specific form like conventional or irregular war. Furthermore, it might well be acceptable to a bulk of nations as Clausewitz provides a (if not the) traditional definition of war, which is shared by a large portion of the international (experts) community. A definition of cyber warfare would thus likely include its elements in some form.

Clausewitz defines war in the very first chapter of *On War* as an "act of violence to compel our opponent to fulfil our will" (Clausewitz 1989, p. 75). If one breaks down the definition, five distinct elements can be identified. Four are obvious: the use of violence as a means ('act of violence'), an attacker ('our'), a victim ('opponent') and the object of compelling the victim to fulfil our will ('compel our opponent to fulfil our will'). The fifth element is derived through the implication of the last passage of this definition. Specifically, the need to compel someone implies that the opposing entities must have a somewhat different position on a certain issue. The fifth element, hence, acknowledges the existence of an issue of conflict.

3 Stuxnet as an Act of War

Building on Clausewitz' definition and in order to legitimately term Stuxnet an act of war, it needs to be shown that the malicious code is deployed in an issue of conflict; is directed against a victim; is developed by an attacker; is used to fulfil the attacker's will; and is coded to be violent.

---

[4] Just one other suitable, yet evolving, alternative would be a contemporary law and effect-based approach, which qualifies a cyber attack as warfare if it caused physical damage with long-term consequences or injury to humans (Owens and Lin 2009, p. 251).

3.1 Issue of Conflict

The issue of conflict likely to be associated with the deployment of Stuxnet is that of Iran's uranium enrichment program (UEP). This claim is largely compelling due to the net relationship between the software code and Iran's UEP illustrated throughout the chapter. The following passages lay the ground for such links by specifically addressing the larger picture in which Stuxnet might be situated, which is the political conflict between various members of the international community and Iran over the Iranian UEP.

Several nations and institutions made political statements on various occasions directed towards Iran to stop its enrichment program, which the international community argues goes beyond the legitimate peaceful use of this technology determined in the Nuclear Non-Proliferation Treaty (NPT). Till date, six United Nations Security Council (UNSC) resolutions have been directed against Iran's program. These resolutions demand Iran to "suspend all enrichment-related" activities (e.g., UNSC [United Nations Security Council] 2006). The particular stance of the USA and Israel, who are identified as potential attackers later in this paper, can be summed up in an announcement by a senior official of the Obama administration, which was given in 2010: "I'm glad to hear they are having troubles with their centrifuge machines, and the U.S. and its allies are doing everything we can to make it more complicated" (Broad et al. 2011, p. 2).

Iran, however, refuses to stop the program, arguing that its aim is the generation of enriched uranium for peaceful purposes only, a right granted by the NPT. One development showing Iran's pursuit of the program is the completion of the Bushehr nuclear power plant in late 2010 (Reznichenko 2010).

3.2 Victim

Leading Stuxnet analyst Ralph Langner claims that it is "beyond reasonable doubt" that Stuxnet is designed to target Iran's UEP (Langner 2010a). The most persuasive evidences leading to such a conclusion are presented in the following.

Looking at the technical aspects of the malware, one of the main hints that Stuxnet had a specific target is the existence of a routine it launches—colloquially called 'code 417' (see also subheading 'Act of Violence'). Langner identifies the centrifuges in Natanz, where Iran's main fuel enrichment plant is located, as a likely destination for the malicious software as it houses a centrifuge cascade made up of 164 machines; exactly the amount of machines destructively affected by code 417 (Langner 2010b, c).

Two other technical clues are traced in an ISIS report from December (Albright et al. 2010, pp. 3–4). Both concern specific frequency values which were found to be programmed into the Stuxnet code. Surprisingly for most, the nominal frequency (1,064 Hz) as well as the maximal value frequency (1,410 Hz) specified in the code blocs is identical to the centrifuge configurations in Iran's main enrichment facility.

The hypothesis of Iran as the intended victim of Stuxnet is also supported by a statistical analysis conducted by Symantec. In order to find out where Stuxnet infects computers, the company monitored the traffic sent by the malware to its Command and Control servers via the internet. Since commencement of recording in September 2010, the database listed about 100,000 contaminated computers; over 60,000 of which were based in Iran (Falliere et al. 2011).

Iran's President Ahmadinejad admitted that Iran's enrichment centrifuges had been hit by a damaging software attack (Erdbrink 2010). Although he did not name Stuxnet directly, the time of his statement in late September 2010 makes Stuxnet a likely cause as it coincides with the shutdown of almost 1,000 centrifuges in Natanz (Albright et al. 2010) and the discovery of Stuxnet in its present form (Falliere et al. 2010).

3.3 Attacker

The expertise and intelligence required to design a worm of Stuxnet's complexity and effectiveness limits its potential origin to a very small circle of suspects. In particular, three indicators point to Israel and the USA as the likely sponsors of Stuxnet (Langner 2010a).

Firstly, to program the malicious code with a reasonable chance of successfully corrupting Iranian IR-1 centrifuges in Natanz, the developers needed to have a profound knowledge of the on-site plant layout. This is because of the configuration process of so-called programmable logic controllers (PLCs), which is unique for each industrial control system constructed (Falliere et al. 2011, p. 3). Such knowledge is held by two groups of people: the planner(s) of the plant and those who possess an "extreme amount of intelligence" about the facility (Langner 2010a).

Secondly, a comprehensive understanding of the functionality of IR-1 centrifuges, as well as a test-side (replica for experimental purposes) is necessary to create a malware as effective as Stuxnet. The actors in possession of such a machine are, again, few. Known holders include Iran, North Korea and Libya, which obtained the centrifuge due to the selling of the P-1, a copy of the IR-1, through A. Q. Khan in 1976. Furthermore, the USA got hold of it after Libya gave up its nuclear program in 2003. However, the US technicians were unable to run the P-1 properly. Another state that acquired the machine but could also manage to master its technology was Israel. Moreover, an American expert confirms, though anonymously, that Israelis in fact "used machines of the P-1 style to test the effectiveness of Stuxnet" (Broad et al. 2011, p. 4).

Thirdly, the developers of Stuxnet needed to have insider knowledge of specific software developed by Siemens that was widely used to control the IR-1. Interestingly, the German manufacturer cooperated with the US national laboratories in Idaho in 2008 to identify vulnerabilities within this control software. Although Siemens and the US laboratory declared that such collaboration was a routine exercise, activities of such nature did provide the USA with an opportunity to gain information on unknown holes in the software that were subsequently exploited by Stuxnet (Broad et al. 2011, p. 1).

3.4 Attacker's Will

Under the assumption that the two likely attackers are USA and Israel, the will of these two nations can be found in their interest to halt or even to reverse Iran's uranium enrichment processes. Recent political developments underpin this urge.

In early 2008, Israel displayed what can be interpreted as its intent to interrupt the Iranian production of weapons-grade uranium with means beyond sanctions and talks. Israel asked Washington during several meetings for a support of bunker-busters, a weapon capable of destroying subterranean targets such as Iran's enrichment facilities in Natanz (Sanger 2009, p. 2). Furthermore, airborne refuelling equipment and the right to enter Iraqi airspace was requested. Combined with the context, these actions pointed already towards Israel contemplating air strikes against Iran's nuclear facilities. The Bush administration, however, refused two of these requests and only agreed to provide assistance with refuelling tools. In June 2008, the supplied fuel equipment was used by the Israeli air force running test flights over the Mediterranean Sea—an action that "spooked a lot of people", according to a White House official (Sanger 2009, p. 2). The reason for the close attention paid by the USA was an analysis indicating that the distance flown by the jets roughly equals the distance from Israel to the enrichment side in Iran (Sanger 2009, p. 2).

Ultimately, Israel never did carry out any attacks on Iran's nuclear facilities. The reason for that may or may not be an initiative authorized by Bush, which commenced at the time Israel carried out its manoeuvres in 2008. This covered program aimed to "undermine the electrical and computer systems around Natanz" (Sanger 2009). Before actually taking over office, current President Barack Obama, was briefed on this issue and sped up the initiative after being appointed to office. Eventually, the program was set up to achieve a goal with striking resemblance to that of Stuxnet. Hence, it is not unreasonable to think that the malware code was at least partly developed under the auspices of this program.

3.5 Act of Violence

Stuxnet represents a violent act because of the same characteristics defining it as a 'malicious' software, a term that has been used without in-depth justification thus far. The following section aims to provide this vindication.

More generally speaking, the code is written to target industrial control systems used in gas and power plants (Falliere et al. 2010, p. 1). Its goal is to reprogram these systems by modifying the code on the programmable logic controllers, which in turn controls the machines attached to it. By doing so, the code can alter the operational process to function as it likes to, most probably somewhat "out of their specific boundaries" (Falliere et al. 2010, p. 2).

Aside from the various code elements used to infiltrate undetected into the PLCs—each able to characterise Stuxnet as an act of violence by its own—three infection routines inside the code that aim to modify PLCs make the use of Stuxnet a violent act.

A PLC is controlled by an external device (e.g. laptop) through specific control software. Using this software, the programmer can access and reconfigure the data on the controller. To change data, the software runs routines to download the current configuration from the PLC and save it on the local hard drive, where the programmer alters and finally uploads it back on the PLC. Stuxnet infects this circle by replacing the original routine with its malicious copy. It is, thereby, able to intercept and start communications between the software and the PLC, respectively. Stuxnet uses this communication first to alter the data blocks on the PLC and second to hide the changes it made. To alter the content of the PLC the malicious program employs three routines—two similar ones to target PLCs with the central processing unit type named 6ES7-315-2 (short: 315) and one for PLC belonging to the 6ES7-417 family (short: 417). These routines are described by Langner as the dual warhead of Stuxnet (Broad et al. 2011, p. 3).

4 Conclusion

The purpose of this chapter was twofold. Firstly, to find a definition for an act of war in cyber space and, secondly, to examine whether Stuxnet can be characterised as warfare on the basis of such. As no suitable classification currently exists, Clausewitz's definition of war was taken as a basis as it is considered both potentially accepted by many nations and applicable to the field of cyber space. In presenting the evidence and findings of computer experts and journalists, it is observed that within the real context in which the code manifested itself, Stuxnet satisfies all elements of Clausewitz's definition. It is, therefore, justified to term Stuxnet an act of war in the international debate.

This conclusion is, however, limited in at least two ways. The first limitation concerns the lack of empirical information used to base our judgements on. Although the arguments are well researched and substantive, they are to varying degrees subject to speculation. The cover of anonymity provided by the world of bits and bytes and the secrecy of military and clandestine operations are but two explanations for the vagueness of some of the evidence available (Douglas 2008). Further research must be conducted to make empirical information more cogent and arguments more robust. The second limitation relates to the definition used.

The application of Clausewitz' definition of an act of war characterises Stuxnet solely as an act of war; not an act of war in cyber space. To justify the latter term in the international discussion, there needs to be a consensus about what constitutes warfare in the realm of cyber space among international actors.

References

Albright, D., Brannan, P., & Walrond, C. (2010). Did stuxnet take out 1,000 centrifuges at the Natanz enrichment plant? Institute for Science and International Security, ISIS Report, December 22.

Broad, W. J., Markoff, J., & Sanger, D. E. (2011). Israeli test on worm called crucial in Iran nuclear delay. *New York Times*. Retrieved February 18, 2011,.from www.nytimes.com/2011/01/16/world/middleeast/16stuxnet.html

Douglas, K. et al. (2008). Analyzing anonymity in cyberspace. In L. Armistead (Ed.), *3rd International Conference on Information Warfare and Security Proceedings* (pp. 221–232).

Erdbrink, T. (2010). Ahmadinejad: Iran's nuclear program hit by sabotage, Washington Post. Retrieved February 21, 2011, from www.washingtonpost.com/wp-dyn/content/article/2010/11/29/AR2010112903468.html

Falliere, N., Murchu, L. O., & Chien, E. (2010). W32.Stuxnet Dossier, Version 1.0. Symantec Corporation.

Falliere, N., Murchu, L. O., & Chien, E. (2011). W32.Stuxnet Dossier, Version 1.4. Symantec Corporation.

Infosecurity. (2010). Stuxnet—a new age in cyber warfare says Eugene Kaspersky. Retrieved February 21, 2011, from www.infosecurity-magazine.com/view/12757/stuxnet-a-new-age-in-cyber-warfare-says-eugene-kaspersky/

Langner, R. (2010a). Year-end roundup. Retrieved February 21, 2011, from www.langner.com/en/blog/page/2/

Langner, R. (2010b). Potential 417 target, K-1000-60/3000-3. Retrieved February 20, 2011, from www.langner.com/en/2010/11/13/potential-417-target-k-1000-603000-3/

Langner, R. (2010c). Breaking news, 417 = centrifuge safety system. Retrieved February 20, 2011, from www.langner.com/en/2010/12/27/breaking-news-417-centrifuge-safety-system/

Libicki, M. C. (2009). Cyberdeterrence and Cyberwar, Appendix A, RAND Corporation (pp. 179–180).

Mehr News Agency. (2010). Iran successfully battling cyber attack. Retrieved February 21, 2011, from www.mehrnews.com/en/NewsDetail.aspx?pr=s&query=stuxnet%20&NewsID=1158506

Owens, W. A., Dam, K. W., & Lin, H. S. (2009). *Technology, policy, law and ethnics regarding US acquisition and use of cyberattack capabilities*. Washington: National Academy Press.

Reznichenko, A. (2010). Iran installs reactor cap at Bushehr NPP, RIA Novosti. Retrieved February 21, 2011, from http://en.rian.ru/world/20101123/161458962.html

Sanger, D. E. (2009). U.S. rejected aid for Israeli raid on Iranian nuclear site. *New York Times*. Retrieved February 23, 2011, from www.nytimes.com/2009/01/11/washington/11iran.html

UNSC [United Nations Security Council]. (2006). Resolution 1696. Retrieved February 20, 2011, from www.un.org/News/Press/docs/2006/sc8792.doc.htm

Ventre, D. (2009). *Information Warfare*. London/Hobocken.

Von Clausewitz, C. (1989). *On war* (M. E. Howard & P. Paret, Trans.). Princeton, Book one, Chapter one, p. 75.

A New Way of Conducting War: Cyberwar, Is That Real?

Hakan Mehmetcik

Abstract There are numerous discussions on both the reality and impact of cyberwar. Most of the critics are based on the Clausewitzian perspective of war in which its political nature must exist, an act of war has to be characteristically violent and has instrumental purposefulness. Therefore cyberwar is generally regarded as a conduct of action that simply doesn't match with these Clausewitzian criteria of war. However during the last two decades, with the advancement of information technology and widening connecters of the world, many incidents such as Estonian and Georgian cases of cyberattacks, Stuxnet worms, and many other politically motivated cyberattacks, show us that we need to think carefully about the terminology that being used by scholars, experts and policy makers. In this chapter, I aim to discuss about the term "cyberwar" within a broader theory of war in International Relations studies. In doing so, my aim is to bring together related International Relations Theories and the contemporary cyberwar discussion and discuss the issue within a theoretical perspective.

H. Mehmetcik (✉)
Isik University, Istanbul, Turkey
e-mail: hakan.mehmetcik@isikun.edu.tr

J.-F. Kremer and B. Müller (eds.), *Cyberspace and International Relations*,
DOI: 10.1007/978-3-642-37481-4_8, © Springer-Verlag Berlin Heidelberg 2014

1 Introduction

In his book *The Third Wave*, Alvin Toffler saw the development in human history fitting into three phases; agricultural society, industrial society, and information society. In this classification of societies as one type comes and pushes the older one aside, industrial society emerged in Europe with the Industrial Revolution leaving agricultural society behind whereas information society has emerged as a post-industrial society with the rise of the Digital Revolution (Toffler 1984). What distinguished industrial society from the old agricultural society were mass productions and mass consumptions. Similarly, what distinguished today's information society from the old industrial one is that our society today is highly interconnected and unavoidably interdepended. Long after Marshall McLuhan who popularized the concept of *global village* and considered its social effects even in the early 1960s, (Carey 1992; McLuhan and Powers 1992; Grosswiler 1997; McLuhan and Fiore 2001, 2005; McLuhan 2011) today it is a common belief that we live in *a wired society*. As a result of this development, cyberspace, which is basically a globally interdepended and interconnected digital information and communications infrastructure, touches practically everything and everyone today. There are, for sure, many benefits and opportunities cyberspace offers us. However, the fact that modern society is highly depended on digital information and communications infrastructure has made an exponential increase in vulnerabilities and threats as well. The cyberspace has become increasingly securitized and now it is a common tendency to see threats to cyberspace as serious national and international security challenges. One direct consequences of this trend is that cyberspace has increasingly militarized and the militarization has been causing counter cyber insecurity within wider international relations[1] (Valeriano and Maness 2012). For instance, more than 30 countries have already built or have been building cyber defense and offense capabilities. The US military today has the largest concentration of expertise and legal authority with respect to cyberspace, which is convincing enough that Pentagon treats cyber space as a war fighting domain (O'Connell 2012). In May, 2008 the establishment of NATO Cooperative Cyber Defense Centre of Excellence (NATO CCD COE), in October, 2010 the establishment of the US Cyber Command (USCYBERCOM), and many other countries' military and institutional efforts to establish similar security related posts powerfully indicate the securitization and militarization of cyberspace.

As a result of these developments, cyberwar, as a new way of conducting war based on new high-tech model of warfare, is one of the most attention-grabbing discussions in the field. Basically, the cyberwar discussion can be divided into

[1] International Relations starting with uppercase letters refers to the academic study of the phenomena as a branch of Social Science and will be used as IR hereafter, while international relations starting with lowercase letters refers to the events under study.

two distinct poles: pro-cyberwar and anti-cyberwar sides. As there are numerous studies, reports, and policy declarations on cyber security, the pro-cyberwar side takes cyberspace as a real and unavoidable security issue and insists that militaries should be ready for eventual and unavoidable future cyberwars. On the other hand, as being anti-cyberwar side, there are some scholars who claim that the threat has been overstated, overused and hyped and there is no reason to foresee such unavoidable future cyberwars that militaries should be ready for. Moreover, as a concept, cyberwar cannot be a war in terms of classic theory of war (Ranum 2003; Libicki 2007; Schneier 2010; Yoran 2010; Rid 2012a, b). My aim here is not to discuss whether or not the threat perception is hyped or real and plausible, but rather whether or not the term cyberwar is conceptually correct in terms of war and conflict theories in IR. That is, I aim to discuss the conceptual part of the issue in a broader theoretical perspective since the military effect of cyberspace is not just about changes in administration and operations but also changes in thought about the concept of war (Creveld 1991). Therefore, when we term any conflict or cyberattacks and counter attacks in cyberspace as such thing *an act of war* or any war related term such as *cyberwar* we need to think about the concept of war. Indeed, there is a debate about the concept of war with respect to cyber space and within this existing debate, skeptics take into account the classic theories of war, like Clausewitzian theory, and claim that cyberwar is not really a war after all it doesn't match any criteria of the classic conceptions. On the other hand, some other experts and scholars find this traditionalist definitions inadequate and try to expand the conceptualization to cover new way of war (Lawson 2011).

Nonetheless, many contemporary discussions on cyberspace and cyberwar actually fail to distinguish between Clausewitz concept of war, as a political act of violence, and warfare, as the technique of applying that violence. The former is mainly a philosophical discussion whereas the latter is completely technical one (Echevarria 2007:57). Therefore, this chapter wants to move further from a descriptive account of the technicality, and intends to provide the reader a conceptual map, whose primary scope is to clarify the terminology in addition to the justification for use of the concepts. In this reasoning my question is very simple: "What is the definition of war in a theoretical point of view and is cyber-war really a war in terms of these definitions?" To answer to this simple question, I present some of classic and contemporary definitions of war and attempt to explain, on the light of these definitions, why Clausewitz's theory still applicable to our contemporary world by relating it to the cyberwar discussion.

2 Definitions of War

Literally, it is hard to define war because it has a variety of related, but different meanings since war is not a constant itself even though it is a persistent feature of world politics. It varies over time and space in frequency, duration, severity, causes, consequences, and other dimensions (Levy and Thompson 2011). In his book "The State, War, and the State of War" K. J. Holsti points out this changing faces of war. The wars of eighteenth century are not the same with the wars of nineteenth or twentieth century whereas wars of twentieth century are not the same with the one of twenty-first century. They have very different profile not just in terms of severity, causes, consequences, but also in terms of other dimensions such as how to be declared, waged and ended (Holsti 1996). Levy and Thomson draw attention that war evolves and coevolves as threat environments, political organizations, military organizations, political economies, weaponry and warfare evolve (Levy and Thompson 2011). Thus, war emerges in different places and times, in totally different ways by depending on these factors. For example at the end of the third millennium BCE, horse drawn chariot as a means of transport and warfare characterized the wars at that times (Tignor et al. 2010). As a weaponry technology advancement and change in wars, such as gunpowder and later use of canons made observable change in the character of wars in the early fifteenth century. Napoleon's introduction of national armies as a new military organization made war more national and more lethal. Again military advancement such as using airplanes and tanks made two world wars totally different in every sense from the earlier examples, even in comparison to one another. The use of atomic bombs at the end of World War II and its advancement and proliferations in the upcoming years made us think about nuclear wars. Similarly, since the first Gulf War in 1991, with the performance of high-tech weapons, the orthodox view of warfare has been totally transformed (Sanger 2012). The use of drones within the USA's War on Terror is considered as a new way of war. What about cyberspace? Does it has such a revolutionizing effects on war as a fifth domain after land, sea, air, and aerospace (Kramer et al. 2009)?

As I have already mentioned earlier my main intention is not to discuss whether or not the cyber threats and the possibilities of cyberwar is hyped or real but challenge with the conception itself. The reason of this is the belief that once the analytical enterprise has failed to provide a guidance because lack of the criteria that can simply be applied to the subject at stake, any discussion of threat perception for war or cyberwar is superfluous in its essence. Reconceptualization and justification of these concepts seems more appropriate before analyzing the issue as an act of war. In that sense what above narration about changing face of war shows us that war has been changing, evolving not just in terms of times and places but also in terms of severity, causes, means, security and political environments, characters, weaponries, and domains. Then, the question is whether or not *the nature of war* is changing as well. Echevarria says no to this question and mentions that there should be some distinctions and separations between the nature of war (its essence) and the character of war (the way of waging a war); the former is constant, while the latter changes over time, giving rise to different forms or styles (Echevarria 2007). Clausewitz, himself tried to find out the general rules and laws behind it on his well known book *On War* believing that the nature of war is constant.

Let's move to the definitions of war at this point. We see that war characteristically differ from time-to-time or space-to-space. However, a scholarly work, which tries to identify general rules and laws behind war, should begin with a definition. With respect to the definition, indeed, there are some attentions that have focused on definition and conceptualization of war (Malinowski 1941; Wright 1965; Lider 1977; Levy 1983; Clausewitz 1989; Holsti 1996; Kelly 2000; Beer 2001; Bull 2002; Vasquez 2009; Levy and Thompson 2011). As one of those attempts, Vasquez (2009) provides us a well-organized chapter in his book *The War Puzzle Revisited.* As he points that one of the early definitions of war comes from Cicero who defined war as "contending by force". As another early definition Grotius saw war not as content but as "a legal condition". Having a departure from these two early definitions of war Wright defined war as "the legal condition that equally permits two or more hostile groups to carry on a conflict by armed force" (Wright 1965). Malinowski put it as "an armed contest between two independent political units, by means of organized military force, in the pursuit of a tribal or national policy" (Levy 1983). Levy and Thomson defines war as situations in which "two or more political units engage in the sustained and coordinated use of violence regardless of the motivations of violence"(Levy and Thompson 2011). Hedley Bull defines war as "organized violence carried on by political units against each other" (Bull 2002).

Vazquez mentioned that "probably the best way to move from an everyday definition of war to a working scholarly definition is to try to think of what phenomena it would be most useful to study to learn about war and what phenomena would make the effort too diffuse and divert it from its main focus" (Vasquez 2009). With respect to this inference, I believe that Clausewitz's definition is still critical to our basic knowledge of war. Indeed, Clausewitz's book, *On War*, is still one of the basic work that occupies the center of the ongoing debates over the nature of war and warfare. His primary aim was to examine the main elements of war by establishing a theory of absolute or ideal war. Clausewitz saw war as "a mere continuation of policy by other means" and "an act of violence intended to compel our opponent to fulfill our will" (Clausewitz 1989). Other than these two famous sentences, what we may deduce from Clausewitz is that basically three principal variables that shape any war. First one is the political nature of war. This is what differs war from other kind of fighting. War is a political act as like cultural, economic, legal, and ethical circumstances determined by politics (Echevarria 2007). Therefore, Clausewitz defines war as mere continuation of political activity by other means. This includes the fact that war fighting occurs among political communities, which have capability to pose political will. The second one is the purpose. In general the purpose of any war is to make our opponent defenseless so that they do what we want them to do. In this regard war basically aims at disarming and overthrowing of the enemy. We can call this as an end in war. The third one is that war is basically institutionalization of violence and therefore every war consist some degree of violence. Within Clausewitzian abstraction the ideal war has limitless violence but in the reality it differs in degree and this is what that brings it closer to reality.

3 Application of Clausewitz Assumptions to Cyberwar

In a well known Rand Cooperation paper, David Ronfeldt and John Arquilla introduced the concept of cyberwar. They define cyberwar as "knowledge-related conflict at the military level" by implying that "cyberwar may be the same thing to the twenty-first century what "blitzkrieg" was to the twentieth century" (Arquilla and Ronfeldt 1993). After 20 years this paper came out, we have now many works on the issue, yet, as I mentioned earlier, not surprisingly there are some skeptics who see cyber-attacks as something only aims three old-fashioned objectives: espionage, subversion, and sabotage. The main argument is here that none of cyber-attacks we have witnessed until now met any of Clausewitzian criteria of war (Rid 2012a, b). Thus the argument goes on claiming that cyber-attacks cannot be seen as stand-alone acts of war. Think about Georgian case. In the wake of Russian and Georgian conflict several government web sites including Presidency and Ministry of Foreign Affairs' were compromised by self mobilized cyber attacks. What about cyber attacks on Estonia in 2007? After the relocation of a Soviet era monument, The Bronze Soldier of Tallinn, several Estonian web sites including parliament's, banks', ministries', newspapers' were under cyber attacks for weeks. Stuxnet, targeting Iranian nuclear program, is the closest example of what we can call cyber warfare but still far away from it. Any of these or many other incidents we have seen until now do not match with Clausewitz criteria. These are the main critical arguments about cyberwar as a concept. A counter argument to this claims that "like air warfare, cyberwar will only become more destructive overtime" meaning that cyber warfare tactics, techniques, and procedures are being developed and get sophisticated enough to conduct war fighting activity in cyber space in the future (Arquilla 2012). Thus, sooner or later cyber warfare will have the capacity equal to kinetic warfare instruments. There are many countries already have military capacity to launch damaging cyber attacks to some degrees and many other not-have countries strive to acquire certain level of military capacity. All of these efforts increasingly militarize cyberspace. My argument, on the other hand, is that Clausewitzian criteria have been taken in a wrong way in evaluating the past incidents. First of all, the misuse and misconception of cyberwar is one thing we need to think about. What is cyberwar really? Were the past incidents examples of a stand-alone act of war in cyber space? What is the possibility of having a pure cyberwar, a conflict conducted by only employing cyber warfare? We can find answers to these questions by bridging Clausewitz's assumptions of the nature of war to cyberwar discussion.

Nevertheless, before looking at whether and how cyberwar is or might be consistent with the definition of war Clausewitz formulated, we need to have a proper definition of the term to draw a conceptual boundary. The question of what cyberwar is or what constitutes a cyberwar, however, is still an elusive one. One useful definition of cyberwar provided by J. Nye who defines cyberwar as "hostile actions in cyberspace that have effects that amplify or are equivalent to major kinetic violence" (Nye 2011). One indirect definition can be found in the *Tallinn*

Manuel Draft.[2] In this report, the expert groups defined cyber attack as "the employment of cyber capabilities with the primary purpose of achieving objectives in or by the use of cyberspace" (Schmitt 2012). These two definitions are useful yet miss some crucial points too. Therefore, I have derived my own definition as a foundation and a perspective for this analysis. So, in my definition, "cyberwar is a network based conflict with high-tech model of warfare, which includes or be limited to cyber warfare, between specialized groups causing harm, damage and destruction with a primary purpose of achieving objectives set by political units". With respect to this, couple of things is important to define an act as a stand-alone act of war in cyber space. First of all it is a network based conflict implemented by military like organized groups. As an act of war, within a cyber conflict, we need to have a special group, therefore I call it military like organized group, since under current technological conditions in military affairs cyber warfare is still designated to be used alongside with kinetic instruments of war (Valeriano and Maness 2012). Moreover, actually what we assume as kinetic instruments of war today are hugely depended on cyberspace. Think about todays military equipment used by our militaries or command and control system of weaponries such as nuclear command and control systems or drones' command and control systems. Therefore, there isn't certain distinction between cyber and kinetic instruments of warfare and, for the time being, cyber warfare is a vital complementary instrument to the current war fighting. Apart from this fact, even when we talk about a pure cyberwar, which requires huge money, ground operatives and vast infrastructures, individuals cannot conduct it. What individuals conduct are actions that constitute cyber crimes. Like in any war, an act of war within the context of cyberwar requires special organized forces. In this kind of war, armies consisting of mostly technicians may be armed with mostly computers instead of being armed with machine guns. But still when it comes to war fighting content it is a conflict between specialized groups. It aims to reach the objectives set by political units and it causes or aims to cause violence in terms of harm, damage and destruction.

Having a definition, we can discuss in details why and how cyberwar, which has now a conceptual boundary, may be an act of war in terms of Clausewitzian conception. At the outset when it comes to political nature of war as a Clausewitzian term, war is a phenomenon that occurs only between political communities in a military contest. "The contest in war is not a contest of individual against individual, but an organized whole, consisting manifold parts" (Clausewitz 1989). In this sense war is a collective action. A collective action is important in at least two ways. First and foremost, collectivities behave differently from individuals. Especially when it comes to state and its bureaucracy, as a special collectivity,

[2] The Tallinn Manual on the International Law Applicable to Cyber Warfare, is a report written by an independent International Group of Experts, under NATO Cooperative Cyber Defense Centre of Excellence. This report is not published yet and only available as a draft and not an official document but is the result of a three-year effort to examine how extant international law norms apply to this new form of warfare.

differences are vast and vital. Last but not least, in the absence of certain level of social organization, fighting a war is quite impossible (Vasquez 2009). Conflict and some degree of violence can occur at all level of social organization from individual to international society. When two individuals have a fight resulting from a conflict of interest we called it a fight. It may involve exchange of physical blows or the use of weapons but it is still called as fight. Families or larger groups may have conflict of interest resulting with physical blows too. Yet we still call them as fight no matter how violent they are. What differs war from this kind of fight is that within war there is a high level of social organization. Therefore, war is a phenomenon that occurs only between communities. One additional characteristic is that these communities must be political one. Every collective action does not cause a war unless they are political. When a group of country X's citizens come together and attack to country Z, this is not a stand-alone act of war unless these people act for X's government. They constitute a collectivity, for sure, but not a political one. In this way we distinguish interpersonal, individual conflicts or gang fights or organized crimes, and war. So, war requires a certain level of social-political organization. However, this does not necessarily imply statehood. Therefore, Clausewitz's concept of war in terms of political nature is not limited to state on state conflict and also seems to be applicable for non-state actors as long as they have capacity to implement collective political actions. Indeed, for example, within a civil war, political groups intending to become states can be defined as a political community in Clausewitzian term whereas gangs, individual criminals (one big question mark stand still with terrorist organizations) are not regarded as political community.

An implication of this classic concept of war to the cyberwar discussion, how we deal with the threat to society posed by freelance hackers, or at certain level by terrorist organizations is a tricky one. Yet, we may turn to the second aspect of this political nature to answer this question at hand. As Clausewitz point out "… all that is connected with their creation, maintenance, and application- belongs to military activity" (Clausewitz 1989). Thus, to identify as an act of war, any hostile action must not just be implemented by a political community, namely by a state or state like community but it must also be an armed conflict. Putting this further clarification in this way, we reaffirm that war is a phenomenon, which occurs only between political communities in a military contest. Cyber related concepts are subjected to the same logic of reasoning. Therefore when it comes to the term cyberwar we can wittingly point that it occurs only between political communities in a military context.

Nonetheless, there seems to be some technical problems here. As most of the experts on the subject agree on that it is often not easy task to find out perpetrators of a cyber-attack. For example in Estonian or Georgian cases, it is widely believed that the perpetrators were Russian even though it has neither officially been accepted by Russia nor has been proven that there was any Russian State involvement. One another issue is the fact that cyber-attacks are generally made against private companies but not often against governments. Especially this is the case where some of the critical infrastructure owned and run mostly by private sectors

(Lifland 2012). Furthermore what constitutes the differences between cyber-espionage, cyber subversion and cyber-attack, as a stand-alone act of war, is indefinite. Cyber espionage or cyber subversion cannot be treated as cyber attacks even if they occur in state on state context because states do not go to war over espionage and subversion (Libicki 2009). However, these are technical problems that will be solved by the evaluations of the subject as a security issue. The same problems to some extent do still exist for conventional war fighting as well. My point is even though there are some unsolved technical, and juridical issues, in terms of Clausewitz's definition of war political nature can be applicable to cyberwar as long as organized armed groups implement it.

As the second assumption of the Clausewitzian theory, war is a phenomenon that has a conscious political aim, a purpose. The key adjective is political which implies the primacy of politics. Lets turn back to my earlier abstraction. We said that when a group of country X's citizens come together and attack to country Z, this is not a stand-alone act of war unless these people act for X's government. We implied that they constitute a collectivity, for sure, but not a political one. Above we also rehearsed that action must be in military context. Then the reformulation goes when a group of country X's citizens come together and attack to country Z, this is not a stand-alone act of war unless these people constitute an organized armed group and act under the command of country X's government. The question of aiming at what stands still and it is about the aim of war fighting. As Clausewitz suggests war is "in the first place, that under all circumstances, regarded not as an independent thing, but as a political instrument" and intends "to compel our opponent to fulfill our will". With respect to cyberwar, what can be a political aim? Schmitt points out that there are two purposes for a cyber-attack in terms of military strategy: (i) to gain advantage by attacking in cyberspace without any intention of escalating the tension; (ii) to prepare the battle space for a conventional attack aiming at disrupt, blind, or mislead opponents (Schmitt 1998). On the other hand, Richard J. Harknet draw attention to more general purpose that cyberwar (he uses the term netwar instead) involves attempts to destroy an enemy's *societal connectivity* and protect one's own including communication, financial transaction, transportation, and basic infrastructure links that are critically important for the functions and continuity of today's modern society (Harknett 1996). So, cyberwar has a very powerful political aim; defend, attack or exploit the societal connectivity on which modern societies is certainly depended. It is worth to mention that as Vasquez put it "war is fought only over certain types of issues and that these issues may change depending on the particular historical needs, culture, or law of an era" (Vasquez 2009). Cyberspace today in this sense is one of the domains in which states operate and not willing to give up in light of the costs of fighting a war.

Thirdly war is a phenomenon that involves violence and therefore it is "continuation of policy by other means". Clausewitz described violence as a *pulsation* and there might be change in degree in terms of violence from war to war with some increases and decreases. Echevarria (2007) uses weather as a metaphor to describe how the level of violence can change in a war but we can still call it war; "Like war, the weather consists of a few common and inescapable elements, such as barometric pressure, heat index, dew point, wind velocity, and so on. Nevertheless, the difference between a brief summer shower and a hurricane is significant, so much so, in fact, that we prepare for each quite differently. Indeed, the difference in degree is so great, the danger to our lives and property so much higher in the latter, that we might do well to consider showers and hurricanes different in kind, though both are certainly stormy weather. We might apply some of the same rules of thumb for each kind of weather, but also many different ones" (Echevarria 2007). Clausewitz himself drew attention that "war can have all degrees of importance and intensity in terms of violence, ranging from a war of extermination down to simple armed observation" (Clausewitz 1989). In this term, William M. Darley rightfully cited that according to Clausewitz, what distinguished mere political contention from war is violence. Clausewitz equates the Platonic abstraction of "ideal war" with "pure violence." However by utilizing war as political intercourse, carried on with other means, we can initially suggest that in contrast to total war, which is characterized by pure violence, any conflict without violence should be viewed as "pure politics" which is a name for a war without violence in terms of Clausewitz conception (Darley 2006). So, we can define a cyber conflict with small amount of violence as "limited war" or with large amount of violence as "ideal war" or "total war" in terms of Clausewitz definition of war. Clausewitz tells us that "war is an act of force, and there is no logical limit to the application of that force" (Clausewitz 1989). That is, it becomes a matter of political decision what degree of violence should be done once a hostile action being implemented. Contrary to common misuse of violence as Clausewitzian criteria, causing no violence does not determine an act of war. Therefore the right question must be whether or not cyber attacks can cause violence. That is, the question is whether it is possible to cause certain level of violence by implementing a cyber attack. With regard to this question, it is a common acknowledge that cyber attacks have the capacity to cause harm, damage and destruction and as so violence. Cyber attacks may not direct cause of death but their consequences may lead to injuries and loss of life (Valeriano and Maness 2012). Even though, at least for now, the violence caused by any cyber attack cannot be compared to the violence in a conventional war, tomorrow's military will be able to do more damage with a keyboard and some incidences such as Stuxnet have already demonstrated this potential (Walt 2010).

Let's look at some example to point out the capacity in clearer way. It is worth to mention once again that these examples are brought forward to show the capacity of cyber attacks in terms of creating violent consequences. The aim is not to justify pro-cyberwar view explained above. For example think of the news about the incident in which US Air Force lost contact for a while with 50 intercontinental ballistic missiles due to a deficit in command and control system that are not designed a decade ago considering a cyber attack since cyber threat was non existent at those times (Ambinder 2010). Think about the possibility of canceling out a missile defense system designed to knock down rockets and missiles by using cyber space. Myriam D. Cavelty has presented fictious stories that represent possible future cyber attacks scenarios. One of them is following: "A 12 year old hacks into the system that runs the Roosevelt Dam, near Phoenix, Arizona, which contains nearly 500 trillion gallons of water. The cities Mesa and Tempe are downstream, with a combined population of one million—the child accidently opens the floodgates: 100,000 people die in the torrents of rampant Salt River" (Cavelty 2007). This story partly mad up, however, vividly demonstrates the reality that networks run most of vital infrastructures, which are vulnerable to cyber attacks. Think about what any concrete military action in cyber space may cause. Moreover, cyberwar may well become the dominant method of waging certain phases of a conflict, as it was the case in the war between Georgia and Russia (Alexander 2008). Another example of this kind would have been NATO's operation to Libya in 2010. Before NATO's intervention to Libya, according to official statements US officials and military personals discussed a pre cyber attack that could have left Libyan air defense system defenseless. But Obama administration did not go with this option bearing in mind two factors. First of all they feared that it might set a precedent for other nations, in particular Russia or China, to carry out such offensives of their own. Secondly, there was not enough time to wage a comprehensive cyber attacks (Schmitt and Shanker 2011). This example would have been a perfect case of cyber war. It had a political aim, bringing down the Kaddafi government, it was in state on state content, with a military contest, and it could have absolutely caused some degree of violence.

Turning back to the issue of violence in any war, in its essence, it may vary over different examples but it is not an ordinary one in any case. That is, the violence caused by an ordinary incident or accident differs greatly from the violence caused by a war. This means that war is a special kind of contest with rules and norms (Vasquez 2009). We have rules about how to wage a war, how to end it and how to behave during a war. In this term there is a very long way to go to complete the international regulations, arrangements, norms and agreements on cyberspace and cyberwar (Schmitt 1998). The emphasis on cyber space as a war fighting domain is in tension with the international law governing the use of force (O'Connell 2012). Even on the surface the two distinct camps—pro cyber versus anti cyber—have different argument on the international law applicable to cyber space as well. While later sees the issue as cyber crime, cyber espionage, and subversion and argue that it should be subjected to mostly international law and rules other than the one governing use of force and self defense, the former argues that territorial sovereignty applies to cyber space and the law governing self defense and use of force are applicable to cyber space as a result. Because this discussion is beyond the space of my chapter I leave it here.

Before moving into the conclusion, I particularly find useful pinning down once again what all these tell us about the Clausewitz concept of war and how it may speak for the contemporary discussion on cyberwar. First of all, war is not just political but it is also an organized activity, collective and social, not individual one. Therefore, cyber attacks launched by individuals or groups without any military involvements are subjected to cyber crime or cyber espionage. When it comes to cyberwar, it should be in a military context. Secondly, war has a political purpose as an end. Cyber attacks with private interests such as subversions and know-how theft are again among cyber crimes. Cyber attacks which aims political ends, such as the one in Estonian or Georgian cases or the one in the case of Stuxnet are example of this kind. Thirdly, war consists some degree of violence. This violence is not random, but implemented with rules and customs and the degree of it may vary. Cyber attacks may not cause of death and may not be as lethal as conventional attacks are. However, the way our society designed reveals that cyber attacks may cause violent consequences. The securitization and militarization of cyber space lead us think of this possibility.

4 Conclusion

War is a concept whose history as old as human history itself. As like human being is constantly changing, adapting and evolving, war has changed in every term over centuries. As human being encountered with new security environment, war evolved. As human being was able to maintain new kind of political and military organizations, war evolved. As human being was able to create the way to support huge armies by maintaining new political economies, war evolved. As human being find the way to build more advanced and lethal weaponries, war evolved. As human being was able to create different type of societies, war evolved. In this evolution story, we have had many different kind of war from tribal war to nuclear war, from war of independence to civil war, from local war to world war. Cyberwar may be the last and newest type of war for twenty-first century because what distinct feature of the century is that our global society is totally wired today. One quick implication of this fact is that our society becomes vulnerable to any cyber-attacks. This opens the way that the issue has been taken as a security challenge and handled by militaries. That is, cyber space has increasingly been securitized and militarized. This makes us to have to think about the possibility of cyberwar.

However, the proper use of conception to place cyberwar into a broader theory of war and conflict is a complex question. Do we really need to have a clear concept of cyberwar? Yes, we certainly do. "Clear concepts are useful for constructing propositions, theories, and analytical frameworks" (Baldwin 1997). Once we have defined the conceptual boundaries of cyberwar, then we can construct good policies over it. For instance, if you use a conception that includes individual hacking activities in cyber space as an act of war, and retailed with counter attacks—it can be conventional or cyber- then you probably end up with unnecessary conflicts within international affairs. If you use the term cyberwar for every incident that you encounter, it is likely turn to be grossly "overused or mismanaged, and you start to diverse resources toward a mythical fear and away from real threats" (Valeriano and Maness 2012). If you use the term cyberwar unwittingly, you probably plunge into tensions with sustained and widespread accepted norms of international law. Therefore clear concepts are utmost important.

Therefore by looking at classic theories of war, we would not just attain the general rules and norms behind any war as a theory building, but also could have a clear concept of cyberwar. With regard to this, Clausewitz theory, as an abstraction for rules, still contributes to our knowledge of war and is avant-garde when it comes to conceptualization of cyberwar. But Clausewitz himself pointed out that "from a pure concept of war you might try to deduce absolute terms for the objective you should aim at and for the means of achieving it; but if you did so the continuous interaction would land you in extremes that represented nothing but a play of the imagination issuing from an almost invisible sequence of logical subtleties" (Clausewitz 1989). That is, a theory is an abstraction and represents mainly the extremes and that's why it does not always match with the reality and that's why theories are philosophical phenomenon but not practical.

Clausewitz's description identifies political nature, political aim and violence as the essential set of the nature of war. According to Clausewitz war is mere continuation of politics by other means. However war not just political but it is also an organized activity, not individual one. Thus, first of all, it is derived as a phenomenon that it occurs only between political communities, in a military context. Secondly "war is no act of blind passion, but is dominated by the political object" (Clausewitz 1989) and therefore it is seen as a continuation of politics by different means. That is, war has a political purpose as an end and aims generally at forcing our opponents to do what we want them to do, leaving them defenceless. Lastly, war consists violence. The degree of violence may vary and determine the differences between war and politics. As a continuation of politics war sometimes provokes very little amount of violence or it may consist a larger amount. "War is, therefore, like a chameleon in character, it changes its color in some degree in each particular case" (Clausewitz 1989).

With respect to these Clausewitzian assumptions, any cyber attack can be regarded as an act of war only if it constitutes these traits as conceptual bases. Having said this, my definition of cyberwar touches these traits as an attempt to not just conceptualize but also to justify the usage. Thus, I define the term cyberwar as a network based conflict with high-tech model of warfare, which includes or be limited to cyber warfare, between specialized groups causing harm, damage and destruction with a primary purpose of achieving objectives set by political units. Within definitions cyberwar is treated as something that occurs between political units in a military context. This inference should be read bearing in mind that cyber space has increasingly being militarized. Cyber attacks launched by individuals or hacker groups consist cyber crimes and are not treated as acts of war. Therefore, to argue and discuss such incidents within cyberwar discussion is not appropriate. Cyber warfare can be used alongside with conventional instruments of war—think about Georgian Case- or as pure cyber instruments—think about Stuxnet virus. However, the aims of employing cyber warfare is the same with conventional war fighting, force our opponents to do what we want them to do. Thus, as it is case in any conventional war, cyberwar has always a political aim. With respect to violence, what important is that cyber attacks have capacity to originate violence equal to kinetic actions either by directly causing of death or by causing fatal consequences. Moreover, as a part of Clausewitz assumptions, violence may vary in degree. The possibility of war fighting without causing any death is possible within Clausewitzian conception. Therefore, the argument that cyberwar is not a war because we have not seen violence equal to kinetic act of war is baseless in terms of Clausewitz theory of war. Reading of Clausewitz with respect to violence shows us that as a continuation of politics war fighting includes violence but the degree can change so much that sometimes it is vast sometimes it is unobservable.

Throughout history new technologies have abruptly changed the face of war, such as the chariot, gunpowder, tanks, aircraft, nuclear technology and drones. Now we have cyberspace and cyber technology in our hands to as revolutionary developments in the battleground. However, conceptualization and theorization are utmost important to handle these changes in a broader IR studies. This work has attempted to touch upon the issue by not concerning with testing hypotheses or constructing theories, but by clarifying the meaning of concepts and bridging a very classic theory of war with this contemporary discussion.

References

Alexander, D. (2008). Cyberwar comes of age. *Military Technology*, *32*, 78–85.

Ambinder, M. (2010). *Failure shuts down squadron of nuclear missiles*. The Atlantic. Available via. URL http://www.theatlantic.com/politics/archive/10/10/power-failure-shuts-down-squadron-of-icbms/65207/ Accessed 18 Dec 2012.

Arquilla, J. (2012). *Cyberwar is already upon us*. Available via foreign policy. http://www.foreignpolicy.com/articles/2012/02/27/cyberwar_is_already_upon_us Accessed 17 Dec 2012.

Arquilla, J., & Ronfeldt, D. (1993). *Cyberwar is coming!* Santa Monica: Rand Corporation.

Baldwin, D. A. (1997). The concept of security. *Review of International Studies*, *23*, 5–26.

Beer, F. A. (2001). *Meanings of war and peace*. College Station: Texas A&M University Press.

Bull, H. (2002). *The anarchical society* (3rd ed.). New York: Columbia University Press.

Carey, J. W. (1992). *Communication as culture, revised edition: essays on media and society*, London: Routledge.

Cavelty, M. D. (2007). *Cyber-security and threat politics: US efforts to secure the information age* (1st ed.). London: Routledge.

Creveld, M. V. (1991). *Technology and war: From 2000 B.C. to the present*, Revised & Expansion edition. Touchstone.

Darley, W. M. (2006). Clausewitz's theory of war and information operations. *FJQ*, 73–81.

Echevarria, A. J. (2007). *Clausewitz and contemporary war*. Oxford: Oxford University Press.

Grosswiler, P. (1997). *Method is the message: Rethinking mcluhan through critical theory*. Montreal: Black Rose Books.

Harknett, R. J. (1996). *Information warfare and deterrence*. *Parameters Autumn*, *26*, 93–107.

Holsti, K. J. (1996). *The state, war, and the state of war*. Cambridge: Cambridge University Press.

Kelly, R. C. (2000). Warless societies and the origin of war. Ann Arbor: University of Michigan Press.

Kramer, F. D., Starr, S. H., & Wentz, L. (Eds.). (2009). *Cyberpower and national security* (1st ed.). Potomac Books Inc.

Lawson, S. (2011). *Cyber war and the expanding definition of war.* Available via Forbes, http://www.forbes.com/sites/seanlawson/2011/10/26/cyber-war-and-the-expanding-definition-of-war/ Accessed 19 Dec 2012.

Levy, J. S. (1983). *War in the modern great power system, 1495–1975* (illustrated ed.). Univ Press of Kentucky.

Levy, J. S., & Thompson, W. R. (2011). *The arc of war: origins, escalation, and transformation*. Chicago: University of Chicago Press.

Libicki, M. C. (2007). *Conquest in cyberspace: national security and information warfare* (1st ed.). Cambridge: Cambridge University Press.

Libicki, M. C. (2009). *Cyberdeterrence and cyberwar.* Santa Monica: Rand Corporation.

Libicki, M. C. (2012). Cyberspace is not a warfighting domain. *I/S: A Journal of Law and Policy for the Information Society, 8*, 325–340.

Lider, J. (1977). *On the nature of war.* England: Gower Pub Co.

Lifland, A. (2012). Cyberwar: The future of conflict. (AMERICAS). *Harvard International Review, 33.*

Lynn, W. J. (2011). *The pentagon's cyberstrategy, one year later*. Available via foreign affairs. http://www.foreignaffairs.com/articles/68305/william-j-lynn-iii/the-pentagons-cyberstrategy-one-year-later Accessed 28 Sept 2012.

Malinowski, B. (1941). An anthropological analysis of war. *American Sociological Society, 46*(4), 521–550.

McLuhan, M. (2011). *The gutenberg galaxy* (Centennial ed.). Toronto: University of Toronto Press, Scholarly Publishing Division.

McLuhan, M., & Fiore, Q. (2001). *War and peace in the global village*. New York: Gingko Pr Inc.

McLuhan, M., & Fiore, Q. (2005). *The medium is the massage*. New York: Gingko Press.

McLuhan, M., & Powers, B. R. (1992). *The global village: transformations in world life and media in the 21st century* (Reprint. ed.). Oxford: Oxford University Press.

Nye, J. S. (2011). Nuclear lessons for cyber security? *Strategic Studies Quarterly, 5*(4), 18–38.

O'Connell, M. E. (2012). Cyber security without cyberwar. *Journal of Conflict and Security Law, 17*, 187–209.

Ranum, M. (2003). *The myth of homeland security* (1st ed.). Indianapolis: Wiley.

Rid, T. (2012a). *Think again: Cyberwar.* Available via Foreign Policy. http://www.foreignpolicy.com/articles/2012/02/27/cyberwar. Accessed 17 Dec 2012.

Rid, T. (2012b). Cyber war will not take place. *Journal of Strategic Studies, 35*(1), 5–32. DOI:10.1080/01402390.2011.608939.

Sanger, D. E. (2012). *Confront and conceal: Obama's secret wars and surprising use of American power*. New York: Crown.

Schmitt, M. N. (1998). Computer network attack and the use of force in international law: thoughts on a normative framework. *Colum. J. Transnat'l L., 37*, 885.

Schmitt, M. (2012). *Tallinn manual on the international law applicable to cyber warfare*. Unpublished, Tallinn.

Schmitt, E., & Shanker, T. (2011). *U.S. debated cyberwarfare against Libya.* Available via The New York Times. http://www.nytimes.com/2011/10/18/world/africa/cyber-warfare-against-libya-was-debated-by-us.html?_r=0 Accessed 12 Dec 2012.

Schneier, B., 2010. *Threat of "cyberwar" has been hugely hyped.* Available via CNN. http://edition.cnn.com/2010/OPINION/07/07/schneier.cyberwar.hyped/index.html Accessed 17 Dec 2012.

Tignor, R., Adelman, J., Aron, S., Brown, P., Elman, B., Kotkin, S., Liu, X., Marchand, S., Pittman, H., Prakash, G., Shaw, B., & Tsin, M. (2010). *Worlds together, worlds apart: A history of the world: 600–1850* (3rd ed.). W. W. Norton & Company.

Toffler, A. (1984). *The third wave*. Bantam.

Valeriano, B., & Maness, R. (2012). *The fog of cyberwar*. Available via Foreign Affairs. http://www.foreignaffairs.com/articles/138443/brandon-valeriano-and-ryan-maness/the-fog-of-cyberwar Accessed 16 Dec 2012.

Vasquez, J. A. (2009). *The war puzzle revisited* (1st ed.). Cambridge: Cambridge University Press.

Von Clausewitz, C. (1989) *On war* (Reprint. ed.). Princeton: Princeton University Press.

Walt, S. M. (2010). *What does Stuxnet tell us about the future of cyber-warfare?* Available via Foreign Policy Blogs. http://walt.foreignpolicy.com/node/460701 Accessed 10 Dec 2012.

Wright, Q. (1965). *Study of war* (2nd Revised ed.). Chicago: University of Chicago Press.

Yoran, A. (2010). *Cyberwar or not cyberwar? And why that is the question?* Available via Forbes.http://www.forbes.com/sites/firewall/2010/03/25/cyberwar-or-not-cyberwar-and-why-that-is-the-question/ Accessed 29 Sep 2012.

Peacekeeping 4.0: Harnessing the Potential of Big Data, Social Media, and Cyber Technologies

John Karlsrud

Abstract Since the Cold War, peacekeeping has evolved from first-generation peacekeeping that focused on monitoring peace agreements, to third-generation multidimensional peacekeeping operations tasked with rebuilding states and their institutions during and after conflict. However, peacekeeping today is lagging behind the changes marking our time. Big Data, including social media, and the many actors in the field may provide peacekeeping and peacebuilding operations with information and tools to enable them to respond better, faster and more effectively, saving lives and building states. These tools are already well known in the areas of humanitarian action, social activism, and development. Also the United Nations, through the Global Pulse initiative, has begun to discover the potential of "Big Data for Development," which may in time help prevent violent conflict. However, less has been done in the area of peacekeeping. UN member states should push for change so that the world organization and other multilateral actors can get their act together, mounting a *fourth* generation of peacekeeping operations that can utilize the potentials of Big Data, social media and modern technology—"Peacekeeping 4.0." The chapter details some of the initiatives that can be harnessed and further developed, and offers policy recommendations for member states, the UN Security Council, and UN peacekeeping at UN headquarters and at field levels.

J. Karlsrud (✉)
Norwegian Institute of International Affairs, Oslo, Norway
e-mail: jka@nupi.no

J.-F. Kremer and B. Müller (eds.), *Cyberspace and International Relations*,
DOI: 10.1007/978-3-642-37481-4_9,

1 Introduction

The world has entered the age of "Big Data." Today, the amount of fresh data being produced increases exponentially, doubling every 20 months (UN Global Pulse 2012a, p. 8). In 2012, "the volume of digital content grows to 2.7 zettabytes (ZB), up 48 % from 2011" (International Data Corporation 2011). The data are produced by the entry into the Digital Age: our digital lives produce "digital exhaust" (ibid.)—our everyday actions produce digital traces that can be, and are being, gathered, analyzed, and turned into actionable data.

This development is less than a decade old, and calls for new and innovative approaches. Such data give us the potential to learn about people's everyday lives, also in countries that are poverty-stricken or ridden by conflict. "Big data" include postings to social media sites, videos, and blog posts posted on the internet—but also the amounts people are using to top up SIM cards, food prices, and transaction records of online purchases, to mention only some examples. Furthermore, these data can be cross-correlated with the frequency of registered violent incidents as well as more traditional statistical indicators such as coverage of mobile phone users, mortality rates, and GDP per capita (The Economist 2010a, b, c).

Global Pulse has developed a useful taxonomy of new forms of data:

(1) "Data Exhaust—passively collected transactional data from people's use of digital services like mobile phones, purchases, web searches, etc., and/or operational metrics and other real-time data collected by UN agencies, NGOs and other aid organisations to monitor their projects and programmes (e.g. stock levels, school attendance); these digital services create networked sensors of human behaviour;
(2) Online Information—web content such as news media and social media interactions (e.g. blogs, Twitter), news articles, obituaries, e-commerce, job postings; this approach considers web usage and content as a sensor of human intent, sentiments, perceptions, and want.
(3) Physical Sensors—satellite or infrared imagery of changing landscapes, traffic patterns, light emissions, urban development and topographic changes, etc.; this approach focuses on remote sensing of changes in human activity
(4) Citizen Reporting or Crowd-sourced Data—Information actively produced or submitted by citizens through mobile phone-based surveys, hotlines, user-generated maps, etc.; While not passively produced, this is a key information source for verification and feedback" (UN Global Pulse 2012a, p. 16).

Brought together, the data can enable international organizations to follow and possibly prevent evolving situations and crises. This potential has been recognized; and, following the financial crisis, the UN Secretary-General created UN Global Pulse to explore opportunities for using real-time data to gain a more accurate understanding of population wellbeing, especially related to the impacts of global crises. The availability of real-time data holds great promise for helping us detect the early signs of stress on vulnerable populations. It represents an unprecedented opportunity to track the human impacts of crises *as they unfold*, and to get real-time feedback on how well policy responses are working (UN Global Pulse 2012b). As such, research undertaken by UN Global Pulse, notably though its networks of country-level "Pulse Labs," may give the UN a better ability to follow, respond to and mitigate the impact of natural disasters and complex crises.

However, more than 90 % of the information will be unstructured, potentially rich in useful information. Turning structured and unstructured information into actionable data requires efficient ways of structuring and analyzing the information in real time in a *data ecosystem* (WEF 2010, p. 4). This process is often called "reality mining" (UN Global Pulse 2012a, p. 18; Eagle and Pentland 2006) or "data mining"—discovering patterns in large data sets (Cheshire 2011; Helbing and Balietti 2012). So, how can the UN and other multilateral actors make use of this data? Cooperation has been initiated with Google and other large corporations that are at the forefront in harvesting actionable data from the "data deluge" (The Economist 2010b).

Concurrently with this development, the digital divide is closing at an increasing speed. According to the World Bank, 44.9 out of every 100 people in sub-Saharan Africa had a mobile subscription in 2010 (World Bank 2012a), and by 2016 this figure will reach 91.3 (Portio Research 2012), although the high number may mask persons have more than one subscription. The percentage of population with access to internet is also increasing (World Bank 2012b). This means that the amount of both structured and unstructured data that can be analyzed and can inform multilateral efforts for conflict prevention and international security is increasing rapidly and can give a more even and realistic picture of the situation in question. However, there is a need to be realistic. There is great variance in the access to data between countries such as Syria and the Democratic Republic of Congo, and many have more than one mobile subscription to strengthen their resilience against patchy networks.

Other co-influencing factors are the rapid spread of 3G networks in developing countries and affordable smart phones at prices down to $50 or less (Jidenma 2011). There is also a current global mega-trend of access to the internet through mobile devices: "in a world where there are 6.3 bn mobile users and 2.3 bn internet users, the default access mode to broadband services is mobile" (Ulf Ewaldsson, Ericsson, quoted in ITU 2012a). According to the International Telecommunication Union, "the ubiquitous mobile phone provides an important foundation for the uptake of mobilebased Internet [in the developing world]. With the majority of countries worldwide having launched 3G mobile-broadband services, the prospects are promising" (ITU 2012b, p. 39, Evans 2012).

In the areas of conflict prevention, humanitarian action, and development, the UN has made some initial steps. But what then is the situation in the areas of peacekeeping and peacebuilding? Unfortunately, little progress has been made so far. Notwithstanding the inclusion of surveillance drones in one peacekeeping mission, the development of Joint Mission Analysis Cells and Joint Operations Centres (which I will return to in the next section), the use of mobile phones in community alert networks in eastern Congo, and the heightened focus on the strategic planning and coordination capacity of peacekeeping and peacebuilding operations, much work remains before peacekeeping operations can be said to be tapping the potential of big data, social media, and cyber-technology effectively, entering the age of "Peacekeeping 4.0."

The good part of this story is that much work already has been undertaken in the similar and parallel fields of conflict prevention, humanitarian action and development. Many lessons from these fields could easily be imported, while other innovative approaches can be accessed through increased cooperation and coordination. Accomplishing this will require overcoming various bureaucratic hurdles and turfism, driven by support from engaged member states and the Secretary-General.

Finally, the uptake of digital information in the planning of UN peace operations may also have implications for how the interaction between the UN, member states and civil society is theorized. IR theorists have increasingly underscored the importance of civil society actors as potential norm entrepreneurs (Keck and Sikkink 1998), and more recent research looking at the relationship between media and international organizations emphasize the potential role civil society and new technology can play in democratizing the access to information, but also the potential for groups spreading disinformation and incite hatred.

This chapter will seek to explore what chances the availability of Big Data and new technologies offer for peacekeeping and as well as inherent challenges. The chapter proceeds as follows: First, I narrow in on some key initiatives in the areas of conflict prevention, humanitarian action, and development that can be relevant to peacekeeping. The following section provides a short background on peacekeeping and its evolution from the end of the Cold War until present, noting some of the steps taken to date. Thirdly, I discuss some of the challenges and opportunities facing policymakers, and relate these to the area of peacekeeping in particular. Finally, the chapter sums up and offers some recommendations for policymakers among member states, in the UN, and among civil society, as well as pointing out areas in need of further research, to enable the UN to enter the era of fourth generation peacekeeping—"Peacekeeping 4.0."

2 Cyberization of Conflict Prevention, Humanitarian Action, and Development

The age of Big Data and social media has dawned on the fields of humanitarian activity, social activism, and development. Here the application of big data and social media has advanced a great deal further than in the areas of peacekeeping and peacebuilding, particularly among civil society organizations (CSOs) and other independent actors.

One of these initiatives is Ushahidi. Ushahidi is a "web based reporting system that utilizes crowdsourced data to formulate visual map information of a crisis on a real-time basis" (Ushahidi 2012a). Ushahidi, which means "testimony" in

Swahili, was originally a website established after the election violence in Kenya in 2008 to map incidents of violence (Ushahidi 2012b). Using crowdsourcing as a method means that everyone with access to common digital communication channels can contribute data.[1] The data can be provided via text messages, email, twitter and web-forms. One recent example is Syria Tracker—a website set up to monitor violent incidents involving civilians in Syria: "Syria Tracker is a crowdsourced effort developed by individuals concerned about the harm inflicted upon civilians in Syria" (Syria Tracker 2012). Ushahidi and Syria Tracker are part of a tendency of "how non-state actors are increasingly collaborating online to tackle issues traditionally managed by governments" (Leson 2012).

Also in the area of monitoring and evaluation, internet platforms are being established to ease the sharing and coordination of information. One example is the ActivityInfo website established by UNICEF, OCHA, and bedatadriven; it "that helps humanitarian organizations to collect, manage, map and analyze indicators…and allow for real time monitoring of the humanitarian situation in the eastern part of the Democratic Republic of Congo" (ActivityInfo 2012).

Analyzing the use of Google searches or Twitter messages can give strong indications of evolving situations, or whether an epidemic is spreading. Paul and Dredze (2011) found a very strong correlation coefficient (0.958) between tweets and official flu statistics, where the tweets were in real time and the statistics available only afterwards. Analyzing trending topics in Google searches or Facebook and blog posts can also yield significant data (Ginsberg et al. 2009). Google Dengue Trends uses aggregated Google search data to estimate dengue activity (Google 2012a); there is a similar service for influenza (Google 2012b).

Following the earthquake in Port-au-Prince, Haiti, researchers from Sweden's Karolinska Institutet and Columbia University in New York used mobile phone data, tracking 1.9 million SIM cards (Bengtsson et al. 2011, p. 2). They were able to follow the population flows and destinations of 648,717 people who had been displaced (ibid.:3). Later that year, the same team followed population movement after a cholera outbreak (Bengtsson et al. 2010, p. 2).

Multilateral actors have started to catch on. The UN Secretary-General has created UN Global Pulse; the World Bank has begun discussing how big data can be used for development (World Bank 2012c), and has established "Mapping for Results" to visualize and track its programs and projects on the ground (World Bank 2012d). However, much remains to be done. In 2009, the UN Global Pulse Initiative launched the Rapid Impact and Vulnerability Analysis Fund (RIVAF). However, a recent report published by the initiative reveals a focus on the use of traditional indicators, and a lack of focus on conflict and post-conflict countries, even though many of the UN agencies, funds, and programs involved in the

---

[1] The term "crowdsourcing" was coined by Jeff Howe as "the act of taking a job traditionally performed by a designated agent (usually an employee) and outsourcing it to an undefined, generally large group of people in the form of an open call" (Howe 2008, p. 99). In the context of mapping this allows data to be submitted by a wide range of stakeholders not directly engaged in the project.

RIVAF initiative operate in precisely such locations (UN Global Pulse 2011). Further work is necessary in this area, also to focus the energies of development-oriented organizations to conflict and post-conflict countries and utilize the potential offered by big data, social media, and cyber-technology.

The UN has engaged with the Crisis Mappers community since 2010 (UN 2012a, p. 4, Crisis Mappers 2012); among other things, the Standby Task Force has supported OCHA crowdsourcing data for South Sudan, collecting "a total of 1,767 unique rows of data and 15,271 unique pieces of information records" in a mere 3 days (Standby Task Force 2012). At a recent meeting in New York to discuss the status of implementation of the UN's Crisis Information Strategy, it was agreed that there is a need for Crisis Information Managers, and that the efforts towards convergence in crisis information management could support the "endeavours of 'One UN' and better coordination within the UN and the international community in general" (Swiss Mission to the United Nations 2012). A Crisis Management Training Course has since been established, with the first course being given in February 2013 at the International Peace Support Training Centre (IPSTC) in Nairobi, Kenya. The course will train civilians, military and police "working in multi-dimensional peace and humanitarian operations … to integrate new information technology into an information management system [and] demonstrate the opportunities and challenges of new ICTs [Information and Communication Technology] and social media tools…" (ICT4Peace 2012a). The challenge now will be to get the UN onboard and send staff to these courses, providing the organization with staff trained personnel that can enable it to make use of Big Data, ICTs and social media in its operations. The UN in Sudan has taken one step in this direction. With support of the United Kingdom, UNDP has run a Crisis Recovery and Mapping Analysis project since 2007 (UNDP 2012a), aimed at supporting both the UN country team (UNCT) and national authorities in making their activities more evidence-based and conflict-responsive (see also Bott and Young 2012).[2]

In Georgia, the Caucasus Research Resource Centers and Saferworld have joined forces with developers to produce *Elva*, combining "the data-rich mapping of Ushahidi with the meticulous requirements of human-rights researchers" (Sifry 2012). The platform is used to create a community safety network where a community representative, using SMS, can report violent or security incidents on a weekly basis. A similar initiative was developed by Columbia University in connection with the *Voix des Kivus* program in the Democratic Republic of Congo (DRC) to "overcome the problems associated with the collection of conflict data" (van der Wind and Humphreys 2012). It involved distributing prepaid cellphones, solar chargers, and code sheets to community representatives in 18 villages in Eastern Congo (ibid.). For both projects, protecting the identity of those reporting against possible reprisals became an important concern (ibid., p. 24; see also Puig 2012).

Together with the crisis mapping community, OCHA is experimenting with developing twitter dashboards for humanitarian crises. These use "Machine

[2] For more on the use of crowdsourcing in conflict, *inter alia* by UNDP in Kyrgyzstan and Liberia, see Kahl et al. (2012), p. 34.

Learning (ML) techniques and social computing methods… to extract relevant information from twitter and aggregate this information according to Cluster for analytical purposes" (Meier 2012). A similar dashboard for peacekeeping operations "that looks across social media content and perhaps uses corporate data" could be envisaged (Interview with Meier 2012).

There is a mushrooming of efforts to make use of big data and social media in countries in crisis. Civil society actors are at the forefront of this development, and this section has detailed some of their efforts. Concurrently, social media is strengthening the opportunities of rebels to communicate their message internally, to domestic and external supporters, and directly to traditional media outlets (Wilson and Dunn 2011). These trends points to the increasing role non-state actors may play in international relations and deserves further scrutiny. In the next section I will trace the development of modern-day peacekeeping and explore to what degree big data, social media and modern technology is being adapted.

3 The Development of Modern-day Peacekeeping

Ramsbotham et al. divide peacekeeping into three generations. First-generation peacekeeping missions were deployed during the Cold War, typically with lightly armed forces to monitor borders and establish buffer zones (Ramsbotham et al. 2005, p. 134). Second-generation peacekeeping was "multilateral, multidimensional and multinational/multicultural" (ibid., p. 136) and mainly supported countries experiencing internal conflict. Peacekeeping operations after the Cold War expanded in size, drew on resources from a wider range of troop-contributing countries, and included police and civilians who helped strengthen national institutions. Third-generation peacekeeping sought to remedy the failures of Bosnia and Rwanda, making peacekeeping operations more robust so as to be able to protect civilians. And after many years of discussions, the UN General Assembly adopted the principle of the Responsibility to Protect in 2005 (UNGA 2005). It also became increasingly clear that the international community would need to reinforce the ability of states to respond to the needs of their citizens, taking on a peacebuilding agenda that included the strengthening of institutions, rule of law, and democratization. UN Secretary-General Boutros-Ghali set this process in motion with his seminal report *Agenda for Peace* in 1992 (Boutros-Ghali 1992), and most peacekeeping operations today have a wide range of such tasks included in their mandates. There is now an evolving understanding that "peacekeepers are peacebuilders" (UN 2012b, p. 10) who should implement early peacebuilding tasks.[3]

---

[3] As defined by the Secretary-General in his opening remarks of the Security Council discussion on peacebuilding, 13 October 2010, where he stressed that peacekeeping missions should be enabled "to have an impact as 'early peacebuilders.'" The meeting in the Security Council was held to discuss the latest *Progress Report of the Secretary-General on Peacebuilding in the Immediate Aftermath of Conflict* (UN 2010).

In their September 2010 submission to the Special Committee on Peacekeeping—the "Committee of 34" (C-34)—the UN Department of Peacekeeping Operations (DPKO) and Department of Field Support (DFS) noted:

> [p]eacekeeping has evolved from a primarily military model of observing ceasefires and separating forces to incorporate a mix of military, police and civilian capabilities to support the implementation of comprehensive peace agreements and help lay the foundations for sustainable peace and legitimate government (UN DPKO/DFS 2011, p. 1).

Strengthening the ability of states not to revert to conflict saves lives and costs. The recently established peacekeeping operation in South Sudan has an explicit and comprehensive peacebuilding mandate to support the Government of South Sudan in peacebuilding. It states that that the UN should "develop an early strategy in support of national peacebuilding priorities" which "can deliver prioritized support that reflects the specific peacebuilding needs and priorities of the Republic of South Sudan" (UN Security Council 2011).

Other innovations in peacekeeping include the Joint Mission Analysis Cell (JMAC) and the Joint Operations Centre (JOC). The JMAC is "a joint uniformed/civilian entity that manages the collection, collation, analysis and dissemination of the mission's operational information analysis" UN DPKO 2008, p. 18). The JMAC is intended to serve the key decisionmakers in a UN peacekeeping mission with information and analysis. The JOC is "a joint military, police, and civilian entity which monitors situation reports and operational reports from all sources within a UN peacekeeping operation on behalf of the HOM [Head of Mission]" and should act as the mission crisis management centre in times of crises (UN DPKO 2006).

The JMAC adds an analytical capacity not previously included in peacekeeping operations. Traditionally, UN member states have been wary of UN peacekeeping operations gaining intelligence-gathering and analysis capabilities (Ramjoué 2011). However, this attitude has gradually shifted, and there is increasing understanding that such capabilities can better enable the peacekeeping operations to implement their mandate and protect civilians (ibid.). The establishment of JMACs and JOCs can be seen as an effect of this evolving understanding. The JMAC and to a certain degree the JOC could be envisaged as foci for cooperation with other actors as regards accessing and analyzing big data and social media at the field level. These examples above, as well as the attempts of reform of peacekeeping show that there is a growing recognition of the role that Big Data, social media, ICTs and other modern technologies can play also in peacekeeping. In the next section I will look in more detail at efforts to reform peacekeeping over the last two decades.

3.1 Peacekeeping Reform Efforts

Currently, the UN is engaged in 16 peacekeeping (UN DPKO 2012) and 13 political and peacebuilding missions across the globe (UN DPA 2012). Many of these have created their own Facebook and Twitter profiles as part of their public relations strategy. MINUSTAH, UNAMA, UNAMID and UNMISS have Facebook profiles where they post news and stories about the operations; UNAMID and MINUSTAH also have Twitter profiles. However, it seems that the potential offered by these social media sites for yielding real-time information on the sentiments of the people of a country not yet has not been fully realized or utilized. Following an initiative of the United Kingdom, the UN Department of Political Affairs has begun weekly briefings to the UN Security Council on emerging issues under the label "Horizon-scanning." These are "closed consultations in which DPA presents thematic and country-specific issues of concern vis-à-vis threats to international peace and security, including some that are already on the council agenda and others that are not" (Romita 2011, p. 11). Practice here is uneven, and has not been continued under all presidencies of the Security Council, but it has been generally appreciated. This is not the first time the Security Council receives such briefings: in fact, this was a weekly practice in the 1990s (Security Council Report 2010).

UN Security Resolution 1706 on 31 August 2006 mandated the use of aerial surveillance "to monitor transborder activities of armed groups along the Sudanese borders with Chad and the Central African Republic in particular through regular ground and aerial reconnaissance activities" (UN Security Council 2006, p. 4). Some EUFOR troops had aerial surveillance drones, and this capability was retained by MINURCAT II with the re-hatting of the forces there. This was probably the first time a UN operation used drones for the protection of civilians. During the rebel attacks that occurred in the course of the operation, the force was able to follow the movements of rebels and position its troops accordingly. These experiences should be reviewed closely when considering future operations in theaters where low-level threats across vast areas are a dominant feature (see also Dorn 2011). The combination of aerial reconnaissance and helicopters could significantly lessen the need for large numbers of troops—an important contribution in times of financial austerity.

On the ground, the UN is also developing new tools and approaches. In DRC, the UN has established Early Warning Centres (EWCs) across eastern DRC, intended to "function as a hub for situational awareness in the Company Operating Base (COB) to optimise operational capacities for [the] protection of civilians" (Kjeksrud and Ravndal 2010, p. 14) based on an initiative of the Indian military contingent in North Kivu (ibid., p. 26). The UN is collaborating with the main telecommunication operators, and the EWCs have established Community Alert Networks that can provide protection alerts: "MONUSCO provides cell phones on closed networks to community Focal Points to create a direct, 24 h-a-day link to the CLAs or MONUSCO commanders and are entrusted to relay information in case of an outbreak of violence" (Weir and Hunt 2012, p. 3). These "work as an extension of the EWC providing MONUC [now MONUSCO] with timely information about aggressive activities of armed groups" (Kjeksrud and Ravndal 2010, p. 27). The mission has also engaged more than 100 Community Liaison Assistants (CLAs; previously known as Community Liaison Interpreters), who are integrated in the Early Warning Centers. They are local persons employed and trained by the UN, tasked with improving communications (due to the poor language skills of international troops), facilitating interaction and confidence-building between MONUSCO and local communities, and setting up communication networks and providing early warning on protection risks and advice on local population needs. CLAs are equipped with telephones and radios, and proven very effective in identifying threats and needs (Reynaert 2011, p. 26). They have been recognized as a critical asset to MONUSCO, but also face various challenges, including lack of transportation and functioning equipment, phone credits, and demands exceeding their capacity (Weir 2012, p. 4).

These three initiatives have enabled real-time monitoring of the situation on the ground and can greatly augment a mission's situational awareness and ability to respond to emerging threats to civilian populations. However, there are also some serious concerns with regard to these innovative practices—for example, Community Liaison Assistants risk personal retaliation from groups that can see them as providing highly sensitive and possibly incriminating information (Weir and Hunt 2012; Reynaert 2011).

In an effort to further reform peacekeeping, UN DPKO and DFS issued a consultation non-paper in 2009 (UN DPKO/DFS 2009). Although not explicitly mentioning the possibility of accessing and analyzing social media data and other big data, it did note that there was a critical lack of capacity in peacekeeping operations in "Information-gathering—observation/surveillance, including high resolution; night operations capability; data management and analysis" (ibid., p. 27). It noted that DPKO and DFS, along the vision of a capability-oriented approach, would "[p]ursue options, in consultation with Member States, to enhance information-gathering, analysis and security-risk assessment capacity, including drawing on information provided by contributing countries" (ibid., p. 25). Member states have discussed this in the General Assembly Special Committee on Peacekeeping Operations (the aforementioned C-34), and expressed concern regarding the danger that modern technology potentially can represent against the sovereignty of the host country:

> The Special Committee stresses that use of technology aimed at enhancing the safety and security of peacekeepers must **uphold the principles of the Charter** of the United Nations and fundamental principles of peacekeeping. The Special Committee looks forward to further consideration of the related legal, operational, technical and financial aspects, in particular the element of the **consent of the countries concerned** with regard to the application of such means in the field, and notes the Secretariat's intention to use assets to enhance situational awareness, if available, on a case-by-case basis (UN 2012c, my emphases).

In this section we have e.g. seen tentative steps towards establishing crowd-sourced networks in DRC and utilizing modern technologies, as exemplified with the use of drones in Chad and soon in DRC. These steps should be scrutinized as potential elements of peacekeeping 4.0. In the next section I will look at some of the challenges and opportunities that are inherent in these and other potentially innovative initiatives for peacekeeping.

4 Challenges and Opportunities

Accessing, analyzing, and using big data present many challenges. In particular, the statistical challenges abound: non-representative samples, sampling selection bias, danger of *apophenia*—"seeing patterns where none actually exist" (UN Global Pulse 2012a, p. 30), the reliability of crowd-sourced information, and so forth (ibid.; Heldt 2012). However, these challenges can to a certain degree be mitigated and are already known to those familiar with handling more traditional data. To access data generated by individual users, systems need to be put in place that can guarantee the privacy of the individuals who generate the data (Tene and Polonetsky 2012; Tene and Polonetsky forthcoming; The Economist 2010c). This is all the more important in a conflict setting, where, for instance, the state may be very interested in finding out just who is reporting alleged violations of human rights.

Ben Wagner argues that during the Jasmine Revolution in Tunisia "hybrid models of communicating protest—that combine the Internet, television and mobile phones—seem to have been the most resilient" (Wagner 2011, p. 1299). He also asserts that "regulatory regimes of media and communications technologies coevolved with the protests" (ibid., p. 1295). Repressive regimes will seek to monitor and use modern technologies to pursue and stop their opponents, turning these technologies into modern swords of Damocles for those who use them. This has been a key trend throughout the Arab Spring (Wagner 2012), and efforts to crack down on activists have been supported by some Western companies, even during the public outcry against the Tunisian government crackdown on the opposition (ibid; see also Elgin and Silver 2012).

There are also institutional and technical challenges. That crisis management information is in many cases owned by private corporations has implications for data retention, use, and release. Many corporations are not willing to share, as they consider the data a business secret. UN Global Pulse has put forward the concept of "data philanthropy" and wants to persuade corporations to share their data (Kirkpatrick 2011). Corporations, UN agencies, and CSOs may not have data stored in a way that enables direct sharing and access with online platforms, or they may have data stored in formats not readily amenable to being shared and integrated on online platforms. Member states should adapt their regulative frameworks to this new-found reality and open up. States are important repositories of data. Here I may note that Brazil and Norway are among the states that have made a commitment to open up some of their data sites for access and engagement with the general public (Data.gov 2012).

One of the main challenges today is the sheer scale of information available, and the ability/inability to sift through this information, verify it, confirm it, structure it and present it in a comprehensible manner, real-time. The UN is in a particularly sensitive situation, as it must carefully consider member-state opinions, and balance between being a guardian of international norms and respecting the sovereignty of its members. But even within these confines, there is ample room for improving how the UN collects, manages, analyzes, and shares information and data.

The DPKO has recognized some challenges in information management in crises, including "clear data governance, handling of sensitive information, lack of a data privacy policy in the UN, difficulties of information verification and taking subsequent action over, within tight timeframes, unverified and often error ridden data, and infrastructural challenges" (ICT4Peace 2012b). Many of these challenges are manageable, but overcoming them will require unified action by member states and the UN bureaucracy. During the fighting in Libya and with regards to Syria, UN officials admit that they have been following websites like Syria Tracker, but they also remain very skeptical as to the validity and potential bias of the information found there (Interview senior UN DPKO official 2012; see also Stauffacher et al. 2011).

Since the beginning of this millennium there has been growing interest in measuring the impact, effectiveness, and efficiency of peacekeeping and peacebuilding operations. The crowd-seeding examples from Eastern Congo and Georgia above could drastically improve the UN's ability to understand the local-level situation in the states it is supporting. Some have suggested using mobile networks for perception surveys—sending out questions such as "have you seen any incidents of physical violence/can you trust the police in your area/do you feel safe in the area you live?" and combining the results with GIS data. These data could also be used in establishing benchmarks and measuring progress towards these in peacekeeping and peacebuilding operations (Interview UN PBSO official 2012).

On 1 October 2012, UN Global Pulse established its second Pulse Lab, in Jakarta. The Pulse Lab will cooperate with the Government of Indonesia, the private sector and in particular mobile network providers, NGOs and other UN actors, to "explore topics related to changes in social welfare, especially with regard to food prices, fuel prices (for both transport and cooking), employment and urban poverty" (UN Global Pulse 2012c). The mobile network providers' "anonymized Call Detail Records will be supplied to Global Pulse" (Interview UN OICT official 2012). With these anonymized data, the Pulse Lab will have access to near-real-time data on the geographical position of the population and will use and leverage the UN Spatial Data Infrastructure (UNSDI) Gazetteer Framework developed by the Commonwealth Scientific and Industrial Research Organisation (CSIRO) of Australia in cooperation with the UN Office of Information and Communications Technology (OICT), and supported by the Australian Agency for International Development (AusAID) (UN Global Pulse 2012c; Interview UN OICT official 2012):

> CSIRO and AusAID are building an information framework for Indonesia which links together gazetteers (databases of place names and their locations) with spatial data (information tied to geographic locations) to help deliver the right information from multiple sources in a timely matter to those that need it (CSIRO 2011).

The gazetteer framework will be accessible to government actors, NGOs, aid agencies, and local communities through an online portal. It will link formal government collected information with crowd-sourced datasets and the mobile network data. The aim is to be able to be alerted to and address information challenges that are common to poverty reduction, humanitarian action, sustainable development initiatives, and environmental protection activities alike (Interview UN OICT official 2012).

Besides forming a part of the cooperation with UN Global Pulse, the initiative is also the first phase of the larger UN Spatial Data Infrastructure initiative, where the long-term goal is to "scale up the Indonesian pilot project to build critical global information infrastructure for improving national and global (UN) spatial information access and use" (CSIRO 2011). For example, in case of another tsunami, the UN and other humanitarian actors will be able to know instantly the areas that people have relocated to. This initiative is expected to indicate the potentials available when the UN has access to large amounts of anonymized data and should be followed closely. Here an important challenge is that re-identification of the anonymized data is still rather simple (Letouzé 2012).

The UN has decided to establish a UN Operations and Crisis Centre (UNOCC), to be situated in the Executive Office of the Secretary-General (UN 2011, p. 5). The UNOCC is expected to "provide senior managers across the system with situational awareness of UN operations and major world events; facilitate coordinated response to crises in the field; and provide senior managers a 24/7 executive communications service" (UNDP 2012b). The UNOCC is planned to be operational during the first half of 2013 (Interview senior UN DPKO official 2012). Building on the existing UN DPKO Situation Centre (SitCen) (ibid.), it "will draw from existing capacities from the Executive Office of the Secretary-General, the Department of Peacekeeping Operations, the Department of Field Support, the Department of Safety and Security, the Department of Political Affairs, the Department of Public Information, the Office for the Coordination of Humanitarian Affairs and the United Nations Development Programme" (UN 2011, p. 5). However, UNICEF has decided to opt out (Interview senior UN DPKO official 2012), and will continue to run its Operations Centre, established in January 1996 as part of the Office of Emergency Programmes. According to UNICEF,

> [The] Operations Centre (OPSCEN) is a 24-h, 7 days-a-week information gathering and dissemination hub within the Office of Emergency Programmes. The centre monitors humanitarian crises, political events and security-related incidents around the world with a view to ensuring the safety of staff, and providing both field offices and senior decision-makers with critical information related to humanitarian emergencies (UNICEF 2012).

UNDP has also established an Early Warning and Response unit in the Bureau for Conflict Prevention and Recovery that is looking into how big data can be included in its work (Interview UNDP official 2012). However, with so many excellent initiatives being developed concurrently, the UN faces a challenge in coordinating its various mechanisms.

Another challenge connected with the establishment of the UNOCC will be to establish instant contact with field missions and UN Country Teams. UN DPKO currently operates with code cables and other archaic forms of communication. To be effective and inform decision-making not only in New York but also on the ground, the new UNOCC will need effective and efficient means of communication and clear entry points. At present there is a practice of nominating a crisis manager in UN peacekeeping missions, but this "could be the Chief of Staff or someone else" (Interview senior UN DPKO official 2012). This approach will have to be streamlined; and here it would be natural for the UNOCC to relate to the Crisis Management Officer in the Joint Operations Centre, in the Joint Mission Analysis Cell, in the Strategic Planning Unit, or all of them. These would then have responsibility for correlating information received from Headquarters with other sources of information in the field, as well as disseminating information to senior decision-makers within the mission and with the UN Country Team. This would better enable the UN to "move to real-time planning an action in peacekeeping" (ibid.). In countries without a peacekeeping mission, similar arrangements must be established, and the UN Country Team should have a dedicated Crisis Information Officer included in the Office of the Resident Coordinator.

In general, turfism is unfortunately one of the main challenges for the UN. As noted by one interviewee:

> We have a group of people working on remittances and a completely different group of people working on conflict prevention—getting these to work together is like moving mountains. Thankfully initiatives like UN Global Pulse are starting to challenge these divisions... great that you are creating an innovation unit, everybody else is resisting it because it is not their turf (Interview UNDP official 2012).

Theoretically, the use of new technologies, big data and social media in peacekeeping also contributes to the pluralism of actors in international relations. Civil society, rebels, and other non-state actors may be able to strengthen their ability to influence the global public, member states and international organizations. This is a promising area for further empirical inquiry with potentially important implications for the theorizing of the relationship between these actors in international relations.

5 Conclusions and Recommendations

The Arab Spring has brought increased attention to social media like Facebook and Twitter, although their impact on the rebellion in Egypt remains inconclusive (Wilson and Dunn 2011). These new media will be important arenas for discussion and debate for people wanting change. The ability of these media to mobilize international attention and support also shows how social media are part of and contribute to a reality where information is crossing borders in real time. While the full potential of social media and big data still is unknown, it is conceivable that they can lead to real change—in coordination of humanitarian aid, understanding and preventing conflict, and supporting democratization processes. However, it must be borne in mind that social media are only platforms—they can serve as media outlets for repressive movements as well as democratic ones. Individual mass communication in real time on a global scale also contributes to the increasing access to information that can help to improve our understanding of social, political, and economic change. That politics have been moved from closed rooms and assemblies to social media is a challenge not just for states, but also for the UN and other multilateral organizations.

The data deluge can be overwhelming, and the precision of the information can be low, even when processed. However, as Mark Fugate, the head of the US Federal Emergency Management Agency (FEMA), says: "Disasters are like horseshoes, hand grenades and thermal nuclear devices, you just need to be close—preferably more than less" (InPublicSafety 2012) Big and open data are potential sources for understanding, responding to, and preventing crises, and for supporting countries in complex crises. In our technological societies, potentially useful information is everywhere—Facebook, Twitter and the internet are obvious sources, but also mobile phone use, food prices, and other indicators can offer important insights into the vulnerability of people and states. Some of this information is openly available, whereas other data sources are owned or controlled by corporations, states, or CSOs. Properly used, this information can support and improve the work of humanitarian, development, peacekeeping, and peacebuilding actors.

The UN has taken the first steps to adapt to these new realities. To enable change, all parts of the UN will need to improve the coordination of data and find new ways of working together. Several funds, agencies, and programs are reforming the ways they generate and manage data, and are also trying to find better ways of using and understanding social media and open data. Big data and social media offer many avenues for insight into how people cope with crises. Their various types of resilience and ability to withstand external shocks are being demonstrated, but also their vulnerabilities. Big data can give real-time access to changes of sentiment in the population, functioning as an early warning mechanism. Being able to access, analyze, and use big data should be imperative for peacekeeping and peacebuilding operations, which by definition find themselves operating in volatile situations. UN Global Pulse has summarized the potential as follows:

1. "**Early warning**: early detection of anomalies in how populations use digital devices and services can enable faster response in times of crisis;
2. **Real-time awareness**: Big Data can paint a fine-grained and current representation of reality which can inform the design and targeting of programs and policies;
3. **Real-time feedback**: the ability to monitor a population in real time makes it possible to understand where policies and programs are failing and make the necessary adjustments." (UN Global Pulse 2012a, p. 39).

The United Nations and other multilateral institutions do not easily reform themselves. Although progress may be made in one area, moving those lessons into implementation and across the system can prove very hard indeed. Momentum can be achieved only with external pressure, from member states as well as from CSOs. To enable the UN in general, and UN peacekeeping and peacebuilding operations in particular, to make use of this potential, member states will need to press for change in multilateral forums. Here are the first steps to be taken:

1. Ensure that the UN Operations and Crisis Centre at UN HQ in New York includes and serves all parts of the UN, including Secretariat organizations like OCHA, DPKO and DPA, as well as UN funds, programs and agencies including UNICEF;
2. Adding relevant capacity such as Crisis Information Managers to JMAC/JOC/Strategic Planning Unit in peacekeeping and peacebuilding operations for better coordination with humanitarian and development partners;
3. Establishing a second-track focus on the field level to enable people-centered prevention and the use of big data and social media on the tactical and operational levels;
4. The UN and its member states must ensure that the potentials of big data and new media are taken into consideration and integrated in the work on developing post-2015 goals and indicators, and indicators for the "New Deal" Peacebuilding and Statebuilding Goals (PSGs);
5. The UN and member states must look for ways to include other data streams, such as mobile phone usage, satellite and surveillance drone imagery, and local food prices;
6. Enhance intra-UN and cooperation with external partners—e.g. between UN Global Pulse, UN Statistics Division, World Bank; International Monetary Fund; International Statistics Institute; the Partnership in Statistics for Development in the twenty-first century (Paris 21), and national statistical bureaus; building on, *inter alia,* the work done to measure the achievement of the Millennium Development Goals;
7. Continue efforts to harmonize UN system-wide ICT practices with support from the UN member states, as set out in the UN ICT Strategy issued in late 2010 (UN OICT 2010);
8. Strengthen cooperation between UN Global Pulse, DPKO, DPA, agencies, funds and programs with leading actors like Crisis Mappers, Ushahidi, Twitter, Google and others;
9. Start a discussion in the General Assembly about open access to member-state data;
10. Support the UN Global Pulse call for data philanthropy, encouraging corporations to share data in a manner that can ensure privacy.

References

ActivityInfo. (2012) *About*. http://www.activityinfo.org/content/. Retrieved August 12, 2012.

Bengtsson, L., Lu, X., Garfield, R., Thorson, A., & von Schreeb, J. (2010). *UPDATE: 23 October, 2010 Saint-Marc Cholera outbreak analyses of ongoing population movements from the Saint-Marc area, Haiti.* New York: Columbia University, Schools of Nursing and Public Health; Lund: Karolinska Institute, Center for Disaster Medicine.

Bengtsson, L., Lu, X., Thorson, A., Garfield, R., & von Schreeb, J. (2011). Improved response to disasters and outbreaks by tracking population movements with mobile phone network data: A post-earthquake geospatial study in Haiti. *PLoS Medicine 8*(8).

Bott, M., & Young, G. (2012). The role of crowd sourcing for better governance in international development. *PRAXIS, 27*, 56–59.

Boutros-Ghali, B. (1992). *An agenda for peace: Preventive diplomacy, peacemaking, and peace-keeping.* Report of the Secretary-General pursuant to the statement adopted by the summit meeting of the Security Council on 31 January 1992. New York: United Nations.

Cheshire, T. (2011). The news forecast: Can you predict the future by mining millions of web pages for data? *Wired.* Retrieved December 19, 2012, from http://www.wired.co.uk/magazine/archive/2011/12/features/the-news-forecast?page=all

Crisis Mappers. (2012). Retrieved August 15, 2012, from http://crisismappers.net/

CSIRO. (2011). Social protection for vulnerable communities. Retrievd October 19, 2012 from http://www.csiro.au/gazetteer#

Data.Gov. (2012). *Open data sites.* Retrieved August 28, 2012, from http://www.data.gov/opendatasites/

Dorn, A. W. (2011). *Keeping watch: Monitoring, technology & innovation in UN peace operations.* Tokyo: United Nations University Press.

Eagle, N., & Pentland, A. (2006). Reality mining: Sensing complex social systems. *Personal and Ubiquitous Computing, 10*(4), 255–268.

Elgin, B., & Vernon Silver, V. (2012). Syria Crackdown gets Italy firm's aid with U.S.-Europe spy gear. *Bloomberg News.* Retrieved October 26, 2012, from http://www.bloomberg.com/news/2011-11-03/syria-crackdown-gets-italy-firm-s-aid-with-u-s-europe-spy-gear.html

Evans, J. (2012). *In five years, most Africans will have smartphones.* Retrieved October 26, 2012, from http://techcrunch.com/2012/06/09/feature-phones-are-not-the-future/

Ginsberg, J., Mohebbi, M. H., Patel, R. S., Brammer, L., Smolinski, M. S., & Brilliant, L. (2009). Detecting influenza epidemics using search engine query data. *Nature, 457*, 1012–1015.

Google. (2012a). *Google dengue trends.* Retrieved August 28, 2012, from http://www.google.org/denguetrends/

Google. (2012b). *Google flu trends.* Retrieved August 28, 2012, from http://www.google.org/flutrends/

Helbing, D., & Balietti, S. (2012). *From social data mining to forecasting socio-economic crisis.* Retrieved December 19, 2012, from http://arxiv.org/abs/1012.0178

Heldt, B. (2012). *Mass atrocities early warning systems: Data gathering, data verification and other challenges.* Working Paper Series. Stockholm: Folke Bernadotte Academy.

Howe, J. (2008). *Crowdsourcing: Why the power of the crowd is driving the future of business.* New York: CrownBusiness.

ICT4Peace. (2012a). *Crisis information management training course.* Retrieved December 21, 2012, from http://cl.ly/3e1s1c2Y1c1d

ICT4Peace. (2012b). *Report of the crisis information management CiMAG retreat, 10–12 June 2012.* Retrieved August 28, 2012, from http://ict4peace.org/updates/report-of-the-crisis-information-management-cimag-retreat-10-12-june-2012

India Today. (2012). *Samsung to launch cheaper smart phones for India.* Retrieved October 26, 2012, from http://indiatoday.intoday.in/story/samsung-to-launch-cheaper-smartphones-for-india/1/178457.html

InPublicSafety. (2012). *FEMA's Fugate says social media is valuable, but 'No Tweet Stops the Bleeding'.* Retreived August 28, 2012 from http://inpublicsafety.com/2012/02/femas-fugate-says-social-media-is-valuable-but-no-tweet-stops-the-bleeding/

International Data Corporation. (2011). *IDC predicts 2012 will be the year of mobile and cloud platform wars as IT vendors vie for leadership while the industry redefines itself.* Retrieved August 12, 2012, from http://www.idc.com/getdoc.jsp?containerId=prUS23177411

ITU. (2012a). *Forging the future. Panel proceedings at the ITU Telecom World 2012, Dubai 14–18 October 2012.* Retrieved October 26, 2012, from http://world2012.itu.int/summary1

ITU. (2012b). *Measuring the information society 2012.* Geneva: International Telecommunication Union.

Jidenma, N. (2011). *Affordable smart phones to drive Africa's Internet adoption.* Retrieved October 26, 2012, from http://thenextweb.com/africa/2011/08/21/affordable-smart-phones-to-drive-africas-internet-adoption/

Kahl, A., McConnell, C., & Tsuma, W. (2012). Crowdsourcing as a tool in conflict prevention. *Conflict Trends, 1*, 27–34.

Keck, M. E., & Sikkink, S. (1998). *Activists beyond borders: Advocacy networks in international politics.* Ithaca: Cornell University Press.

Kirkpatrick, R. (2011). Data philanthropy: Public & private sector data Sharing for global resilience. *UN Global Pulse,* 16 September 2011. Retrieved August 28, 2012, from http://www.unglobalpulse.org/blog/data-philanthropy-public-private-sector-data-sharing-global-resilience

Kjeksrud, S., & Ravndal, J. A. (2010). *Protection of Civilians in practice—emerging lessons from the UN Mission in the DR Congo.* Oslo: Norwegian Defense Research Establishment (FFI).

Leson, H. (2012). *Crowdsourcing for Change?* Retrieved August 15, 2012, from http://www.isn.ethz.ch/isn/Digital-Library/Podcasts/Detail//?ots591=40db1b50-7439-887d-706e-8ec00590bdb9&lng=en&id=135915

Letouzé, E. (2012). *Can big data from cellphones help prevent conflict?* Retrieved December 13, 2012, from http://theglobalobservatory.org/component/myblog/can-big-data-from-cellphones-help-prevent-conflict-/blogger/Emmanuel%20Letouz%C3%A9/

Meier, P. (2012). Towards a Twitter dashboard for the humanitarian cluster system. *iRevolution.* Retrieved October 29, 2012, from http://irevolution.net/2012/07/30/twitter-for-humanitarian-cluster/

Paul, M. J., & Dredze, M. (2011). *You are what you tweet: Analyzing Twitter for public health.* Presented at the Fifth International AAAI Conference on Weblogs and Social Media, 17–21 July 2011, Barcelona. Retrieved August 28, 2012, from http://www.aaai.org/ocs/index.php/ICWSM/ICWSM11/paper/view/2880

Portio Research. (2012). *Portio research mobile factbook 2012.* Retrieved August 12, 2012, from http://www.portioresearch.com/media/1797/Mobile%20Factbook%202012.pdf

Puig, H. (2012). Conflict sensitive crowdsourcing. *Let them talk.* Retrieved October 29, 2012, from http://letthemtalkdotorg.wordpress.com/2012/07/05/conflict-sensitive-crowdsourcing/

Ramjoué, M. (2011). Improving United Nations intelligence: Lessons from the field. *GCSP Policy Paper* n°19, August 2011. Geneva: Geneva Centre for Security Policy.

Ramsbotham, O., Woodhouse, T., & Miall, H. (2005). *Contemporary conflict resolution* (2nd ed.). Cambridge: Polity Press.

Reynaert, J. (2011). *MONUC/MONUSCO and Civilian protection in the Kivus.* International Peace Information Service: Antwerpen.

Romita, P. (2011). *The UN Security Council and conflict prevention: A primer.* New York: International Peace Institute.

Security Council Report. (2010). Conflict prevention: Horizon scanning. *November 2010 Forecast.* October 29, 2010. Retrieved August 14, 2012, from www.securitycouncilreport.org/site/c.glKWLeMTIsG/b.6355203/k.97F7/November_2010brConflict_Prevention_Horizon_Scanning.htm

Sifry, M. L. (2012). In Georgia's troubled border region, text messaging is Fostering Community safety. *techPresident.* Retrieved October 29, 2010, from http://techpresident.com/news/wegov/22789/georgias-troubled-border-region-text-messaging-fostering-community-safety

Standby Task Force. (2012). *OCHA South Sudan deployment: Curating data for disaster preparedness.* Retrieved August 28, 2012, from http://blog.standbytaskforce.com/ocha-south-sudan-deployment-curating-data-for-preparedness/

Stauffacher, D. et al. (Eds.) (2011). *Peacebuilding in the information age: Sifting hype from reality.* Geneva: ICT for Peace Foundation.

Swiss Mission to the United Nations. (2012). *Report on high-level dialogue with UN Member States on the status of the UN Crisis Information Management Strategy (CiMS) using inter alia social media tools, crisis mapping and crowdsourcing.* New York: Swiss Mission to the United Nations.

Syria Tracker. (2012). *About Syria tracker*. Retrieved August 14, 2012, from https://syriatracker.crowdmap.com/page/index/1

Tene, O., & Polonetsky, J. (2012). Privacy in the age of big data: A time for big decisions. *Stanford Law Review Online 63*, 63–69.

Tene, O., & Polonetsky, J. (forthcoming). Big Data for All: Privacy and User Control in the Age of Analytics. *Northwestern Journal of Technology and Intellectual Property*.

The Economist. (2010a). *Data, data everywhere*. 25 February 2010. Retrieved August 12, 2012, from http://www.economist.com/node/15557443

The Economist. (2010b). *The data deluge*. 25 February 2010. Retrieved August 12, 2012, from http://www.economist.com/node/15579717

The Economist. (2010c). *New rules for big data*. 25 February 2010. Retrieved August 28, 2012, from http://www.economist.com/node/15557487

UN. (2011). *A/66/619/Add.1. Implementation of the recommendations of the Special Committee on Peacekeeping Operations: Report of the Secretary-General: Addendum, 16 December 2011*. New York: United Nations.

UN. (2012a). *Crisis information management strategy.* Powerpoint presentation. Retrieved August 28, 2012, from http://ict4peace.org/wp-content/uploads/2012/07/High-level-meeting-on-CIM-Strategy-July-2012-FINAL-1.pdf

UN. (2012b). *Peace: keep it. Build it. The contribution of United Nations Peacekeeping to early peacebuilding: Strategy.* New York: UN Department of Peacekeeping Operations and Department of Field Support.

UN. (2012c). *Report of the special committee on peacekeeping. A/66/19*. New York: United Nations.

UN Department of Political Affairs. (2012). *Fact sheet as of 30 June 2012*. Retrieved August 2, 2012, from http://www.un.org/wcm/webdav/site/undpa/shared/undpa/pdf/Political%20Missions%20July%202012.pdf

Un, D. P. K. O. (2006). *DPKO policy directive: Joint Operations Centres and Joint Mission Analysis Cells*. New York: United Nations Department of Peacekeeping Operations.

Un, D. P. K. O. (2008). *Policy: Authority, command and control in United Nations Peacekeeping Operations*. New York: United Nations Department of Peacekeeping Operations.

UN DPKO. (2012). *Fact Sheet as of 30 June 2012*. Retrieved August 2, 2012, from http://www.un.org/en/peacekeeping/resources/statistics/factsheet.shtml/

UN DPKO/DFS. (2009). *A new partnership agenda: Charting a new horizon for UN peacekeeping*. New York: United Nations Department of Peacekeeping and Department of Field Support.

UN DPKO/DFS. (2011). *Peacekeeping and peacebuilding: Clarifying the nexus*. New York: UN Department of Peacekeeping Operations and Department of Field Support.

UN Global Pulse. (2011). *Rapid impact and vulnerability analysis fund (RIVAF): Final report*. New York: UN Global Pulse.

UN Global Pulse. (2012a). *Big data for development: Challenges and opportunities*. New York: UN Global Pulse.

UN Global Pulse. (2012b). *About*. Retrieved August 12, 2012, from http://www.unglobalpulse.org/about-new

UN Global Pulse. (2012c). *Jakarta*. Retrieved October 29, 2012, from http://www.unglobalpulse.org/pulse-lab/jakarta

UN OICT. (2010). *Shaping the future of information and communications technology for the United Nations Secretariat*. New York: UN Office of Information and Communications Technology.

UN Security Council. (2006). *Resolution 1706*. UN Document S/RES/1706, 31 August 2006. New York: United Nations.

UN Security Council. (2011). *Resolution 1996*. UN Document S/RES/1996, 8 July 2011. New York: United Nations.

UNDP. (2012a). *Enhancing national capacities for conflict mapping, analysis and transformation in Sudan—CRMA Phase II*. Retrieved August 28, 2012, from http://www.sd.undp.org/projects/dg13.htm

UNDP. (2012b). *Reporting officer*. Retrieved October 25, 2012, from http://jobs.undp.org/cj_view_job.cfm?cur_job_id=31078

UNGA. (2005). *A/RES/60/1: 2005 World summit outcome*. New York: United Nations General Assembly.

UNICEF. (2012). *UNICEF's office of emergency programmes (EMOPS)*. Retrieved October 26, 2012, from http://www.unicef.org/emerg/index_33578.html

Ushahidi. (2012a). *Our team*. Retrieved August 14, 2012, from http://ushahidi.com/index.php/about-us/team

Ushahidi. (2012b). *About us*. Retrieved August 14, 2012, from http://ushahidi.com/about-us

van der Wind, P., & Humphreys, M. (2012). *Crowdseeding conflict data: An application of an SMS-based data system to estimate the conflict effects of development aid*. New York: Columbia University.

Wagner, B. (2011). "I Have Understood You": The co-evolution of expression and control on the Internet, television and mobile phones during the jasmine revolution in Tunisia. *International Journal of Communication*, *5*, 1295–1302.

Wagner, B. (2012). *After the Arab spring: New paths for human rights and the Internet in European Foreign Policy*. Brussels: European Union.

WEF. (2010). *Big data, big impact: New possibilities for international development*. Davos: World Economic Forum.

Weir, E. A. (2012). *DR Congo: Local communities on the front line*. Washington D.C: Refugees International.

Weir, E. A., & Hunt, C. (2012). *DR Congo: Support community-based tools for MONUSCO*. Washington D.C: Refugees International.

Wilson, C., & Dunn, A. (2011). Digital media in the Egyptian revolution: Descriptive analysis from the Tahrir data Sets. *International Journal of Communications*, *5*, 1248–1272.

World Bank. (2012a). *Mobile cellular subscriptions (per 100 people)*. etrieved August 12, 2012, from http://data.worldbank.org/

World Bank. (2012b). *Internet users (per 100 people)*. Retrieved August 12, 2012, from http://data.worldbank.org/

World Bank. (2012c). *Building with bits rather than atoms: 'Big Data' alternatives for infrastructure development in the 21st century*. Retrieved August 28, 2012, from http://web.worldbank.org/WBSITE/EXTERNAL/EXTABOUTUS/ORGANIZATION/EXTPREMNET/0,,contentMDK:23150444~menuPK:2880846~pagePK:64159605~piPK:64157667~theSitePK:489961,00.html

World Bank. (2012d). *Mapping for results*. Retrieved August 28, 2012, from http://maps.worldbank.org/

Interviews

Interview with Patrick Meier, 27 Aug 2012.
Interview with senior UN DPKO official, New York, 23 August 2012.
Interview with UN OICT official, 14 Sep 2012.
Interview with UN PBSO official, 22 August 2012.
Interview with UNDP official, 31 August 2012.

US Leadership in Cyberspace: Transnational Cyber Security and Global Governance

Ryan David Kiggins

Abstract This chapter examines US cyber security policy in light of transnational cyber security, deterrence theory, and hegemonic stability theory. Recent work on US cyber security policy has argued for or against deterrence theory as a basis for US cyber security policy. Deterrence theory, as a state level theory of national security, focuses attention on strategic choice enabling policymakers to manage state level responses to perceived threats. The problem is that the Internet is a transnational medium and, increasingly, an important global medium for economic exchange, being treated as a duty free zone under WTO agreements. Thinking about cyber security at the level of the state elides threats to the Internet as a global commercial medium. Framing cyber security as a transnational security issue may assist in developing a comprehensive US cyber security policy that incorporates deterrence and US leadership. The role of the US in the global economic order is to provide leadership ensuring stability necessary or economic and information exchange to occur. From the standpoint of transnational security, the US should fulfill its role as leader of collective hegemony, by leading cyber space stakeholders to develop norms and rules for global cyber security governance regimes and institutions that will teach states the norms and rules necessary for a stable and secure cyber domain through which global information and economic exchange will continue to flourish.

R. D. Kiggins (✉)
Williams College, Williamstown, MA, USA
e-mail: rykigg@ufl.edu

J.-F. Kremer and B. Müller (eds.), *Cyberspace and International Relations*,
DOI: 10.1007/978-3-642-37481-4_10,

1 Introduction

Deployment of the Stuxnet computer virus, the "first digital warhead," is a watershed event for transnational security (Nakashima 2012). A new domain of state on state and state on non-state actor conflict adds a new dimension to national security and transnational security considerations. Stuxnet, allegedly, the product of Israeli and US cooperation, was tested at Israel's military facility at Dimona in the Negev Desert before being uploaded from a thumb drive into computer networks at Iranian nuclear fuel production facilities (Broad et al. 2011). The Stuxnet virus was designed to seize control of the supervisory control and data acquisition (SCADA) software managing the operational performance of the centrifuges, then command centrifuges to spin faster than design limits causing, in some instances, kinetic events where centrifuges broke apart (Ibid.). Before Iranian experts discovered Stuxnet, the malicious software reportedly disabled 984 nuclear centrifuges operated by the Iranian government for the purpose of enriching uranium (Ibid.). Assuming the reports are accurate as to the source of Stuxnet, rather than dropping bombs from airplanes or launching cruise missiles to kinetically destroy Iranian nuclear enrichment assets, policymakers in the US and Israel chose, instead, to launch a pre-emptive strike through cyber space.

Stuxnet combined with ongoing the efforts of other state and non-state cyber operators to gain access to information stored on government and corporate computer networks around the globe, or to gain control over those networks when desired, underscores the collective vulnerability (and opportunity) of states in an era of rapid globalization driven, in part, by advances in information and telecommunications technologies (Nakashima 2012). Globalization combined with information technologies deepens interdependency placing limits on what single state actors can accomplish in cyber space to ensure security (Nye 2011a).

Nye (2011b) argues that cooperation among states will be needed to comprehensively address new cyber threats that emerge, but cautions that such cooperation will evolve slowly over time. The problem is that the risk of a catastrophic cyber event is such that waiting for cyber security cooperation to evolve over time may prove too late. How might cyber security cooperation among states emerge more rapidly? Relying on hegemonic stability theory, the case is made, in what follows, that US leadership in the cyber domain is crucial to achieving transnational cyber security through coordinated efforts at cyber threat reduction through constructing shared cyber security norms. US policymakers must adopt a strategic approach for cyber security at the transnational level that is grounded in developing cooperation among cyber stakeholders and that compliments extant US national cyber security strategy.

In what follows, current US cyber security policy is reviewed and the limits to a deterrence theory based US cyber security policy are explained. Cyber security is, next, reconceptualized as a transnational security issue requiring leadership-enabled cooperation among state actors in response. Viewing cyber security as a transnational security issue, underscores the linkages among cyber security, transnational commerce, and Internet governance. In effect, transnational cyber security is a problem for global governance where states cooperate to eliminate and reduce cyber threats to achieve decreased and more manageable risks thereby providing certainty to users that the Internet is a stable, reliable, and secure medium for global information and economic exchange.

2 Cyber Vulnerability, US Cyber Security Policy, and the Limits of Cyber Deterrence

Cyber space is an artificially created domain of information and economic exchange. As is the case for international relations, cyber space is a domain characterized by the condition of anarchy, the absence of a central authority. However, cyber space, as an anarchical domain, and similar to international relations, is not devoid of rules, "At the most basic level, [cyber space] is governed by rules of physics as well as code, which give it predictability and finite characteristics" (Deibert and Rohozinski 2010, 256). Governance is built into the computer network system from which cyber space emerges. Cyber space is formed through the internetworking of computers and software that governs communication among networked computers to achieve pooling of scare computing resources (Abbate 2000). The upshot of globalized networked computing is that lower costs associated with information retrieval, consumer and producer accessibility to global markets, and transnational communication is gained. These gains are achieved on a system designed with efficiency being, instead of security, the primary concern clearing the way for cyber actors to exploit vulnerabilities in network and software design for the purpose of controlling information in order to gain advantage. As the development of cyber space into a critical domain of information and economic exchange has occurred during the first decades of the globalized post-Cold War era, the capability to control information stored on the Internet through pricing, altering, or securitizing information has become a point of contention among cyber actors of all stripes including state and non-state actors.

Cyber attacks can be defined as attempts to gain control over information stored on computer networks that comprise the Internet. The deployment of the Stuxnet computer virus against Iranian nuclear program assets illustrates a cyber attack through exploiting design flaws in computer network, hardware, and software design to achieve actor objectives. By altering information stored on Iranian computer networks, the safe and efficient operability of Iranian nuclear centrifuges became problematic. Similarly, non-state actors operating in cyber space share objectives with states to control information through pricing, altering, or securitizing information possessing technical skill on par with that available to states. The hacktivist group known as "Anonymous" is renown as much for its technical expertise as for its brazen cyber attacks. States are far from the most powerful actors in this new domain of conflict given that technical skill is widely distributed among state and non-state actors and the fact that cyber operators can remain anonymous (Singh 2010). Rather, there is relative parity in capability among cyber actors to control information through cyber attack (Morgan 2012a, b). Criminals engage in widespread computer fraud costing consumers and businesses billions of dollars a year (Osborne 2012; Schwartz 2012). While cyber spies ply their trade to steal information including the intellectual property of commercial enterprises or government secured information to gain competitive advantage (Rogin 2012; Stoll 1990). Terrorists probe for computer network weaknesses that can be exploited for political ends (Verton 2003; Weimann 2006). The problem facing cyber strategists is protecting information stored on computer networks accessible through the Internet. This problem is comprised of technical and policy elements. This chapter focuses on policy, specifically, US cyber security policy.

2.1 US Cyber Security Policy

Upon taking office in January 2009, President Barak Obama ordered a review of US cyber security policy. In May 2009, President Obama accepted the policy review and directed that US government departments and agencies begin coordinating cyber security efforts through The White House Cyber security Coordinator (WHCC). The WHCC is charged with ensuring that all US government departments and agencies are implementing cyber security technologies and protocols consistent with US cyber security strategy. US cyber security strategy is to enhance US cyber capabilities to identify, defend against, and deter would be cyber attackers. Identification and defense occur on the level of the state whereas deterrence straddles the state level and the transnational level. US policymakers recently recognized that an effective cyber security strategy must include "collective deterrence" predicated on cooperation in a multistakeholder framework (*Department of Defense Strategy for Operating in Cyber space* 2011, 9). "By sharing timely indicators about cyber events, threat signatures of malicious code, and information about emerging actors and threats, allies and international partners can increase collective cyber defense" (*Department of Defense Strategy for Operating in Cyber space* 2011, 9). The challenge is how to foster the sort of multistakeholder cooperation that enhances cyber defense and deterrence.

Within the United States, a veritable cottage industry has emerged in which US vulnerability to cyber attacks including cyber war, cyber terror, cyber espionage, cyber crime, or just plain cyber Armageddon is proclaimed and pleas are made for robust government action to fortify US cyber defenses (Adams 1998; Armistead 2010; Clarke and Knake 2010; Demchak and Dombroski 2011; Gerstein 2005; Katin-Borland 2012; Rattray 2001). Building off this cottage industry, work on the topic of US cyber security policy has focused on identifying a theory of international relations that may serve as a policy guide, leading some to advocate for deterrence theory (Crosston 2011; Kugler 2009; Sterner 2011; Taipale 2009). Others (Cimbala 2011; Libicki 2007, 2009, 2011) have argued that deterrence theory is inapplicable to cyber security, but Nye (2011b) is more sanguine noting that deterrence theory may prove effective where state on state cyber conflict is concerned. Nye hedges, however, that the fungibility of deterrence to non-state actor perpetrated cyber attacks or other transnational issue areas that cyber touches is limited. Why is deterrence theory not an adequate policy guide beyond the issue area of state on state cyber attacks? There are two hurdles that may vitiate deterrence theory from serving as a suitable US cyber security policy guide beyond state on state cyber attacks. Examining both hurdles is preceded by a brief overview of deterrence theory. This will be followed by an examination of the problem of credibility and the problem of arbitrary threshold. My aim is examine the merits of each problem in an effort to delineate the precise limits of deterrence as a US cyber security policy guide.

2.2 The Limits of Cyber Deterrence

Within the academic discipline of international relations, Waltz (1959), proposed that theories of international relations could be categorized as first image, second image, or third image theory according to the primary unit of analysis (individual, state, or system—respectively) advanced by the theory. The primary unit of analysis is the object from which deductions are formulated about how the object will interact with other objects given a set of constraints or conditions. This schema of theory categorization is often referred to as levels of analysis, as in, the level of politics at which an object or unit of analysis is situated and for which international relations theory is intentionally designed to describe, explain and prescribe policy. Deterrence theory posits that the principal actors in international relations are states, making states the primary unit of analysis for deterrence theory (Huth and Russett 1984; Jervis 1998; Morgan 1983; Schelling 1980).[1] Under Waltz's international relations classification scheme, deterrence theory would be categorized as a second image or state level theory designed to prescribe policy for state actors. Achen and Snidal (1989) note that deterrence theory, after identifying its primary unit of analysis, moves to posit certain conditions concerning its unit of analysis. Deterrence theory advances that states are rational, that states are unitary actors "(changes in personnel, in decision-making patterns, or in bureaucratic politics are not the explanatory focus)," and, as such, engage in cost benefit analysis to determine the best course of action given constraints and preference optimization strategies (Achen and Snidal 1989, 151). Deterrence theory treats states as functionally equivalent, with known capabilities, and willingness to use those capabilities, for the purpose of predicting that, under certain conditions, deterrence is a viable state strategy. States are actors in cyber space and this fact mitigates the

[1] There is a rich literature that investigates and debates the merits of deterrence theory including Fearon (2002), Harvey (1998), Huth (1999), Huth and Russett (1993), Jervis (1989), Lebow and Stein (1989), and Lebow (2009).

issue of deterrence theory applicability as a guide to US cyber security policy. The appeal of deterrence theory to US cyber security policy is in its "logical cohesion and consistency" (Achen and Snidal 1989, 153).

The logic of deterrence theory is that a potential foe is dissuaded from launching an assault when the "threatened punishment exceeds the gains from attacking" (Achen and Snidal 1989, 151). Treating actors in cyber space as rational actors that have an objective in mind, that order preferences to determine optimal strategies for achieving that objective, is a framework that assists policymakers in simplifying and making sense of cyber threats—a necessary step in determining policy response. Perhaps the weakness of deterrence theory is to be found in its strength. In order to successfully deter certain conditions must be present including an assessment by potential initiators of an attack of the credibility of a threat to inflict punishment in response, accurate identification of the object to which punishment is directed, the capability to carry out the punishment, and the capability to limit the effects of punishment to the intended object. Unique features of cyber space, presently, work against these deterrence conditions and these features cut to the heart of deterrence theory as a suitable US cyber security policy guide. This claim will become clearer through examining the two hurdles of credibility and arbitrary threshold.

Within deterrence theory, credibility stipulates that perpetrators of attacks must believe that the punishment will be carried out precisely as the defender has indicated. It is unlikely that actors in cyber space dismiss the resolve of US policymakers to respond to a cyber attack utilizing any and all means at their disposal and proportional to the damage inflicted by the cyber attack. Credibility, however, is more than asserting resolve; credibility includes an assessment by a potential attacker that a defender has the capability to carry out the punishment. Capability to carry out a punishment is comprised of the following three elements: identification of perpetrator/s, selection of the appropriate response, and execution of the response. The US has the luxury of superlative technical skill among its cyber operators in government service and the experience to execute cyber operations as evidenced by Stuxnet. What the US lacks, as all other cyber operators, is the technology to identify whom or what perpetrated a cyber attack beyond identifying where a computer used to initiate an attack is located geographically. It's not as if cyber operators are wearing uniforms with country identifying insignia operating clearly marked military vehicles or, in this case, computers that make country identification of a cyber attacker recognizable. Current technology allows investigators to trace an attack to the country of origin but not determine whether or not a cyber operator acting as an official or member of a state sponsored group typed the commands in the computer keyboard that initiated a cyber attack. Cyber operators are able to remain anonymous behind computer screens and keyboards, the only identifying feature of a cyber operator may be the consistencies in software programming that are the telltales of a particular programmer or group of programmers. The inability to identify cyber attackers is known as the problem of attribution. Lacking attribution of an attack limits the effectiveness of deterrence by neutering retaliation. Threat credibility in cyber space is undercut by the problem of attribution.

Being able to attribute a cyber attack determines the type of response, including which state capability or capabilities are to be utilized, and, accordingly, how the response is executed given selected state capabilities. Was a cyber attack perpetrated by a teenage hacker getting kicks showing off for friends, by a terrorist group bent on sowing fear, or by another state in a tit for tat scenario, to commit espionage, or preparing for war by degrading US technological superiority on which US military depends for gaining advantage during kinetic hostilities? How a policymaker or group of policymakers answers these questions determines the course of policy designed to respond to a cyber attack. The inability to answer these questions limits what policymakers can conjure up as punishment in response to a cyber attack. The problem of attribution negates the first element of extending credible threats, which effectively neuters the second and third elements of extending credible threats. If credibility of threats is rendered ineffective through the anonymity afforded cyber operators, an effective deterrence is limited. Unfortunately, US policymakers have further limited the effectiveness of deterrence on this front by imposing an arbitrary threshold that, when met, triggers a US imposed punishment up to and including military force.

US policymakers have determined that the same laws that apply to war in the domains of air, land, sea, and space, apply to the cyber domain and have reserved the right to utilize military force in response to a cyber attack. In November 2011, the US Department of Defense released the *Department of Defense Cyber space Policy Report* in which it is determined that, "Without question, some activities conducted in cyber space could constitute a use of force, and may as well invoke a state's inherent right to lawful self-defense." An unattributed US military official clarified "use of force" in a news story on the aforementioned US Department of Defense report that during or, as a consequence of a cyber attack, "If you shut down our power grid, maybe we will put a missile down one of your smokestacks" (Gorman and Barnes 2011, 1). Consequently, US policymakers have committed to a threshold that if other states, operating in cyber space, cross, US response may include a military attack utilizing missiles, bombs, or land invasion. The effect of a cyber attack must be such that loss of human life or significant damage to critical infrastructures (power systems, water systems, transportation systems) warrants retaliatory strike. This threshold has the effect of circumscribing the credibility of the US threat to retaliate to a cyber attack. Other states now know how far they can pursue cyber operations without risking US retaliation. For example, on 21 September 2012, US Senator Joe Lieberman, Chair of the US Senate Homeland Security Committee, identified Iran as the perpetrator of cyber attacks on US banking institutions and state owned oil companies throughout the Middle East, including Saudi Aramco (Nakashima 2012). As of the writing of this chapter, the Iranian cyber attacks continue. While the loss of data was of significant cost to these commercial enterprises, the cyber attacks warranted little more than condemnation from US policymakers as the Iranian cyber attack did not cross the threshold, in the estimation of US policymakers, set by US policymakers that would trigger a direct response and forceful response from the US. This problem of arbitrary threshold undercuts US cyber deterrence. Stunningly, US policymakers have recently admitted that their own threshold is unclear; US policymakers are unclear as to what criteria are used to assess a cyber attack in an effort to determine a response (Gorman and Barnes 2011). This admission ties back to the problem of credibility begging the question of how credible US threats to retaliate. Lacking threat credibility due to an arbitrary and unclear threshold that triggers a response vitiates deterrence theory as a US cyber security policy guide.

To be fair, deterrence theory is a response to a set of historical, social, and strategic circumstances unique to the Cold War where two nuclear-armed states vied for relative advantage under the risk that nuclear war could break out at any time. Each state relied on the credibility of threat backed by stockpiles of accurately directed nuclear-armed intercontinental ballistic missiles ready to be used in a massive nuclear retaliatory-strike. Updating the theory to the cyber domain includes overcoming the problem of attribution and refusing to set arbitrary thresholds that provide other cyber actors operational space in which to maneuver with cover. Offense, indeed, is favored in cyber space (Nye 2011b). There is one other issue confronting deterrence theory as a suitable US cyber security policy guide. Deterrence theory elides the purpose of cyber space as a transnational domain comprised of a multitude of actors that use the domain for information and economic exchange. Viewing cyber space in this light clears ground to propose an international relations theory that is designed to explain, describe, and prescribe policy at the system level of analysis. Moreover, pooling capabilities may lead to cooperation that produces technological breakthroughs that overcome the hurdle of credibility while negotiation settles on norms for what counts as a threshold and identifies appropriate responses depending on the severity of damage incurred during a cyber attack. In the next section I defend the claim that cyber space is a transnational domain in which information and economic exchange reflects the primary purpose of the technology. I then propose that US power, exercised through leading other states to form multi-stakeholder coalitions may initiate transnational cooperation for state supported programs to develop technology that overcomes the problem of attribution and results in transnational agreement concerning cyber attack thresholds and norms governing the use of cyber weapons or conventional weapons for retaliation. In conclusion, I will argue that cyber security is a transnational governance issue.

3 Transnational Cyber Security

Viewing cyber space as a transnational domain entails understanding the social purpose of the Internet in the post-Cold War era. The Internet was initially developed as a distributed communications system designed to continue operating in the event of nuclear attack on the United States. The initial social purpose of the Internet was to serve as a communications and control system through which US policymakers could direct nuclear war operations. Elsewhere I have shown (Kiggins 2011), that as the Cold War came to a close and the US government began to decrease finding for its Cold War military-industrial complex, the Internet became something of a budgetary hot potato as it was tossed from the US Defense Department to the National

Science Foundation and from there, ultimately finding a home in a private–public partnership overseen by the US Commerce department. From defense to commerce is a striking journey and speaks to the view of the Internet held by US policymakers in the post-Cold War era. The view of the Internet held by US policymakers can be explained by the Open Door interpretation of US diplomatic history.

The Open Door holds that US policymakers subscribe to a worldview where the security of the United States rests on sustained economic and political expansion abroad (Beard 1934; Williams 1959; also see Bacevich 2002; Layne 2006, 1998). Adas (2006) has shown that US policymakers from the founding of the United States through the present consistently leverage technology in pursuit of that expansion. Beginning in late 1994 and continuing to the present, US policymakers initiated and sustain a policy to repurpose the Internet as a platform for the expansion of American products and political ideals (Kiggins 2011). From the view of US policymakers, the social purpose of the Internet in the post-Cold War era is to serve as a platform for expanding free-market commerce and free speech, for globally expanding information and economic exchange (Kiggins 2011). To ensure the Internet is used in accordance with this social purpose, US policymakers have constructed a discourse around the Internet founded on the principle of openness (Antonova 2008; McCarthy 2011). US policymakers discursively promote and protect the Internet as an open domain in order to create global institutional conditions that are favorable for global expansion of information and economic exchange consistent with the worldview of US policymakers. Castells (1999) has shown how the Internet assists globalization by linking states in a deepening web of economic interdependence that characterizes this era of global capitalism shaped by the United States and other allied advanced industrialized democracies. Evidence of the growing economic import of the Internet supports the claim that the Internet is an increasingly vital global platform for exchange.

By 2015, total international trade over the Internet, more commonly referred to as global electronic commerce, is projected to be \$1.4 trillion and is expected to continue to grow at a 13.5 % compounded annual growth rate for the foreseeable future (Enright 2011). Mann and Kierkegaard (2006, 25) estimate that global electronic commerce adds roughly .25 basis points of growth to annual GDP for industrialized nations. In the case of the United States, that translates to over \$400 billion added to US GDP per year. While 53 % of all global electronic commerce transactions occur in the United States, Japan, and the United Kingdom, developing countries such as Brazil, China, Russia, and Mexico are projected to experience electronic commerce growth at an annual rate of 26 % for the foreseeable future (Enright 2011). A shift is underway where global electronic commerce moves from the developed world to the developing world driven, in part, by successful economic development strategies that are creating consumer classes in those countries and, in part, by the expansion of mobile telecommunications networks throughout the developing world. More consumers, on a global scale, plug into cyber space through their new mobile devices such smart phones and tablet computers reflecting a shift from desktop computing to cloud computing. This shift will deepen interdependence, shrinking the distance between private Internet based computing and public Internet based computing (Castells 1999, 1996).

With this shift in computing, global consumption patterns may change, and, with that change in consumption patterns may come change in global trade, economic production, employment, and political institutions (Ibid.). The Arab spring could be construed as reflecting these tectonic shifts in the global political economy that are amplified and accelerated by cyber based and enabled communications technologies. Combined, the Stuxnet virus, the cyber attack on Google and thirty-three other US enterprises, and the growing import of the Internet to global trade and information flows argue against a state-centric framework of cyber security that elides the role that the Internet plays in deepening linkages among state and non-state actors (Keohane and Nye 2001).

For my purposes, cyber security means the absence of conflict among actors such that a condition of certainty and stability ensues within the cyber domain that enables global information and economic exchange. Framing cyber security in this manner more accurately reflects that cyber security is a transnational security issue where all cyber users share vulnerability to cyber attack. Owing to the interdependent nature of cyber security, better to think of cyber security as a transnational security issue where states forge cooperation to achieve a secure cyber space. How to achieve policy coordination among state actors on cyber security may be answered by hegemonic stability theory. Hegemonic stability theory may compliment deterrence theory by prescribing US cyber security policy at the system level.

4 The Need for US Leadership

Some may quibble that hegemonic stability theory is an outdated theory of international relations that is no longer applicable. On the contrary, hegemonic stability theory remains applicable precisely for the reason that US policymakers continue to think in terms of US leadership being essential to global security as is evident with how the Obama Administration has framed US cyber security policy. The Obama administration is clear in its 2011 *Cyber space Policy Review* that, "It is the fundamental responsibility of our government to address strategic vulnerabilities in cyber space and ensure that the United States and the world realize the full potential of the information technology revolution." This means that, "The United States must signal to the world that it is serious about addressing this challenge with strong leadership and vision." To be clear, the US is not acting out of some altruistic or benevolent notion of global leadership. US policymakers understand that pooling scarce resources generates economies of scale toward achieving national and global security. Leadership is the catalyst to the multistakeholder processes by which the pooling of scare resources, in this case technical expertise and information sharing accelerates the rate at which national and global cyber security may be achieved.

Global institutions create conditions in which states may cooperate (Keohane 1984). As it stands currently, cyber security institutions remain underdeveloped. Consequently, states are confronted with a security dilemma where cyber arms races and low-level cyber conflict threatens state information technology networks and the stability of cyber space as an open medium for information and economic exchange.

At the time of writing, Iran is now in its 5th week of a concerted cyber campaign against economic and financial assets of the United States, Saudi Arabia, Israel, and other states in response to the use of cyber weapons by the US and Israel with tacit support from Saudi Arab against Iranian nuclear weapons program assets (Gorman 2012). Elements of Russia successfully prosecuted cyber attacks against Estonia in 2007 and Georgia in 2008 driving home the point to policymakers worldwide that cyber is a new domain of conflict. As more states demonstrate their cyber weapons capability, other states recognize their cyber vulnerability and respond by acquiring cyber weapons and cyber defense capability in a perpetual cycle of response and counter-response. Escaping the affects of this security dilemma is possible through the formation of international institutions (Keohane 1984; Keohane and Nye 2001). Hegemonic stability theory describes the role that hegemons may fill in processes by which international institutions are formed.

Hegemonic stability theory is best viewed as school of thought to which international relations scholars from a range of ontological and epistemological backgrounds contribute. The logic of hegemonic stability theory is that, "there can be no liberal international economy unless there is a leader that uses its resources and influence to establish and maintain an international economy based on free trade, monetary stability, and freedom of capital movement" (Gilpin 2001, 99; also see Ikenberry 2011; Kagan 2012; Keohane 1980, 1982; Kindleberger 1973, 1981; Krasner 1976).[2] For my purposes, hegemony refers to absolute and relative power preponderance such that there is one state that sets the terms for conflict and cooperation among all other states. On the view of David Lake, hegemonic stability theory is "a research program composed of two, analytically distinct theories. *Leadership theory* builds upon the theory of public goods and focuses on the production of international stability" while "*Hegemony theory* seeks to explain patterns of international economic openness" by focusing on how dominant states impose the norms and rules of the international economic order (Lake 1993, 460). Describing hegemonic stability theory in this manner has the advantage of conceptual clarity but overlooks instances when patterns of international economic openness are expanded in the global political economy through a combination of hegemony and leadership.

Significantly, Keohane (1984) cautions that hegemony is not a necessary condition for cooperation among states, however, Keohane (1980) previously noted that cooperation could occur under conditions of hegemony. Indeed, it may be to the advantage of hegemons to foster and participate in cooperation among actors for the purpose of creating conditions where other actors bandwagon with the hegemon's desired policy preferences, thereby lending an air of legitimacy to hegemony. The influence of hegemony may be sustained through cooperation, which speaks to an inconvenient and persistent puzzle for international relations: the resiliency of US preponderant power, notwithstanding predictions that the US is in relative decline (Stone et al. 2008). Others have noted that US power is crucial to sustaining

[2] Important critiques of hegemonic stability theory include Conybeare (1983), Lake (1983), Snidal (1985), Milner (1998).

the extant liberal international economic order (Clark 2009; Duedeny and Ikenberry 1999; Ikenberry 2011; Lake 2011; Norrloff 2010). Ruggie (1983) demonstrates how liberalism became embedded in the international economic order by virtue of US power shortly after the close of World War II. According to Gilpin (2001), there is extensive empirical support developed by economists showing that the global economic order functions most efficiently when a dominant power enforces norms and rules that govern economic exchange. What strategy should hegemons purse to enforce global norms and rules? Destradi (2010) provides a useful analysis that sharpens the conceptual distinctions between the strategies of empire, hegemony, and leadership. Accounting for available power resources to US policymakers, the social purpose for the Internet, and, hence, the cyber domain as envisaged by US policymakers in a transnational and hierarchically ordered international system, Destradi's framework offers a path that illuminate a US cyber security strategy at the systemic level that compliments deterrence theory at the level of the state. A brief overview of Destradi's framework seems prudent at this point.

Destradi (2010) is primarily concerned with examining strategies that rising powers such as China, India, or Brazil, may pursue at the regional level of international politics. I apply Destradi's ideal-type to the systemic level to show three possible strategies that US policymakers could pursue in cyber space, a new domain or region of conflict and cooperation among states. States pursuing a strategy of empire are wholly concerned with national interest and security in an anarchical condition employing hard power through the application of military force and threat to achieve desired outcomes (Ibid.) Imperial powers seek to dominate and impose outcomes on other states. In contrast to empire, and the contrast is, admittedly, "subtle," states pursuing a strategy of hegemony employ tactics that range "from the exertion of pressure to the provision of material incentives, up to the discursive propagation of the hegemon's norms and values" (Destradi 2010, 912–913). The difference between hegemony and leadership is that outcomes always reflect the hegemons goals (Idid.). In pursuing a strategy of leadership, dominant states use soft power to lead other states to engage in a process whereby states negotiate and renegotiate their common policy goals. Soft power has been defined as "getting others to want the outcomes you want" (Nye 2004, 5; Destradi 2010). Soft power is effective when states share values and "the attraction to shared values and the justness and duty of contributing to the achievement of those values" shapes the preferences of states to support the leading role that the hegemon fills in the processes of negotiation and renegotiation of common policy goals (Nye 2004, 7; Destradi 2010). Keohane (1982), Ikenberry (2011), and Ruggie (1983) have independently shown that US policymakers chose to pursue a strategy of leadership in the post-World War II era rather than a strategy of hegemony or empire by cooperating with other states to forge shared values for a liberal international economic order that included limits on US power imposed through international institutions and regimes.

In his seminal work on power in international relations, Nye argues that, "it is a mistake to think of power—the ability to affect others to obtain preferred outcomes—simply as 'power over' rather than 'power with' others" Nye (2011b, 90). The United States leads a collective hegemony comprised of advanced industrialized democracies that coordinate and enforce the norms and rules institutionalized within the, present, liberal international economic order for the purpose of governing the global political economy. Stone et al. (2008) lend support to this view, finding that leading states will form coalitions for the purpose of forging new institutions rather than resort to using hegemonic power to impose new institutions. That is, leading states will persuade others to pool power in an effort to address issues affecting the stability of the extent liberal international economic order. The liberal "international [economic] order is a global public good—something everyone can consume without diminishing its availability to others" and that as the largest consumer of international economic order, the US must take the lead to ensure its continued provision "because of the difficulties of organizing collective action when large numbers are involved" (Nye 2002, 239–240). As the largest consumer of the international economic order, the US has a vested interest in its stability and continued provision and given that the cyber domain is and will increasingly be a critical part of the international economic order, the US has a vested interest in ensuring that the cyber domain is secure. Not strictly in the sense of protecting sensitive political, economic, or national security information from theft or preventing the loss of control of critical SCADA software that operate the nation's power grid, water supply, or transportation systems—all are critical aspects of a comprehensive cyber security policy; but, more broadly, in the sense of *keeping the cyber lanes of communication and commerce open.*

Indeed, as the liberal international economic order becomes more reliant on global electronic commerce and information exchange, think cloud computing married with smart phone and tablet based computing, communication, and media convergence all combining to plug ever increasing numbers of consumers into the global political economy, keeping the cyber lanes of communication and commerce open will be as critical to the future stability of the liberal international economic order as has been keeping international sea-lanes of communication and commerce open. Cyber space, as a medium for global information and economic exchange, is a global public good requiring leadership to avoid the Balkanization of the domain. US leadership in cyber space is not without precedent having been decisive establishing cyber space as an open medium for international trade by persuading other state actors to pool power to ensure that the Internet is protected under by World Trade Organization (WTO) as a duty-free trade zone (Kiggins 2011). US cyber security policy must evolve into a more comprehensive posture that combines deterrence with global governance. I now turn to transnational cyber security as a global governance issue.

5 Cyber Security as a Global Governance Issue

Global governance, in the post-Cold War era, grew into a site of scholarship, analysis, and policymaking as a response to the perceived exigencies attendant to globalization of information and economic exchange. Global governance is an essentially contested term with multiple meanings and definitions (Dingwerth and Pattberg 2006; Finkelstein 1995; Gilpin 2002; Held and McGrew 2002; Rosenau 1995). One widely used definition views, "global governance is conceived to include systems of rule at all levels of human activity—from the family to the international organization—in which the pursuit of goals through the exercise of controls has transnational repercussions" (Rosenau 1995, 13). The problem with this definition twofold: 1) the definition is broad, global governance could "be virtually anything" (Finkelstein 1995, 368); 2) Rosenau's definition ignores how power may influence which norms ultimately structure global governance institutions (Gilpin 2001). Held and McGrew (2002) argue that the debate over what is the definition of global governance reflects the ongoing debate about the role and efficacy of the state in an era characterized by globalization of information and economic exchange. Cyber space is terrain on which the contestation over norms that govern the role of the state in global political economy comes to a head through merging transnational politics of information exchange, economic exchange, and security. Cooperation continues among states in governance of transnational information exchange, economic exchange, and security.

Information exchange occurring through cyber space traverses geographic space administered by states. States exist by virtue of mutual agreement among peers on the meaning of sovereignty. States are sovereign in that exclusive right to use force to coerce is reserved to the apparatuses of states within a specified and mutually recognized geographic space or territory. Within each state, disparate regulatory traditions have developed over time that govern information exchange, economic exchange, and use of force to achieve security (Hart 1988; Zacher 2002). As information and economic exchange have globalized through digitalization, first with the printed word, then the telegraph, followed by computer network and satellite assisted voice and data transmissions, states have been compelled to cooperate to ensure that differences in the treatment of information and economic exchange by disparate regulatory traditions does not impede the global flow of information, goods, and services (Zacher 1996). For example, states cooperated in the governance of information exchange by forming the International Telecommunications Union as a global governance institution charged with universalizing technical standards and regulations to facilitate reliable, quick, and efficient information exchange (Mueller and Thompson 2004; Rauen et al. 2011).

Similarly, in the realm of economic exchange, states cooperate in order to achieve market efficiencies and absolute gains from trade (as opposed to relative gains, where my loss is your gain). During the post-World War Two era, regional and global multistakeholder coalitions have formed to promote a more open global trade system consistent with the principle of international economic openness supported and sustained by hegemony. For example, the General Agreement on tariffs and Trade (GATT) was formed in 1948 to promote fair treatment of goods and services exchanged among member states. In 1994, GATT was folded into the World Trade Organization (WTO), the current global governance institution that mediates trade disputes among member states and provides a forum in which cooperation among states produces the norms and rules that govern global economic exchange.

At the regional level, the European Union, a customs union where tariffs have been eliminated on goods and services exchanged among member states, exemplifies what can be accomplished among states motivated to cooperate in the realm of economic exchange. Cyber space has been repurposed in the post-Cold War era as a domain for economic exchange being treated as a duty-free trade zone under WTO agreements (Kiggins 2011). From the view of US policymakers, and open global trade system is essential to global peace and prosperity and US policymakers have promoted global trade cooperation among states in order to achieve this aim (Bacevich 2002; Beard 1934; Ikenberry 2011; Layne 2006; Williams 1972).

States routinely cooperate within the issue area of transnational security having formed the United Nations to promote collective security globally and, at the regional level, formed alliances such as the North Atlantic Treaty Organization (NATO) to promote regional security. In my view, what sets apart the transnational issue areas of information exchange and economic exchange from that of cyber security is a lack of inertia among states to cooperate, to coordinate global governance, on the issue of cyber security. It is here that US power, exercised by leading other states to form a multistakeholder coalition for the purpose of promoting transnational cyber security norms could prove decisive at forming global governance structures within the issue area of transnational cyber security. US policymakers should aggressively pursue opportunities to persuade other states to accept and partner with the US in promoting cyber security norms that enhance threat credibility and clarify retaliation threshold. Within the transnational issue areas of information exchange and economic exchange, US power has proved decisive at ensuring governance institutions within each issue area reflect the norm of openness—long promoted, defended, and expanded through US led hegemony in the post-WWII era. The role of leadership in global governance is to promote and protect the constitutive rules (openness) that shape the regulative rules (cyber attack threshold, use of force, form of punishment) of global regimes.

Leading other actors in the formation and operation of a multistakeholder cyber security coalition includes the addressing the following tasks. First, international cooperation could be leveraged to develop a cyber weapons non-proliferation regime. This would have the effect of limiting the number of cyber threats to which a state must develop counter measures. Second, increased cooperation on cyber security could pool resources and capabilities in an effort to overcome the problem of attribution. This would have the effect of distributing costs associated with overcoming technical hurdles among participants. Third, cooperation is needed among states to develop consensus on a norm or set of norms that govern the sharing of information, arrest, extradition, and prosecution of criminal acts in cyber space. Crimes committed in cyber space often cross international borders, criminals may be located in one country while committing fraud or theft in another country through cyber space. Combined, three and four would have the effect of mitigating the problem of attribution and strengthening threat credibility issued by state actors. Fifth, US policymakers need to determine specific criteria for retaliation to cyber attacks so that US power in cyber space can be demonstrated as a credible deterrent. Threatening to send a missile down a smoke stack is a far cry from actually doing so.

In the end, perhaps the collective vulnerability of states in cyber space will contribute to the balkanization of the domain into disparate networks in which norms for identifying users and granting of network privileges is conducted by a coordinated network administrator behind a virtual, heavily fortified, and defended wall. Indeed, an outcome to the formation of a US led cyber security multistakeholder coalition may be just that, increased state control. This risk aside, in the absence of leadership that protects and promotes the Internet as an open domain, ensures cyber security cooperation reflects this normative and social purpose for the Internet, and leverages international institutions to teach states which norms to follow in global governance of cyber space (see Finnemore 1996), the Internet as it is known and experienced today, may cease to function as an open medium for global information and economic exchange; likely succumbing to the necessity of achieving cyber security through exerting absolute state control over the domain. Ironically, US hegemonic power, exercised through leadership, may be the best hope for preserving an open Internet, for keeping the cyber lanes of communication and commerce open.

6 Conclusion

This chapter has argued that US cyber security may best be achieved through the formulation of a more comprehensive cyber security policy that combines deterrence theory with leadership theory as described in hegemonic stability theory. A more comprehensive cyber security policy takes into account the transnational nature and social purpose of the Internet in the post-Cold War era in addition to the requirement to inflict punishment on cyber attackers as a deterrent to future cyber attacks. The social purpose of the Internet in the post-Cold War era is to serve as an open medium for global information and economic exchange and the growth in information flows and electronic commerce bear this out. The advantage of deterrence theory is to be found in its logical coherence, which affords policymakers a simple and easily explained framework for cyber security. A deterrence theory based cyber security policy is challenging given that threat credibility is undermined by the lack of technical capability to attribute cyber attacks and the lack of a clear threshold that stipulates the form of retaliation. In addition, deterrence theory elides the very transnational nature of cyber space where the domain is confronted by disparate regulatory traditions and approaches to security across states. Hegemonic stability theory offers a systemic level policy approach that compliments deterrence theory by taking into account the transnational nature of cyber space and proposing that, through leadership, a multistakeholder cyber security coalition could be formed in an effort to produce consensus concerning global cyber security norms that would govern cyber weapon proliferation, cyber crime investigation and punishment, and shared costs for overcoming the problem of attribution making deterrence more effective through strengthening threat credibility. The risk associated with forming a US led multistakeholder cyber security coalition is balkanization of the Internet into chunks of cyber space more easily controlled by states in order to achieve security balanced against keeping the cyber lanes of communication and commerce open within the multistakeholder coalition. Ironically, it may be US hegemony that offers the best hope for keeping cyber space open, stable, and secure.

References

Abbate, J. (2000). *Inventing the Internet*. Cambridge: MIT press.

Achen, C. H., & Snidal, D. (1989). Rational deterrence theory and comparative case studies. *World Politics, 41*(2), 143–169.

Adams, J. (1998). *The next world war: Computers are the weapons and front line is everywhere*. New York: Simon and Schuster.

Adas, M. (2006). *Dominance by design: Technological imperatives and America's civilizing mission*. Cambridge: Belknap Press of Harvard University Press.

Antonova, S. (2008). *Powerscape of internet governance: How was global multistakeholderism invented in ICANN?*. Saarbruken: VDM Verlag Dr. Mueller Aktiengesellschaft & Co. KG.

Armistead, L. (2010). *Information operations matters: Best practices* (1st ed.). Washington, DC: Potomac Books.

Bacevich, A. J. (2002). *American empire: The realities and consequences of U.S diplomacy*. Cambridge: Harvard University Press.

Beard, C. A. (1934). *The idea of national interest*. New York: The MacMillan Co.

Broad, W. J., Markoff, J., Sanger, D. E. (2011). Israeli Test on Worm Called Crucial in Iran Nuclear Delay. *The New York Times*. http://www.nytimes.com/2011/01/16/. world/middleeast /16stuxnet.html?pagewanted = all&_r = 0. Accessed 12 Dec 2012.

Castells, M. (1996). *The rise of the network society*. Cambridge: Blackwell Publishers.

Castells, M., & United Nations Research Institute for Social Development. (1999). *Information technology, globalization and social development*. Geneva: United Nations Research Institute for Social Development.

Cimbala, S. J. (2011). Nuclear Crisis Management and "Cyberwar" Phishing for Trouble?. *Strategic studies quarterly* (Spring), pp. 117–131.

Clark, I. (2009). Bringing hegemony back in: The United States and international order. *International Affairs, 85*(1), 23–36.

Clarke, R. A., & Knake, R. (2010). *Cyber war: The next threat to national security and what to do about it*. New York: Ecco/Harper Collin.

Conybeare, J. A. C. (1983). Tariff protection in developed and developing countries: A cross-sectional and longitudinal analysis. *International Organization, 37*, 441–463.

Crosston, M. D. (2011). World Gone Cyber MAD: How 'Mutually Assured Debilitation' Is the Best Hope for Cyber Deterrence. *Strategic studies quarterly* (Spring), pp. 100–116.

Deibert, R., & Rohozinski, R. (2010). Under cover of the net: The hidden governance mechanisms of cyber space. In A. L. Clunan & H. A. Trinkunas (Eds.), *Ungoverned spaces: Alternatives to state authority in an era of softened sovereignty* (pp. 255–272). Palo Alto: Stanford University Press.

Demchak, C. C. & Dombrowski, P. (2011). Rise of a cybered westphalian age. *Strategic studies quarterly* (Spring), pp. 32–61.

Destradi, S. (2010). Regional powers and their strategies: empire, hegemony, and leadership. *Review of International Studies, 36*, 903–930.

Deudney, D., & Ikenberry, G. J. (1999). The nature and sources of liberal international order. *Review of International Studies, 25*(2), 179–196.

Dingwerth, K., & Pattberg, P. (2006). Global governance as a perspective on world politics. *Global Governance, 12*, 185–203.

Enright, A. (2011). Global e-Commerce to Reach $1.4 Trillion in 2015. *International marketing*. http://www.internetretailer.com/2011/06/07/global-e-commerce-reach-14-trillion-2015. Accessed 30 Oct 2012.

Fearon, J. (2002). Selection effects and deterrence. *International Interactions, 28*(1), 5–29.

Finkelstein, L. S. (1995). What is global governance? *Global Governance, 1*, 367–372.

Finnemore, M. (1996). *National interests in international society*. Ithaca: Cornell University Press.

Gerstein, D. M. (2005). *Securing America's future: National strategy in the information age*. Westport: Praeger Security International.

Gilpin, R. (2001). *Global political economy: Understanding the global economic order*. Princeton: Princeton University Press.

Gilpin, R. (2002). A realist perspective on international governance. In D. A. M. Held (Ed.), *Governing globalization: Power, authority, and global governance* (pp. 237–248). Cambridge: Polity.

Gorman, S. & Barnes, J. E. (2011). Cyber combat: Act of war. *Wall Street Journal*. http://online.wsj.com/article/SB10001424052702304563104576355623135782718.html. Accessed 29 Oct 2012.

Hart, J. A. (1988). The politics of global competition in the telecommunications industry. *The Information Society, 5*(3), 169–201.

Harvey, F. P. (1998). Rigor mortis or rigor, more tests: Necessity, sufficiency, and deterrence logic". *International Studies Quarterly, 42*(4), 675–707.

Held, D. & McGrew, A. G. (2002). *Governing globalization: Power, authority and global governance*. Cambridge: Polity.

Huth, P., & Russett, B. (1984). What makes deterrence work? Cases from 1900 to 1980. *World Politics, 36*(July), 496–526.

Huth, P. & Russett, B. (1993). General deterrence between enduring rivals: Testing three competing models. *American Political Science Review, 87*, 61–73.

Huth, P. K. (1999). Deterrence and international conflict: Empirical findings and theoretical debates. *Annual Review of Political Science, 2*(1), 25–48.

Ikenberry, G. J. (2011). *Liberal leviathan: The origins, crisis, and transformation of the American world order*. Princeton: Princeton University Press.

Jervis, R. (1998). The utility of nuclear deterrence. *International Security, 13*(2), 80–90.

Jervis, R. (1989). Rational deterrence theory: Theory and evidence. *World Politics, 61*(January), 183–207.

Kagan, R. (2012). *The world America made*. New York: Alfred A. Knopf.

Katin-Borland, N. (2012). Cyberwar: A real and growing threat. In S. S. Costigan & J. Perry (Eds.), *Cyber spaces and global affairs* (pp. 3–22). London: Ashgate.

Keohane, R. O. (1980). The theory of hegemonic stability and changes in international economic regimes, 1967–77. In O. R. Holsti, R. M. Siverson, & A. L. George (Eds.), *Change in the international system* (pp. 131–162). Boulder: West View Press.

Keohane, R. O. (1982). Hegemonic leadership and U.S. Foreign economic policy. In W. P., Avery, & D. P., Rapkin (Eds.), *America in a changing world political economy* (pp. 49–76). New York: Longman.

Keohane, R. O. (1984). *After hegemony: Cooperation and discord in the world political economy*. Princeton: Princeton University Press.

Keohane, R. O., & Nye, J. S. (2001). *Power and interdependence* (3rd ed.). New York: Longman.

Kiggins, R. D. (2011). Wired world: US policy and the open door internet. Dissertation, University of Florida, Gainesville.

Kindleberger, C. P. (1973). *The world in depression, 1929–1939*. Boston: Little Brown.

Kindleberger, C. P. (1981). Dominance and leadership in the international economy. *International Studies Quarterly, 25*(June), 242–254.

Krasner, S. D. (1976). State power and the structure of international trade. *World Politics, 28*, 317–347.

Kugler, R. L. (2009). Deterrence of cyber attacks. In F. D. Kramer, S. H. Starr, & L. K. Wentz (Eds.), *Cyber power and national security* (pp. 309–340). Washington: NDU Press.

Lake, D. A. (1983). International economic structures and American foreign policy, 1887–1934. *World Politics, 35*, 687–713.
Lake, D. A. (1993). Leadership, hegemony, and the international economy: Naked emperor or tattered monarch with potential? *International Studies Quarterly, 37*(4), 459–489.
Lake, D. A. (2011). Dominance and subordination in world politics: Authority, liberalism, and stability in the modern international order. In *Prepared for the Author's workshop on the 30th anniversary of Robert Gilpin's war and change in world politics*. Princeton University, Princeton, Oct 27–29, 2011. http://weber.ucsd.edu/~dlake/papers.html. Accessed 12 Dec 2012.
Layne, C. (1998). Rethinking American grand strategy; hegemony or balance of power in the twenty-first century? *World Policy Journal* (Summer), *15*, 8–28.
Layne, C. (2006). *The peace of illusions: American grand strategy from 1940 to the present*. Ithaca: Cornell University Press.
Lebow, R. N. (2009) The golden age of deterrence theory. *The Routledge Handbook of Security Studies, 5*, 393–398.
Lebow, R. N., & Stein, J. G. (1989). Rational deterrence theory: I think. *Therefore I Deter. World Politics, 61*(January), 208–224.
Libicki, M. C. (2007). *Conquest in cyber space: national security and information warfare*. New York: Cambridge University Press.
Libicki, M. C. (2009). *Cyberdeterrence and cyberwar*. Santa Monica: RAND Corporation.
Libicki, M. C. (2011). Cyberwar as a confidence game. *Strategic Studies Quarterly* (Spring), *5*, 132–146.
Mann, C. L., & Kirkegaard, J. F. (2006). *Accelerating the globalization of America: the role for information technology*. Washington: Institute for International Economics.
McCarthy, D. R. (2011). Open networks and the open door: American foreign policy and the narration of the internet. *Foreign Policy Analysis, 7*(1), 88–111.
Milner, H. V. (1998). International political economy: Beyond hegemonic stability. *Foreign Policy, 110*(Spring), 112–123.
Morgan, P. M. (2012a). *1983. Deterrence: A conceptual analysis* (rev ed.). Beverly Hills: Sage Publications.
Morgan, P. M. (2012b). *1983. Deterrence: A conceptual analysis* (rev ed.). Beverly Hills: Sage Publications.
Morgan, P. M. (2012b). The state of deterrence in international politics today. *Contemporary Security Policy, 33*(1), 85–107.
Mueller, M., & Thompson, D. (2004). ICANN and intelsat: Global communication technologies and their incorporation into international regimes. In S. Braman (Ed.), *The emergent global information policy regime* (pp. 62–85). New York: Palgrave/Macmillan.
Nakashima, E. (2012). U.S. Accelerating Cyberweapon Research. *The Washington Post*. http://articles.washingtonpost.com/2012-03-18/world/35447948_1_military-weapons-air-defense-target-system. Accessed 12 Dec 2012.
Norrloff, C. (2010). *America's global advantage: US hegemony and international cooperation*. New York: Cambridge University Press.
Nye, J. S, Jr. (2002). The American national interest and global public goods. *International Affairs, 78*(2), 233–244.
Nye, J. S, Jr. (2004). *Soft power: The means to success in world politics*. New York: Public Affairs.
Nye, J. S, Jr. (2011a). *The future of power*. New York: Public Affairs.
Nye, J. S., Jr. (2011b). Nuclear lessons for cyber security. *Strategic Studies Quarterly* (Winter), *4*, 18–28.
Osborne, C. (2012). Cybercrime costs U.S. Consumers $20.7 billion. *CNet News*. http://news.cnet.com/8301-1009_3-57506216-83/cybercrime-costs-u.s-consumers-$20.7-billion/. Accessed 26 Oct 2012.
Rattray, G. J. (2001). *Strategic warfare in cyber space*. Cambridge: The MIT Press.
Rauen, C. V., Hiratuka, C., & Fracalanza, P. S. (2011). Universalization of telecommunications services: Public policies in the OECD and in Brazil. *International Journal of Development Issues, 10*(2), 108–122.

Rogin, J. (2012). NSA Chief: Cybercrime constitutes the greatest transfer of wealth in history. http://thecable.foreignpolicy.com/posts/2012/07/09/nsa_chief_cybercrime_constitutes_the_greatest_transfer_of_wealth_in_history. Accessed 8 Oct 2012.
Rosenau, J. N. (1995). Governance in the twenty-first century. *Global Governance, 1*, 13–43.
Ruggie, J. G. (1983). International regimes, transactions, and change: embedded liberalism in the postwar economic order. In S. D. Krasner (Ed.), *International regimes*. Ithaca: Cornell University Press.
Schelling, T. C. (1980). *The strategy of conflict*. Cambridge: Harvard University Press.
Singh, J. P. (2010). Negotiating internet governance: Security implications of multilateral approaches. In A. L. Clunan & H. A. Trinkunas (Eds.), *Ungoverned spaces: Alternatives to state authority in an era of softened sovereignty* (pp. 232–254). Palo Alto: Stanford University Press.
Snidal, Duncan. (1985). The limits of hegemonic stability theory. *International Organization, 39*(4), 579–614.
Sterner, E. (2011). Retaliatory deterrence in cyber space. *Strategic Studies Quarterly* (Spring), *5*, 62–80.
Stone, R. W., Slantchev, B. L., & London, T. R. (2008). Choosing how to cooperate: A repeated public-goods model of international relations. *International Studies Quarterly, 52*, 335–362.
Schwartz, M. J. (2012). Cybercrime attacks, costs escalating. *Information Week*. http://www.informationweek.com/security/attacks/cybercrime-attacks-costs-escalating/ 240008658. Accessed 8 Oct 2012.
Stoll, C. (1990). *The cuckoo's egg*. New York: Pocket Books.
Taipale, K. A. (2009). Cyber-deterrence. Available at SSRN: http://ssrn.com/abstract=1336045. Last accessed, 23 July 2013.
Verton, D. (2003). *Black ice: The invisible threat of cyber-terrorism*. New York: McGraw-Hill/Osborne.
Waltz, K. (1959). *Man, the state and war: A theoretical analysis*. New York: Columbia University Press.
Weimann, G. (2006). *Terror on the internet: The new arena, the new challenges*. Washington, DC: United States Institute of Peace Press.
Williams, W. A. (1959) 1972. *The tragedy of American diplomacy*. 2d rev. and enl. ed. New York: Dell Pub. Co.
Zacher, M. W. (2002). Capitalism, technology, and liberalization: The international telecommunications regime, 1865–1998. In J. N. Rosenau & J. P. Singh (Eds.), *Information technologies and global politics: The changing scope of power and governance* (pp. 189–210). New York: SUNY Press.
Zacher, M. W., & Sutton, B. A. (1996). Mutual interests, normative continuities, and regime theory: Cooperation in international transportation and communications industries. *European Journal of International Relations, 2*(1), 5–46.

Hierarchies in Networks: Emerging Hybrids of Networks and Hierarchies for Producing Internet Security

Andreas Schmidt

Abstract Networked governance is the default modus operandi in Internet governance. Even the provisioning of Internet security heavily relies on non-hierarchical, networked forms of organisation. Responses to large-scale botnets show the prevalence of networked governance and provide insight into its strengths and limitations. Networked governance can be defined as a semi-permanent, voluntary negotiation system that allows interdependent actors to opt for collaboration or unilateral action in the absence of an overarching authority. This chapter analyses the ability of traditional powerful actors such as state authorities and large enterprises to provide Internet security and exert power in the cyber-domain. The chapter outlines potential anchor points for traditional powerful actors to introduce more elements of hierarchy and control into Internet security provisioning networks. Empirically, the chapter describes emerging hybrids of networks and hierarchies in Internet security provisioning.

A. Schmidt (✉)
Delft University of Technology, Delft, The Netherlands
e-mail: a.schmidt@tudelft.nl

J.-F. Kremer and B. Müller (eds.), *Cyberspace and International Relations*,
DOI: 10.1007/978-3-642-37481-4_11, © Springer-Verlag Berlin Heidelberg 2014

1 Introduction

Empirical research has shown the prevalence of networked governance in Internet security provisioning institutions (Mueller et al. 2013). The characteristics of current Internet security problems, the global distribution of both attacking resources and those needed for responding to security incidents require a networked approach. In recent years, however, discussions on Internet security do no longer only engage technical forums, but also G8 meetings and international conferences of senior policy-makers. Internet security has become a concern of national security politics. One can therefore hypothesize that state authorities attempt to achieve more important, if not pivotal roles in Internet security. Given the distributed control over decisive technical resources, states cannot merely incorporate the tasks of existing security networks into the portfolio of their bureaucracies.

The existing international relations literature (Eilstrup-Sangiovanni 2007; Raustiala 2002 and Slaughter 1997, 2004) has not adequately explored the interplay of networks and hierarchies in the domain of Internet and information security. Likewise have literatures on networked organisation and security and policing studies so far ignored the issues of governance of the Internet and its security (Bryden and Caparini 2006 and Krahmann 2005, 2010). This chapter is therefore concerned with the question how traditional powerful actors could theoretically and do practically alter existing networked forms of Internet security provisioning.

This chapter is organised as follows. The first part analyses hierarchies within networks from a theoretical perspective. It starts with a section on models of security provisioning, in which networked security is presented as but one way of providing security. The second section of the theoretical part discusses how networks can be altered by traditional powerful actors to the latter's advantage. The second part of the chapter is devoted to some empirics in Internet security provisioning. The chapter argues that in anti-botnet response endeavours a relatively egalitarian network of actors is replaced by networked approaches with increasingly hierarchical elements. Two subsequent empirical sections depict the arguable rapprochement between national security communities and Internet security communities. The chapter concludes with a call for a more in-depth analysis of both theoretical and empirical aspects of hierarchisation of networks.

2 Security, Networks and Hierarchies in International Relations

2.1 Models of International Security

Different degrees in hierarchies in security governance have been a classic topic in the studies of international relations. Starting from the idea of international anarchy—an unregulated sphere among rivalling, potentially aggressive nation states—, international relations theory has come up with several models to explain the absence of war. Prominent ideal-type systems for international security[1] are balance-of-power relations, collective security, hegemonic peace, and international regimes. This list needs to be supplemented by networked security.

Based on the construct of international anarchy, balance-of-power is the first model to provide a secure international sphere, albeit in a precarious manner. In an assumed world, in which individual actors, i.e. states, are not restrained and civilized by institutional means such as global hierarchy, a benevolent hegemon, international cooperation or regimes, states are incentivized to maximise their influence and are even compelled to behave aggressively and therefore increase the insecurity for their peer contenders in the international arena. The ominous international anarchy forces individual states into building up their own defence, response and attack capacities. At best, the capacity build-up results in a durable balance of power, in which no state dares to deploy its forceful means for the fear of a harmful retaliation of attacked and by-standing actors. Mutually assured destruction is the most vicious form of a stable balance-of-power formation.

Contrasting the balance-of-power model in terms of organisational precision is the collective security model, in which threats for states emerging from other states are mitigated by the establishment of regional or global authorities responsible for protecting international peace. The League of Nations and the United Nations have implemented a federated variant of this idea. The centralised version of collective security model has been outlined by Grenville Clark and Louis Sohn in their book *World Peace Through World Law,* a concept of a world government with coercive authority, a kind of super-empowered UN with substantial executive forces to overcome the governance problem created by the invention of nuclear and hydrogen bombs (Clark and Sohn 1958).

Endowed with a more exclusive decision making body and coercive authority on a scale similar to a collective security system of agreeing states, is the hegemonic state. Ideally, the hegemon amasses power second to none, choses to only exert it by and large in benevolent ways and thereby acts as the guarantor of a hopefully just and peaceful existing order. Third states that oppose this order may face the forceful response of the hegemon, while aligned states are protected by the hegemon against attacks from third parties. The price for enjoying this gift of stable order in addition their required support for the hegemon, however is to endure the shortcomings of the existing order. The "benevolent hegemon"—a role frequently attributed to the United States after the end of US-Soviet conflict—ensures global security and prosperity as global public goods (Mandelbaum 2006; Nye 1990). Using the concepts of institutional economic theory, a state's hegemony establishes a "hierarchy between polities [that] reduces transaction costs and mitigates opportunism" (Lake 2009, p. 275).

The fourth fundamental way to ensure a peaceful international order mixes some of the characteristics of the previously described approaches. Lacking stable

[1] International security is here used in its narrow sense as the absence of violent conflict in contrast to e.g. the broader Galtungian notion of international peace as the absence of structural violence.

orders provided by the models of collective security or hegemonic peace, states can still reduce their mutual distrust that could eventually result in an arms race and thus spiralling societal cost for security provisioning. By engaging in international cooperation and establishing international regimes and norms, states can manage to balance their security interests, reduce mutual distrust and establish an international order that does not resemble a zero-sum game. For many international issues, the various forms of international regimes are the default organisational form of international problem solving.

Resembling international regimes, networks in various forms have entered the sphere of global politics as an organisational form.[2] The concept of transgovernmental networks reflects the widening and deepening of international collaboration and intensification of communication at medium and lower level of hierarchies in national bureaucracies. These TGNs manage to produce outcomes beneficial to the states involved. During the last decade, security and policing studies have observed a diversification of how security is provided, away from the state as the sole provider of public security towards a system where the state is supplemented by private actors such as security services and mercenaries. In national security circles, the term "networked security" refers to "loose institutional arrangements and non-hierarchical structures of information exchange" (Gruszczak 2008) that are established e.g. in anti-terrorism activities or to re-establish security in formerly failed state such as Afghanistan (Jung 2009). However, the idea of networked governance goes beyond the idea of networks as a governmental tool.

In practice, Internet security is provided in a highly networked way. Anarchy on the Internet has quite likely never existed. Content distributed by it may have been unregulated for while, but the technical integrity and functionality has been ensured by a community of technical experts ever since these risks have become obvious. This collaboration has resulted in a kind of distributed, bottom-up collective security provisioning. As the previous sections have shown, this model is challenged in a number of was.

So far, there is no established and globally accepted cyber hegemon.[3] Not an act to foster cyber-peace, the US has with its apparent involvement in the Stuxnet attacks showcased how attacks on ICT systems with ICT systems can be used in international conflicts to project coercive force on opponent states. On a regional level, Russia might have attempted similar outcomes with its alleged involvement in the cyberattacks on Estonia in 2007 and on Georgia a year later. The cyberattacks on Iran could be interpreted as a move towards cyber hegemony, which would perpetuate the military dominance of the US from the physical to the digital world. Hegemonic cyber-peace would describe a world in which no country would dare to launch cyber attacks against third countries for the fear of retaliation by the

---

[2] An example for networked organisation in the domain of Internet security is the anti-Spam London Action Plan. (Tabatabaie et al. 2012).

[3] This article was written in late 2012, early 2013. An analysis after the PRISM revelations might come to different conclusions

hegemon, who would be legitimized by an adapted international law and optionally authorized by an international body. This model assumes that cyberspace is a potential place for interstate conflicts and to exchange coercive means to bring down opponents. It is arguable whether such cyber hegemony will come into existence in the near future. Nye argues that the US most likely has the most sophisticated attack capabilities, but is on the other hand more vulnerable to cyber attacks than other countries (Nye 2011a).

There is no collective security organisation akin to the UN or the OSCE to balance national security interests in cybersecurity. Warnings about an imminent cyber-arms-race date back almost as long as prophecies of doom brought by forthcoming digital Pearl Harbours, which usually also served as a call for a nation, usually the US, to start or speed up the build-up of cyber defence and attack capabilities (Brito and Watkins 2011; Deibert 2010 and Minkwitz and Schöfbänker 2000). Apparently, these early warnings for a cyber-arms race have been to no avail. Nation states are in the midst of an "[accelerating] global cyber arms race", according to Cybercom's director of intelligence (Benitez 2012). Founder and CEO of security company Kaspersky Lab, Evgeny Kaspersky, has called for a new dedicated organisation. The "International Cyber-Security Organisation" should act as an "independent global platform for international cooperation and treaties on non-usage of cyber-weapons, and cyber-security regulations for critical infrastructures" ("CeBIT 2012: Eugene Kaspersky calls for international cyber-security organisation," 2012).

2.2 *Hierarchies in Networked Security*

The responses to Internet security incidents rely on networks. The question about which forms of organisation emerge when ideal-type forms such as networks and hierarchies merge has been raised by authors such as Steven Weber or David Ronfeldt.[4] Nevertheless, existing networks literature does not provide a detailed look on the relationship between traditional powerful actors, such as states and large corporations, and networked governance in transnational forms of organisation. Likewise, IR literature that embraces networked governance still focuses on governmental and state authorities (Mueller et al. 2013). A number of key questions, e.g. whether the networked approach and the decreased importance of states in Internet security is temporary or permanent, have therefore remained unanswered. This article aims at analysing the relations between hierarchies and networks within the networked approach by (a) developing a model of how traditional powerful actors

[4] Compare Ronfeldts blog entries on Michel Bouwens' concept of the Partner State (http://twotheories.blogspot.com/2011/07/bauwens-partner-state-part-1-of-2-vis.html, http://twotheories.blogspot.com/2011/10/bauwens-partner-state-part-3-of-3-vis.html), and his TIMN framework and emerging hybrid organisational forms (http://twotheories.blogspot.com/2009/06/timn-and-emergence-of-collaborative.html, http://twotheories.blogspot.com/2009/05/organizational-forms-compared-my.html, http://twotheories.blogspot.com/2009/04/uick-comments-one-on-sta-other-on-timn.html).

theoretically interact with inevitable security networks and alter them to their advantage and (b) analyse recent developments in Internet security and their effect on the qualities of Internet security provisioning networks.

Hierarchies can be defined "as a continuum on which one actor has more or less political authority over other actors" (Lake 2009, p. 264). This more political, less sociological conceptualization is closely related to the idea of political authority, which "is most simply understood as rightful or legitimate rule" akin to what can be found within firms, governmental bureaucracies or between governments and citizens (Lake 2009, p. 265). The conceptual lines between political authority and political power are blurry, making them all closely related. Joseph Nye has recently linked power to "behavioural outcomes", defining power as the ability to achieve preferred outcomes by affecting others ("domain") on certain areas ("scope") by coercion, reward, or attraction ("means") (Nye 2011b, p. 21). Despite similarities, hierarchy is not synonymous to power, at least not with Lake's conceptualisation. The difference is that hierarchy refers to an organisational structure that is characterized by institutionalized asymmetric power-relationships between higher positions in the hierarchies and those at lower regions in the hierarchy; in addition, this ability to achieve preferred outcome is deemed legitimate.

There are a number of reasons for a nation state or a national government to alter existing power relations. Incentives for creating a hierarchy could either be nurtured by discontent with the outcomes or efficiencies of a given security provisioning institutions; large corporations might use a less equal network to achieve results that better suit their interests. Hierarchies are a way to decrease transactions costs within a certain institution. Next to this efficiency or effectiveness argument, establishing hierarchy can be seen as the means of an actor to create greater influence on a domain. Much akin to their ability to print money via their central banks, states can create authority, hierarchy and thus power by printing laws, at least in domestic affairs. Major schools of international relations state that states seek or at least would favour to improve their relative power status. With the emergence of security networks and the inevitability of the networked approach in Internet security, states need to react to named institutions that tend to undermine the traditional capacities of states in security governance.

For a nation state that seeks to hierarchify existing global networked security provisioning institutions, there are two ways to achieve this. First, states can alter existing governance networks in a way that grants them more influence or power over other actors.[5] In opposition to earlier normative interpretations of networks as more egalitarian structures, networks can very well have asymmetrically distributed power structures among its members (Kahler 2009). In addition, contrary to initial beliefs, open source software and similar projects for distributed production of intangible goods are now known for substantial levels of hierarchy and authority (Dafermos 2012 and Weber 2004). Authority in these open source production networks has been established by needs for increasing efficiency, ensuring quality, streamlining internal communication and similar means to reduce transaction costs (Dafermos 2012 and Weber 2004).

---

[5] According Joseph Nye, influence is usually used synonymic to power (Nye 2011b, p. 11).

Network theory provides the recipes for actors willing to increase their influence within networks. The centrality of an actor, the number, density and intensity of connections of a network node, e.g. facilitated by seizing a first-mover advantage (Wong and Lake 2009), decide over its power status within the network. This common finding of network studies applies to states in international networks as well (Slaughter 2009, p. 112). Accordingly, her recommendation for US policy is to increase its "capacity for connection, rather the splendid isolation or hegemonic domination" (Slaughter 2009, p. 113). It does not go much beyond these high-level recommendations, though, just as one would expect with an *Foreign Affairs* article.

An obvious prerequisite to gain influence in networks is to be part of them at first. Traditional powerful actors embed themselves into existing networks. This has been happening in the cybercrime area and with police forces and law enforcement. In addition, we have also seen attempts by military and intelligence organisation to liaise with these Internet security communities. The same holds true for large corporations that required the support of the Internet security community after attacks on their systems. To give an example, Siemens has increased its visibility and information sharing with ICT security communities as a result of Stuxnet, and Apple has only recently participated in major conferences of the security community for the first time, abandoning its usual go-it-alone policy after a year with several exposed vulnerabilities of its operation system platform. (Jackson Higgins 2012a, b)

Once actors are a node in Internet security networks, they can start influencing the way these networks operate and thus in the long run alter existing networked security governance models. New combinations of hierarchy and networked approaches are to emerge. An example is the replacement of more egalitarian types of collaboration such as peer-production with hierarchical forms of social production such as crowdsourcing. Malware reverse engineering, a necessity in the response to any major attack on ICT systems, can be co-produced, shared and discussed openly among experts on their security mailing lists. In the crowdsourced variant, a security company would request for input and attempt to create their own contributory network. The difference between open community-based production and crowdsourcing is that the terms of collaboration and production are defined by the platform owner and crowdsourcing party.

Crowdsourcing is but one example of how existing collaborative networks can be altered by actors. Theoretically, any of the defining characteristics of networks can be adjusted and thereby the nature of the network. Networks differ from hierarchies by their different permeability for membership candidates, a more flat and decentralised organisational structure, low degree of legalisation, trust as the ultimate glue between members, a consensus-oriented decision making process, fast and direct flows of communication, and lower set-up costs and time. Furthermore, as empirical accounts of the Conficker response or the Estonian cyberattacks have shown (Schmidt 2012), security incident response networks actually resemble communities that slightly differ from ideal-type networks and come with a unique mix of access criteria, vetting of membership candidates, conflict resolution, decision making, ownership of shared information, and access to community outcomes.

The following table illustrates the differences among hierarchies and networks for a number of criteria.[6]

Criteria	Network	Hierarchy
Membership	More permeable (less so for security networks)	Less permeably
Structure	Decentralised, flat; elements of internal authority	Centralised, hierarchical
Legalisation	Low	High
Unit relations	Trust-based (in security communities, trust is based on keeping rules)	Rule-based
Scope	Narrow	Broad
Decision making	Consensus; slow, complicated; frequent renegotiation	Few; fast
Communication	Fast, efficient; ineffective for repetitive tasks, competing agendas	Slow, constrained, complicated
Scalability	High (low for security networks)	
Set-up costs	Low; hardly no overhead; (medium for trust-based security networks)	High
Set-up time	Low (moderated for trust building)	High
Adaptability	High	Low

The table only depicts ideal types of network and hierarchies. For real-world examples, the characteristics of these criteria of networks and hierarchies might differ. In the case of Internet security response networks, membership and scalability differ form ordinary networks. Individuals with certain functional roles ("with something to bring in").

Response activities are usually driven by distinctive communities or even ad-hoc groups, whose members are part of a wider security network. Instead of altering the norms of existing security communities—communities are cohesive and densely connected nodes (Porter et al. 2009, p. 1086)—hierarchical organisations could try to set up new communities within security networks that follow rules favourable to their own goals. These rules can be enforced by market pressure, rule of law or other leverages. Such altered communities can exist in parallel to existing ones that are characterised by more traditional security community governance norms. Thereby, a national security organisation could more easily control membership and access criteria and other important criteria. Presumably highly important for national security organisations is the proper vetting of the member base. While technology-oriented mailing-list-based communities do not discriminate nationality, those dedicated to national security issues could do so more likely.

The second fundamental strategy is to decrease the importance of existing security provisioning networks. Fundamental strategies to achieve this are the creation of new response technologies, alternative technical and political response institutions.

[6] The content of the table is partly based on (Eilstrup-Sangiovanni 2007, pp. 5–6).

The current state of technology requires a highly decentralized, if not distributed approach. Awareness about the current state of the Internet, the attacks going on, the malware flooding around, require distributed monitoring of networks. Since the emergence of botnet in the early-mid 2000s, capacities to detect and monitor botnets have been increased. So called honeynets or honeypots installed at different segments on the Internet by different parties, give insight into the malware floating around the Internet; appliances installed in the facilities of Internet service and backend providers analyse network traffic and watch out for suspicious patterns not only within single networks, but on the Internet worldwide; the ever close connection and increasing data exchange with operating systems running on end users' machines, allows OS vendors to analyse Internet traffic and to detect malicious content. So far however, these intermediating traffic analysis systems are not controlled by states, let alone a single state.[7] A technological innovation that would support the state's role would first of all decrease the reliance on distributed input from technical experts around the world and allow for a more centralised form of monitoring and problem detection. Once a certain degree of centralisation is achieved, a state would have more hierarchical counterparts whose behaviour could be incentivised to ensure outcomes in the state's favour.

The importance of technological response networks can also be reduced by establishing non technical response institutions to prevent security incidents in the first place, such as deterrence or the establishment of international norms such as state responsibility. The question whether deterrence can be applied to the world of information technology has been a standard topic of Internet security literature. While in the beginning, authors tended to deny the transferability of deterrence mainly because of the alleged impossibility to identify attackers—the so-called attribution problem—the idea to codify more extensive obligations for states to assist each other during incidents has recently gained popularity among pundits. Cold-war wisdom comes to rescue here. Other than frequently stated, the attribution problem, the problem to identify the perpetrators of an attack beyond any doubt, doesn't exclude the build-up of plausible, deterring threats (Healey 2012 and Nye 2011a). "Active response"—a popular topic in recent security discourses—might actually result in an upping of existing deterrence, such as the capability to damage a state's reputation that is allegedly very likely responsible for the attacks (Nye 2011a, pp. 33–34).

3 Hierarchies in Botnet Responses

While the previous sections have delved into theoretical perspectives of hierarchies within networks, the following sections discuss some empirical developments in the area of Internet security provisioning. This section starts with a look

[7] The NSA reportedly has, however, installed traffic analysis systems at major US Internet exchange points. (American Civil Liberties Union 2006).

at the response to the Conficker botnet. Botnets are widely known for their role as a facilitator spam, cybercrime and DDoS attacks. In late 2008, a particularly large botnet plagued networks and computers worldwide. Even more remarkable than the sophisticated attack techniques used by the botnet's malware were the efforts by networks of security experts to respond to and mitigate the problems this botnet posed. The response to the Conficker botnet heavily relied on networked governance in what could pose as an ideal-type form of security provisioning by a networked of relatively equal players and without significant involvement of state authorities (Mueller et al. 2013 and Schmidt 2012).

The response to the Estonian cyberattacks in 2007 relied on a similar bottom-up approach with little involvement of corporate and state hierarchies (Schmidt 2013). Hence, "at least at that moment of Internet history, states played hardly any role in responding to attacks on an infrastructure so densely interwoven into many societal practices, either at the operational or governance level" (Mueller et al. 2013). However, the response to the Conficker botnet was but one ad-hoc effort to mitigate the impact of a botnet, more were to come and a few among them included a more hierarchical elements than the Conficker response. Since 2009, much of the organisational design of the anti-Conficker approach has been reused in other anti-botnet endeavours. In general, we see states attaching themselves to these networks of operators and technical experts and taking roles of varying prominence in these networks. US law enforcement has been particular keen to link up to these technical communities and vice versa. Response activities to post-Conficker botnets such as the DNS Changer scam (von Eitzen 2011), the BredoLab (Schwartz 2010), Mariposa (Kolakowski 2010; Sully and Thompson 2010) and the ZeuS botnets (Lennon 2012) are characterised by an increased role of law enforcement agencies.

The DNS Changer malware was first discovered in 2007. Thc malware intercepts DNS requests made by other software on its host computer and redirects users to illegitimate websites controlled by the DNS Charger gang, where web ads would be served to the visitors. The malware had infected some 4 M computers, and served their users with faked ads from their 350,000 servers, leaving $14 M advertisement costs for their victims (FBI New York Field Office 2011). The DNS Changer Working Group (DCWG) botnet included many of the players of the Conficker Working Group, complemented by a significant role for the FBI and the National Cyber-Forensics & Training Alliance, a non-profit partnership between law enforcement and technical experts from industry and academia. In November 2011, FBI announced its "Operation Ghost Click", which would lead to the seizure of a block of IPv4 addresses by Dutch prosecution authorities on behalf of the FBI. Eventually, a court order temporarily transferred operational control of the domain names used by the DNS Charger gang to one of DCWG's members, the Internet Systems Consortium (ISC). This transfer allowed the DCWG to inform users that their machines had been infected. Other than the Conficker response, the work of the DCWG led to arrests, namely of 6 Estonians and 1 Russian (FBI New York Field Office 2011 and Forward-Looking Threat Research Team 2012).

Bredolab was a significant botnet comprising millions of infected machines until it was dismantled in late 2010. After a weeks-long investigation, Dutch police and prosecution ordered the take down of the command-and-control servers of the Bredolab botnet in October 2010. The technical analysis and operations were seemingly performed by Govcert, Dutch IT security company Fox-IT and the Internet hoster Leaseweb. Police claimed 30 M computers according to the press release issued by the Dutch police Team hight Tech Crime (Openbaar Ministerie 2010), however, these numbers were more likely much lower.[8] The investigation into Bredolab, called "Operation Tolling", was part of a wider campaign against botnets by Dutch authorities. The Dutch police even had a dedicated communications team with the goal to raise awareness of the botnet problem in the wider public (Korps Landelijke Politiediensten 2011). Law scholars, civil society Internet activists, and AV vendors criticised the police for taking over infected machines and sending warning messages to their users.[9]

In late 2010, the Mariposa botnet was brought down by a joint effort of Canadian, Spanish, and US security experts collaborating with the FBI and Guardia Civil (Larraz 2010; Leyden 2010 and Sinha et al. 2010). One of the largest botnets ever, Mariposa consisted of 11 m unique IP addresses over the entire lifespan of the botnet and was used for the usual cybercrime variants, including spam, theft of online credentials, and DDoS attacks (Sully and Thompson 2010). To respond to the Mariposa botnet, the technical community again formed an ad-hoc working group that resembled the Conficker Working Group. The working group was initiated by a small Canadian anti-botnet solution vendor Defence Intelligence and supplemented by Spanish security company Panda Security, network company Neustar, Directi, and by academics of Georgia Tech's Information Security Center, plus a number of unnamed researchers from other institutions. (Sully and Thompson 2010, p. 10) As Defence Intelligence later frankly admitted, they first aimed at turning the detection and analysis of the Mariposa malware into a marketing success. In the course of the response they learned that turning a collective effort into a unilateral marketing success undermines the mutual trust that is required for such international anti-botnet campaigns. Defence Intelligence seemingly wanted to steer the group, but lacked the authority to actually enforce the direction it wanted the group to head into (Sully and Thompson 2010, p. 16). Eventually, the botnet was brought down, the botherders and the developer of the underlying Mariposa software kit arrested.

In spring 2012, a working group lead by Microsoft initiated the seizure of the, as Microsoft stated it, "Zeus botnet" (Boscovich 2012). The consortium was lead by Microsoft's Digital Crimes Unit and supported by the company's Malware Protection Center, the US Financial Services Information Sharing and Analysis

---

[8] Michel van Eeten, a researcher with a long list of publications on quantitative dimensions of malware, estimated some 3 M infected machines. He assumes that the Dutch police did not take into account that temporary assignment of DNS number gives any infected machine several IP addresses over time and that therefore the number of unique IP addresses is not equal to the number of actually infected machines (van Eeten 2010).

[9] "Politie overtrad wet bij oprollen botnet", NU.NL, Oct 28, 2010, http://www.nu.nl/Internet/2366129/politie-overtrad-wet-bij-oprollen-botnet.html.

Center (FS-ISAC) and Electronic Payments Association (NACHA), ICT security company Kyrus Tech Inc, which was responsible for the malware analysis (Krebs 2012), and AV vendor F-Secure. Additional intelligence came from global ISPs and CERTs (Cf. Boscovich 2012). The consortium eventually dismantled a botnet created with Zeus-malware variants Ice-IX and SpyEye (Bijl 2012). Zeus is a malware toolkit, a type of software that miscreants can use to create their own malware and with which they can then create their own botnets (Macdonald and Manky 2010). Microsoft's stated primary goal was to not bring down the botnet entirely, but to primarily "inflict costs on cybercriminals". These goals conflicted with some of the other network partners with more perseverance and an interest in the permanent take down. Some of them e.g. had build up hidden online personae that were then exposed by the texts in the law suit filing. Analyst and blogger Rik Ferguson of AV company Trendmicro pointed at the importance of close collaboration with law enforcement and stated successful collaboration with LE agency requires more time, but leads to more sustainable results (Ferguson 2012). Ferguson blames Microsoft for prematurely exposing identities of perpetrators, thereby severely harming due legal process and the ability to prosecute perpetrators. Dutch ICT security company Fox-IT blamed Microsoft outright of obstructing criminal investigations (Bijl 2012 and de Natris, 2012). Fox-IT labelled Microsoft's "Operation B71" as ineffective, short-sighted, marketing-oriented and as a blow to the established trust and effectiveness of the security community by snubbing the community of using shared information only with the agreement of the sharer.

In general, the networked approach in Internet security mirrors a general trend in policing and security that has been observed in the last two decades, in which the statal monopoly of force has been riddled in a number of areas (Kempa et al. 1999 and Krahmann 2005). State authorities have been relegated to a marginal position or even a virtually non-existing role in the Conficker case. However, the response activities after Conficker appear to have more hierarchical elements than the combined efforts of Conficker Working Group and the global security communities and networks. Reflecting changes in the way how actors responded to Internet security incidents, the altered, more prominent roles of both law enforcement and large companies comes to mind. In the response endeavours after Conficker, state authorities have increasingly embedded themselves into existing response communities of the larger Internet security network. Likewise, large companies have tried to push egalitarian rules of the security community and to take a leading role in these response communities. In the Bredolab case, the Dutch High Tech Crime Team took the driving seat. The most significant changes from an organisational prospective were the takedowns of the Bredolab botnet under the guidance of the Dutch police and Microsoft's blatant breach of community code in the 'ZeuS botnet' takedowns. The number of cases certainly is too small to see a statistical trend in these developments. Qualitatively, it is however significant that some embedded player attempt to design botnet response activities in their own way.

In terms of rhetoric, the rollback of Internet security governance by states is even more apparent. A number of influential policy-makers have called for a built-up of contingency capabilities that would provide public authorities and national security institutions with far-reaching capabilities in the area of surveillance, identification and communication traffic control (Gorman and Barnes 2011; McConnell 2010 and Pear 2012). Unsurprisingly, such political rhetoric makes its way into actual Internet security policies and operations in other, non-botnet areas of Internet security as the subsequent sections demonstrate.

4 Rapprochement of National Security and Technical Security Communities

4.1 The Estonian Cyber Defence League

Incumbent security institutions such as police, military and intelligence agencies have stood on the side-lines of response efforts against infrastructural security incidents for years. Their contribution to mitigating large-scale Internet security incidents such as the Conficker botnet or the Estonian cyber attacks was virtually non-existent. Nevertheless, governments have started to grasp the importance of the global Internet security community for re-establishing the availability and functionality of common Internet-based services in times of attacks. With Internet security moving up to the very top of national political agendas, these communities are slowly becoming a focal point of national cyber-security politics. Estonia spearheaded this trend right after it had lived through its 2007 cyberattacks. One of the consequences the Estonian government drew from the incident was to establish the Estonian Cyber Defence League (CDL).[10]

Far from setting up an operational team of hackers or cyber warriors, the Cyber Defence League creates an organisational umbrella for the otherwise loosely coupled community of technical experts that had saved the Estonian Internet infrastructure from a full-fledged halt in April and May 2007. While the Estonian ministry of defence issued sharp rhetoric after the attacks, its contribution to solving this "national security situation"[11] was marginal. It took days until the Ministry of Defence asked the technical community for a thorough briefing on the situation. In the later days, its task was to exchange information with its foreign peers in Western embassies and capitals. Political circles cried "cyberwar" (Poulsen 2007), but couldn't do anything, while technical circles managed the situation and mitigated the attacks (Davis 2007 and Schmidt 2013).

Not everything was perfect with the response of the Estonian technical community. For one, the Estonian technical community wasn't appropriately connected to

---

[10] For a more extensive analysis of the Estonian cyber-security policies after 2007, cf. (Czosseck et al. 2011). The cyberattacks themselves and the defensive responses to them are described in greater depth in (Schmidt 2013).

[11] Estonian Minister of Defense, Jaak Aaviksso, cited in (Landler and Markoff 2007).

the international networking community, which was needed to mitigate the DDoS attacks. Secondly, the information and communication within the Estonian community was highly centralised and lacking back-up capacities. Had the attackers managed to knock off the central node, the Estonian CERT, the Estonian defence activities would likely have slumped down very soon. Third, high-level members of Estonian ministries were aware of strong indications that Russian communities were planning DDoS attacks on Estonian Internet services (Gomez 2012). Such early warning could have been used to reach out to the Russian government and request assistance to hinder these attacks from happening in the first place.[12] However, the early warning got stuck somewhere in-between the lower and highest ranks of the Estonian ministries (Schmidt 2013).

The CDL establishes an organisational link between Estonia's civil technical community and its military establishment. After the 2007 attacks, the community of Estonian Internet security experts was formalised under the umbrella of the Cyber Defence League in 2009. In 2011, the CDL became part of the Estonian Defence League (DL) as its Cyber Defence Unit (Estonian Ministry of Defence 2011). The Estonian Defence League is an 11,000 persons, all-volunteer paramilitary defence organisation armed with mostly machine guns and antitank weapons. The Defence League was set up after World War I as a response to frequent occupations in the Estonian history and is aimed at guaranteeing national sovereignty. The commander of the DL is appointed by leading Estonian militaries (Estonian Defence League 2010).

The CDL does not act by itself as an independent, authoritative force. If the CDL wanted to, it would have to overrule the links between its technical members and their respective employers or affiliated organisations and break the legal employer-employee relationship. The CDL's members, who are mostly employees of Estonian private and public organisations, would be drafted and had to implement orders of CDL leadership in their employers' infrastructure. Instead, the CDL acts as "coordinator and supervisor of the activity of volunteer cyber protection specialists" and it "would not provide counterforce itself, but would instead act only in an advisory capacity" (Estonian Ministry of Defence 2011). The civilian side of CDL's ambiguous character is represented by its very leadership. The members of the CDL are lead by the same person that also supervises the Estonian CERT and reports to the ministry of economic affairs.

The rationale behind the foundation of the CDL is to "harness… the skills and resources of security specialists and enthusiasts for a constructive purpose" (Ottis 2010). Of the shortcomings of the 2007 response model described above, the organisational form of the Cyber Defence League mainly addresses the vulnerability of the response organisation, in which CERT EE held a central, indispensable role. But not everyone who participated in the 2007 response efforts was pleased with the at least rhetorical paramilitarisation of the Estonian Internet security community, and preferred to not take part in the CDL. The informal beer-and-sauna protocol has been supplemented by paramilitary traditions. Volunteers dedicate their efforts no

[12] Cp. the discussion on state responsibilities for non-state cyberattacks in (Healey 2012).

longer only to "keep the Internet secure"—a frequently mentioned motivation of contributors to the Conficker response in interviews with the author—, but also to help their respective homelands. Internet security has become a national cause.

4.2 Developments in the U.S

The developments in Estonia have not gone unnoticed by those who perceive ICT insecurity as a potential threat for national security. In the US, there have likewise been attempts to establish technical communities and gather security enthusiasts for the national cause. The importance of technical communities is increasingly recognized by national security circles (Gomez 2012; Klimburg 2011 and Lawson and Gehl 2011). The Estonian CDL model, however, is built on institutional, cultural, and historical ground unique to Estonia. In order to achieve an "integrated national cyber capability", Alexander Klimburg argues, these technical experts, if not coerced or co-opted, "must be motivated to cooperate with government aims", and mutual trust needed to be build up among them and governments (Klimburg 2011, p. 55). "Mobilising cyber power", as his article is titled, requires the collaboration of these technical experts. Indeed, infrastructural Internet security requires support of private actors responsible for or operating the various technical systems that eventually make up the global network of networks (Schmidt 2012).

Some of these technical experts have been influenced, if not deeply rooted in what is commonly labelled as Californian ideology, which traditionally is sceptical of governmental authorities. Foreign policy strategists in Washington have faced the need for Silicon Valley's cooperation with the US government once before. New York Times columnist Thomas Friedman expressed the scepticism of U.S. foreign policy circles towards Silicon Valley's then apolitical stance: "There is a disturbing complacency here toward Washington, government and even the nation. There is no geography in Silicon Valley, or geopolitics" (Friedman 1998). A couple of years later, major players of the US IT industry and traditional US security organisations had joined forces. The "War on Terror" following the 9/11 attack lead to numerous task forces pondering ways to exploit information technology to uncover terrorist networks and their activities.[13] The IT industry had every economic incentive to support its alignment with governments and the ubiquitous use of ICT for national security purposes (American Civil Liberties Union 2004, pp. 27–29).

The challenge for national security circles this time however is not to align mere companies, a task that could be solved with ease by a proven mix of rewarding and sanctioning incentives such as governmental purchasing power and anti-trust or tax investigations. In the case of Internet security, the indispensable actor required by national governments to achieve their national security goals are the networks of security experts, not only companies. Internet security communities usually comprise individual experts dedicated to certain technologies, Internet services, or

[13] The Markle Foundation Task Force has been a broad and visible example (Markle Foundation-Task Force on National Security in the Information Age 2002).

problem-specific ad-hoc task forces. These individual experts happen to exchange information via access-restricted mailing lists and collaborate, driven by their individual motivation, usually with company backing or at least connivance.

There are historic examples how to include volunteering individuals into an overall national undertaking. Again, the post-9/11 policies provide illustrative examples. Organized watch programmes and citizen awareness campaigns aimed at balancing governmental lack of sensors to detect potential terror suspects.[14] The idea of recruiting informants from specific sectors with broad access to specific parts of individuals' lives gained a foothold in Washington soon after 9/11. The idea behind planned programs like 'Citizen Corps" or the "Terrorism Information and Prevention System" was to get individuals "directly involved in homeland defense" (American Civil Liberties Union 2004, p. 4). Using a term that was only coined more recently, these programs aimed at crowdsourcing the monitoring of human traffic in societal systems with the results being appropriated by the platform owners, i.e. national security organisations.

Recent developments suggest that the existing security community landscape is being altered by several policy approaches. It is not obvious, however, whether they are driven by an underlying strategy or are the result of incidental policy projects in different branches and levels of the US administration. An example of such a newly formed network is the Cyber Security Forum Initiative (CSFI). CSFI is a the result of a private initiative, and incorporated as a US non-profit organisation. The Forum, which appears to have close links to US military, aims at educating the US military on cyber warfare and facilitating collaboration and information sharing inside government, military, law-enforcement and industry.[15] While it is a "volunteer group" (Klimburg 2011) just like the Conficker Working Group, it differs from the widespread type of mailing-list-based Internet security groups in important aspects. Different from these mailings-list-based communities, thorough vetting is no prerequisite for basic membership of CSFI (only for specific projects of the initiative), nor is active contribution required to remain part of the group. This allows CSFI to gather some "5,000 Cyber Security and Cyber Warfare professionals",[16] which are, inconceivable for traditional operational-security groups, managed via the LinkedIn social network. Another characteristic of CSFI is its close cooperation with military organisations, exemplified by frequent postings for jobs usually requiring US clearances and related to US military, a joint recruitment sessions with NATO Cooperative Cyber Defence Centre of Excellence,[17] and a dedicated "cyber-warfare division".

While CSFI is a private initiative, the second example of changes of relations between states and security communities is more obvious. DARPA's Cyber Fast Track program signifies a departure from usual bureaucratic governmental

---

[14] Keith Alexander used the term of "bad packets" that need to be detected on the Internet by ISPs. Cheryl Pellerin, "Cybersecurity Involves Federal, Industry Partners, Allies", defense.gov, November 8, 2012, http://www.defense.gov/news/newsarticle.aspx?id=118479.

[15] CSFI, "About CSFI", http://www.csfi.us/?page=about (Retrieved June 1, 2011).

[16] (CSFI, ibd.).

[17] CCDCOE, "Recruiting Cyber Power Workshop", 2011, http://www.ccdcoe.org/ICCC/CSFI_CCDCOE_Workshop.pdf.

contracting. The program, directed by former hacker Peiter Zatko, grants funding for short, fixed-price projects to individual researchers and entrepreneurs in the security community. The stated primary goal of this project is to create useful knowledge for the security community.[18] Such funding and collaboration might well alter or ensure the perception of the Pentagon as a trustworthy organisation in the security community. In the long run, such programs might help to shape political mentalities and dispositions in the information security community. Mentalities among members of the ICT security community can determine whether ICT-based national security incidents are played out along the interests of national security communities or not.[19].

From the perspective of those concerned with ICT-related aspects of national security, the geopolitical implications of the activities of security industry requires need to concern. Publicly, these concerns have so far only been shared in journalistic outlets, though by journalists apparently well connected with Washington's political cybersecurity establishment. In a piece that was published in several online subsidiaries of IDG publishing house, Jeff Bardin, Chief Intelligence Office of security company Treadstone 71, accused US security companies for their arguably treacherous support in dismantling "cyber-weaponry" such as Stuxnet, Flame, Duqu, or Gauss, directed at Iran, an "enemy and well-defined adversary" of the U.S. In addition, Bardin fingerpointed at Russian citizen Evgeny Kaspersky, founder and CEO of London-based AV and security company Kaspersky for his alleged loyalty and proximity to the Kremlin. His ongoing loyalty would root in his former affiliation with Russian intelligence agency FSB and would still be visibly by his AV company's exclusive interest in US-originating malware, while ignoring cyber-weaponry developed in his home country (Bardin 2012). Such a nationalistic stance on malware analysis was first seen in Wired magazine, where Noah Shachtman, a long-standing and usually sober observer of information security issues (Shachtman 2011), raised questions about the links of Kaspersky to the Kremlin (Shachtman 2012). Wired repeated its allegations against Evgeny Kaspersky by adding him to the list of "Wired's Most Dangerous".[20] Such rumor-based reporting and shaming of actors with possibly lacking loyalty to US-security interests might well shape the stance of members of individuals and companies in the IT security community. Naming and shaming of unwanted actors is a proven and one of the harshest means to alter the behaviour of another actor in a networks and communities without organisational hierarchies.

---

[18] DARPA, Research Announcement, Cyber Fast Track (CFT), DARPA-RA-11-52 August 3, 2011, https://www.fbo.gov/utils/view?id=48b671dacf69d07facc107e40840878d (Retrieved Jun 25, 2012).

[19] The role of mentalities—not so much for the effects of governmental programs as they did not play a role here—is illustrated in the case of Wikileaks and Adrian Lamo. Lamo passed logs of private chats, which he had with Bradley Manning and in which the latter revealed self-compromising information, to U.S. authorities and the Wired magazine (Calabresi 2010). In January 2013, Lamo rationalized his actions, calling it "needful" and claims that it was "his duty" to "interdict the freedom of the man in the IM window." His handing over of Manning to public authorities happened "in deference to the hubris of believing that the masses only await our touch in order to to be enlightened" (Lamo 2013).

[20] Russia Today, "Wired's Most Dangerous: Russia's cyber-security mogul behind Flame virus downfall hits top 15", December 22, 2012, http://rt.com/news/kaspersky-most-dangerous-people-606/.

5 Conclusion

Actors can reply to technological changes that threaten to erode their previous power resources. Brenden Kuerbis doctoral thesis (Kuerbis 2011) has highlighted how new security technologies "can alter power relations and economic dependencies among stakeholders" (Kuerbis and Mueller 2011, p. 125). This chapter has aimed at understanding possibly ways for traditional powerful actors to interact with Internet security networks and alter them to their advantage both theoretically and empirically. The motivation for this has not been to provide an early draft of "il Internet security principe", but to provide a tool to better analyse ongoing developments in the field of Internet security and the role of the security community therein from a power perspective.

As a first facet of the analysis, this article first related networked security to other ideal-type models of security provisioning in the international sphere. The characteristic of Internet security is its reliance on the networked approach. Previous ways to provide security as described in the section Models of international security don't apply to the empirics of Internet security. There is neither cyber hegemony, nor collective cyber security, nor cyber anarchy. Internet security instead is provided predominantly in a networked approach. Within such networked approaches, governments and large corporations can alter networks in various ways to make them more amenable to their interests. In general, these actors can theoretically aim at altering any of the characteristics that define networks that are more egalitarian or try to reduce the importance or even replace these networks by altering the underlying technologies, reduce the importance of established security response communities or replace them with more hierarchical communities.

In the second part of the chapter, the analysis of networked security provisioning in the Conficker case has shown that the currently predominant organisational form for Internet security provisioning is based on networked governance. Response to Internet security incidents largely relies on the contribution of a global community of technical experts with affiliations to various sectors and of law enforcement agencies. However, Conficker's governance model with its relatively levelled power structure appears to be increasingly replaced by a form of networked governance in which states and governments have a greater say. Activities of Developments in the U.S. with close links to them in the national security communities indicate that U.S. authorities are aware of their dependence on these technical communities and aim for a greater role within these networks.

The empirical data presented in the second half of this chapter is certainly not rigidly selected and therefore only provides indications that allow to build the hypothesis that a hierarchisation within networked production of Internet security is underway. To actually prove such a thesis requires a more elaborated theoretical model and, even more so, more rigid data selection, collection and analysis. In our previous paper we have already stipulated the importance to better understand the networked organisational form as the basis for Internet governance and its contribution to growth, resilience of transnational communications (Mueller et al. 2013). The forces and developments in the field of Internet security highlight the necessity to better understand the intersection of networks and hierarchies or rather the effects that powerful hierarchies and interested market forces have on the networked governance approach.

References

American Civil Liberties Union. (2004, August). *The surveillance-industrial complex: How the American government is conscripting businesses and individuals in the construction of a surveillance society*. New York. Retrieved November 8, 2008, from http://www.aclu.org/FilesPDFs/surveillance_report.pdf.

American Civil Liberties Union. (2006, January 31). Eavesdropping 2010: What can the NSA do? [Web page] Retrieved January 2, 2013, from http://www.aclu.org/files/pdfs/eavesdropping101.pdf.

Bardin, J. (2012, August 16). Giving aid and comfort. *Infosec island* [Web page]. Retrieved from http://www.infosecisland.com/blogview/22211-Giving-Aid-and-Comfort-to-the-Enemy.html.

Benitez, J. (2012, April 11). Pentagon expanding international partnership to address 'global cyber arms race. *ACUS website*. Retrieved from http://www.acus.org/natosource/pentagon-expanding-international-partnerships-address-global-cyber-arms-race.

Bijl, J. (2012, April 12). Critical analysis of Microsoft operation B71. *Fox IT blog* [Web page]. Retrieved from http://blog.fox-it.com/2012/04/12/critical-analysis-of-microsoft-operation b71/.

Boscovich, R. D. (2012, March 25). Microsoft and financial services industry leaders target cybercriminal operations from Zeus botnets. *The official Microsoft blog* [Web page]. Retrieved from http://blogs.technet.com/b/microsoft_blog/archive/2012/03/25/microsoft-and-financial-services-industry-leaders-target-cybercriminal-operations-from-zeus-botnets.asp.

Brito, J., & Watkins, T. (2011, April). Loving the cyber bomb? The dangers of threat inflation in cybersecurity policy. Retrieved November 2, 2012, from http://mercatus.org/publication/loving-cyber-bomb-dangers-threat-inflation-cybersecurity-policy.

Bryden, A., & Caparini, M. (2006). *Private actors and security governance*. Münster: Lit Verlag.

Calabresi, M. (2010, December 2). WikiLeaks' war on secrecy: Truth's consequences. *Time magazine* [Web page]. Retrieved December 3, 2011, from http://www.time.com/time/magazine/article/0,9171,2034488,00.html.

CeBIT 2012: Eugene Kaspersky Calls for International Cyber-security Organisation. (2012, March 9). *Bizcomm*, Retrieved March 15, 2012, from http://www.bizcommunity.com/Article/82/391/72039.html.

Clark, G., & Sohn, L. B. (1958). *World peace through world law*. Cambridge: Harvard University Press.

Czosseck, C., Ottis, R., & Talihärm, A. (2011). Estonia after the 2007 cyber attacks: Legal, strategic and organisational changes in cyber security. In *Proceedings of the 10th European conference on information warfare and security at the Tallinn University of Technology Tallinn, Estonia 7–8 july* 2011 (pp. 57–64). Retrieved September 4, 2012, from http://www.ccdcoe.org/articles/2011/Czosseck_Ottis_Taliharm_Estonia_After_the_2007_Cyber_Attacks.PDF.

Dafermos, G. (2012). Authority in peer production: The emergence of governance in the freebsd project. *Journal of Peer Production*, (1). Retrieved January 1, 2012, from http://peerproduction.net/issues/issue-1/peer-reviewed-papers/.

Davis, J. (2007). Hackers take down the most wired country in Europe. *Wired Magazine*, 15, 9.

Deibert, R. (2010). Militarizing cyberspace-to preserve the open internet we must stop the cyber arms race. *Technology Review*. Retrieved January 10, 2012, from http://www.technologyreview.in/web/25901.

de Natris, W. (2012, May 22). Public private cooperaration: The Zeus take down example. *Personal blog* [Web page]. Retrieved January 10, 2013, from http://woutdenatris.wordpress.com/2012/05/22/public-private-cooperaration-the-zeus-take-down-example.

Eilstrup-Sangiovanni, M. (2007, October). *Varieties of cooperation: Government networks in international security*. Florence: European University Institute, Robert Schuman Centre for Advanced Studies. EUI Working Papers RSCAS 2007/24. Retrieved April 20, 2009, from http://cadmus.iue.it/dspace/handle/1814/7503.

Estonian Defence League. (2010, December 20). Estonian defence league. Retrieved December 21, 2010, from http://en.wikipedia.org/wiki/Estonian_Defense_League.

Estonian Ministry of Defence (2011, January 20). Government formed cyber defence unit of the defence league. *Website of ministry of defence* [Web page]. Retrieved January 25, 2011, from http://www.mod.gov.ee/en/government-formed-cyber-defence-unit-of-the-defence-league.

FBI New York Field Office (2011, November 9). Manhattan U.S. Attorney charges seven individuals for engineering sophisticated Internet fraud scheme that infected millions of computers worldwide and manipulated Internet advertising business. Retrieved May 13, 2012, from http://www.fbi.gov/newyork/press-releases/2011/manhattan-u.s.-attorney-charges-seven-individuals-for-engineering-sophisticated-internet-fraud-scheme-that-infected-millions-of-computers-worldwide-and-manipulated-internet-advertising-business.

Ferguson, R. (2012, March 27). Don't be dumb, keep schtumm!. *CounterMeasures-trend micro blog* [Web page]. Retrieved January 10, 2013, from http://countermeasures.trendmicro.eu/dont-be-dumb-keep-schtumm/.

Forward-Looking Threat Research Team (2012). *Operation Ghost Click-the Rove Digital takedown* (Trend Micro Incorporated Research Paper). Retrieved September 19, 2012, from http://www.trendmicro.com/cloud-content/us/pdfs/security-intelligence/white-papers/wp_the_rove_digital_takedown.pdf.

Friedman, T. (1998). Techno-Nothings. *New York Times,* p. 13. Retrieved October 7, 2003, from http://www.gsu.edu/~poljsd/3400/3400readings/techno-nothings.html.

Gomez, W. (Transcript author). (2012). Building a secure cyber future: Attacks on Estonia, five years on. (Transcript of the ACUS workshop on May 23, 20012, Washington D.C). The Atlantic Council of the United States. Retrieved August 24, 2012, from http://www.acus.org/print/70435.

Gorman, S., & Barnes, J. E. (2011, May 31). Cyber combat can count as act of war. *Wallstreet Journal,* Retrieved from http://professional.wsj.com/article/SB10001424052702304563104576355623135782718.html.

Gruszczak, A. (2008). Networked security governance: Reflections on the EU's counterterrorism approach. *Journal of Global Change and Governance, 1*(3), 1–23.

Healey, J. (2012, January). Beyond attribution: Seeking national responsibility for cyber attacks. *Atlantic council issue brief.* Retrieved April 3, 2012, from http://www.acus.org/publication/beyond-attribution-seeking-national-responsibility-cyberspace.

Jackson Higgins, K. (2012a, July 26). Apple makes black hat debut. *Dark reading* [Web page]. Retrieved July 30, 2012, from http://www.darkreading.com/mobile-security/167901113/security/vulnerabilities/240004456/apple-makes-black-hat-debut.html.

Jackson Higgins, K. (2012b, June 6). Siemens enhances security in post-stuxnet SCADA world. *Dark reading* [Web page]. Retrieved June 20, 2012, from http://www.darkreading.com/advanced-threats/167901091/security/vulnerabilities/240001644/siemens-enhances-security-in-post-stuxnet-scada-world.html.

Jung (2009). The "networked security" concept–stocktaking and perspectives. *European Security and Defence*, (1), 7–12. Retrieved June 28, 2009, from http://www.europeansecurityanddefence.info/Ausgaben/2009/01_2009/01_Jung/ESD_0109_Jung.pdf.

Kahler, M. (2009). Networked politics: Agency, power, and governance. In M. Kahler (Ed.), *Networked politics: Agency, power, and governance* (pp. 1–21) [Web]. Cornell: Cornell University Press.

Kempa, M., Carrier, R., Wood, J., & Shearing, C. (1999). Reflections of the evolving concept of 'private policing'. *European Journal on Criminal Policy and Research, 7*(2), 197–223. doi:10.1023/A:1008705411061.

Klimburg, A. (2011). Mobilising cyber power. *Survival, 53*(1), 41–60. doi:10.1080/00396338.2011.555595.

Kolakowski, N. (2010, March 3). Spain, IT security companies sting Mariposa botnet. *eWeek*. Retrieved August 2, 2012, from http://www.eweek.com/c/a/Security/Spain-IT-Security-Companies-Sting-Mariposa-Botnet-390027.

Korps Landelijke Politiediensten (2011, February 16). *Evaluatie tolling-Innovatieve hoogtepunten en processuele lessen*. Retrieved October 7, 2012, from https://rejo.zenger.nl/files/0000034/20110216-evaluatie-tolling.pdf.

Krahmann, E. (2005). Security governance and networks: New theoretical perspectives in transatlantic security. *Cambridge Review of International Affairs, 18*(1), 15–30. doi:10.1080/09557570500059514.

Krahmann, E. (2010). *States, citizens and the privatization of security*. Cambridge: Cambridge University Press.

Krebs, B. (2012, April 16). Microsoft responds to critics over botnet bruhaha. *KrebsOnSecurity* [Web page]. Retrieved January 10, 2013, from http://krebsonsecurity.com/2012/04/microsoft-responds-to-critics-over-botnet-bruhaha/.

Kuerbis, B. (2011). *Securing Critical Internet Resources: Influencing Internet Governance through Social Networks and Delegation* (Doctoral Thesis). Syracuse University, iSchool-Information Science and Technology.

Kuerbis, B., & Mueller, M. (2011). Negotiating a new governance hierarchy: An analysis of the conflicting incentives to secure Internet routing. *Communications and Strategies, 81*, 125–142.

Lake, D. A. (2009). Hobbesian hierarchy: The political economy of political organization. *Annual Review of Political Science, 12*, 263–283. doi:10.1146/annurev.polisci.12.041707.193640.

Lamo, A. (2013, January 3). Bradley Manning and me: Why I cannot regret turning in the WikiLeaks suspect. *The guardian* [Web page]. Retrieved January 11, 2013, from http://www.guardian.co.uk/commentisfree/2013/jan/03/bradley-manning-wikileaks-suspect-adrian-lamo.

Landler, M., & Markoff, J. (2007). In Estonia, what may be the first war in cyberspace. *International Herald Tribune*. Retrieved November 4, 2010, from http://www.iht.com/articles/2007/05/28/business/cyberwar.php.

Larraz, T. (2010, March 3). Spanish "botnet" potent enough to attack country: Police. *Reuters*. Retrieved January 16, 2013, from http://www.reuters.com/article/2010/03/03/us-crime-hackers-idUSTRE6214ST20100303.

Lawson, S., & Gehl, R. W. (2011, May). *Convergence security: Cyber-Surveillance and the biopolitical production of security*. Paper prepared for Workshop on Cyber-Surveillance in Everyday Life: An International Workshop, May 12–15, 2011, University of Toronto.

Lennon, M. (2012, March 26). Microsoft leads sting operation to disrupt Zeus botnets. *SecurityWeek*. Retrieved May 13, 2012, from http://www.securityweek.com/microsoft-and-partners-disrupt-zeus-botnets-sting-operation.

Leyden, J. (2010, March 3). How FBI, police busted massive botnet. *The register*. Retrieved January 10, 2013, from http://www.theregister.co.uk/2010/03/03/mariposa_botnet_bust_analysis/.

Macdonald, D., & Manky, D. (2010, February). Zeus: God of DIY botnets. *Fortiguard blog* [Web page]. Retrieved January 10, 2013, from http://www.fortiguard.com/analysis/zeusanalysis.html.

Mandelbaum, M. (2006). *The case for Goliath: How America acts as the world's government in the twenty-first century*. New York: PublicAffairs.

Markle Foundation-Task Force on National Security in the Information Age (2002, October). *Protecting America's freedom in the information age. A report of the markle foundation task force*.

McConnell, M. (2010, February 28). Mike McConnell on how to win the cyber-war we're losing. *Washington Post*, Retrieved November 4, 2012, from http://www.washingtonpost.com/wp-dyn/content/article/2010/02/25/AR2010022502493.html.

Minkwitz, O., & Schöfbänker, G. (2000). *Information warfare: Die Rüstungskontrolle steht vor neuen Herausforderungen. Für eine Informationskriegsordnung: Frühzeitige Rüstungskontrolle statt Rüstungswettlauf.* Berlin: Forschungsgruppe Informationsgesellschaft und Sicherheitspolitik. FoG:IS Arbeitspapier 2.

Mueller, M., Schmidt, A., & Kuerbis, B. (2013). Internet security and networked governance in international relations. *International Studies Review, 15*(1), 86–104.

Nye, J. S. (1990). *Bound to lead: The changing nature of American power*. New York: Basic Books.
Nye, J. S. (2011a). Nuclear lessons for cyber security? *Strategic Studies Quarterly, 5*(4), 18–38.
Nye, J. S. (2011b). Power and foreign policy. *Journal of Political Power, 4*(1), 9–24. doi:10.1080/2158379X.2011.555960.
Openbaar Ministerie (2010, October 25). Nationale recherche haalt berucht botnet neer. Retrieved January 10, 2013, from http://www.om.nl/actueel/nieuws-_en/@154337/nationale_recherche_0.
Ottis, R. (2010, November 19). Cyber security conference in Georgia. *Personal blog-conflicts in cyberspace* [Web page]. Retrieved January 11, 2013, from http://conflictsincyberspace.blogspot.com/2010/11/cyber-security-conference-in-georgia.html.
Pear, R. (2012, April 26). House votes to approve disputed hacking bill. *New York Times*, Retrieved January 11, 2013, from http://www.nytimes.com/2012/04/27/us/politics/house-defies-veto-threat-on-hacking-bill.html.
Porter, M. A., Onnela, J. P., & Mucha, P. J. (2009). Communities in networks. *Notices of the AMS, 56*(9), 1082–1097.
Poulsen, K. (2007, August 22). 'Cyberwar' and Estonia's panic attack. *Wired, threat level*. Retrieved November 10, 2010, from http://www.wired.com/threatlevel/2007/08/cyber-war-and-e/.
Raustiala, K. (2002). The architecture of international cooperation: Transgovernmental networks and the future of international law. *Virginia Journal of International Law, 43*. Retrieved July 4, 2012, from http://ssrn.com/abstract_id=333381.
Schmidt, A. (2012). At the boundaries of peer production: The organization of Internet security production in the cases of Estonia 2007 and Conficker. *Telecommunications Policy, 36*(6), 451–461. doi:10.1016/j.telpol.2012.02.001.
Schmidt, A. (2013). The Estonian cyberattacks. In J. Healey (Ed.), *The fierce domain–conflicts in cyberspace 1986–2012* (pp. 1986–2012). Washington, D.C.: Atlantic Council.
Schwartz, M. J. (2010, October 27). Bredolab botnet busted. *InformationWeek*. Retrieved May 13, 2012, from http://www.informationweek.com/story/showArticle.jhtml?articleID=228000096.
Shachtman, N. (2011, June). *Pirates of the ISPs: Tactics for turning online crooks into international pariahs*. Washington, D.C.: Brookings. Retrieved March 10, 2012, from http://www.brookings.edu/papers/2011/0725_cybersecurity_shachtman.aspx.
Shachtman, N. (2012, July). Russia's top cyber sleuth foils US spies, helps Kremlin pals. *Wired*. Retrieved January 11, 2013, from http://www.wired.com/dangerroom/2012/07/ff_kaspersky/all/.
Sinha, P., Boukhtouta, A., Belarde, V. H., & Debbabi, M. (2010). Insights from the analysis of the Mariposa botnet. In *CRiSIS 2010, fifth international conference on risks and security of Internet and systems, Montreal, Canada, October 10–13, 2010* (pp. 1–9). doi:10.1109/CRISIS.2010.5764915.
Slaughter, A. M. (1997). The real new world order. *Foreign Affairs, 76*(5), 183–197.
Slaughter, A. M. (2004). *A new world order*. Princeton: Princeton University Press.
Slaughter, A. M. (2009). America's edge-power in the networked century. *Foreign Affairs, 88*(1), 94–113.
Sully, M., & Thompson, M. (2010, February). *The deconstruction of the Mariposa botnet*. Defence Intelligence. Retrieved September 16, 2012, from http://defintel.com/docs/Mariposa_White_Paper.pdf.
Tabatabaie, S., van Eeten, M., & Asghari, H. (2012). *Transgovernmental networks in cybersecurity: A quantitative analysis of the London Action Plan against spam*. Paper presented at the 2012 Annual Convention of the International Studies Association.
van Eeten, M. (2010, November 1). Dutch police inflates Bredolab botnet success by factor of ten, and then some. *Internet governance project*. Retrieved November 2, 2010, from http://www.internetgovernance.org/2010/11/01/dutch-police-inflates-bredolab-botnet-success-by-factor-of-ten-and-then-some.
von Eitzen, C. (2011, November 10). Operation Ghost Click: FBI busts DNSChanger botnet. *The H Security*. Retrieved May 13, 2012, from http://www.h-online.com/security/news/item/Operation-Ghost-Click-FBI-busts-DNSChanger-botnet-1376746.html.
Weber, S. (2004). *The success of open source*. Cambridge: Harvard University Press.
Wong, W., & Lake, D. (2009). The politics of networks: Interests, power, and human rights norms. In *Networked politics: Agency, power, and governance*. Ithaca: Cornell University Press.

How the 2010 Attack on Google Changed the US Government's Threat Perception of Economic Cyber Espionage

Oliver Read

Abstract In 2010 economic cyber-espionage emerged as a top national security threat for the US government. Analysis suggests that the government's swift mobilization of resources to block the problem stems from a major event in January 2010: Google's announcement that hackers in China had penetrated its computer systems. Following that incident, the government's threat perception of economic cyber-espionage changed and led to new efforts to counter the problem. This argument is substantiated in two main steps. In step one, it is shown how the American government conceptualized the threat of economic cyber-espionage *before* and *after* the announcement. In step two, we trace how this perception-shift led to a series of countermeasures. During both steps, we adopt an analytical framework called threat politics, which maintains that influential actors in and around government play a crucial role in convincing key policymakers how to perceive and respond to threats.

O. Read (✉)
Global Public Policy Institute, Berlin, Germany
e-mail: oread@gppi.net

J.-F. Kremer and B. Müller (eds.), *Cyberspace and International Relations*,
DOI: 10.1007/978-3-642-37481-4_12,

1 Introduction

For many United States policymakers, online intellectual property theft is leading to America's slow, agonizing death by a thousand cuts. Intelligence officials have estimated that US businesses lose between $100 and 250 billion annually in sales from intellectual property theft in cyberspace (Anderlini et al. 2011). Each year more data than the amount stored in the US Library of Congress is stolen from American firms and universities (Lynn 2010, 100; Perlroth 2012). Policymakers have piled most of the blame on China, who they say has instituted a program to steal high-tech trade secrets from the US to boost Chinese economic competiveness, undermining American innovation and threatening national security.

A more technical term for intellectual property theft performed online is economic cyber-espionage, one of multiple topics that constitute the nebulous issue area of cyber-security. Understanding cyber-security means realizing that cyber space undergirds almost every domain of contemporary society, supporting the global economy, civil infrastructure, public safety and military forces. Cyber-security involves protecting the computer networks on which all these sectors depend, as well as the information stored in these networks and transferred through them. Economic cyber-espionage is the practice of infiltrating these networks with the aim of acquiring trade, technological or economic information to benefit a foreign country or foreign agent (Cornell University Law School 2012).[1] Economic espionage differs from traditional espionage, defined as the appropriation of classified information that belongs to governments (Burstein 2009, 6).

Until recently, US policymakers did not consider economic cyber-espionage a national security priority. From the early 1990s until 2010, presiding administrations concentrated on blocking online attacks to the nation's critical infrastructure. In 2010, under the Barack Obama administration, the issue of economic cyber-espionage emerged as a top national security threat for the government; it now shares space with critical infrastructure protection on the list of acute cyber-security concerns. After 2010, the administration championed a bill to strengthen the 1996 Economic Espionage Act by increasing the penalty for misappropriating trade secrets. It has also advocated international norms that frown upon intellectual property theft. In the US Congress, lawmakers introduced a bevy of bills pertaining to economic cyber-espionage.

Striking about these proposals is that economic cyber-espionage is not a new problem. Since the 1990s, particularly at the turn of the century, security professionals have warned about the deleterious effects of economic cyber-espionage to national security. From a social scientific perspective, all the energy paid to online intellectual property theft invokes the question, why did the US government not take more decisive action to block the economic cyber-espionage problem before 2010?

Analysis suggests that recent efforts stem from a major event in January 2010: Google's announcement that hackers in China had penetrated its computer systems

---

[1] Cornell University Law School's definition of "economic espionage" refers to the practice generally, not necessarily online or offline.

and stolen valuable source code, at the same time tapping into the email accounts of human rights activists in China, the US and Europe. Google reported that at least 20 other firms had been hit, but industry investigations later found that the same cyber-campaign had targeted 34 other US-based tech companies, including Adobe, Symantec and Yahoo (Cha and Nakashima 2010). A well-known computer security company later dubbed the campaign Operation Aurora (Kurtz 2010).

On the surface, that the US government abruptly changed its tune on economic cyber-espionage is not surprising. The government was protecting its own from a powerful competitor, China. However, this explanation ignores many questions. It fails to account for why the government did not respond more decisively following other intrusions into economically significant corporate networks, why it chose some countermeasures over others, or who inside and outside government helped craft those countermeasures. Answering these questions enables us to grasp the process whereby policymakers took action against economic cyber-espionage in 2010.

In this chapter, we trace that process. While doing so, we assume that threats such as economic espionage are socially constructed. They are social facts that "depend on human agreement that they exist" (Ruggie 1998, 856). If policymakers en masse decided that economic espionage did not pose an existential threat, the issue would not draw so much attention. Our task is to track how and why economic cyber-espionage moved onto the government's list of security priorities and which key actors induced the move. This chapter posits that American government officials have taken action against economic cyber-espionage because following the Google announcement they came to perceive the issue as more urgent. Following the 2010 Google incident, or Operation Aurora, the US government's threat perception of economic cyber-espionage changed and led to new efforts to counter the problem.

This argument is substantiated in two main steps. In step one, we establish through discourse analysis how the American government conceptualized the threat of economic cyber-espionage *before* and *after* Aurora. In step two, we detail how this perception-shift led to a series of countermeasures meant to prevent economic cyber-espionage. During both steps, we adopt an analytical framework called *threat politics*, which maintains that influential actors in and around government play a crucial role in convincing key policymakers how to perceive and respond to threats. The whole project—a case study of the Google event—uses the process-tracing method. For George and Bennett, "The process-tracing method attempts to identify the intervening casual process—the casual chain and causal mechanism—between an independent variable (or variables) and the outcome of the dependent variable" (2005, 206). To collect data, secondary sources were used (policy papers, hearing transcripts, articles, legislative texts and government documents).

This chapter comprises four sections. The first provides background on Operation Aurora, the industry name for the attack against Google and other US companies that took place in 2009 and was disclosed in January 2010. In section two, we expound the threat politics framework, the theoretical lens used to explain the recent energy devoted to preventing economic cyber-espionage. The framework derives from the Copenhagen School's securitization theory, which argues that key political actors can transform a marginal issue into a national security issue that justifies extraordinary measures. Our framework is predicated on the idea that to make sense of an issue, people break it down and use some of its aspects to compose easily consumable narratives, or frames, which act as filters through which people can understand the world around them. Actors construct frames to both conceptualize issues and propose actions for addressing them. People do the same when trying to comprehend threats; they frame the threat in understandable narratives *and* propose solutions for dealing it. Every so often, for instance after a major event, opportunities crop up for influential people in and around government to formulate threat frames and convince key government policymakers to adopt this perspective. If policymakers like what they hear, they implement the proposed countermeasures.

In accordance with step one, section three compares the economic cyber-espionage threat frame for the US government *before* and *after* Google announced the hack. The purpose of this section is to demonstrate empirically that a perception-shift occurred. It is shown that before Google announced the hack, while the US government had identified and discussed economic cyber-espionage as an issue, it did not vigorously address it. In theoretical terms, the economic cyber-espionage threat frame before the Google announcement was vague and lacked a concrete action-plan. The government instead directed attention to the foreign intelligence threat from the late 1970s through the mid-90s and later critical infrastructure protection from the mid-90s until 2010. Following Google's 2010 announcement, the government put economic cyber-espionage on its priority list and mobilized resources to block the problem. Through our theoretical lens, we observe a more elaborate threat frame. Its diagnosis contains China, human rights and America's competitive edge, while its prognosis involves intellectual property enforcement, the diffusion of international norms and voluntary codes of conduct for business.

Reflecting step two, section four explains the change in perception and the subsequent countermeasures. Following 2010 Google's announcement, three sets of actors—Google, influential government officials and consultants and think tanks—collectively elaborated the economic cyber-espionage threat frame, specifying who was behind the threat, what was being threatened and which solutions could mitigate the problem. The reason that this elaborated threat frame resonated with key policymakers is that it included the sensitive issues of China, American jobs and human rights.

In the last section, a model is presented that illustrates one explanation for the efforts to block economic cyber-espionage. To be sure, alternative explanations are plausible. One is that these efforts simply coincide with the Google announcement. The US government was already building economic cyber-espionage into its cyber-security policy framework when, by chance, the Google incident occurred, which is why it opportunistically used China and human rights to strengthen its case. This argument supposes that the government would have placed corporate espionage onto its priority list regardless of the Google event. In fact, many policymakers might argue as much if asked whether the event really animated recent responses to economic cyber-espionage. But this scenario is hard to imagine. Although economic cyber-espionage concerned security professionals inside and outside government as early as the 1990s, the US government never prioritized the issue to the extent that it took decisive action to block it. The issue never made its way onto the "decision agenda" over the span of 30 years; why would that have changed so suddenly? Absent the Google hack in 2010, the US government's approach to economic cyber-espionage would have likely stayed the course.

If we do assume that the Google event amounts to a watershed moment for economic cyber-espionage policy, there are alternative theories to our framework that can explain how the US government decided on countermeasures. Through a rational lens, one could argue that policymakers, when poring over the problem of economic cyber-espionage, decided that advocating international norms was the most cost effective solution. One could also look to garbage can theory, which would view the US government as an "organized anarchy" within which there are competing interests and "fluid participation" (Cohen et al. 1972, 2). According to the authors:

> The garbage can process is one in which problems, solutions, and participants move from one choice opportunity to another in such a way that the nature of the choice, the time it takes, and the problems it solves all depend on a relatively complicated intermeshing of elements. These include the mix of choices available at any one time, the mix of problems that have access to the organization, the mix of solutions looking for problems, and the outside demands on the decision makers (16).

Put differently, the actions taken to counter economic cyber-espionage result from the structure of the decision situation, not the influence of key framing actors. The trouble with this and the former explanation is that they do not sufficiently appreciate the role of private actors, namely Google, who coupled the problem of economic cyber-espionage with China and censorship, creating a marriage that does not appear in the available government documentation before January 2010. Key actors are key to this story, and because they are, a theoretical framework that prioritizes influential political players provides a sound footing for this project.

2 Threat Politics

For this project we employ a theoretical framework developed by Myriam Dunn Cavelty (2008) and grounded in the Copenhagen School's securitization theory, which falls under the constructivism heading. Our *threat politics framework* goes beyond securitization theory to include insights from framing theory, the Paris School and agenda setting theory to plug holes in the Copenhagen School project. In this section, securitization theory is first summarized in order to establish the fundamental logic of our framework. After this, the framework is expounded piece by piece.

Securitization theory rests on the premise that saying something can produce an effect, "as in betting, giving a promise, naming a ship" (Wæver 1995, 51). The Copenhagen School authors extend this premise to the field of security studies and argue that when key actors apply security-related language to an issue, that issue can come to be perceived as threatening to the extent that urgent measures are taken to address it. In the context of international security, issues perceived as threatening are generally regarded as jeopardizing the survival of states (Hansen and Nissenbaum 2009, 1158), while the urgent measures designed to counter these issues are enacted by policymakers.

Actors play an essential role in this process of shaping the perception of certain issues to represent a security threat. When an actor's negative framing of an issue gains resonance, the issue will move from being politicized or even non-politicized into the realm of high politics, where it legitimates extraordinary measures that go beyond the limits of normal procedure (Buzan et al. 1998, 23–24). For the Copenhagen School, security is the discursive practice of framing an issue as a security issue. Securitization is the process whereby a key actor or set of actors convincingly present an issue as a security issue, leading to extraordinary measures. Buzan, Wæver and de Wilde argue that extraordinary measures constitute going beyond "the normal political rules of the game (e.g., in the form of secrecy, levying taxes or conscription, placing limitations on otherwise inviolable rights, or focusing society's energy and resources on a specific task)" (24). The authors say that for an issue to be securitized, policymakers do not necessarily need to have taken extraordinary measures; they only need to be able to take such steps (25).

The task of the analyst then is not only to judge an objective threat. It is also to track how and why an issue moves from being marginal to politicized to existentially threatening, as well as which actors induce this move. Consistent with this logic, our theoretical framework assumes that people in a position of influence shape the perception of certain issues to represent a security threat. Our model, though, augments securitization theory by folding in concepts from framing theory, the Paris School and agenda setting theory, allowing us to construct a causal chain that explains the process by which an identified threat generates countermeasures.

The causal chain begins when a problem is recognized (for example, following a major event like an attack) or when big changes in government or the public mood occur. On these occasions, windows of opportunity open up for influential actors to devise explanations for, and solutions to, the perceived problem or shifts in the political stream. These actors compose conceptual schemata (or threat frames) through which others can understand the problem and ways to block it. Following a struggle during which all these influential actors lobby to have their threat frames accepted as the truth, key government officials embrace the threat frames that are easy to understand and that dovetail with their beliefs. At this point, key policymakers place the issue on their priority list. Provided the accepted threat frames contain solutions to the issue, we expect to see these solutions implemented in the form of countermeasures. The model also conveys threat frames as dependent and independent variables. Threat frames are dependent when they are caused by framing actors, and they are independent when they result in countermeasures.

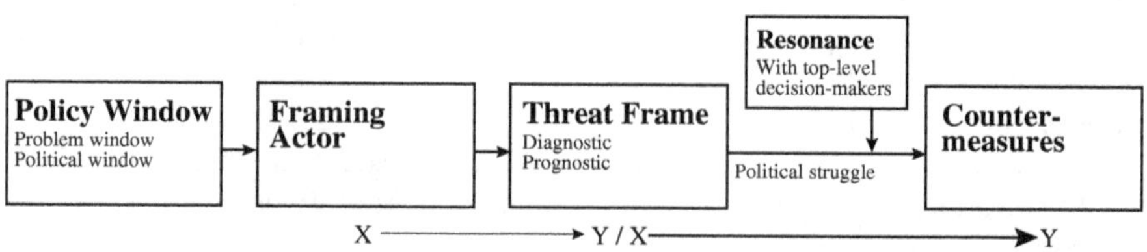

2.1 Threat Frame

The threat frame component of our model comes from framing theory, the underlying principle of which is that people conceptualize issues in different ways (Chong and Druckman 2007, 103). To make sense of an issue, people break it down and extract some its parts to compose easily-consumable narratives. These narratives, or frames, act as filters through which people can understand the world around them. Framing refers to the process of frame construction. We bring into our framework the framing theory analysis of Benford and Snow, who argue that frames have at least two core tasks—"diagnostic framing" and "prognostic framing" (2000, 615–617). Diagnostic framing involves identifying a perceived problem and ascribing whom or what is to blame; in prognostic framing, actors propose solutions to the problem and assign strategies for realizing the proposed solution (2000, 617). We are interested in the construction of frames that pertain to security threats, a process known as threat framing. Threat framing refers to the struggle for a shared narrative or an "interpretative schemata" (Cavelty 2008, 30), the function of which is to diagnose a problem, propose a plan of action for dealing with the problem and assign specific actors to manage the response.

The reason for incorporating threat framing into the Copenhagen School framework is two-fold. First, framing theory enables the analyst to zero in on the winning, socially constructed presentation that moves an issue out of the politicized realm and into the area of high politics. Second, framing theory provides a stronger mechanism to explain how threat frames effect countermeasures. When threat frames proposing action plans resonate among policymakers who enact laws, chances are good that policymakers will try to turn the action plan into policy. In this way, threat frames function as independent variables. When studying threat frames as independent variables, we investigate how they result in countermeasures. At the same time, threat frames can function as dependent variables. When studying them as dependent variables, we need to identify the key actors who frame an issue (Cavelty 2008, 30–33).

2.2 Framing Actors

Framing actors refer to influential actors in and around government who are in a position to piece together coherent narratives about security issues. Framing actors in our model derive largely from the Paris School's professionals of security: influential actors who compete to have their voices heard and their arguments accepted as the truth—to achieve "discursive hegemony" (Cavelty 2008, 27). Paris School subscribers contend that bureaucratic actors socially construct security issues by means of ordinary practices and processes (van Munster 2007, 236; Wæver 2004), arguing that the analyst should go beyond discourse and look into non-discursive practices. The Copenhagen School's securitization process cannot be separated from objective factors, namely the amount of social capital that particular people are endowed with (Aradau 2001). Not just anyone can securitize an issue. Professionals of security can and do.

Animated by a commitment to act as the protector of society, these actors seek out new security problems and in so doing construct narratives through the conflation of heterogeneous events and statistics (Aradau 2001). Because many positions of authority exist within a state's machinery, we expect political wrangling over how security problems should be perceived and dealt with. Professionals of security engage in a political struggle to have their discourses accepted as *the truth*. In the model, rather than using the Paris Schools' term "professional of security," we refer to these actors as "framing actors." These actors are supplied with symbolic capital, are in a position to piece together disparate developments to construct a specific threat frame, and have access to the policymakers who enact countermeasures. Framing actors include politicians, experts, pressure groups or the media (Eriksson 2001, 212).

2.3 Policy Window

The idea of policy windows comes from agenda setting theory, which seeks to explain why some issues get moved from the political agenda, where they are discussed, to the decision agenda, where action is required. Policy windows are opportunities for key actors to insert their ideas into the government docket. Policy windows open up for two reasons (Durant and Diehl 1989, 180; Soroka 1999, 768). One is a shift in the "political stream," which amounts to election results, successful campaigns by pressure groups or fluctuations in the public mood. We call these *political windows*. Policy windows also open when actors become aware of problems by virtue of, for instance, a major event or an important study. We call these *problem windows*. Changes in the political stream or the development of new problems change the perception of the status quo, compelling framing actors—in agenda-setting theory, "policy entrepreneurs" (Durant and Diehl 1989, 190)—to use this opportunity to conflate a narrative that either frames or re-frames an issue. Policy windows open in advance of the framing or reframing process, and the analyst should be able to track when policy windows open and how that leads to actions by actors (Cavelty 2008, 37).

2.4 Resonance and Countermeasures

Threat frames vary in how they resonate with their intended audience (Benford and Snow 2000, 619). The degree to which a frame appeals to an audience depends on two factors, the frame's received credibility and received salience. A frame is credible when it is presented without overt contradictions, substantiated with empirical evidence, and when those actors who advocate the frame's central message come across as reputable and sincere. A frame is salient when the intended audience comprehends the frame's meaning and is spurred to follow a directive. Further, for a frame to be salient, it should dovetail with the beliefs, values and everyday experiences of those for whom the message is intended. Should the threat frame that resonates with key policymakers contain prognoses for the perceived problem, these solutions will be translated into countermeasures such as laws, executive orders and bureaucratic changes.

3 Operation Aurora

In January 2010 Google disclosed on its official blog that attackers in China had broken into its internal system to steal intellectual property and access the Gmail accounts of human rights activists inside and outside of China (Drummond 2010a). In this blog post, Google lawyer David Drummond wrote that the attack also targeted businesses in the finance, technology and chemical sectors, among others. Industry reports released later said that the operation, which took place the last half of 2009, affected at least 34 firms, including Yahoo, Adobe, Northrop–Grumman and Dow Chemical (Cha and Nakashima 2010). Computer security experts corroborated Google's assertion that the assault originated in China, even claiming to have traced the hack to a Chinese university (Markoff and Barboza 2010).

According to McAfee, a known computer security firm, the hackers carried out the sophisticated and well-resourced attack to steal intellectual property from political and business targets, the kind of operation known as an "advanced persistent threat" (Mandiant 2011; Damballa 2011; Kurtz 2010). Targeted employees at Google and other firms received tailored emails or instant messages from seemingly friendly senders. Those emails and instant messages contained links that when clicked would forward the employee to a website hosted in Taiwan. There, the employee's browser downloaded malicious code onto his or her computer, creating a hidden backdoor through which hackers could enter and then prowl in the employee's computer and the system it was part of. Dmitri Alperovitch, vice president of threat research at McAfee, later named the attack Operation Aurora (Kurtz 2010).

On top of appropriating valuable proprietary information, the attackers tried tapping into the Gmail accounts of Chinese human rights activists as well as users in the US and Europe who support human rights in China. In response, Google stated that it would no longer comply with the Chinese government to censor search engine results, and that it was considering closing down its offices in the country. Two months later, during negotiations between it and China, Google followed through with its promise to stop suppressing content on google.cn and decided to redirect users in China to an uncensored server in Hong Kong (Drummond 2010b).

Around this time, The Washington Post reported that Google had requested support from the US National Security Agency to analyze the security breach, although the details of this agreement remain unclear (Nakashima 2010). The US government's public response following Google's announcement emphasized the censorship angle of the incident. In a widely publicized speech on "Internet freedom," rife with references to China, Secretary of State Hilary Clinton called on China to investigate the Google hack and refuse "politically motivated censorship" (BBC 2010; Burns 2010; Clinton 2010).

4 The US Government's Perception of Economic Cyber-Espionage Before and After Aurora

Following the 2010 Google incident, or Operation Aurora, the US government's threat perception of economic cyber-espionage changed and led to new efforts to counter the problem. Through discourse analysis, the following section demonstrates empirically how the American government conceptualized the threat of economic cyber-espionage *before* Aurora (part one) and *after* Aurora (part two).

Part one shows that before Google announced the hack, while the US government had identified economic cyber-espionage as a problem, it did not vigorously address the issue. Economic cyber-espionage was considered a problem that generated more rumination than action. In theoretical terms, the economic cyber-espionage threat image before the Google announcement was vague and lacked clear prognoses. The government directed attention to the foreign intelligence threat from the late 1970s through the mid-90s and later critical infrastructure protection from the mid-90s until 2010.

Part two demonstrates that following Google's 2010 announcement, the US government put economic cyber-espionage on its priority list and mobilized resources to stem the problem. Through our theoretical lens, we observe a more elaborate threat frame: Its diagnosis contains China, human rights and America's competitive edge, while its prognosis contains the diffusion of intellectual property theft enforcement, voluntary codes of conduct for business and international norms.

4.1 Threat Frame Before Aurora

From the late 1970s through the early 90s, by virtue of the Cold War or because the Internet was not widely accessible to the public, the US government interpreted computer security mostly as the blocking of foreign nations from stealing sensitive information belonging to it and its contractors. The Carter administration took an early first step to guard against this foreign intelligence threat when in 1977 it issued presidential directive 24, intended to protect unclassified information "transmitted by and between Government agencies and contractors that would be useful to an adversary" (Carter 1977). Computer security registered more with the Reagan administration, for whom the threat also included the theft of classified government information. Issued in 1984, National Security Decision Directive 145 (Reagan 1984) arguably best illuminates the way the administration understood cyber-security. The directive reads that while "microelectronics technology" promises to improve efficiency within the government and private sector, "it also poses significant security challenges." It continues:

> Telecommunications and automated information processing systems are highly susceptible to interception, unauthorized electronic access, and related forms of technical exploitation, as well as other dimensions of the hostile intelligence threat. The technology to exploit these electronic systems is widespread and is used extensively by foreign nations and can be employed, as well, by terrorist groups and criminal elements. Government systems as well as those which process the private or proprietary information of US persons and businesses can become targets for foreign exploitation.

The directive called for "initial objectives of policies, and an organizational structure to guide the conduct of national activities directed toward safeguarding systems which process or communicate sensitive information from hostile exploitation." It also established a steering group at the cabinet level to assess the computer systems used to manage "sensitive government or government-derived information," as well as to "identify categories of sensitive non-government information, the loss of which could adversely affect the national security interest." The language in the National Security Decision Directive 145 indicates that the administration associated computer security primarily with the foreign intelligence threat; enemies were after classified and sensitive information cached in the systems of government and its contractors. The administration after Reagan, this one under George H W Bush, conceptualized computer security in much the same manner. The foreign intelligence threat remained the highest priority, and the government's strategy stayed the same. This continuation of policies is evidenced by the 1990 National Security Directive 42 (Bush 1992), the text of which is virtually identical to Reagan's National Security Decision Directive 145.

Largely in response to the 1995 Oklahoma City bombing, an attack on the Alfred P. Murrah Federal Building that killed 168 people, the Clinton administration shifted its gaze from the foreign intelligence threat to the protection of critical infrastructure (Cavelty 2008, 98–103; Jenkins 2011). Critical infrastructure describes the "systems and assets, whether physical or virtual, so vital to the United States that the incapacity or destruction of such systems and assets would have a debilitating impact on security, national economic security, national public health or safety, or any combination of those matters" (US Department of Homeland Security 2011). In 1996, Clinton created the President's Commission on Critical Infrastructure Protection and charged it with "recommending a national strategy for protecting and assuring critical infrastructures from physical and cyber threats" (US Department of Justice 1999). The commission offered its recommendations in 1997, and the president implemented nearly all of them in presidential directives 62 and 63 (Bendrath 2001). Several years later in 2000, the Clinton administration released another report specific to cyber-security, *Defending America's Cyberspace—National Plan for Information Systems Protection*

(Clinton 2000). Released soon before the inauguration of George W Bush, this paper again emphasizes critical infrastructure protection:

> We are at risk. The United States depends more on computers today then ever before. The pace of the technological drive to install computer controls in every critical infrastructure far outstrips our potential to design computer security software, train information technology security personnel, or develop and promulgate computer security recommended practices and standards. We have created a gaping vulnerability in our national security and economic stability. This affects not only our computer-controlled systems for electrical power, telecommunications, and nearly every utility, but also the vital databases that maintain our medical data, criminal records, and proprietary information. We are vulnerable to mischief-making hackers, hardware and software failures, cyber criminals and, most alarmingly, to deliberate attack from nation states and terrorists (1).

The following year in 2001, the attacks of September 11 killed thousands while rattling the ailing US economy, crippling businesses in New York and devastating vast amounts of property. It also served to keep critical infrastructure protection at the center of the government's approach to cyber-security. The Bush administration folded cyber-security into its broader strategy of protecting critical infrastructure, laid out in two documents. The first is the 2002 *National Strategy for Homeland Security*, which called critical infrastructure protection a "critical mission area" (Bush 2002). The second is the 2003 *National Strategy for the Physical Protection of Critical Infrastructures and Key Assets*, which "identifies a clear set of national goals and objectives and outlines the guiding principles that will underpin our efforts to secure the infrastructures and assets vital to our national security, governance, public health and safety, economy, and public confidence" (Bush 2003a, vii). Also in 2003, the administration released its *National Strategy to Secure Cyberspace.* As in the two papers just mentioned, protecting critical infrastructure receives top billing:

> Our Nation's critical infrastructures are composed of public and private institutions in the sectors of agriculture, food, water, public health, emergency services, government, defense industrial base, information and telecommunications, energy, transportation, banking and finance, chemicals and hazardous materials, and postal and shipping. Cyberspace is their nervous system—the control system of our country (Bush 2003b, vii).

This chapter has three main objectives: (1) "Prevent cyber attacks against America's critical infrastructures," (2) "Reduce national vulnerability to cyber attacks," and (3) "Minimize damage and recovery time from cyber attacks that do occur" (viii). It is in this context that the document discusses espionage. The concern is over enemies stealing information to be used to attack the US: "In peacetime America's enemies will conduct espionage against our government, university research centers, and private companies. Activities would likely include mapping U.S. information systems, identifying key targets, lacing our infrastructure with 'back doors' and other means of access" (50).

Several years later in 2008, the administration established the Comprehensive National Cybersecurity Initiative (CNCI), perhaps the most expansive set of cybersecurity measures instituted during the Bush tenure. Authorized through the National

Security Presidential Directive 54, the CNCI focused on securing government information. At the time, some US congressional committees took issue with it because the directive was classified and cost billions of dollars (Aftergood 2010; Senate Armed Services Committee 2008). The CNCI defined the government's offensive and defensive cyber space goals and affected a host of federal agencies. Guarding government networks from intrusion and disruption lies at the heart of the CNCI (Lewis et al. 2008, 15). Consistent with that objective, the directive tasked the recently conceived Department of Homeland Security with defending the government's computer systems using data encryption, intrusion monitoring technologies and other tools. For its part, the National Security Agency, Central Intelligence Agency and Federal Bureau of Investigation were to monitor the Internet traffic of federal agencies. The directive also instructed the Pentagon to draw up retaliatory plans in case a foreign country attacked US government networks (Nakashima 2008). In short, the CNCI indicates where the government's cyber-security priorities were—on securing.gov and.mil networks from intrusion and disruption. Not only that, it was instructive for the Obama administration, which used the directive as its starting point for cyber-security upon assuming office in 2009 (US National Security Council 2010).

In May 2009, the Obama administration published a paper that outlined a new, holistic framework for securing the nation's digital infrastructure. Though the recommendations built upon the CNCI directive, the new administration distanced itself from its predecessor. It pledged to make its approach more transparent, affirmed that this approach would be "anchored" in the White House and tried easing concerns about privacy (Sanger and Markoff 2009; Vijayan 2010). Titled *Cyberspace Policy Review*, the paper was released following a 60-day assessment of the government's cyber-security policies and structures, during which the administration collected input from the legislative and executive branches, state governments, academia, the private sector and civil rights groups (Obama 2009, iii). More than previous administrations, the authors brought in the threat of intellectual property theft and warned of its effects to economic security, even using statistics: "Industry estimates of losses from intellectual property to data theft in 2008 range as high as \$1 trillion" (2). However, the paper did not clarify if this threat refers to economic cyber-espionage or to the piracy of entertainment products, nor did it distinguish tech companies like Google from military contractors. As a concept, economic cyber-espionage is fuzzy. Moreover, the report's recommended near-term and mid-term action items did not include measures specific to economic cyber-espionage, listing measures concerned with bureaucratic restructuring, public-private relationships for critical infrastructure protection, capacity building, civil liberties and emergency response. That the document mentioned economic cyber-espionage but not solutions to it indicates that the issue had not yet moved onto the government's decision agenda.

All this said, while the Obama administration and the four before it associated computer security chiefly with critical infrastructure protection or traditional espionage, security professionals in and near government did not neglect economic cyber-espionage. The issue concerned security experts as early as the 1990s. In 1992, during a House committee hearing, then CIA director Robert Gates said that since the end of the Cold War, the foreign intelligence threat has become "more diversified and more complex," with foreign intelligence services now targeting the American technology "important for economic as well as military reasons" (US Senate 1996). In the mid-1990s, FBI director Louis Freeh testified that "industrial espionage" can damage America's "competitive advantage" (US Senate 1996). From 1995 to 2008, Congress tasked the intelligence community with compiling reports on the "foreign economic collection and industrial espionage" (Burstein 2009, 13). Released every year until 2008, these reports increasingly warned about the threat of economic cyber-espionage to the US economy, particularly starting in the early 2000s. Further, by the mid-1990s the connection between economic cyber-espionage and national security had been made. In 1996 Congress enacted the Economic Espionage Act, which "prohibits individuals from 'knowingly' committing a wide range of acts associated with the misappropriation of trade secrets for the benefit of any foreign government, foreign instrumentality, or foreign agent" (US Senate 2011). A 1996 report on the Espionage Act by the House states:

> There can be no question that the development of proprietary economic information is an integral part of America's economic w.ell-being. Moreover, the nation's economic interests are a part of its national security interests. Thus, threats to the nation's economic interest are threats to the nation's vital security interests (Burstein 2009, 16–17).

These reports and transcripts demonstrate that the US government was discussing economic cyber-espionage back in the 1990s. A threat frame for economic cyber-espionage existed. The threat subject constituted foreign governments, foreign firms and criminals, while US national and economic security made up the referent object (that which is threatened). Economic cyber-espionage was unquestionably on the government agenda. On the other hand, from the 1990s until 2010, though it perceived economic cyber-espionage as problematic, the US government did not devise novel policies to deal with it, even as the frequency and cost of intellectual property theft rose (Anderlini et al. 2011), and as increasingly sophisticated communication technology empowered an array of actors with malicious intent. Protecting critical infrastructure got priority at the time. In essence, while the economic cyber-espionage threat frame was *out there*, it lacked precise prescriptions and failed to impress key policy actors. It was more a condition than a problem to be dealt with. At least until 2010, it never appeared on the decision agenda.

4.2 Threat Frame After Aurora

In January 2010, Google disclosed that hackers in China had broken into its computer systems and stolen source code from the company, while also tapping into the Gmail accounts of human rights activists in China, the US and Europe. Through analysis of policy-relevant documentation drafted since the 2010 announcement, we can distinguish a more coherent, easily-consumable threat image. With regard to a diagnosis, state actors, foreign firms and foreign criminals make up the threat subjects and are primarily connected with China's indigenous innovation program—China's endeavor to promote domestic innovation and reduce its reliance on foreign technologies (Palmer 2010; Lubman 2011); the referent object is America's competitive edge and the private sector's opportunities to innovate, which connotes a threat to basic human rights. Prognoses in the threat frame include prescriptions that fall into three policy areas: (1) intellectual property enforcement, (2) voluntary codes of conduct for business and (3) international norms building.

After January 2010, the Obama administration started to show special concern for intellectual property enforcement. Two reports illustrate the government's position on economic espionage. One is the *Joint Strategic Plan on Intellectual Property Enforcement* (Obama 2010). Released in June 2010, five months after the Google announcement, and put together in coordination with multiple federal agencies, including the Department of Homeland Security and the State Department, this report was the first of its kind. In it, economic espionage falls under the broader national security problem of intellectual property infringement: "Intellectual property infringement can undermine our national and economic security. This includes counterfeit products entering the supply chain of the U.S. military, and economic espionage and theft of trade secrets by foreign citizens and companies" (4). The threat subject constitutes foreign countries and foreign firms. The authors even provide a watch list that includes China as a leading suspect. As to the referent object, the report states that economic espionage threatens US national and economic security and American jobs (4).

Although this document contains the same diagnosis for economic espionage that appears in documents released before the Google announcement, it also contains five policy recommendations, including enhancing foreign law enforcement cooperation, working with international organizations and using trade policy tools to strengthen intellectual property rights enforcement (22). After the release of this report, the administration established in February 2011 a cabinet-level intellectual property advisory committee and expanded the National Intellectual Property Rights Coordination Center, a task force in the Department of Homeland Security.

In March 2011, the administration published a follow-up to the *Joint Strategic Plan* titled *White Paper on Intellectual Property Enforcement Legislative Recommendations*, in which the government labels economic espionage "one of the most serious intellectual property crimes" (Obama 2011a, 4). It recommends that Congress amend the 1996 Economic Espionage Act to increase the statutory maximum sentence for economic espionage from 15 to 20 years in prison, a suggestion that US senators translated into a bill called the Economic Espionage Penalty Enhancement Act (US Senate 2011). The House introduced a similar bill in 2012 (US House 2012). These countermeasures add up to intellectual property enforcement, one of three prescriptive policy areas in the post-Aurora threat frame.

In a report released the following month, April 2011, another prescriptive policy area is evident. This one involves standardizing the security practices of the private sector in the name of national security, controversial because businesses commonly object to regulation and argue that it hinders innovation and hurts growth (Lewis et al. 2011, 5; Smith 2011). The Obama administration laid out its stance on standardization in the report, *Cybersecurity, Innovation and the Internet Economy*, prepared by a task force at the US Commerce Department (2011a, iv). The report defines a new sector of cyber-security, the Internet and Information Innovation Sector, or I3S, made up of firms that depend on the Internet but do not help manage critical infrastructure (10). To "mitigate threats in the I3S," the government advocates "voluntary codes of conduct" for the private sector. "By increasing the adoption of standards and best practices," the administration said after releasing the report that it is "working with the private sector to promote innovation and business growth, while at the same time better protecting companies and consumers from hackers and cyber theft" (US Department of Commerce 2011b). The private sector lauded this recommendation for endorsing a "flexible, non-regulatory" framework (Smith 2011). Google and multiple other firms helped to develop the Obama framework, therefore the recommended voluntary codes of conduct come as no surprise. As will be discussed later, however, some security experts have called for tougher regulation, therefore it is significant that the voluntary framework won the day.

After this April 2011 report came a May 2011 report, *International Strategy for Cyberspace—Prosperity, Security, and Openness in a Networked World*. It makes apparent that the US government will try to prevent economic cyber-espionage through a diplomatic push to spread international cyber-security norms that might one day become a set of conventional expectations (Segal 2012, 14). Its most comprehensive paper on cyber-security strategy, the report states the following goal:

> The United States will work internationally to promote an open, interoperable, secure, and reliable information and communications infrastructure that supports international trade and commerce, strengthens international security, and fosters free expression and innovation. To achieve that goal, we will build and sustain an environment in which norms of responsible behavior guide states' actions, sustain partnerships, and support the rule of law in cyberspace (Obama 2011b, 8).

In putting forward a grand cyber strategy, the administration lists priority issues to tackle, among them "promoting international standards and [an] innovative, open market" online. Under this category is economic cyber-espionage. This is arguably the first time that economic cyber-espionage has appeared as a priority in a government report on cyber-security. As a broad measure to counter the problem, which "can erode competitiveness in the global economy, and businesses' opportunities to innovate," the administration states that the US "will take measures to identify and respond to such actions to help build an international environment that recognizes such acts as unlawful and impermissible, and hold such actors accountable" (17–18).

Elsewhere in the report, the administration overtly weds economic cyber-espionage with human rights and Internet freedom, or "a single Internet where all of humanity has equal access to knowledge and ideas" (US Department of State 2011). Under the goal "Internet Freedom: Supporting Fundamental Freedoms and Privacy," the report reads:

> Ensuring the integrity of information as it flows over the Internet gives users confidence in the network and keeps the Internet open as a reliable platform for innovation that drives growth in the global economy and encourages the exchange of ideas among people around the world (24).

When associated with an open Internet, economic cyber-espionage can be understood as a moral issue. Internet freedom has been a key aspect of the State Department's 21st century statecraft, the diplomatic practice of incorporating more technology (for instance, social networking) into traditional foreign policy. A primary target of America's Internet freedom project is China (Jacobs 2011).

By early 2011, in statements and publications, policymakers were embracing an understanding of economic cyber-espionage fused with China and its scheme to pilfer information from the US to boost economic competitiveness. In April 2011, the House Foreign Affairs Subcommittee on Oversight and Investigations organized a hearing on "Communist Chinese Cyber-Attacks, Cyber-Espionage and Theft of American Technology." In the opening statement, Congressman Dana Rohrabacher (2011) said: "The Communist Chinese Government has defined us as the enemy. It is buying, building and stealing whatever it takes to contain and destroy us. Again, the Chinese Government has defined us as the enemy." This inclination to equate economic cyber-espionage with China came up again during an October 2011 congressional hearing on "Cyber Threats and Ongoing Efforts to Protect the Nation. House Permanent Select Committee on Intelligence Chairman Mike Rogers (2011) gave an opening statement in which he said that his chief concern is not critical infrastructure protection. It is the "death by a thousand cuts that we are suffering right now from cyber espionage being conducted every day against nearly every sector of our economy." He then impugns China and turns to the Google 2010 incident for proof.

> You don't have to look far these days to find a press report about another firm, like Google, whose networks have been penetrated by Chinese cyber espionage and have lost valuable corporate intellectual property. ... Attributing this espionage isn't easy, but talk to any private sector cyber analyst, and they will tell you there is little doubt that this is a massive campaign being conducted by the Chinese government. I don't believe that there is a precedent in history for such a massive and sustained intelligence effort by a government to blatantly steal commercial data and intellectual property.

Also in October 2011, the Office of the National Counterintelligence Executive (2011)—with input from 13 other US government agencies, including the FBI, CIA, State Department and National Security Agency—released a report to Congress about economic cyber-espionage in 2009-2011. Titled *Foreign Spies Stealing US Economic Secrets in Cyberspace*, the report states that much of the cyber-espionage targeting sensitive economic information in the US stems from China (1)—an allegation that policymakers had only insinuated in the past (Shanker 2011). In the paper, which cites the 2010 Google incident as verification of the cyber espionage carried out by China, the authors state that "Chinese leaders consider the first two decades of the 21st century to be a window of strategic opportunity for their country to focus on economic growth, independent innovation, scientific and technical advancement, and growth of the renewable energy sector" (5).

The report asserts that, in addition to Chinese actors, Russian intelligence services covertly collect economic and technology information from US firms, but it does not flesh out this accusation. The report also acknowledges that US partners carry out economic cyber-espionage against the US. "Certain allies and other countries that enjoy broad access to US Government agencies and the private sector conduct economic espionage to acquire sensitive US information and technologies. Some of these states have advanced cyber capabilities" (6). No more particulars are given.

5 How Aurora Led to Economic Cyber-Espionage Countermeasures

The threat frame just described resonated with top policymakers, who moved economic cyber-espionage onto their priority list of national security threats. In this section, the process whereby the Google incident led to measures designed to counter economic cyber-espionage is explained. According to the threat politics framework, the opening of a policy window prompts framing actors to formulate or reformulate threat frames concerning an issue. Threat frames perform two tasks, to diagnose the problem and propose solutions to it. The threat frames that resonate with top-level policymakers will effect countermeasures. Threat frames function as both dependent and independent variables—dependent in that they are caused by framing actors and independent in that they cause countermeasures.

In part one of this section, the policy window that was opened by virtue of Google's 2010 announcement is described. In part two, it is argued that three sets of actors—Google, influential government officials and consultants and think tanks—collectively elaborated the economic cyber-espionage threat frame, specifying the threat subject and solutions to the problem. Put differently, the framing actors (the independent variables, or X) caused the elaborated threat frame (the dependent variable, or Y). In part three, evidence is provided to show why the more specific threat frame resonated with key policymakers and led to countermeasures. The reason is that the revised threat frame included the sensitive issues of China, American jobs and human rights. In other words, the elaborated threat frame (now the independent variable, or X) caused the countermeasures (the dependent variables, or Y). The arguments in parts one, two and three appear in the model below.

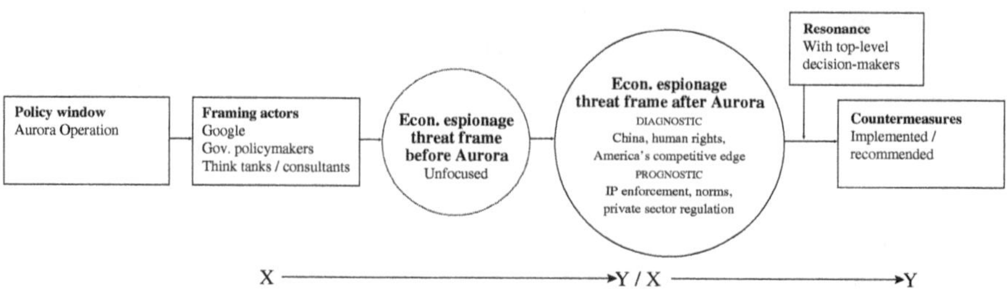

5.1 Policy Window: Operation Aurora

A vital question for this chapter's central argument is whether the 2010 Google announcement was the catalyst for the government's change of tune on economic cyber-espionage, or whether these efforts resulted from another event, or an aggregation of events, or whether these efforts would have come along irrespective of any events. The Google incident was a crucial turning point for three reasons. First, of the nearly 70 major cyber events since 2006 as reported by the Center for Strategic and International Studies, a Washington think tank and arguably the most influential voice on cyber-security for the Obama administration, only two involved intellectual property theft before January 2010 (Lewis 2011).[2] Furthermore, they were relatively minor. The Google incident has been perceived as the first major economic espionage incident. Second, after January 2010, many if not most government reports and analyses have referenced the Google hack as reason for action on economic cyber-espionage and Internet freedom. Third, the American media intensely covered the Google-China story for weeks following the announcement, the interest no doubt fed by the increasing anxiety about cyber-war that began in the years before. The media response arguably fueled the government's decision to take action against economic cyber-espionage.

5.2 Framing Actors → Elaborated Threat Frame

Three sets of actors—Google, influential government officials and think thanks and consultants—played significant roles in elaborating the economic cyber-espionage threat frame.

5.2.1 Google

One framing actor is Google. When it divulged the hack on the Official Google Blog, the firm stated that attackers in China had stolen intellectual property from it and 20 others. According to the blog, the hackers also tried tapping into the Gmail accounts of Chinese human rights activists and users in the US and Europe who support human rights in China. By framing the breach in these terms, Google married the economic cyber-espionage problem with China and human rights, producing a novel conception of economic cyber-espionage that the US government has embraced. The prime example is the 2011 report *Cybersecurity, Innovation and the Internet Economy*, which proposes an approach to cyber-security entailing the diffusion of international norms and Internet freedom. Because conversations between Google and the US government following the attack are confidential,

[2] This chapter was written in October 2012.

we cannot prove that Google directly influenced the US government's strategy for tackling economic cyber-espionage. Still, that Google turned to the National Security Agency for advice shows that there was communication (Markoff 2010), as does the fact that at least one high-profile State Department official left the agency to head up a Google think tank (Larson 2010).

5.2.2 Influential US Government Officials

Influential government officials have also colored in the economic cyber-espionage threat image. In 2011, for example, the Commission on Cybersecurity for the 44th Presidency, which assembled lawmakers, consultants and academics to provide policy recommendations to the Obama administration, labeled espionage and cyber crime the nation's "greatest threats" (Lewis et al. 2011, 2). Another commission that has written about economic cyber-espionage is the US-China Economic and Security Review Commission (2010). During a hearing in 2011, it invited experts to shed light on indigenous innovation. Some policymakers in Washington suspect that in pursuing this long-term strategy, China is stealing American intellectual property rather than investing in its own innovation. This is a prevalent theme in congressional hearings and reports issued by, for instance, the Office of the National Counterintelligence Executive (2011) and the US International Trade Commission (2011).

On the executive side, actors in the Defense of Department and State Department have influenced the economic cyber-espionage threat frame following Aurora. In the fall of 2010, for instance, US Deputy Secretary of Defense William Lynn III published an essay in Foreign Affairs on "defending the new domain." What needs defending, he wrote, is three-fold: US military capabilities, critical infrastructure and economic vitality, which sustains military capabilities. Lynn wrote that intellectual property theft "may be the most significant cyberthreat that the United States will face over the long term," citing the Google incident to prove his point, as well as an often-mentioned statistic that "Every year, an amount of intellectual property contained in the Library of Congress is stolen from networks maintained by U.S. businesses, universities, and governmental agencies" (Lynn 2010, 100). In the piece, while his diagnosis for the problem is clear (foreign actors threaten US national security), he does not propose a solution for economic cyber-espionage, concentrating instead on Pentagon efforts to safeguard.mil networks.

As to the State Department, after Google's announcement, Secretary Clinton called on China to investigate the incident and refuse "politically motivated censorship" (BBC 2010; Burns 2010), in effect coupling censorship and the economic cyber-espionage problem. Further, with its call for global Internet freedom, the State Department's fingerprints appear on the administration's May 2011 cybersecurity strategy report, in which the authors express a principled approach for achieving "innovative, open markets" (Obama 2011b, 17); in the report, this broad goal subsumes the more specific aim to "protect intellectual property, including commercial trade secrets, from theft" (17–18). The use of the word "open" is significant. It connotes freedom and opportunity, not only in the context of market access, but also with respect to the Internet generally. In her 2010 speech on Internet freedom, Clinton uses "open" and "openness" when referencing government transparency, democracy and the aptness of some governments to exploit the Internet's uninhibited nature to "crush dissent and deny human rights" (Clinton 2010). When associated with an open and free Internet, economic cyber-espionage can be understood as a moral issue.

5.2.3 Think Tanks and Consultants

Security professionals in think tanks and consulting firms represent another type of actor to refine the economic cyber-espionage threat frame after January 2010, presenting the issue as an urgent security threat connected principally to China and proposing prescriptions to the problem. One example is the computer security firm McAfee, where security professionals took it upon themselves to investigate the Google hack and bestow the name Operation Aurora. The same month the attack was announced, McAfee's former chief technology officer George Kurtz wrote in a blog post that Operation Aurora had changed "the cyberthreat landscape." He wrote that "These attacks have demonstrated that companies of all sectors are very lucrative targets. Many are highly vulnerable to these targeted attacks that offer loot that is extremely valuable: intellectual property" (Kurtz 2010). He went on to state that intellectual property theft now represents an additional security concern for companies:

> All I can say is wow. The world has changed. Everyone's threat model now needs to be adapted to the new reality of these advanced persistent threats. In addition to worrying about Eastern European cybercriminals trying to siphon off credit card databases, you have to focus on protecting all of your core intellectual property, private nonfinancial customer information and anything else of intangible value.

The official report from McAfee (2010) on the incident follows this line of reasoning that intellectual property is a serious problem for the private sector but goes one step further to argue that intellectual property theft threatens global capitalism:

> Numerous sources of intellectual property (IP) exist inside today's global companies, including trade secrets, proprietary formulas, copyrights, trademarks, and source code, to name a few. To say these IP sources represent the heart and core value of companies worldwide is an understatement. When these IP sources get compromised, capitalism and commerce are compromised on a global scale (4).

The "countermeasures" (11) that McAfee proposed are technical (for instance, improve the resistance of source code management systems) and perhaps too specific to be adopted by policymakers at the highest levels for government. But to be sure, McAfee pushed the economic cyber-espionage problem that security professionals inside and around the US government have embraced.

Security professionals in Washington have also emphasized the deleterious effects of economic cyber-espionage while coupling them specifically with China. Two examples include Adam Segal of the Council on Foreign Relations and long-time presidential advisor Richard Clarke. Segal has written at length about indigenous innovation as well as testified before Congress on the issue. As for Clarke, he published a commentary in April 2012 for The New York Times titled, "How China Steals our Secrets." In it, Clarke wrote: "But by failing to act, Washington is effectively fulfilling China's research requirements while helping to put Americans out of work" (Clarke 2012). Both Segal and Clarke have pushed for establishing international norms to stem economic cyber-espionage (Snyder 2010; Segal 2011; Segal 2012, 19). These prescriptions have also appeared in the proposed solutions by the government.

Another major actor-set in Washington is the Commission on Cybersecurity for the 44th Presidency, run out of the Center for Strategic and International Studies think tank. Headed by James Lewis, a prolific cyber-security expert, the commission comprised members of government and experts from firms such as Microsoft, IBM and Lockheed Martin (CSIS 2011). In December 2008, the commission published an influential report titled *Securing Cyberspace for the 44th Presidency*, which included recommendations that the Obama administration essentially cut and pasted into later reports. In 2008, the authors called economic cyber-espionage a major threat to US economic security and, in turn, national security (Lewis et al. 2008, 13). After the Google incident, their warning grew more explicit. In a 2011 follow-up to the 2008 report, the authors write:

> The greatest threats remain espionage and cyber crime. Espionage and cyber crime are not acts of war. They are, however, routine occurrences on the Internet. The Internet provides nation-states, their intelligence agencies, and cyber criminals with vastly expanded capabilities to illicitly acquire information. Economic espionage does the most damage: other nations steal technology, research products, and intellectual property. Some cyber spies are nation-state agents, some are proxies acting for a nation-state, and some steal for their own benefit (Lewis et al. 2011, 2).

Since January 2010, when questioned by the media on Google and China, Lewis has warned about the economic cyber-espionage threat, in effect coupling the problem with a threat subject. "This is a big espionage program aimed at getting high-tech information and politically sensitive information—the high-tech information to jump-start China's economy and the political information to ensure the survival of the regime," Lewis told The Washington Post. "This is what China's leadership is after. This reflects China's national priorities" (Cha and Nakashima 2010). Here again the indigenous innovation narrative appears.

Regarding solutions to economic cyber-espionage, the commission recommended that the government regulate the security standards of the private sector. In its 2011 follow-up paper, the commission wrote that "It is facile to assume the gains from innovation enabled by an unrestricted Internet outweigh the losses from economic espionage. It does little to help innovation and growth if foreign competitors can steal by the truckload the results of U.S. investments in research and intellectual property because of weak cybersecurity" (Lewis et al. 2011, 5). The authors, however, write that "Regulation needs to impose the lightest possible burden, be flexible rather than prescriptive, and be developed in partnership with industry (7–8). Yet, as evidenced in the 2011 report *Cybersecurity, Innovation and the Internet Economy*, the administration opted for voluntary codes of conduct for the private sector, a decision that many in the private sector applauded (Smith 2011). Under the logic of our threat politics framework, a political struggle among security professionals may be at work. On one side, the influential CSIS commission proposed stricter regulation of the private sector to block economic cyber-espionage, while on the other side, influential actors in the private sector favored voluntary conduct, an approach that evidently resonated with key policymakers in the Obama administration.

5.3 *Expanded Threat Frame → Countermeasures*

After the incident, framing actors—Google, influential government officials and professionals in think tanks and consulting firms—have established a more specific threat frame for economic cyber-espionage: It brings in China, human rights and the nation's position in the global economy, as well as concrete prognoses to the problem. This elaborated threat frame has resonated with the government, resulting in the government putting the problem on the decision agenda. Based on analysis, the expanded threat frame resonated with top-tier leaders for three reasons.

First, framing actors effectively wedded the problems of China and economic cyber-espionage. China is one of numerous countries (including American allies) with espionage programs targeting information that belongs to the American government and private sector (Fialka 1996; Office of the National Counterintelligence Executive 2011). Yet, when American policymakers think of economic espionage online, they think of China. The thought of Israel, France or even Russia (Anderlini et al. 2011) surreptitiously appropriating commercial intellectual property from American business does not set off the same alarm bells that China does. Because it is China and Chinese firms that commit corporate espionage, the US government feels more compelled to act.

The second, related reason why the expanded threat frame resonated with policymakers is that economic cyber-espionage has been understood to lead to Americans losing their jobs, a line that has been folded into government reports and legislation (US Senate 2011; Obama 2010, 4). The logic is that *unless we do something*, China will use intellectual property stolen from American companies to build up competitor firms, or worse, build up new tech industries that reduce its reliance on American products.

Finally, the elaborated threat frame resonated because it now includes the human rights variable. Economic cyber-espionage has been incorporated into a larger strategy of advancing a global normative institution that frowns upon censorship and promotes "an open, interoperable, secure, and reliable information and communications infrastructure that supports international trade and commerce, strengthens international security, and fosters free expression and innovation" (Obama 2011b, 8). Because human rights has become a serious tension-point between China and the US (MacLeod 2011), it is not surprising that the economic cyber-espionage threat image, now expanded to include Internet freedom, resonated with policymakers.

6 Conclusion

This project has tried to prove that the American government's present-day, energized attempts to deter intellectual property theft stems from a major event: Google's 2010 announcement that hackers in China had penetrated the company's systems to steal valuable source code and tried to access the Gmail accounts of human rights activists in China, Europe and the US. According to industry reports, the hackers in 2009 targeted the intellectual property of 34 additional companies. The computer security firm McAfee later dubbed the intrusions Operation Aurora.

Following this 2010 event, key American policymakers came to perceive economic cyber-espionage as an urgent problem requiring immediate attention. Although security professionals have warned about economic cyber-espionage since the 1990s, the issue after January 2010 was catapulted onto the government's docket of national security priorities. This reprioritizing resulted in measures to block the problem. Following the 2010 Google announcement, the US government's threat perception of economic cyber-espionage changed and led to new efforts to counter the problem.

To arrive at this argument, as well as explain the process whereby the event led to countermeasures, a theoretical framework called threat politics was employed. The core premise of this framework is the idea that people conceptualize, or frame, threats in easy-to-understand narratives. They develop threat frames. Threat frames have two main tasks—to diagnose a threat and propose solutions to it. The threat politics framework expects that every so often, for instance after a major event, influential actors in and around government have opportunities to formulate threat frames and convince key government officials to accept that perspective as the truth. If the threat frame resonates with the key government officials, they will implement the solutions. The framework also assumes that analysts can track threat frames in discourse available in policy-relevant documentation, therefore the current project—a case study of the Google incident—involved analysis of policy papers, transcripts, articles, legislative texts and government documents.

The central argument was substantiated in two steps. The first required showing that a change in perception occurred. In comparing the US government's perception of economic cyber-espionage before and after Aurora, we found that before Aurora, the threat frame was unspecific and lacked concrete prescriptions to the problem of economic cyber-espionage. After Google announced in January 2010 that it and other firms had been hacked, the economic cyber-espionage threat image was made more elaborate. The problem became associated with China's indigenous innovation program, human rights abuses and the blunting of America's competitive edge. The frame also includes concrete solutions to the problem, more precisely intellectual property enforcement, the diffusion of international norms and voluntary codes of conduct for business.

Step two involved detailing how the Google event led to countermeasures. With the threat politics framework, a causal chain was constructed that illustrates the process whereby the event resulted in policy changes. The model depicts the

Google event opening up a policy window, which animated three sets of actors—Google, government security professionals and think tanks and consultants—to rework and elaborate the economic cyber-espionage threat frame. This refined threat image has resonated with key US government policymakers because it includes the sensitive issues of China, American jobs and human rights.

Further research on the political struggle between the framing actors is needed. However, revealing more about this interaction necessitates that the analyst conduct interviews and obtain documentation that may be off limits. This chapter also has not entertained the question of whether the countermeasures implemented or recommended after January 2010 qualify as "extraordinary." Buzan, Wæver and de Wilde argue that extraordinary measures constitute going beyond "the normal political rules of the game" (1998, 24), but what qualifies as extraordinary is open to interpretation (Cavelty 2008, 26).

Future research projects could also gain insight into China's perception of economic cyber-espionage, or the perception of economic cyber-espionage in Europe, India and Brazil. Analysts could also move away from the study of threat perception and explore practical questions inched at in this chapter. What are the benefits or limits of international norms in cyber space? Are voluntary codes of conduct for the private sector the right answer to block online theft? How can the problem of economic cyber-espionage be measured objectively? Future economic-espionage research along both practical and theoretical lines is welcome because, going forward, cyber theft will almost certainly become a more overt sticking point in world politics.

References

Aftergood, S. (2010, March 3). White house offers glimpse of cybersecurity program. Secrecy news. Retrieved 20 Oct 2011 from http://www.fas.org/blog/secrecy/2010/03/wh_cyber.html

Anderlini, J., Marsh, P., Reed, J., Menn, J., Hollinger, P., Schäfer, D. (2011, Feb 1). Industrial espionage: Data out of the door. Financial times. Retrieved 20 Oct 2011 from http://www.ft.com/intl/cms/s/0/ba6c82c0-2e44-11e0-8733-00144feabdc0.html#axzz1ThWqmEDe

Aradau, C. (2001). Migration: The spiral of (In)security. Rubikon March 2001. Retrieved 20 Oct 2011 from http://web.archive.org/web/20070403192142/http://venus.ci.uw.edu.pl/~rubikon/forum/claudia1.htm#_ftnref12

BBC (2010, Jan 21). Hillary Clinton calls on China to probe Google attack. Retrieved 20 Oct 2011 from http://news.bbc.co.uk/2/hi/8472683.stm

Bendrath, R. (2001). The Cyberwar debate: Perception and politics in US critical infrastructure protection. *Information and Security: An International Journal, 7*(2001), 80–103.

Benford, R. D., & Snow, D. A. (2000). Framing processes and social movements: An overview and assessment. *Annual Review of Sociology, 26*(2000), 611–639.

Burns, A. (2010, Jan 14). Clinton weighs in on Google-China clash. Politico. Retrieved 20 Oct 2011 from http://www.politico.com/news/stories/0110/31483.html

Burstein, A. (2009). Trade secrecy as an instrument of national security? Rethinking the foundations of economic espionage. *Arizona State Law Journal, 41*, 937–938.

Bush, G. H. W. (1992). National policy for the security of national security telecommunications and information systems. Federation of American scientists. Retrieved 20 Oct 2011 from http://www.fas.org/irp/offdocs/nsd/nsd_42.htm

Bush, G. W. (2002). *National strategy for homeland security*. Washington DC: US Government Publishing Office.
Bush, G. W. (2003a). *National strategy for physical protection of critical infrastructure and key assets*. Washington DC: US Government Publishing Office.
Bush, G. W. (2003b). *National strategy to secure cyberspace*. Washington DC: US Government Publishing Office.
Buzan, B., Wæver, O., & de Wilde, J. (1998). *Security: A new framework for analysis*. Boulder: Lynne Rienner.
Carter, J. (1977). Presidential directive 16 Dec 1977. Federation of American scientists. Retrieved 20 Oct 2011 from http://www.fas.org/irp/offdocs/pd/index.html
Cavelty, M. D. (2008). *Cyber-security and threat politics: US efforts to secure the information age*. New York: Routledge.
Cha, A. E., Nakashima, E. (2010, Jan 14). Google China Cyberattack part of vast espionage campaign, Experts say. Washington post. Retrieved 20 Oct 2011 from http://www.washingtonpost.com/wp-dyn/content/article/2010/01/13/AR2010011300359.html
Chong, D., & Druckman, J. N. (2007). Framing Theory. *Annual Review of Political Science, 10*(2007), 103–126.
Clarke, R. A. (2012, April 2). How China steals our secrets. New York Times. Retrieved 20 Oct 2011 from http://www.nytimes.com/2012/04/03/opinion/how-china-steals-our-secrets.html?ref=computersecurity
Clinton, H. (2010). Speech on internet freedom. Washington DC, 21 January 2010. Retrieved 20 Oct 2011 from http://www.state.gov/secretary/rm/2010/01/135519.htm
Clinton, W. (2000). *Defending America's cyberspace—national plan for information systems protection*. Washington DC: US Government Publishing Office.
Cohen, M. D., March, J. G., & Olsen, J. P. (1972). A garbage can model of organizational choice. *Administrative Science Quarterly, 17*(1972), 1–25.
Cornell University Law School (2012). Economic espionage, Legal Information Institute. Retrieved 21 Oct 2012 from http://www.law.cornell.edu/wex/economic_espionage
CSIS (2011). Cybersecurity commission members. Retrieved 21 Oct 2012 from http://csis.org/node/30500
Damballa, (2011). Advanced persistent threats (APT). Accessed 21 Oct 2012. http://www.damballa.com/knowledge/advanced-persistent-threats.php
Drummond, D. (2010a, Jan 12). A new approach to China. Official Google blog. Accessed 21 Oct 2012. http://googleblog.blogspot.com/2010/01/new-approach-to-china.html
Drummond, D. (2010b, March 22). A New Approach to China: An update. Official Google blog. Accessed 21 Oct 2012. http://googleblog.blogspot.com/2010/03/new-approach-to-china-update.html
Durant, R. F., & Diehl, P. F. (1989). Agendas, alternatives, and public policy: Lessons from the U.S. foreign policy Arena. *Journal of Public Policy, 9*(2), 179–205.
Eriksson, J. (2001). Cyberplagues, IT, and security: Threat politics in the information age. *Journal of Contingencies and Crisis Management, 9*(4), 200–210.
Fialka, J. J. (1996). Stealing the spark: Why economic espionage works in America. *The Washington Quarterly, 4*(10), 172–189.
George, A. L., & Bennett, A. (2005). *Case studies and theory development in the social sciences*. Cambridge: MIT Press.
Hansen, L., & Nissenbaum, H. (2009). Digital disaster, cyber security, and the Copenhagen school. *International Studies Quarterly, 53*(4), 1155–1175.
Jacobs, A. (2011, Feb 17), China assails New US policy on internet freedom. The New York Times. Accessed 21 Oct 2012. http://www.nytimes.com/2011/02/18/world/asia/18beijing.html
Jenkins, J. P. (2011) Oklahoma city bombing. encyclopedia britannica. Accessed 21 Oct 2012. http://www.britannica.com/EBchecked/topic/735994/Oklahoma-City-bombing
Kurtz, G. (2010, Jan 14). Operation "Aurora" Hit Google, others. McAfee, Blog central. Accessed 21 Oct 2012. http://blogs.mcafee.com/corporate/cto/operation-%E2%80%9Caurora%E2%80% 9D-hit-google-others
Larson, C. (2010, Sep 7). State department innovator goes to Google. Foreign policy. Accessed 21 Oct 2012. http://www.foreignpolicy.com/articles/2010/09/07/jared_cohen?page=0,0

Lewis, J. A., Langevin, J. R., McCaul, M. T., & Raduege, H. (2011). *Cybersecurity two years later*. Washington DC: CSIS.

Lewis, J. A. (2011, June 21). Significant cyber incidents since 2006. CSIS. Accessed 21 Oct 2012. http://csis.org/publication/cyber-events-2006

Lewis, J. A., Langevin, J. R., McCaul, M. T., Charney, S., & Raduege, H. (2008). *Securing cyberspace for the 44th presidency*. Washington DC: CSIS.

Lubman, S. (2011, July 22). Changes to China's "Indigenous Innovation" policy: Don't get Too excited. Wall Street Journal. Accessed 21 Oct 2012. http://blogs.wsj.com/chinarealtime/2011/07/22/changes-to-chinas-indigenous-innovation-policy-dont-get-too-excited/?mod=google_news_blog

Lynn, W. J. (2010). Defending the new domain. Foreign affairs September/October.

MacLeod, C. (2011, April 28). US and China miles apart on human rights. USA today. Accessed 21 Oct 2012. http://www.usatoday.com/news/world/2011-04-29-china-human-rights-dissidents-talks_n.htm

Mandiant, (2011) Advanced persistent threat. Accessed 21 Oct 2012. http://www.mandiant.com/services/advanced_persistent_threat/

Markoff, J. (2010, Feb 4). Google asks spy agency for help with inquiry into Cyberattacks. The New York Times. Accessed 21 Oct 2012. http://www.nytimes.com/2010/02/05/science/05google.html

Markoff, J., Barboza, D. (2010, Feb 18). 2 China schools said to be tied to online attacks. The New York Times. Accessed 21 Oct 2012. http://www.nytimes.com/2010/02/19/technology/19china.html

McAfee. (2010). Protecting your critical assets—Lessons learned from "Operation Aurora." White Paper, McAfee Labs and McAfee Foundstone Professional Services.

Nakashima, E. (2008, Jan 26). Bush order expands network monitoring.Washington Post. Accessed 21 Oct 2012. http://www.washingtonpost.com/wp-dyn/content/article/2008/01/25/AR2008012503261.html

Nakashima, E. (2010, Feb 4). Google to enlist NSA to help it ward off cyberattacks. Washington Post. Accessed 21 Oct 2012. http://www.washingtonpost.com/wp-dyn/content/article/2010/02/03/AR2010020304057.html

Obama, B. (2009). *Cyberspace policy review*. Washington DC: US Government Publishing Office.

Obama, B. (2010). *2010 joint strategic plan on intellectual property enforcement*. Washington DC: US Government Publishing Office.

Obama, B. (2011a). *Administration's white paper on intellectual property enforcement*. Washington DC: US Government Publishing Office.

Obama, B. (2011b). *International strategy for cyberspace—prosperity, security, and openness in a networked world*. Washington DC: US Government Printing Office.

Office of the National Counterintelligence Executive. (2011). *Foreign spies stealing US economic secrets in cyberspace*. Washington DC: US Government Printing Office.

Palmer, D. (2010, May 12). US to press China on indigenous innovation. Reuters. Accessed 21 Oct 2012. http://www.reuters.com/article/2010/05/12/us-usa-china-trade-idUSTRE64B52A20100512

Perlroth, N. (2012, Feb 14). How much have foreign Hackers Stolen? The New York Times. Accessed 21 Oct 2012. http://bits.blogs.nytimes.com/2012/02/14/how-much-have-foreign-hackers-stolen/?ref=computersecurity

Reagan, R. (1984). National security decision directive number 145. Federation of American scientists. Accessed 21 Oct 2012. http://www.fas.org/irp/offdocs/nsdd145.htm

Rogers, M. (2011). Opening statement, cyber threats and ongoing efforts to protect the nation, US house of representatives permanent select committee on intelligence, 3 Oct 2011.

Rohrabacher, D. (2011). Opening statement, communist Chinese cyber-attacks, cyber-espionage and theft of American technology, House committee on foreign affairs, 15 April 2011.

Ruggie, J. G. (1998). What makes the world hang together? Neo-utilitarianism and the social constructivist challenge. *International Organization, 52*(4), 855–885.

Sanger, D.E., Markoff, J. (2009, May 29). Obama outlines coordinated cyber-security plan. The New York Times. Accessed 21 Oct 2012. http://www.nytimes.com/2009/05/30/us/politics/30cyber.html

Segal, Adam. (2012). *Chinese computer games. Foreign affairs March/April, 2012*, 14–20.

Segal, A. (2011, June 21). The role of cybersecurity in US-China relations. East Asia Forum. Accessed 21 Oct 2012. http://www.eastasiaforum.org/2011/06/21/the-role-of-cyber-security-in-us-china-relations/

Senate Armed Services Committee (2008). Report 110-335, National Defense Authorization act for Fiscal Year 2009. Washington DC.

Shanker, T. (2011, Nov 3). US report accuses China and Russia of internet spying. The New York Times. Accessed 21 Oct 2012. http://www.nytimes.com/2011/11/04/world/us-report-accuses-china-and-russia-of-internet-spying.html?_r=1&ref=computersecurity

Smith, J. (2011, June 8). Commerce department calls for voluntary Cybersecurity codes. National Journal. Accessed 20 Oct 2012. http://www.nationaljournal.com/tech/commerce-department-calls-for-voluntary-cybersecurity-codes-20110608

Snyder, W. (2010, Oct 14). Richard clarke again calls for imputed responsibility and a new protocol for the internet. Crossroads. Accessed 21 Oct 2012. http://blog.cybersecuritylaw.us/2010/10/14/richard-clarke-again-calls-for-imputed-responsibility-and-a-new-protocol-for-the-internet-the-regist/

Soroka, S. (1999). Policy agenda-setting theory revisited: A critique of Howlett on downs, baumgartner and Jones, and Kingdon. *Canadian Journal of Political Science, 32*(4), 763–772.

US-China Economic and Security Review Commission (2010). 2010 Report to Congress. Washington DC.

US Department of Commerce. (2011a). *Cybersecurity*. Washington, DC: Innovation and the internet Economy.

US Department of Commerce (2011b). Press release: Commerce department proposes new policy framework to strengthen cybersecurity protections for businesses online. Washington DC, 8 June 2011.

US Department of Homeland Security (2011). Critical infrastructure structures. department of homeland security. Accessed 21 Oct 2012. http://www.dhs.gov/critical-infrastructure-sectors

US Department of Justice (1999) Critical infrastructure protection. Accessed 13 Aug 2011. http://www.justice.gov/criminal/cybercrime/critinfr.htm#Vc

US Department of State (2011) Internet freedom. Accessed 27 July 2011. http://www.state.gov/e/eeb/cip/netfreedom/index.htm

US House (2012). HR 6029: Foreign and economic espionage penalty enhancement Act of 2012. GovTrack.us. Accessed 20 Oct 2012. http://www.govtrack.us/congress/bills/112/hr6029

US International Trade Commission. (2011). *China: effects of intellectual property infringement and indigenous innovation policies on the US economy*. DC: Washington.

US National Security Council (2010). The comprehensive national cybersecurity initiative." whitehouse.gov. Accessed 21 Oct 2012. http://www.whitehouse.gov/cybersecurity/comprehensive-national-cybersecurity-initiative

US Senate (1996). Report 104-359: The industrial espionage Act of 1996. Accessed 21 Oct 2012. http://www.fas.org/irp/congress/1996_rpt/s104359.htm

US Senate (2011). S678: Economic espionage penalty enhancement Act 2011. GovTrack.us. Accessed 21 Oct 2012. http://www.govtrack.us/congress/bills/112/s678

van Munster, R. (2007). Security on a shoestring: A Hitchhiker's guide to critical schools of security in Europe. *Cooperation and Conflict: Journal of the Nordic International Studies Association, 42*(2), 235–243.

Vijayan, J. (2010, March 2). Obama administration partially lifts secrecy on classified cybersecurity project. Computerworld. Accessed 21 Oct 2012. http://www.computerworld.com/s/article/9164818/Obama_administration_partially_lifts_secrecy_on_classified_cybersecurity_project

Wæver, O. (2004). Aberystwyth, Paris, Copenhagen: New schools in security theory and their origins between core and periphery. Montreal, 17–29 March 2004

Wæver, O. (1995). Securitization and desecuritization. In R. Lipshutz (Ed.), *On security*. New York: Columbia University Press.

Cooperative International Approaches to Network Security: Understanding and Assessing OECD and ITU Efforts to Promote Shared Cybersecurity

Stephen D. McDowell, Zoheb Nensey and Philip E. Steinberg

Abstract States have accentuated efforts to build cybersecurity strategies and offensive and defensive capabilities in the last two decades. While states have balanced efforts to promote mobility of capital, people, and goods and services with security measures to protect fixed investment and national assets, these efforts suggest a shift in the mix of openness and control. While this balance has long been a part of states' foreign policy and international relations, the promotion of network security highlights some core tensions between international conflict and cooperation in promoting cybersecurity. The Organization for Economic Cooperation and Development (OECD), and the International Telecommunications Union (ITU) have emphasized cooperation among participants in preventing harm to the network and in enhancing a "culture of security." The ITU has a longstanding principle of preventing harm to the network, and Anthony Rutkowski argues that this extends to new online networks and services. These international efforts aim to build a broad international community of participants promoting the security of physical networks, applications and uses, content, and data about individuals. The chapter examines these international efforts to advance cooperative approaches to network security and cybersecurity. It assesses these multilateral efforts in light of recent moves by states to advance more strategic national approaches to network security.

S. D. McDowell (✉) · Z. Nensey
School of Communication,
Florida State University, University Center Building C, Suite 3100,
Tallahassee, FL 32306-2664, USA
e-mail: steve.mcdowell@cci.fsu.edu

Z. Nensey
School of Communication, Florida State University,
University Center Building C, Suite 3100,
Tallahassee, FL 32306-2664, USA
e-mail: zoheb.nensey@gmail.com

P. E. Steinberg
Department of Geography, Durham University, Science Laboratories, South Road,
Durham, Dh1 3LE, UK
e-mail: steinbergphil@gmail.com

J.-F. Kremer and B. Müller (eds.), *Cyberspace and International Relations*,
DOI: 10.1007/978-3-642-37481-4_13,

1 Introduction

A wide variety of organizations have addressed concerns of their constituents over questions of network security, whether in telecommunications network services or in internet-based communications. States have accentuated efforts to build cybersecurity strategies and capabilities in the last two decades. While states have balanced efforts to promote mobility of capital, people, and goods and services with security to protect fixed investment and national assets, these efforts suggest a shift in the mix of openness and control. While this balance has long been a part of the foreign policy, trade policy, and international relations, the differing ways to promote network security highlight some core tensions between strategies of unilateral action and cooperation (Keohane 1984).

The chapter examines two international efforts to advance cooperative approaches to network security. After introducing some of the important characteristics of electronic networks and the related complexities of network security, it discusses recent arguments and claims about the desirability and feasibility of international cooperation in cybersecurity. It reviews and assesses multilateral efforts in the OECD and ITU, in light of this broader debate. The most useful steps in promoting shared or cooperative approaches to cybersecurity may come in regional agreements, or in measures taken in specific sectors in online space.

2 Network Security and Cybersecurity in the Infosphere

Increasing concerns about cybersecurity over the past decade can be contrasted with the general claims of openness that were widely made in the 1990s, when it was asserted that borders would not matter in the infosphere and that network-based communication and information technologies would be used to facilitate open flows of goods, services, and information, communication and people. However, it is useful to begin an examination of network security with a more accurate understanding of both the limits of a perspective based only on openness, and also the challenges of defining security in a network context.

While states and relations among states are building blocks of the international state system, the connections among different states and the movement and mobility of information, people, goods, and money have also been a core element of the inter-state system. Networks of transportation, communication, finance, and institutions, as well as infrastructures for energy, water, etc., have directed and defined these flows. Generically, some characteristics of networks are notable, especially when contrasted with the idea of states being defined in part by national borders:

Networks are made up of connections between different nodes or points;
There may be multiple connections between different points, not just one path;
Often networks are inter-networking, connections between some networks (regional and national) and other networks (like the internet);

Multiple uses and applications may make use of a network infrastructure, such as finance or transportation networks;
Networks require common standards and protocols to support diverse exchanges, uses, and applications;
Investment in infrastructure affects the direction, pace, and capacity of movement and mobility;
The characteristics used in network analysis focus less on users or uses and more on connections and the position of nodes, or the composition of the overall network, such centrality, or density;
Open and diverse networks may have multiple users with point-to-point contacts with others (such as the telephone or mail system), rather than one-to-many distribution dominated by a few (as with broadcast models of communication).

These features of networks pose some fundamental challenges to many conventional ideas of security. While we do not undertake a full review here, security, like positive and negative freedom (Berlin 1958), can entail keeping entities safe from some harm or risk, or safe to act and behave in certain ways. This might include being safe from destruction, harm, threats, or it may include being safe to make certain choices and actions, such as expression, communication, or commerce. Perception and politics are core to security, in that some risks and uncertainties are accepted to be in the realm of the individual, and some risks may be socialized, and in the sphere of the social and political collective. In politics, security is seen as the basic task of governments and governance. The terms sovereignty and security are often used together.

The national sphere in seen in many liberal theories of the state as a space of movement and flow, providing citizens with the security essential for the exercise choice and the enjoyment of civil rights, ideally free from some insecurities. The space within nation-states provides standardized social, economic and political institutions and practices. The nation-state thus can be seen like a walled city, with a clear frontier or edge, beyond which guarantees of security decline. But, physical walls and fenced borders are not the norm and the realities of strong networks and the essential nature of cross-borders flows for the inter-state system create challenges for those who would guarantee security.

Borders have always had a significant role in defining the nation-state geographically and territorially (Braman 2006; Kahin and Nesson 1997). Ports or border crossings serve as channels to allow and disallow mobility of people, goods and services into and out of a nation-state. Borders therefore define the terms and conditions of connections and interactions with other countries. However, when we take into account the role of networks and flows, the movement that occurs is part of the construction of national space as well as the conditions within the national sphere. Braman (2006) notes also that borders are no longer at the geographical frontier. Hence, we must look at a variety of network connections and institutions to understand the significance and locations of national borders and the conditions that they seek to impose on the mobility of people, goods, services and information.

With these considerations in mind, the conceptual and practical problems posed for the promotion of "network security" begin to accumulate. In telecommunications networks in the past, transnational communication was described as an interconnection regime (Zacher and Sutton 1996). States and inter-state organizations set the terms and conditions for connections with carriers in other countries, including technical standards, exchange of traffic, and compensation for traffic, trying to respect and reproduce borders in these interconnection points in what could be continuous technical and service networks. These efforts were animated both by economic and strategic considerations.

The wide scope of security concerns in the network context today includes the network infrastructure in the broadest sense of the term. This might include safety from its physical destruction, but also protection of content as well as security from service interruptions, unintended uses, unintended access, loss of property (IPRs), and information theft. In other words, the different clusters of concern about network security include not just the physical infrastructure but also the information carried on a computer/communication network, applications software, and the networked assets of a specific organizations or user group, as well as civil and human rights concerns such as speech, information search, privacy and identity.

Network security is vaguely defined and may include threats from a variety of users and service providers, using wired or wireless technologies, and involving any form of data (voice, audiovisual, etc.). Network security presents an attempt to balance attempts to secure national assets while reaping the advantages of open exchange, networking and open networking. These benefits, in addition to economic stability and growth, include other political and cultural values. Thus, efforts to achieve a balance that sacrifice commitments to open networking may conceal other significant costs. More broadly, the means to promote network security and security may mean the use of network technologies and applications for tracking and surveillance activities.

3 Perspectives on the Desirability and Feasibility of International Cooperation on Network security

The general characteristics of networks and challenges of promoting network security or cybersecurity with diffuse borders take on additional complexity when considered in the context of the inter-state system and international organization processes. The desirability and feasibility of inter-state cooperation or institution building to promote cybersecurity has been widely debated in a range of forums in recent years (EastWest Institute 2010; Schjolberg and Ghernaouti-Helie 2011).

The challenges of network security also bring out classic differences in perspectives between neo-realist positions and neo-liberal internationalist or institutionalist approaches to understanding international politics. The issues of security in the infosphere are often addressed as either unilateral foreign policy questions (Goodman et al. 2007; Mathieu 2007; U.S. 2002, 2009) or in a stark neo-realist framework (Information Warfare site 2011; Libicki 1996; Rothkopf 1998).

However, proponents and critics of cooperative approaches to cybersecurity do not break down neatly along these theoretic lines, and reasons arising from different perspectives can be cited both for and against the desirability and feasibility of cooperative agreements on cybersecurity (i.e. institutional approaches). The discussion below highlights some views on the *desirability* of building mechanisms for international cooperation, as well as comments on the *feasibility* of specific mechanisms. The comments below draw upon arguments and synthesize some of the main claims of numerous authors who have discussed the idea of cooperative approaches or an international treaty on cybersecurity (Bajaj 2010; Choucri and Goldsmith 2011, 2012; Ford 2010; Hughes 2010; Koh 2012; Nojeim 2010; Nye 2011; Sofaer et al. 2010; Spade 2012).

The desirability of a treaty or some form of institutionalized cooperation is most often phased in terms of the *benefits* such a mechanism would offer in terms of reducing the costs of unilateral and technical approaches to enhancing network security, and also in reducing the *risks* or system failures that might be associated with unilateral technical actions by states to protect electronic communication networks or assets connected to them.

An international agreement with broad participation could *preserve openness* of internet uses and connections, as against multiple and ongoing steps by states to advance their national self-interest in the absence of any international norms or commitments.

Cooperative state action is also desirable in that it could potentially limit the actions of non-state actors or *cyber criminals*. States may not agree to all elements of a cooperative cybersecurity treaty, but they might be able to agree on more narrow elements focused on specific criminal behavior.

A treaty or agreement might also bring online actions of states in line with *the laws of war*, in which case there would be standards for use of certain tools and means during a period when there is no formal declaration of war, and also standards for periods in which there may be a formal declaration of war between states (Hughes 2010; Koh 2012). Network-based attacks and attacks on network-connected control systems could contribute to real physical harm to persons and property, and hence could be considered to be hostilities as covered by institutions governing the conduct of war between states. Koh (2012) of the U.S. State Department argues that international law applies in cyberspace, and it is not a "law-free zone."

On the other hand, major concerns have been voiced by a number of analysts regarding the desirability of developing a cooperative international agreement on cybersecurity. Given the number of states and the diversity of political traditions, there may be *few shared values* or goals that would orient any agreement. As an interstate institution, a cooperative security agreement would *enhance the role of the state*, and likely include greater recognition of state sovereignty and control of networks. These two elements run against the traditions of internet governance that have been followed by the Internet Corporation for Assigned Names and Numbers (ICANN) since the 1990s, and by others organizations before that, which build upon the role of stakeholders rather than the preeminence of states.

Further, much technology development, deployment and use in providing network-based services takes place in the *private sector*, and the innovation, investment and predominant uses are driven by the private sector. The differences between public and private actors cut several ways. Important non-state actors are likely to be side-lined in an interstate agreement, whether the commercial actors or non-governmental organizations and civil society groups that have been active in internet governance. Alternatively, government security policies, whether national or international, may be too directive for non-government actors. Nojeim notes that any approach must consider the different needs of the public and private sectors, and that policies, "towards government systems can be much more prescriptive than policy towards private systems" (Nojeim 2010, p. 119).

This *fragmentation* between public and private responsibilities also affects national policy formation. Spade (2012) suggests that American interest in cybersecurity solutions is critically low—that the United States desperately needs a response to the ability of China to hack networks and shut down critical infrastructure in a matter of days or even hours. In Spade's view, there is fragmented interest in solving the problem, and while the Department of Defense and the Department of Homeland Security have some responsibility to protect .gov and .mil websites, they do not overlap and neither covers all of the private sector. Meanwhile, the private sector views cybersecurity as a government responsibility, while the government views it as a private responsibility. Nye (2011) also notes that non-state political actors may have gained influence: "dependence on complex cybersystems for support of military and economic activities creates new vulnerabilities in large states that can be exploited by nonstate actors" (p. 20).

Any sort of agreement to enhance security could also *reduce or limit benefits* that arise from open and interconnected electronic networks with minimal state governance. The procedures of inter-state institutions would reduce the flexibility of governance, and might shift the presumption that the internet is best governed through limited state participation. One of the substantive elements of the current order is the relative openness of the network, and stronger security institutions would likely result in more state sponsored limitations on speech and commerce.

It is also not clear what the *ideal scope* of an agreement or treaty would be. States are likely to resist any effort to restrict cyberespionage and intelligence gathering activities, especially outside their national sphere where some civil protections and civil liberties may be in place. Cyber warfare goals and tools are also distinct from intelligence gathering, with distinct institutional responses needed.

Just as there are major differences on the desirability of pursuing cooperative approaches to cybersecurity, so too are there claims and questions about the *feasibility* of such an approach. Many of the claims in support of the feasibility of this path focus on the incentives for states to work together, and also argue by comparing the infosphere to other sectors where international agreements or institutions are in place.

Proponents argue that the current condition is one of strong *interdependence* among the providers, users, and governments concerned with electronic networks and resources. While all trans-boundary sectors or issue areas—ranging from abstract processes like finance, trade, investment, to defined spaces like the international seabed, outer space, or the radio magnetic spectrum—have elements contributing to cooperative and competitive approaches to international governance, interdependence may contribute to developing ways for emphasizing shared benefits and channeling conflicts into institutional forums such as dispute resolution bodies.

Beyond the interconnection and interdependence of networks, electronic communication networks are *critical infrastructure* internal to all countries, and so protection of these resources also provides the basis for shared goals.

Also along this line, the *leading states* with largest economies have the most at stake, the most to lose from risks and vulnerabilities to networks and from cyberwarfare. This provides some incentive to explore modalities of international cooperation. Bajaj (2010) argues, "unilateral dominance is cyberspace is not achievable by any country." Similarly: "No government can fight cybercrime or secure its cyberspace in isolation. Cyber security is not a technology problem that can be 'solved'; it is a risk to be managed by a combination of defensive technology, astute analysis and information warfare, and traditional diplomacy" (p. i).

States and private sector actors also have incentives to reduce the high and increasing *costs* of technical approaches to security. While purchases of security hardware, software and services are a form of economic consumption and do stimulate increased investment and expenditures in the overall economy, they also skew the distribution of economic costs, and may also introduce other social, political and cultural costs to providers and users, some more difficult to quantify in the formal economy.

States have shared interests in reducing *risks from non-state actors*, and have shown that sovereign states can work together in certain criminal matters, for instance, to deal with challenges that cross borders. Some norms are emerging in regional agreements, such as the European Commission Convention on Cybercrime. Shared norms have emerged and cooperative bodies are placed in other sectors related to electronic networks, such internet protocols, technical standards, electronic payments, prevention of fraud, or controlling child pornography.

Mechanisms can be developed to *identify elements* of cybersecurity challenges and address these uniquely and at different levels, rather than proceeding to build a total framework at one time (Bajaj 2010, p. ii). Many private organizational measures and international measures are already in place, such as Cyber Emergency Response Team information sharing (Choucri and Goldsmith 2012; Sofaer et al. 2010). Franz-Stefan Cody of the East–West Institute, for instance, proposes a trust-building code of conduct that might coordinate cyber-response centers (Sternstein 2011). Another proposal along this line would be "confidence-building, stability, and risk reduction measures" (Sternstein 2012) as discussed in the Organization for Security and Cooperation in Europe. Sofaer, Clark and Diffie (Sofaer et al. 2010) also argue that cybersecurity agreements are only likely be effective by identifying, "the activities that are most likely to be subjects of such agreements and those that are not" (p. 180).

Critics who raise questions about feasibility point to the *lack of shared norms*, apart from specific interests, among leading states (Goldsmith 2011). If some states are not acting in good faith (Ford 2010), an agreement to limit options for offense and defense may have wider implications for signatory states.

Further problems in feasibility arise from several *information inadequacies*. One is the lack of mechanisms to verify that offensive capabilities are not being developed and deployed (Ford 2010; Nye 2011). Nye (p. 25) calls this a lack of empirical content to form a strategy. Identification of bad actors or "attribution" poses another problem (Koh 2012). The existence of dual use (Koh 2012) or multiple use network capabilities makes identification of offensive capabilities difficult (Ford 2010).

Ford (2010) argues that leading states may have *different understandings* of cybersecurity strategy, and that Russia and China may view this more in terms of influence and broad communication environments rather than in technical terms as in the United States (p. 55). Following this approach, some forms of expression and political speech, including foreign information operations, would be seen as state security threats in Russia and China.

Nye (2011) notes that, "interdependence and vulnerability are twin facts that are likely to persist, but we should expect further technological change to complicate early strategies" (p. 24). Interdependence is not sufficient to lead to cooperative institution building, as the shifting technological tools and environments complicate efforts to build shared information and understandings.

Large states still have incentives to *pursue unilateral advantages* in communication network based activities through technical means, and these seem to outweigh the supposed benefits or incentives to build cooperative security institutions that might serve to limit the autonomy of state action. While the participation of leading states is needed to build multilateral cooperative institutions, these states also are in the strongest position to benefit through the use of unilateral technical means to enhance their security and interests. For instance, Spade (2012) suggests that virtually every major conflict over the last few years has been accompanied by cyberattacks. Spade argues that Russia and China are especially guilty of this, as they have tacitly supported hacking operations in Eastern Europe (in the case of Russia), and in Taiwan, Western Europe, and the United States (in the case of China.) While these hackers do not receive official government sanction, the governments do not punish these criminals or bring them to court. Rather, their activities are considered "patriotic." Spade also suggests that cyberspace is yet another domain that can be used for warfare—just as land, air, sea, and space have all been used for warfare, so can cyberspace. And just as these domains can have an impact upon each other, cyberspace has an especially strong impact.

At best, even with some areas or sectors building some cooperative forums, states will retain rights to use whatever means they deem appropriate to protect their core national interests, consistent with the principle of self-help. Spade (2012) argues that cyber war is different from cyber warfare, largely in that cyber warfare is part of a larger, coordinated strategy that involves the other domains. The problem is that there is no clear definition of what a cyberattack is. There are different parts to cybersecurity and cyber war—there are offensive attacks designed to disable and disrupt, there are defensive measures designed to stop incoming cyber attacks, and lastly, there are offensive attacks that are merely intended to steal information or exploit weaknesses in cyberstructure—and of those, there are plenty.

This brief summary of some of the key claims and elements of arguments for and against the desirability and feasibility of cooperative approaches to cybersecurity provides a conceptual and theoretic context within which to consider the specific programs of two international organizations in this area.

4 The Organization for Economic Cooperation and Development

The OECD has a limited membership, including only industrialized liberal democracies prior to expansion in the 1990s. In 2013 it had 34 member countries, mainly developed market economies in Europe, North America and Asia, but also newer members in Eastern Europe. These countries have many of the most advanced information and communication networks in the world, and their economies depend increasingly over the last decades on networked communication infrastructures. The OECD unit on IICP had been dealing with international electronic information networks since the 1970s, most directly in a series of studies on transborder data flow (TDF) in the 1970s and 1980s, as well as agreements on TDF in 1980 and 1985.

The 1992 OECD Guidelines for the Security of Information Systems are notable for their effort to recognize and not impinge upon state sovereignty. They note: "the Guidelines do not affect the sovereign rights of national governments in respect of national security and public order ("ordre public"), subject always to the requirements of national law." The 1992 Guidelines also recommend a comprehensive program of action by member states to further refine and agree upon security measures and move forward in their implementation. It recommends that countries:

establish measures, practices and procedures to reflect the principles concerning the security of information systems….
consult, co-ordinate and co-operate in the implementation of the Guidelines, including international collaboration to develop compatible standards, measures, practices and procedures for the security of information systems;
agree as expeditiously as possible on specific initiatives for the application of the Guidelines;
disseminate extensively the principles contained in the Guidelines;
review the Guidelines every five years with a view to improving international co-operation on issues relating to the security of information systems (OECD 1992).

Other work in the 1990s by the OECD, also directly connected with Internet technologies, focused more on commercial and economic development. This included the studies and deliberations that grew out of the NII and the Global Information Infrastructure (OECD 1997) discussions, beginning with the "Framework for Global Electronic Commerce" (United States 1996). The OECD undertook a number of efforts to define e-commerce beginning in the late 1990s, as well as to harmonize ways to measure e-commerce among its members. An "OECD Action Plan for Electronic Commerce" emphasized four major areas: enhancing information infrastructure, including "improving access to telecommunications and Internet services at the price, reliability, and speed levels needed for e-commerce"; "building trust for users and consumers of electronic commerce"; "establishing ground rules for the digital marketplace"; and maximizing benefits of electronic commerce (Tigre and O'Connor 2002).

The OECD also issued its *Guidelines for Consumer Protection in Electronic Commerce* (1999). The goals of these guidelines were "to help ensure that online consumers are no less protected when shopping online than when buying from their local store or ordering from a catalogue," and to "reflect existing legal protections available to consumers in more traditional forms of commerce by setting out core characteristics of effective consumer protection for online b2c transactions" (Donohue 2003). The emphases are transparent and effective protection; fair business, advertising and marketing practices; online disclosures; transparent processes for the confirmation of transactions; secure payment mechanisms and information on the level of security; dispute resolution and redress; privacy protection; and education and awareness (Donohue 2003).

This agenda combined a number of significant policy changes to support construction of telecommunications infrastructure and provision of a competitive environment and stable regulatory environment in the context of privatization efforts (versus "excessively generous exclusivity agreements"). Among other issues that OECD experience in e-commerce highlighted were the construction of an "e-commerce conducive business environment," consumer protection, the protection of privacy, ensuring the security of transactions, and the authentication of electronic signatures (Tigre and O'Connor 2002).

Some countries saw the Global Information Infrastructure goals, national information infrastructure planning, and e-commerce applications on the World Wide Web as vehicles to stimulate the next wave of economic development, and to gain competitive advantage for leading national sectors. This view was reinforced by the emphasis placed upon the availability of information and communications technologies deployed in the infrastructures necessary to support e-commerce. For instance, an OECD presentation in 2001 emphasized internet access prices, internet subscription levels, the number of internet hosts per 100 inhabitants, the number of secure internet servers per 100 inhabitants in a country, the level of broadband subscriptions by households, and the level of household ownership of computers (OECD 2001).

The OECD also launched a series of efforts to coordinate electronic commerce promotion among its members. Among the issues and initiatives addressed were the "culture of security," privacy online, network security, cross-border fraud, broadband access, the importance of electronic commerce for development, and measuring the information economy (OECD 2004). A 2005 report outlined national efforts to promote "a culture of security for information systems and networks in OECD countries" (OECD 2005), while a follow-up compared "development of policies for the protection of critical information infrastructures" in Canada, Korea, the United Kingdom, and the United States (OECD 2007).

The shift in emphasis and approaches was also reflected in principles to guide efforts to promote a culture of security in the online world that the OECD published in 2002, and that notably referred to "participants" rather than members states:

- Awareness. Participants should be aware of the need for security of information systems and networks and what they can do to enhance security.
- Responsibility. All participants are responsible for the security of information systems and networks
- Response. Participants should act in a timely and co-operative manner to prevent, detect and respond to security incidents.
- Ethics. Participants should respect the legitimate interests of others.
- Democracy. The security of information systems and networks should be compatible with essential values of a democratic society.
- Risk assessment. Participants should conduct risk assessments.
- Security design and implementation. Participants should incorporate security as an essential element of information systems and networks.
- Security management. Participants should adopt a comprehensive approach to security management.
- Reassessment. Participants should review and reassess the security of information systems and networks, and make appropriate modifications to security policies, practices, measures and procedures.

The contrasts with the 1992 statement are striking. The 2002 OECD Guidelines use the term "participants" rather than referring to "countries." This includes a variety of public and private organizations, with a range of scopes of operation, nationally and internationally.

Other than respecting the legitimate interests of others, there is no direct mention of international cooperation or institutions or agreements. The focus is on the role of actors or participants, rather than on the activities of international organizations or cooperative agreements or mechanisms. Transnational activities, the importance or lack of importance of borders, or the respect or non-respect for borders are not mentioned in the principles. In a sense this either accepts or promotes the idea of a borderless world, but it does not confront directly the question of where states, borders, or international cooperation fit into the framework.

The June 2011 OECD "Communique on Principles for Internet Policy-Making" emphasized openness, transparency and multiple stakeholders' participation, and included a section on encouraging cooperation to promote internet security. The statement addressed security efforts in the context of other goals, including innovation, economic growth, and social progress, and also highlighted the importance of "market-driven security standards":

Policies to address security threats and reduce vulnerabilities are important to the continued vitality of the Internet. The implementation of internationally recognised, market-driven security standards and best practices to promote online security should be encouraged. In addition, breakthrough R&D on novel security systems capable of dealing with the high complexity of ICT networks, information systems and applications should be encouraged. Policies to enhance online security should not disrupt the framework conditions that enable the Internet to operate as a global open platform for innovation, economic growth, and social progress and should not be used as pretence for protectionism. Policies should also aim to enhance individual and collective efforts for self-protection and promote trust and confidence. Their consistency with, and potential impact on, other economic and social dimensions of the Internet should be carefully assessed through a multi-stakeholder process prior to adoption and implementation (OECD 2011).

The OECD's July 2012 "Recommendation of the Council Concerning Guidelines for the Security of Information Systems and Networks: Towards a Culture of Security" arose from a five year review cycle of the 2002 principles and included the same principles as the 2002 statement (OECD 2012a, b, c). The recommendation reviewed the changing conditions and noted that states had made cybersecurity policies a much higher priority in recent years. It noted that the guidelines were intended to be "voluntary, and do not affect the sovereign rights of states," and that no one solution was being proposed, but it did recommend that member countries:

Establish new, or amend existing, policies, practices, measures and procedures to reflect and take into account the Guidelines for the Security of Information Systems and Networks: Towards a Culture of Security by adopting and promoting a culture of security as set out in the Guidelines;

Consult, co-ordinate and co-operate at national and international levels to implement the Guidelines;

Disseminate the Guidelines throughout the public and private sectors, including to governments, business, other organisations, and individual users to promote a culture of security, and to encourage all concerned parties to be responsible and to take necessary steps to implement the Guidelines in a manner appropriate to their individual roles;

Make the Guidelines available to non-member countries in a timely and appropriate manner.

The desirability of collective action and cooperation in security policies is emphasized. However, the benefits of openness are also highlighted in the security guidelines, so that security efforts do not close off the open flow of information, trade and investment.

The Guidelines are presented as practices that each member state and other participant should move toward, rather than the path of pursuing a formal agreement as the main mechanism. The 2012 recommendation does go somewhat further than earlier in asking member states to work together, arising from the increased intensity of concerns about cybersecurity and the possibility that unilateral state actions might diminish the benefits of open flow.

Since the OECD includes a small subset of states, the group shares general approaches to economic growth and governance that have produced the Guidelines as well as ongoing work and discussion, and it would seem to be better suited to make progress toward further institutionalization of this cooperation than would other international organizations. At the same time, the Guidelines lay out norms to move toward national policy harmonization rather than addressing a formal agreement. Although a smaller group of states, the OECD has often set general principles and standards for other international forums. Indeed, the principles of the Culture of Security also appeared in a United Nations (2003) resolution.

The OECD has completed a number of formal agreements or declarations in this sector, most notably the Transborder Data Flow agreements in 1980 and 1985 aimed at keeping borders open for flows of digital data. The lack of stronger resolutions or agreements in the network security sector is notable, however, given that the stakes are high and that many of these countries are also members of the Council of Europe, the North Atlantic Treaty Organization, and Council for Security and Cooperation in Europe.

5 The International Telecommunications Union

The International Telecommunications Union (ITU) is the main multilateral body dealing with telecommunications issues, and especially telecommunications network technology standards. As of 2012 there were 193 member states and over 700 private sector members. Numerous working groups address technology standards in order to allow various technologies and networks from across the world to interconnect with each other. The ITU has therefore been involved in coordinating the discussions among governments and industry players for the many layers and kinds of technology whose interconnection is necessary for web-based services and e-commerce (ITU International Telecommunications Union 2004; Kahin et al. 1995). A number of internet use and governance issues were addressed in the meetings of the World Summit on the Information Society in Geneva in 2003 and Tunis in 2005 (ITU 2005a, b, 2003a, b). The main focus of these meetings was expanding access and applications of relevance for developing countries, as well as issues and modes of internet governance.

Rutkowski (2005) provides a very useful overview of the history of concerns about network security, noting the longstanding commitment of ITU members to cooperation in protecting the network from harm and in identifying network elements or users that have harmed the network:

> *The 1988 International Telecommunication Regulations ... obligates* countries to "avoid technical harm to the operation of the telecommunication facilities of third countries"

> the basic international arrangements for public communication network infrastructures tend to be quite similar whether the technology platform is the electrical telegraph, satellite systems, or internet protocols. The key features include agreement on a common purpose in establishing globally internetworked public networks and services, the role of government in assuring availability, the adherence to some common technical and operational standards, national security considerations, sharing information, prioritization of emergency communications, and settlement mechanisms among providers.

> since the inception of intergovernmental telecommunications collaboration in 1850 at Dresden, the protection of public communication network infrastructures has been "rule no. 1." All cooperating nations have a shared obligation to maintain and protect the public communication infrastructure. (Rutkowski 2005)

An important part of this approach to network security is to identify all components of the network (or network objects), including those that do harm to the network:

> For 155 years, one requirement has always been fundamental. **Every signatory nation has an obligation to implement administrative and enforcement mechanisms whereby those who can cause harm to the network infrastructure or radiocommunications of another country can be authoritatively identified and contacted, to make that information available to other signatories, to take actions to mitigate the harm, and pursue the party causing the harm whether by accident or intent** (Rutkowski 2005).

Rutkowski (2005) argues that, "The core international requirements for infrastructure protection are pretty much the same as they have always been:" global intergovernmental agreements to avoid harm to another country's network, and implementation of effective administrative and enforcement mechanisms to identify and pursue any party causing harm to the network. Rutkowski (2011) provides detailed and historical evidence to outline the elements of ITU agreements concerning network security and demonstrates the longstanding development of these elements. States have obligations to avoid harm to the network and to identify and share information about and pursue any party causing harm to the network. States also have sovereign rights to shut down the network for reasons of national interest or emergency.

The report on the first phase of the World Summit on the Information Society (WSIS) held in Geneva in 2003 included very strong claims of international cooperation, including "new forms of solidarity, partnership and cooperation among governments and other stakeholders, i.e. the private sector, civil society and international organizations. Realizing that the ambitious goal of this Declaration—bridging the digital divide and ensuring harmonious, fair and equitable development for all—will require strong commitment by all stakeholders, we call for digital solidarity, both at national and international levels" (ITU 2003a). The Declaration of Principles from WSIS 2003 also noted the need to promote a culture of security:

> Strengthening the trust framework, including information security and network security, authentication, privacy and consumer protection, is a prerequisite for the development of the Information Society and for building confidence among users of ICTs. A global culture of cyber-security needs to be promoted, developed and implemented in cooperation with all stakeholders and international expert bodies. These efforts should be supported by increased international cooperation. Within this global culture of cyber-security, it is important to enhance security and to ensure the protection of data and privacy, while enhancing access and trade.....
>
> While recognizing the principles of universal and non-discriminatory access to ICTs for all nations, we support the activities of the United Nations to prevent the potential use of ICTs for purposes that are inconsistent with the objectives of maintaining international stability and security, and may adversely affect the integrity of the infrastructure within States, to the detriment of their security. It is necessary to prevent the use of information resources and technologies for criminal and terrorist purposes, while respecting human rights (ITU 2003a)

The 2005 phase two meetings of the WSIS led to the Tunis Commitment, which also included statements on network security. This statement is more comprehensive in presenting security questions and concerns as opportunities in all cases for international cooperation. This includes confronting uses of ICTs for purposes that are "inconsistent with objectives of maintaining international stability and security" and that, "may adversely affect the integrity of infrastructure within States."

> … **we underscore** that ICTs are effective tools to promote peace, security and stability, to enhance democracy, social cohesion, good governance and the rule of law, at national, regional and international levels. ICTs can be used to promote economic growth and enterprise development. Infrastructure development, human capacity building, information security and network security are critical to achieve these goals (ITU 2005a).

The 2005 meeting's "Tunis Agenda for the Information Society" included a more extensive list of statements concerning network security, including the role of all stakeholders. As with the mention of "international cooperation and solidarity at all levels" in the "Tunis Commitment" (paragraph 37), the "Tunis Agenda" directly emphasized both the role of international cooperation and of states. The "Tunis Agenda" outlined a range or priorities concerning security, and in many cases these were offset by competing values such as privacy and human rights. While recognizing both national and international level priorities, national borders were represented as opportunities for cooperation and coordination. As with the OECD, multiple stakeholders were mentioned:

> 39. **We seek** to build confidence and security in the use of ICTs by strengthening the trust framework. **We reaffirm** the necessity to further promote, develop and implement in cooperation with all stakeholders a global culture of cybersecurity, as outlined in UNGA Resolution 57/239 and other relevant regional frameworks. This culture requires national action and increased international cooperation to strengthen security while enhancing the protection of personal information, privacy and data. Continued development of the culture of cybersecurity should enhance access and trade and must take into account the level of social and economic development of each country and respect the development-oriented aspects of the Information Society.
>
> 42. … **We affirm** that measures undertaken to ensure Internet stability and security, to fight cybercrime and to counter spam, must protect and respect the provisions for privacy and freedom of expression as contained in the relevant parts of the Universal Declaration of Human Rights and the Geneva Declaration of Principles.
>
> 45. **We underline** the importance of the security, continuity and stability of the Internet, and the need to protect the Internet and other ICT networks from threats and vulnerabilities. **We affirm** the need for a common understanding of the issues of Internet security, and for further cooperation to facilitate outreach, the collection and dissemination of security-related information and exchange of good practice among all stakeholders on measures to combat security threats, at national and international levels.

The ITU was charged with the responsibility to follow up on action item C5 "Building confidence and security in the use of ICTs." The International Telecommunications Union has also increased emphasis on network security, establishing a "Cybersecurity Gateway" web portal page in 2007 to link to security activities in different ITU sectors (ITU 2012d):

> … a framework within which the international response to the growing challenges to cybersecurity can be coordinated and addressed in response to its role as Facilitator for C.5. GCA benefits from the advice of a High-Level Experts Group (HLEG) composed by world-renowned specialists in cybersecurity, representing expertise from across a broad range of backgrounds in policy-making, government, academia and the private sector.

The Global Cybersecurity Agenda (ITU 2012b) includes five main areas: legal measures, technical and procedural measures, organizational structures, capacity building, and international cooperation. As part of the Cybersecurity Strategy, a High Level Experts Group was formed. Its mandate was to identify approaches to advance collective cybersecurity. Its report deals mainly with cybercrime, and the bulk of the report draws mainly on expanding participation in the Council of Europe Convention on Cybercrime. It does not address the state use of surveillance and monitoring that may be outside of national legal frameworks, nor does it address citizen rights or broader claims of international human rights or civil rights. It does not address the principles laid out in the 2002 OECD principles or the 2003 UN resolution (ITU 2008).

The ITU WSIS resolutions are inclusive, wide ranging documents, while more technical steps are laid out by the expert group. The focus on network security follows from the longstanding mandate of the organization (ITU 2011). Additionally, the broad participation of the WSIS and parallel civil society conferences was a way to promote broader legitimacy for its work from civil society, as well as to reassert a state and interstate role in internet governance.

The ITU continues efforts in coordination, collective action, standardization and regulation in line with its history. Although it has opened up to some non-state actors and pays some note to civil society actors, challenges to standardization—which is envisioned as a closed-system of rules-based exchanges and network community of common interests rather than an ever-expanding, ill-defined network—continue to grow as a way to pursue network security.

The ITU World Conference on International Telecommunications (WCIT) meeting in December 2012 was a review of the International Telecommunication Regulations (ITU 2012a), and was also seen as an attempt to codify some new norms for internet governance. The conference attracted much comment about efforts to expand ITU control of the internet (ITU 2012c). Bennett notes that the system to date had been a "loose, consensus-based system of voluntary agreements" (Bennett 2012). Chinese and Russian proposals were listed in the Final Acts of the 2012 ITU meetings. These proposals (codified in additions to Article 3A of the ITU constitution) would have replaced the ICANN with the ITU-T for the purposes of assigning letters and numbers (ITU 2012). In an era where the ICANN has attempted to be as open as possible and integrate as many voices as possible into the decision-making process, Bennett argues that the Russian and Chinese proposals would drown out the voices of others merely because they are the most powerful individual countries in the ITU (Bennett 2012). In order for an organization to have institutional legitimacy, it must not only have all actors involved (and not just listed on paper), but it must have a way of holding all actors in the organization and in the negotiations accountable (Take 2012). Logically speaking, the most substantial reform that the ITU could make to prevent the sort of political gamesmanship that occurred recently would be to increase the level of transparency and to involve more countries in the treaty negotiations (Take 2012). The proposed treaty was agreed upon by 89 of the 152 countries, and did not enjoy the approval of the United States, India, Japan, Canada, Germany, and several other major states (Pfanner 2012). The ITU in many ways is a potentially useful vehicle for moving forward with international cooperation around internet governance, but the proposed treaty would have empowered some leading states and the expense of other actors.

6 Discussion and Conclusions

The chapter has examined efforts by two international organizations to advance cooperative approaches to network security. Although these efforts have been over-shadowed in recent years by unilateral state efforts to defend ICT resources and develop offensive capabilities, the challenges to and importance of advancing possibilities for multilateral cooperation and governance remain.

The multilateral efforts of the OECD and ITU stand alongside and run against those of leading states to push ahead with more national and technical approaches to network security. However, while these two organizations have advanced cooperative approaches to network security to deal with cybercrime, they do not address directly the militarization of the infosphere, perhaps because the dominant states do not want to rule out the unilateral uses in which they might prevail, and small states with fewer capabilities are unwilling to rule out self help or are unable to limit certain activities. Collective security and arms control have been tried in other issue areas, whether in small groups, treaties, or in the UN, but not so much in this sector. Given an increased state focus on unilateral cybersecurity strategies and tools, this presents major challenges for broad cooperative international approaches or building stronger multilateral institutions to preserve openness and safety and security in the infosphere. Several observations are offered in this regard to conclude the chapter, relating claims about the desirability and feasibility of cooperative approaches to the work of the OECD and ITU.

The OECD and the ITU both have long histories of developing cooperative international approaches to network management, reflecting the general desirability of these mechanisms. Both proceed from the basis of enhancing the benefits of use of electronic networks, and enhancing and preserving the openness of connections to and uses of these networks. Both encourage efforts to address cybercrime and illegitimate uses of the network, but their mandates do not include addressing state actions in war, although the ITU does note that states have the right to protect their interests and sovereignty, as Rutkowski notes, consistent with the laws of war.

The work of the two organizations in many ways runs against the claims of arguments critical of the desirability of cooperative approaches. While states may disagree, they do have shared values in promoting network connectivity in the

ITU, and, in the case of the OECD, maximizing the benefits of promoting trade, investment, technical change, and similar policy directions in member countries. The ITU includes state members, with some non-state observers, while the OECD also includes non-state consultative groups. The OECD Culture of Security Guidelines refer to participants, rather than just the member states, recognizing the importance of private sector actors in building broadly shared approaches to network security and working to minimize the fragmentation between public and private sectors. International cooperative action in the OECD is intended to minimize the costs of security efforts and promote economic development, even though there have been changes in emphasis. While the ITU WSIS documents embrace a large number of issues, the OECD guidelines break the problem area into sectors that can each be addressed in a more limited scope.

Regarding the feasibility of cooperative approaches, both organizations' work, again, proceeds from the assessment of strong interdependence of all countries in interconnected electronic networks, and that these networks constitute critical infrastructure internal to all countries. The OECD and ITU both include the leading market economy states in the developed world, although ITU participation is almost global. Both organizations have mechanisms in place for negotiation although states may disagree on specific policies. It is less clear that the ITU has heard clear messages from leading states to promote efforts to reduce the high and increasing costs of technical approaches to security, while the OECD work is proceeding on multiple fronts. The ITU statements reflect efforts to reduce the risks to safety and security from non-state actors, and the OECD approach encourages work on multiple segments to identify different cybersecurity challenges and work on these as appropriate.

The work of the OECD and ITU addresses in some parts the various claims about the lack of feasibility of cooperative approaches, but not entirely. Although there are some shared norms reflected in the history and purposes of these organizations, there is also a lack of shared norms in the security sector in the ITU, given its more inclusive and diverse membership. Both organizations have extensive policy research and information sharing programs that could be built upon to address the challenges of information inadequacies in network security, but persistent concerns about legitimizing an enhanced role of the states in internet governance limit the possibility for information building and sharing to address questions of verification, attribution, and dual-use network technologies. While the OECD countries have a higher level of agreement concerning political economy and governance, different understandings of cybersecurity strategies remain a crucial challenge for the ITU. While technical change does complicate any efforts at developing cooperative approaches, both organizations have dealt with and addressed technical change and continue to do so. Since both organizations' member states have varying interests, while all have committed in some ways to international treaties obligating states to certain policies and procedures in a wide range of sectors, the nature and scope of the OECD and ITU work is not likely to dissuade states from pursuing unilateral advantages and maintaining the rights to use whatever means they deem appropriate.

In general, the work of these two organizations seems to show that forms of partial, rather than global, approaches to cooperation may be useful next steps in enhancing network security. One approach is *regional agreements* among groups of states such as the OECD that may contribute to the development of shared norms and practices. The OECD is a smaller group, and the active participation of mid-level policy makers over the long haul can build shared understandings of policy problems. Its work can be relatively flexible, as the shifts in emphasis show, and the processes and working groups in place seem more likely to respond to emerging issues, such as efforts to encourage more direct state action and international cooperation in the 2012 reports. This regional approach makes it more likely that common national approaches would emerge among this group, consistent with its efforts at policy coordination and harmonization.

The other approach recommended by many analysts is to pursue *sectoral* talks and agreements in areas such as fraud, intellectual property protection, and actions by certain non-state groups. Certain dimensions of network security, associated with protecting the network and the obligations of states, have a long history in the ITU, and this recognition could provide a basis for updating and refining these mechanisms. WSIS documents balance network security with other values and objectives, making the set of linked issues quite large, but they have been one way to offset suspicion among some groups that the ITU (and the states who are its dominant players) is taking a greater role in internet governance including security issues without due regard to speech rights, privacy, etc. The sharing of best practices, or the network of CERT centers, may provide models for building sectoral work and common knowledge and information as the basis for cooperative approaches.

Overall, the goals and ambitions set for cooperative approaches to network security have often been set so high that the possibility of accomplishing these outcomes in the international context are very slim. These proposals come in the form of proposals for comprehensive treaties or agreements. The investigation of regional and sectoral agreements may be a way to redirect the consideration of challenges and responses in this sector. Another consideration is the historical and incomplete nature of institution building. This is most often a series of decisions and smaller agreements that contribute over time to broader understandings, practices, and institutional formation. Even when relatively stable and developed, total cooperation and participation by states and other actors in an institutional framework (such as trade and investment or dispute resolution) is also not the actual outcome or practice. More historical and nuanced understanding of these processes, as seen in some of the analysis cited here, can also contribute to identifying important next steps.

References

Bajaj, K. (2010). The cybersecurity agenda: Mobilizing for international action. Available via The EastWest Institute. http://www.ewi.info/system/files/Bajaj_Web.pdf.

Bennett, R. (2012). The gathering storm: WCIT and the global regulation of the internet. Available via The Information Technology & Innovation Foundation. Retrieved December 12, 2012. from http://www2.itif.org/2012-gathering-storm-wcit-regulations.pdf.

Berlin, I. (1958). Two concepts of liberty. In Isaiah Berlin (1969), *Four essays on liberty*. Oxford: Oxford University Press.

Braman, S. (2006). Change of state: Information, policy, and power. Cambridge MIT Press.
Choucri, N., & Goldsmith, D. (2012). Lost in cyberspace: Harnessing the internet, international relations, and global security. *Bulletin of the Atomic Scientists, 68*(2), 70–77.
Donohue, M. (2003). Consumer protection across borders: OECD work to build consumer trust in the digital economy. Presentation at the OECD/UN/World Bank Global Forum: Integrating ICT in Development Programmes, Paris, 5 March 2003.
EastWest Institute. (2010). *Protecting the digital economy: The first worldwide cybersecurity summit in Dallas*. Dallas, 2010.
Ford, C. A.(2010). The trouble with cyber arms control. *The New Atlantis Fall, 29*, 52–67.
Goldsmith, J. (2011). Cybersecurity treaties: a skeptical view. In: *Future challenges in national security and law*. http://media.hoover.org/sites/default/files/documents/FutureChallenges_Goldsmith.pdf
Goodman, S. E., Kirk, J. C., & Kirk, M. H. (2007). Cyberspace as a medium for terrorists. *Technological Forecasting and Social Change, 74*(2), 193–210.
Hughes, R. (2010). A treaty for cyberspace. *International Affairs, 86*(2), 523–541.
Mathieu, G. (2007). Cyberterrorism: Hype or reality? *Computer Fraud & Security, 2007*(2), 9–12.
The Information Warfare Site. (2011). Information Warfare Site. http://www.iwar.org.uk/index.htm
International Telecommunications Union. (2012a). *Final acts of the world conference on international telecommunications*. Dubai: International Telecommunications Union.
International Telecommunications Union. (2012b). Global cybersecurity agenda. http://www.itu.int/osg/csd/cybersecurity/gca/new-gca-brochure.pdf.
International Telecommunications Union. (2012c). WCIT-12:vMyth-busting presentation. http://www.itu.int/en/wcit-12/Pages/WCIT-backgroundbriefs.aspx.
International Telecommunications Union. (2003a). *Geneva declaration of principles*. In: First phase of the WSIS. Geneva, 10–12 December 2003. Retrieved from http://www.itu.int/wsis/documents/doc_multi.asp?lang=en&id=1161|0.
International Telecommunications Union. (2003b). *Geneva plan of action*. In: First phase of the WSIS. Geneva, 10–12 December 2003. Retrieved from http://www.itu.int/wsis/documents/doc_multi.asp?lang=en&id=1160|0.
International Telecommunications Union. (2004). *ITU and its activities related to internet-protocol (IP) networks*. Geneva: ITU.
International Telecommunications Union. (2005a). *Tunis commitment*. In: Second phase of the WSIS. Tunis, 16–18 November 2005. Retrieved from http://www.itu.int/wsis/documents/doc_multi.asp?lang=en&id=2266|2267.
International Telecommunications Union. (2005b). *Tunis agenda for the information society*. In: Second phase of the WSIS. Tunis, 16–18 November 2005. Retrieved from http://www.itu.int/wsis/documents/doc_multi.asp?lang=en&id=2266|2267.
International Telecommunications Union. (2008). Global security agenda high level experts group global security report. http://www.itu.int/osg/csd/cybersecurity/gca/global_strategic_report/index.html.
International Telecommunications Union. (2011). The ITU national cybersecurity strategy guide. http://www.itu.int/ITU-D/cyb/cybersecurity/docs/ITUNationalCybersecurityStrategyGuide.pdf.
International Telecommunications Union. (2012d). Cybersecurity gateway. http://groups.itu.int/Default.aspx?alias=groups.itu.int/cybersecurity-gateway.
Kahin, B., & Abbate, J. (Eds.). (1995). *Standards for information infrastructure*. Cambridge: MIT Press.
Kahin, B., & Nesson, C. (1997). *Borders in cyberspace: Information policy and the global information infrastructure*. Cambridge: MIT Press.
Keohane, R. O. (1984). *After hegemony: Cooperation and discord in the world political economy*. Princeton, NJ: Princeton University Press.
Koh, HH. (2012). International law in cyberspace. Remarks at USCYBERCOM Interagency Legal conference, Ft. Meade, MD. Retrieved September 18, 2012. from http://www.state.gov/s/l/releases/remarks/197924.htm.

Libicki, M. (1996). The emerging primacy of information. *Orbis, 40*, 261–274.
Nojeim, G. T. (2010). Cybersecurity and freedom on the internet. *Journal of National Security law and Policy, 4*, 119–137.
Nye, J. S. (2011). Nuclear lessons for cyber security. *Strategic Studies Quarterly, 5*(4), 18–38.
Organization for Economic Cooperation and Development. (1992). OECD guidelines for the security of information systems, 1992. http://www.oecd.org/internet/ieconomy/oecdguidelinesforthesecurityofinformationsystems1992.htm.
Organization for Economic Cooperation and Development. (1999). *Guidelines for consumer protection in electronic commerce*. Paris: OECD.
Organization for Economic Cooperation and Development. (2001). *Business to consumer electronic commerce: An update on the statistics*. Paris: OECD.
Organization for Economic Cooperation and Development. (2002). OECD guidelines for the security of information systems and networks: Towards a culture of security. http://www.oecd.org/dataoecd/16/22/15582260.pdf.
Organization for Economic Cooperation and Development. (2004). Electronic commerce. http://www.oecd.org/development/electroniccommerce.htm.
Organization for Economic Cooperation and Development. (2005). The promotion of a culture of security for information systems and networks: Towards a culture of security. http://oe.cd/2002sg.
Organization for Economic Cooperation and Development. (2007). Development of policies for the protection of critical information infrastructures. In: *Report on OECD ministerial meeting on the future of the internet economy*. Seoul, 17–18 June 2008. Retrieved from http://www.oecd.org/sti/40761118.pdf.
Organization for Economic Cooperation and Development. (2011). Communique on principles for internet policy-making. In: *OECD high level meeting on the internet economy. Paris, 28–29 June 2011*. Retrieved from http://www.oecd.org/internet/innovation/48289796.pdf.
Organization for Economic Cooperation and Development. (2012a). Recommendation of the council concerning guidelines for the security of information systems and networks: Towards a culture of security. acts.oecd.org/instruments/ShowInstrumentView.aspx?InstrumentID=116&Lang=en&Book=False.
Organization for Economic Cooperation and Development. (2012b). Cybersecurity policy making at a turning point: Analysing a new generation of national cybersecurity strategies for the internet economy. OECD Digital Economy Papers. doi:10.1787/5k8zq92vdgtl-en.
Organization for Economic Cooperation and Development. (2012c). The role of the 2002 security guidelines: Towards cybersecurity for an open and interconnected economy. OECD Digital Economy Papers. doi: 10.1787/5k8zq930xr5j-en.
Organization for Economic Cooperation and Development, Committee for Information, Computers, and Communications Policy. (1997). Global information infrastructure—Global information society (GII-GIS) policy requirements. Paris: OECD.
Pfanner, E. (2012). US rejects telecommunications treaty. In: The New York Times, Retrieved December 13 from http://www.nytimes.com/2012/12/14/technology/14iht-treaty14.html?_r=0&adxnnl=1&pagewanted=1&adxnnlx=1363493660-nqCPGplj9 LwTJStzmwbxg.
Rothkopf, D. J .(1998). Cyberpolitik: The changing nature of power in the information age. *Journal of International Affairs, 51*, 325–360.
Rutkowski, A. M. (2005). The ITU treaty provisions for infrastructure protection: How they came to be and why they are relevant today In: ITU meeting on cybersecurity, Geneva, Retrieved 29 June–1 July 2005. from http://www.itu.int/osg/csd/wtpf/wtpf2009/resources/infrastructure_protection_treaty_2%203.pdf.
Rutkowski, A. M. (2011). Public international law of the international telecommunications instruments: Cyber security treaty provisions since 1850. *Info, 13*(1), 13–31.
Schjolber, S., & Ghernaouti-Helie, S. (2011). A global treaty on cybersecurity and cybercrime. (2nd ed.). http://www.cybercrimelaw.net/documents/A_Global_Treaty_on_Cybersecurity_and_Cybercrime,_Second_edition_2011.pdf.
Sofaer, A. D, Clark, D, Diffie, W. (2010). Cybersecurity and international agreements. In: *Proceedings of a workshop on deterring cyberattacks: Informing strategies and developing*

options for U.S. Policy, Committee on Deterring Cyberattacks: Informing Strategies and Developing Options; National Research Council. Available: https://download.nap.edu/catalog.php?record_id=12997.

Spade, J. M. (2012). Information as power: China's cyber power and America's national security. Carlisle Barracks, PA, US Army War College. http://www.carlisle.army.mil/dime/documents/China's%20Cyber%20Power%20and%20America's%20National%20Security%20Web%20Version.pdf.

Sternstein, A. (2011). International cybersecurity treaty might not be achievable, Report says. Available via Nextgov. http://www.nextgov.com/cybersecurity/2011/01/international-cybersecurity-treaty-might-not-be-achievable-report-says/48282/.

Sternstein, A. (2012). U.S., Russia, other nations near agreement on cyber early-warning pact. Available via Nextgov. http://www.nextgov.com/cybersecurity/2012/12/us-russia-other-nations-near-agreement-cyber-early-warning-pact/59977/.

Take, I. (2012). *Regulating the internet infrastructure: A comparative appraisal of the legitimacy of ICANN, ITU, and the WSIS*. Regulation and Governance 6(4).

Tigre, PB and O'Connor, D. (2002). *Policies and institutions for e-commerce readiness: What can developing countries learn from OECD experience?* In: OECD Development Centre, Technical Papers No. 189. Paris: OECD Publishing.

United Nations. (2003). *Creation of a global culture of cyber security*. In: General assembly resolution. www.itu.int/osg/spu/cybersecurity/docs/UN_resolution_57_239.pdf.

United States Department of Homeland Security. (2009). National infrastructure protection plan, partnering to enhance protection and resiliency. http://www.dhs.gov/xlibrary/assets/NIPP_Plan.pdf.

United States. (2002). National strategy to secure cyberspace. http://www.whitehouse.gov/pcipb/.

United States. (1996). A framework for global electronic commerce. http://clinton4.nara.gov/WH/New/Commerce/read.html.

Zacher, M., & Sutton, B. (1996). *Governing global networks: International regimes for transportation and communications*. Cambridge: Cambridge University Press.

Phreak the Speak: The Flawed Communications within Cyber Intelligentsia

Matthew Crosston

> *I would quote Confucius to my new students: "The rectification of names is the most important business of government. If names are not correct, language will not be in accordance with the truth of things." The point has less to do with communicating than it did with thinking—thinking clearly. Clear communication begins with clear thinking. You have to be precise in your language and have the big ideas right if you are going to accomplish anything.*
>
> – Michael V. Hayden (2011)

Abstract This chapter will examine a fundamental dichotomy that has developed within the academic, technical and policy communities when it comes to understanding, advancing, and communicating work on cyberspace within global affairs. This distinct tendency today has technical cyber scholarship partially blind and deaf to important political ramifications while political cyber work remains partially illiterate and mute on cyberspace's technical complexity. This dichotomy not only exists as an intellectual barrier between scholars of the hard and social sciences, it impinges on progressive cooperation between the political and technical communities. Consequently, there is a gap weakening the scope and reach of theoretical and empirical work on cyberspace in general. Indeed, this problem has the potential to become exponentially larger in the immediate future: not only are real-world professionals and scholars having trouble building bridges between obvious mutual interests, but this 'Chinese knowledge wall' separates each group respectively. Just as phreaking involves a subculture of specialists who experiment and toy with telecommunication systems, the intellectual, technical, and governmental worlds need a new generation of 'phreak-scholars' who are adept at building connections between these diverse, inter-related knowledge bases.

M. Crosston (✉)
International Security and Intelligence Studies, Bellevue University, Bellevue, NE, USA
e-mail: matt.crosston@bellevue.edu

J.-F. Kremer and B. Müller (eds.), *Cyberspace and International Relations*,
DOI: 10.1007/978-3-642-37481-4_14, © Springer-Verlag Berlin Heidelberg 2014

1 Introduction

There is a fundamental dichotomy that has developed within the academic, technical and policy communities when it comes to understanding and advancing work on cyberspace within global affairs. While Gen. Hayden is not specifically talking about this dichotomy in the above quote, the lesson he is espousing is a valuable one: today has technical cyber scholarship partially blind and deaf to important political ramifications while political cyber work remains partially illiterate and mute on crucial technical complexity. In short, there is no clear communication between the two and consequently limited clear thinking across this increasingly important discipline. This dichotomy not only exists as an intellectual barrier between scholars of the hard and social sciences: it hinders progressive cooperation between the political and technical communities that impacts the real world. Consequently, this technical-political gap is significantly weakening the scope and reach of theoretical and empirical work on cyberspace.

This problem has the potential to become exponentially larger in the immediate future: not only are real-world professionals and scholars having trouble building bridges between obvious mutual interests but this 'wall of separation' is being concretized institutionally. Just as phreaking involves a subculture of specialists who experiment and toy with telecommunication systems, the intellectual, technical, and governmental worlds need a new generation of 'phreak-scholars' who are adept at building connections between these diverse, inter-related knowledge bases. The failure to do this can result in obstacles that Confucius noted millennia ago: without improved communications the 'truth' of things may be lost.

In many ways this techno-political communication gap across the scholarship is doubly surprising: not only for its emergence but for the current lack of recognition its potential impact might have on the discipline. When one considers how much technology has always had a momentous causal impact on economic, military, political, and environmental reality, and how much that impact has been a mixed blessing and curse, the need for scholars equally adept and comfortable communicating to each other across technical and political lines should have been apparent ages ago (Fritsch 2011). In previous incarnations the divide went unnoticed because of a tolerable research separation: the hard sciences had their areas of concentration while the social sciences had theirs. Thus, it was possible to examine environmental pollution, global climate change, and the loss of biodiversity, for example, strictly from a scientific impact perspective and then allow political scientists, sociologists, historians, and the like to swoop in and discuss the social consequences that might emerge. But the 'digital divide,' for lack of a better term, between political researchers and technical specialists in the cyber domain cannot separate so explicitly without there being a real negative consequence to the overall reach and impact of said projects.

Even more remarkable is how many have noticed particular gaps or exclusions in the cyber domain that cover empirical areas not related to scholarship.

The coming section will examine how peculiarly applicable the language is when discussing such flaws in the technical, political, economic, and governmental spheres of cyber reality, even though they do not in fact go on to make the scholarly communication connection gap. This chapter makes said gap explicit so as to hopefully spur creation of the bridge needed to eliminate it. The cyber discipline is doing a fine job exploring the deficiencies in each of its respective knowledge silos, but it is then failing to deal with the relative absence of cross-communication:

> This overall pattern leads to two challenges. One is the need to reassess the educational requirements and the role of a new cadre of software systems engineers/systems integrators. Underlying this statement is the need to recognize software development as a true engineering discipline… the other challenge is the need to assess the added vulnerability of software-intensive systems to risks of cyber terrorism, to develop appropriate risk management measures for countering such cyber risks, and to develop new and appropriate metrics with which to measure these risks (Chittister and Haimes 2006).

The above quote is a perfect example of whistling past the scholarship connection gap; just as there is a need for new cadres of software systems engineers, there is a bigger need for new cadres of technically-adept political scholars and politically-savvy technical specialists; recognizing such development as a needed part of engineering is matched by the need to inspire scholarly evolution as a crucial part of the cyber domain; the development of new metrics for measuring risk is paralleled by an equal desire to develop phreak-scholars. Such development will create new and more powerful research methods. Instead of only improving the silos of the cyber domain individually, there should be a movement to tackle the discipline holistically.

2 Examining Flaws within Knowledge Silos

The four knowledge silos of technical, political, governmental, and economic competently and explicitly deal with their respective cyber issues, but each also has connectivity issues within their respective scholarship that does not bridge across to the other silos. Ironically, they often deal with ‘internal’ research questions with a writing style which analogizes effectively to this communication gap. In each case, however, the opportunity to tackle the problem is missed.

2.1 Technical

The obvious flaw within the technical knowledge silo is a tendency to dive down so deeply into ‘techno-speak’ that the scholarship cannot help but communicate only to the most dedicated of IT specialists. Even the best technically-oriented cyber papers, ones that try to deal with political and security issues, often have the political/security aspects flooded over by technical jargon:

> Cloud service models describe IT design capabilities and levels of autonomy for customers. There are three accepted industry-wide cloud service models: Software-as-a-Service (SaaS), Platform-as-a-Service (PaaS), and Infrastructure-as-a-Service (IaaS)… All benefit from consolidation into a virtualized cloud environment because these capabilities tend to require much lower processing cycles on servers… Within this model, the cloud provider manages their physical servers; however, customers that employ their own applications in PaaS and their virtual servers in IaaS can maintain and secure the applications and virtual systems, respectively. The implication is that if an organization is already lacking in its security regime, then migrating to a cloud environment will not necessarily improve the overall security posture (Buennemeyer 2011).

I would defy any politically-oriented scholar concerned with cyber to explicitly get something valuable from the above quote other than the very last sentence. The problem, of course, is that the last sentence is based on the 'evidence' provided in great detail preceding it. Because of this formulation and tendency to talk only to colleagues already firmly located within the technical knowledge silo, all collaborative possibilities between silos is largely lost. This is particularly disheartening when considering the fact that the above exemplar, which is quite common to this silo, is in fact engaging in a security-oriented research article. The findings would absolutely be relevant and considerable for the political, governmental, and economic silos seeking to better understand the changing/evolving technical environment from a protection standpoint.

2.2 Political

Unlike the technical silo, where there is either an ignorance or reluctance to properly engage the political silo, cyber research that is politically-oriented suffers most commonly from scholars who are clearly not comfortable getting into any technical depth, even when researching issues that demand technical detail:

> My deeper concern is that the smaller scale cyber war exploits might eventually scale up… This is why I think cyber war is destined to play an increasingly prominent role in future wars. The challenge for cyber warriors today lies in figuring out how to support these various cyber offensives. This won't happen if defenders remain dependent on a cyber space-based version of the Maginot Line: the firewalls designed to detect viruses, worms, and other tools, and keep attackers from intruding into and roaming about one's systems… Instead of debating whether it is real, we need to get down to the serious work of better understanding this new mode of war fighting (Arquilla 2012).

The point is not to denigrate the scholarship within individual silos. Rather, it is to emphasize that even when writing in a manner that seems to beg for cross-silo pollination, scholars do not strive for such connectivity. The above piece is exemplary of the political silo in that it pushes for a 'better understanding' of the cyber domain but does not itself push into areas of technical proficiency. These political discussions of 'technical' issues, therefore, remain at the superficial and cursory level. Perhaps more daunting in overcoming this scholarship connection gap, and also something absent within the technical knowledge silo, is unacceptable research dismissiveness. In the political silo it manifests itself by considering the 'nuts and bolts' of technical detail to be of limited causal importance:

> What is most challenging here is that the execution of the computer program itself behind the attack could be related to any of these categories and thus the technical aspects of the attack *reveal very little.* It does not reveal the source and it does not, importantly, reveal the intent (Harknett 2010).

One of the obvious purposes of this chapter is to push to the side this intellectual self-segregation. It will be difficult enough reorienting the discipline and encouraging institutions to truly engage in the production of new scholars who feel comfortable with their feet in both silos, looking to bridge the two together. But it will be near impossible to accomplish this if either silo finds itself deleteriously looking upon the other and finding it analytically wanting. Cyber could very well be the 21st century discipline ideal for this political-technical merging of the minds: political cyber research would benefit from a deeper understanding of the technical aspects, while all technical research would greatly expand its scope and reach by having a more nuanced appreciation for the political consequences that emerge from technological actions.

2.3 Governmental

In 2012 the 112th Congress passed the Cybersecurity Act. A hefty bill coming in at over 200 pages, it contained several relevant sections on the aims and goals of the United States government (USG) for evolving and improving cyber education and research. Each of the following excerpts highlights consistent misinterpretations and missed opportunities to address the scholarship communication gap. Consequently, unless amended in the near future, said gap is only going to be concretized more deeply:

> The Secretary of Education... shall develop model curriculum standards and guidelines to address cyber safety, cyber security, and cyber ethics for all students enrolled in career and technical institutions in the United States (112th Congress 2012).
>
> The Secretary of Education... shall analyze and develop recommended courses for students interested in pursuing careers in ***information technology, communications, computer science, engineering, mathematics, and science,*** as those subjects relate to cyber security (112th Congress 2012).
>
> Section 238: Cyber Security Research and Development—***[the establishment of research and development programs should] understand human behavioral factors that can affect cybersecurity technology and practices*** (112th Congress 2012).
>
> The May 2009 White House Cyberspace Policy Review asserts "***the Nation also needs a strategy for cyber security designed to shape the international environment*** and bring like-minded nations together on ***a host of issues, such as technical standards and acceptable legal norms regarding territorial jurisdiction, sovereign responsibility, and use of force***". International norms are critical to establishing a secure and thriving infrastructure (112th Congress 2012).

> The cyberspace objectives of the United States include the full range of cyber issues, including issues related to ***governance, standards, cyber security, cybercrime, international security, human rights***, and the free flow of information. (112th Congress 2012)

Closer inspection of these provisions indicates two things quite clearly. First, the USG envisions cyber issues firmly embedded within both the technical and political realms. Second, there is paradoxically no mention in the Cybersecurity Act for developing model curriculum and model courses within non-IT disciplines. There is nothing necessarily wrong with an emphasis on IT-disciplines, until one realizes that most of the cyber security programs currently housed in IT and other Science and Technology disciplines are dominated by curriculum and courses that do not address the explicit social and behavioral science issues mentioned and prioritized in the Cybersecurity Act.

Indeed, the scholarship communication gap between the technical and political experts is, if anything, further institutionalized within higher education. Perhaps the Cybersecurity Act of 2012 is meant to address this current problem. But without serious federal funding to encourage such curriculum and course reform/development it is doubtful universities have the financial backing to truly engage the effort. This is somewhat akin to a technical curriculum dismissiveness toward the political that is equal to the aforementioned political research dismissiveness. In some ways this lack of curriculum engagement is even more detrimental for it ties directly into the production of future cyber scholars and specialists. If the political side is arguably more at fault for the current research connectivity gap, then it is just as arguable that the technical side will be the one responsible for its perpetuation long into the future.

2.4 Economic

Out of the four knowledge silos examined here, it is the economic one that shows the most intriguing promise for connectivity and scholarly bridging. Unfortunately for the cyber domain, it may be the economics field, compared to the other three, which is the least invested in cyber research currently:

> Whereas computer viruses continue to be a problem, criminal attack strategies now more typically rely on malware, propagated in multiple ways via viruses, worms, trojans, and drive-by attacks from compromised websites. Large numbers of infected computers are integrated in versatile botnets, which serve as platforms for sending spam, fraud, and other types of cybercrime… from these developments hybrid forms of governance emerged, in which alternative and traditional forms of regulation complement (and sometimes rival) each other… Currently, these measures amount to a patchwork rather than an integrated approach but they are steps in the right direction (Bauer and Van Eeten 2011).

When economic research engages cyber, it is fuller and more comprehensive. It also tends to be more adept at crossing between technical issues and political perspectives. Perhaps this is because of the heavy quantitative and statistical elements within the study of economics, making the technical nature of cyber problems well within the methodological reach of economic experts. Combine this with the long-standing partnership it has had with political science and economics has a potentially unique cyber comfort zone. The only problem is that the IT, computer science, and political science disciplines have not emulated it.

Arguably, the social and behavioral science fields hold a higher responsibility for making these connections. After all, two of the four political science sub-disciplines (American Politics and International Relations) have long espoused the heavy use of quantitative research methods and statistical data modeling for solving its research questions just like the economics field. Thus, there seems to be little intellectual justification to explain why political science experts are failing so miserably to incorporate the heavily technical elements of the cyber domain into their work. Ultimately, both the technical and political domains must share equal responsibility in overcoming the scholarship communication gap as both domains weaken their own scholarship and miss greater explanatory power by not doing so.

The failure of the technical silo to reach beyond its scientific specialization cuts itself off from most of the civilized intellectual world, rendering itself basically nothing more than applied solutions to specific professional problems. Its dissections of the technical threats within cyber should be much more important and far-reaching than they are presently. The failure of the political silo to overcome its own awkward discomfort with the 'science of cyber' relegates much of the work to limited policy discussions. Even more disturbing, the rationalization of this ignorance encourages an intellectual arrogance within the scholarship that can be nothing but damaging to its long-term impact and relevance when it comes to those aforementioned real-world empirical applications. The failure of the governmental silo is simply a breakdown of its supreme mission: to be the facilitator that connects the political and technical disciplines together, that unites them for the benefit of not just the body of knowledge, but the advancement of society writ large.

Indeed, the knowledge silos must be taken down. Not only because of the individual damage explained in detail above, but because of the virus-like contamination that can spread into sub-specializations within cyber. This is apparent when reviewing such exemplars across the literature that seem to come so close to being able to create obvious analogies to the political-technical problem, only to fall short, never making the correlation explicit. If the failure of connectivity within the silos is a top-down problem, then the failure within the sub-specializations attests to a dearth of bottom-up inspiration as well.

3 Missing Analogies within Various Analytical Frameworks

It is not a new discussion when it comes to introducing technology more effectively into global affairs. Indeed, while not obviously applying to the cyber domain, establishing the mutual relationship between science and technology and foreign affairs has been underway since the 1960s. Most of those discussions, however, have not been about empirical reality or policy applicability but rather about finding nuanced theory to comprehensively incorporate both. Against that backdrop, researching the cyber domain in the 21st century has revealed many analytical frameworks that seem close to crafting applicable analogies for the technical–political communication gap but ultimately fall short in making the connection.

3.1 The Policy-Scholar Gap in Cyber Terrorism

The dangers of cyber terrorism have become of great political interest over the past decade. Interestingly, this increase in research emphasis has created a divergence between scholars and policymakers. While there are many definitions of cyber terrorism, the standpoints and views of the two groups have varied widely. Indeed, due to multidimensional structures, the context of cyber terrorism seems to create different understandings and interpretations by the various parties (Ahmad and Yunos 2012). This divergence of interpretation perfectly mirrors the problem that exists between the information technology and political science groups.

Unlike the technical–political gap, there seems to be both recognition and a building consensus within the policy–scholar cyber terrorism community. For this group has recognized that the concept of cyber terrorism is one that will always be interpreted differently at the different levels of researcher, professional, and policy maker. Therefore, understanding similarities and differences in the perception of what constitutes cyber terrorism can provide insight on how the research variations can communicate to one another (Ahmad and Yunos 2012). This same recognition and building of consensus is deeply needed within the technical and political communities. Just as with cyber terrorism, the discourse generated between these two communities has naturally different viewpoints and emphases. But unlike the cyber terrorism community, the technical and political worlds seem to rarely cross each other or try to create connective themes and discourses.

3.2 The Strategic-Operational Gap in Military Cyber Affairs

Stephen J. Blank of the Army's Strategic Studies Institute has long criticized how battle space designers have factored out strategic political decision-making and as a consequence have created civilian and military elites who seem unable to talk to each other openly (Cullather 2003). What this translates into for Blank is a decade of military operational simulations needing to build in some empathy and understanding of cultures, people and social contexts. But instead this has been tackled by tweaking software, i.e., adding visualization but not comprehension (Cullather 2003).

In many ways this strategic-operational gap perfectly mirrors the innate flaws within technically-oriented cyber research: namely, a reluctance and discomfort when dealing with the people side of cyber. It therefore sticks rigidly to the technological/computing side of problems. One of the most common biases of quantitative research is the temptation to believe all things can be solved as long as there are enough numbers to crunch and data to process. This lack of engagement with the 'personal' side must not persist within the cyber domain for its key relevant impact points are in how they affect human communities.

3.3 The Abstract-Explicit Measurement Gap in Cyber Metrics

Within the realm of network and information security, there is no proposed set of metrics universally accepted and embraced as useful and no framework that lets organizations universally answer their wide variety of questions (Pfleeger 2009).

> …Abstract attributes such as health or safety are difficult to define and measure. In each case, the attribute being measured is usually some combination of characteristics, each of which reflects a narrow aspect of the whole. The difficulty rests not only in finding an appropriate measure but also in understanding how the whole is formed from its parts. Moreover, the measures are often drawn from what is easy or available to measure, not from what is needed… Complicating matters, no common vocabulary or standard way to measure the number and kind of cyber security events currently exists. Some attempts are being made, but with little consistency of effort or viewpoint. Thus, it is better at this point to define a collection of perspectives (Pfleeger 2009).

The real reason for this lack of consensus is because of the inability to move beyond the narrow aspect trying to be measured and focus on the larger, more comprehensive total cyber picture. This is why the present chapter emphasizes the technical–political scholarship communication gap: many of these narrower gaps will be addressed by tackling the gap more completely. Half measures, like the one discussed above, are not a substitute: they result in loosely associated projects that discuss similar ideas but not with each other.

3.4 The Hodgepodge Congressional Gap in Cyber Security Legislation

Some of the missing and contradictory elements of The Cyberscurity Act of 2012, from the 112th Congress, have already been discussed in detail. Its flaws become more understandable when realizing that several cyber bills were presented in the 110th Congress and even more were presented in the 111th. However, no comprehensive cyber security legislation ended up being voted into law. As a result, more than thirty separate pieces of legislation were ultimately forwarded for review before the 112th Congress (Newmeyer 2011).

Some might think the 112th Congress should be congratulated for piecing together multiple bills into a single Cybersecurity Act. But given the endeavor was not a melding of diverse pieces into a coherent whole but was simply a cutting and pasting of multiple pieces into a single document, praise should be withheld. The 2012 law has too many inconsistencies and internal contradictions to create a true academic shift. As the Congressional Research Service itself pointed out, when describing the entire cyber legislation process, there is still no single Congressional committee or executive agency that has primary responsibility for cyber security issues and this has led to a 'hodgepodge' (Newmeyer 2011).

In many ways Congressional problems in crafting a holistic and comprehensive cyber bill from disparate parts is a perfect analogy for the lack of success in building a technical–political scholarly bridge between two related but disconnected cyber research communities. Instead of truly aiming to create works that talk to one another and build upon one another fluidly, projects remain distinct at worst or haphazardly jumbled together at best in a manner which results in hard-to-follow conclusions and confusion as to how to proceed further.

3.5 Glimmers of Hope within the Frameworks

Not all is lost when examining these various frameworks and missed analogies. While no one at present has properly identified the importance of eliminating the technical–political scholarly communication gap, there are some areas of cyber research that nudge thinking in the direction where the gap might finally be addressed. The idea of creating a cyber "neighborhood watch", or a Commons Protection Union, for example, emerged from dissatisfaction with no connectivity between top-down and bottom-up approaches in cyber security (Lukasik 2011).

Top-down approaches were government-driven and policy-related. Bottom-up approaches were about the way processes actually work, rich in detail but perhaps missing the forest for the trees. There is a clear parallel here: the political side of cyber is top-down while the technical side is bottom-up. Just as Lukasik wanted to see a more integrated approach in order to achieve a more substantive user protection, so does the cyber domain need a more integrated union between the technical and political research venues. Greater collaboration leads to more nuanced communication which creates knowledge advancement.

Still others emphasize the need for a comprehensive approach to cyber security where the elements of threat, deterrence, and response are combined. In so doing overlaps of authority are created, aiming to eliminate the gaps (Tikk 2010). This is based more on practical reinforcement along national and international lines of action. In other words, it is arguing for the end of "stovepipes". These empirical stovepipes function the same way as knowledge silos. Whereas Tikk was hoping to create a new environment for solving real-world problems, this chapter hopes to create a new scholarship world. Tikk felt that no further instruments were immediately required on the international level and that national approaches necessitating coordination and possible harmonization could create the needed niche for new organizations to fill (Tikk 2010). This chapter echoes his hopeful sentiment: specialists already exist; the disciplines are well formed; areas of investigation are defined. What is needed most is alternative thinking on how to utilize the already existing resources so as to create a new intellectual harmonization. This is of course not easy but it is still far better than having to create the resources from scratch.

4 On the Scholarship Frontlines: Positive and Negative Cases

4.1 The Joint Harvard-MIT 'Explorations in Cyber International Relations' Project

At first glance the joint Harvard-MIT project seems to be created to answer the very concerns of this chapter. Its ultimate goal is to create a new research discipline that integrates cyberspace into the fabric of international affairs, in all its manifestations, such as to eliminate the current tendency to consider cyberspace and international affairs as two distinct parallel arenas or areas of interaction (Choucri and Goldsmith 2012).

However, the public version of its main strategy emphasizes five strategic initiatives that unfortunately do not deal with education or connecting the two worlds from a scholarship/research perspective:

(1) Treating cyberspace as an operational military domain
(2) Employing new defense operating concepts
(3) Partnering with other US government agencies and the private sector
(4) Building relationships with allies and partners to strengthen collective security
(5) Leveraging the nation's workforce for technological innovation.

These are all tremendously worthwhile and valuable goals and objectives. Again, this chapter does not highlight rigorous pieces of research and fine institutions of higher learning in a detrimental way. It is simply highlighting an important niche that is going unnoticed and whose continued absence in the cyber domain will have an adverse effect on increasing the discipline's body of knowledge. As the Harvard-MIT project states unequivocally: it hopes to change the environment by creating an integrated view of cyber in *real* international relations (Choucri and Goldsmith 2012). In short, this project is built for improving the empirical policy results coming out of cyber research. It is not addressing the absence of a bridge between the two main parties creating that research. This is made explicit when reviewing the project's own chosen 'gap foci' (Choucri and Goldsmith 2012):

> *The cyber theory gap*: There is an enormous disconnect between the cyber realities of today and the theories of the 20th century, which continue to guide national policy and international relations.

The empirical data gap: Well-recognized, there is a powerful disconnect between cyber activities on the one hand and the quality, integration, inconsistency of the data about these activities on the other.

The policy analysis gap: This disconnect is between traditional modes of policy analysis and the realities that focus largely on states and threats through the cyber domain that involve non-state actors.

It is remarkable how unnoticed the technical–political communication gap is when two overwhelmingly powerful institutions create their own gap analysis, exacerbated by the technical–political divide, but do not in fact address the divide explicitly. This communication bridge undoubtedly makes policy analysis, empirical data, and cyber theories more developed and more rigorous. If technical specialists and political experts are able to adeptly address their research aspects together in a language that encourages connectivity, then the entire discipline benefits. The Harvard-MIT project is a policy endeavor that needs its mirror match in the scholarly realm.

4.2 The Bulletin of Atomic Scientists

Even though the Bulletin considers itself a 'non-technical' online magazine that covers global security and public policy issues, it is in fact excellent in its reach, scope, and writing style. It does not directly or explicitly address the technical–political scholarly communication gap but it is becoming increasingly active in addressing cyber issues and seems to be a venue that attracts voices well-suited to overcome the gap in their work. To that end its work is highlighted:

> A safer and more secure cyberspace will not be achieved with one magic technological advance, one new strategy, or one comprehensive arms control agreement. Rather, progress will be incremental and, likely, slow. For now, responsible nations need to use what they know, and they also need to develop new options for protecting themselves against cyber conflict, the implications of which will need to be researched (Lin 2012a, b).

In some ways the history of the Bulletin adapts well to the current need in the cyber domain. Originally, the scientific community felt it was essential to educate society about the danger of atomic weapons, specifically in the way they would inevitably impact foreign policy and global affairs. The Bulletin sought to educate citizens, scientists, policymakers, and journalists in a relatively non-technical way that was still scientifically sound and policy-relevant. If its original aim was to go about the business of educating society to the changing realities of the scientific age, then at present there is no journal more historically and ideally-suited to take on the challenge of addressing the technical–political communication gap in the cyber domain. Whether or not the bulletin truly sees its future tied to this effort, this chapter hopes that it will be considered. For if the previous overview and analysis of knowledge silos, analytical frameworks and institutional frontlines has proven anything, it is that the cyber domain desperately needs someone to take up the banner for building this intellectual bridge.

5 Conclusion

The goal of this contribution to the symposium was to show that so far technology has been insufficiently discussed by major theories of IR/IPE, although it is often implicitly present in many arguments. The paper tried to develop the concept of technology and its mutual relationship with global affairs that goes beyond the traditional conceptions so far applied. It argued for conceptualization of technology as an integral core part of the global system... which in turn impacts the character and behavior of system actors and modifies existing, as well as newly emerging, policy issues.

~ *Stefan Fritsch (2011)*

This chapter has emphasized the lack of thinking epitomized by Fritsch. Some headway is indeed being made, but it is still too limited and too quiet to achieve the impact needed in cyber domain research. The much more prominent trend is knowledge silos sitting in relative isolation, not striving to make connective bridges and not considering it a priority. Inside of those silos are tremendous pieces of scholarship, examining many diverse analytical frameworks, seeking out gaps to fill and trying to profoundly contribute to the body of knowledge. But these pieces focus on lesser gaps that could be bigger contributors by first addressing the 'missing gap': the advances that could be made in cyber scholarship are incalculable if the two main scholarly communities would produce work that is at least attempting to understand the relevant terms, objectives, and realities inherent within *both* fields.

The missed connections within so many research analogies must cease for the benefit of the discipline. So when scholars discuss the need for a comprehensive 'new balance,' an effort that recognizes the action that must be taken across the entirety of the defense community, that 'this necessitates the identification and resolution of entrenched technical and cultural impediments that hamper progress,' these scholars need to realize that there is a much bigger 'new balance' to be achieved, going beyond the purely empirical and purely theoretical (Korns 2009). It is a new balance creating an intimately connected partnership where there is currently, at best, a simple begrudging acknowledgment.

The benefit to research that attempts to bridge these gaps and attempts to engage both the technical and the political is immeasurable:

> The debate over the applicability or non-applicability of international law to cyber war and the need for a cyber-specific international treaty might be irrelevant. Both camps, pro and con, argue about the need for cyber war to have the Law of Armed Conflict or some new international legal project properly cover the cyber domain. Whether one believes the Law of Armed Conflict can or cannot apply, whether one pushes for an international cyber treaty or thinks such treaties will be meaningless, one need is constant: the desire for rules governing cyber war behavior. All camps, however, misread how the structure of the cyber domain precludes strategically 'piggy-backing' on conventional norms of war. These norms are effective because of the ability to differentiate between civilian and military sectors. The cyber domain is not amenable to this separation as it is typified by a fusion where participants, facilities and targets are hopelessly entangled between civilian and military institutions. This has been an important missing explanation as to why the global effort to enhance and clarify cyber norms has remained uneven and inadequate. Thus Duqu's Dilemma: with the focus on establishing legitimate targets and setting limitations on allowable action, the United States and its allies expose themselves to vulnerabilities while engaging a futile endeavor that does not lead to improved cyber control (Crosston 2013).

As illustrated above, this structural issue is more than just semantics. It literally covers who engages cyber war, what can be destroyed in cyber war, who can be a victim during cyber war, even the philosophical and ethical questions meant to be asked about cyber war itself. These are deeply political questions that will have huge impact on the real world. But the understanding of those political questions came only from understanding the technical complexity inherent to the problem. Without being able to engage both aspects, the work itself would have gone nowhere, losing the knowledge contribution in its entirety. The more scholars look to push this evolution the better.

This evolution within the cyber domain, however, will not come easy. There are many natural impediments and obstacles in the way. Most occur innocently but others not so much, as has been discussed within this chapter. How will we know when a new age has come to cyber? What signs can we look for, signaling the age of 'cyber scholar-phreaks,' ushering in research that is higher, deeper, and broader? Hopefully, with admitted bias, books like this one will become ever more common. But more realistically, success in the long-term has to be rooted in the educational and training systems. Perhaps efforts can be made to first have traditionally political conferences accept panels that have a heavy technical emphasis, and vice versa. Eventually this could grow into actual conferences evenly balanced between the political and technical realms, but with those realms actively engaging each other within the event and not self-segregating into their own rooms and auditoriums.

Most importantly, there needs to be a concentrated, ambitious, and talented effort to create curriculum and degree programs that do not institutionalize a Chinese Knowledge Wall between the technical mastery of cyber threats/risks/defense and the political nuance of cyber war/weapons/deterrence. It does not mean that universities must create computer programmers with the foreign policy acumen of a Kissinger. It simply means we must create future scholars who are essentially cyber bilingual: equally capable and comfortable with discussing, debating, and researching the most crucial questions in the cyber domain, regardless of how technically complicated or politically subtle they happen to be.

Though this is a daunting challenge it is also a monumental opportunity. For whichever country becomes adept at producing scholars who can 'phreak the speak' then that country will quickly find itself mastering the future of the cyber domain. Considering that future will have a large role in so much more than just network security (no doubt covering the global economy, foreign affairs, and military engagement just to name a few), this issue should be considered anything but academic.

References

Ahmad, R., & Yunos, Z. (2012). A dynamic cyber terrorism framework. *International Journal of Computer Science and Information Security, 10*(2), 149–158.

Arquilla, J. (2012). Rebuttal cyberwar is already upon us. *Foreign Policy*, Mar/Apr, 84–85.

Bauer, J. M., & Van Eeten, M. (2011). Introduction to the economics of cybersecurity. *Communications and Strategies, 81*, 13–21.

Buennemeyer, T. K. (2011). A strategic approach to network defense: framing the cloud. *Parameters Autumn*, 43–58.

Chittister, C. G., & Haimes, Y. Y. (2006). Cybersecurity: from Ad Hoc patching to lifecycle of software engineering. *Journal of Homeland Security and Emergency Management, 3*(4), 1–20.

Choucri, N., & Goldsmith, D. (2012). Lost in cyberspace: harnessing the internet, international relations, and global security. *Bulletin of the Atomic Scientists, 68*(2), 70–77.

Crosston, M. (2013). Duqu's dilemma: The ambiguity assertion and the futility of sanitized cyber war, *Journal of Military and Strategic Affairs, forthcoming*, 5(1).

Cullather, N. (2003). Bombing at the speed of thought: intelligence in the coming age of cyber-war. *Intelligence and National Security, 18*(4), 141–154.

Fritsch, S. (2011). Technology and global affairs. *International Studies Perspectives, 12*, 27–45.

Harknett, R. J., et al. (2010). Leaving deterrence behind: war-fighting and national cybersecurity. *Journal of Homeland Security and Emergency Management, 7*(1), 1–24.

Hayden, M.V. (2011). The future of things CYBER. *Strategic Studies Quarterly Spring*, 3–7.

Korns, S. W. (2009). Cyber operations: the new balance. *Joint Forces Quarterly, 54*, 97–102.

Lin, H. (2012a). Why computer scientists should care about cyber conflict and us national security policy. *Communications of the ACM, 55*(6), 41–43.

Lin, H. (2012b). A virtual necessity: some modest steps toward greater cybersecurity. *Bulletin of the Atomic Scientists, 68*(5), 75–87.

Lukasik, S. J. (2011). Protecting users of the cyber commons. *Communications of the ACM, 54*(9), 54–61.

Newmeyer, K. P. (2011). Who should lead us cybersecurity efforts? *Prism, 3*(2), 115–126.

Pfleeger, S.L. (2009). Useful cybersecurity metrics. IT Proceeding, May/June, 38–45.

Tikk, E. (2010). Global cybersecurity-thinking about the niche for NATO. *SAIS Review, 30*(2), 105–119.

United States Senate, 112th Congress (2012). Cybersecurity Act of 2012. Washington DC: 1–205.

Reflections on Virtual to Real: Modern Technique, International Security Studies and Cyber Security Environment

Suarez Marcial A. Garcia and Acácio Igor D. Palhares

Abstract This chapter addresses the analysis of the phenomenon of modern technique by Martin Heidegger, especially regarding the issue of information societies and the role of the virtual network with respect to providing information about the political behavior of states, which accordingly affects the international security environment. We propose a debate on international relations theory, specifically from the perspective adopted by the Copenhagen School of International Security Studies. We conduct a study from the perception that cyberspace, as a multiverse, is not uniform, and therefore, the various actors emerge with different capacities for political action depending on the dependency of the states and societies to use new information and communication technologies (NICTs) as well as the interconnections with critical infrastructures (i.e., Critical Information Infrastructure).

S. M. A. Garcia (✉)
Fluminense Federal University, Niterói, Rio de Janeiro, Brazil
e-mail: marcialsuarez@id.uff.br

A. I. D. Palhares
Rio de Janeiro State University, Rio de Janeiro, Brazil
e-mail: igor.acacio@yahoo.com.br

J.-F. Kremer and B. Müller (eds.), *Cyberspace and International Relations*,
DOI: 10.1007/978-3-642-37481-4_15, © Springer-Verlag Berlin Heidelberg 2014

1 One Starting Point: Security and Technology in the Information Age

The main objective is to understand the transformations that the security studies agenda and international security itself experience due to new information and communications technologies (NCIT), a typical paradigm of the Information Age. Dunn (2007) summarizes the position adopted in this session and discusses common points mentioned in the literature regarding the transformations within the Information Age. Accordingly, he posits that the following aspects must be relativized:

a) a change in the nature of power due to the occurrence of technological change as the centrality of military power is now diminished *vis-à-vis* economic power and economic flows;
b) the relative loss of power of the State because it is no longer the only acting entity of international politics and there is now increased opportunity for non-governmental organizations to position their agendas on the international scene;
c) the widening spectrum of general threats to include asymmetric threats, such as that which threatens the State even though there exists an asymmetry of forces, resources and capabilities; that is, attacking points that compromise the functioning of an industrialized society as a whole and not necessarily attacking a military branch. The literature refers to these attack points and their association to NICTs as the critical infrastructures, thereby making them critical information infrastructures. In the words of Dunn and Brunner (2007):

> The information infrastructure—the complex combination of computer networks and communications systems that serve as the underlying infrastructure for organizations, industries, and the economy—has become a key asset in today's security environment. All critical infrastructures are increasingly dependent on the information infrastructure for a variety of information management, communications, and control functions. This dependence has a strong national-security component, since information infrastructure enables both economic vitality and military and civilian government operations. In particular, the information infrastructures of the government and the military depend on commercial telecommunications providers for everything from logistics and transport to various other functions (Dunn and Brunner 2007; 11).

To develop this study, we analyze Martin Heidegger's (1977) interpretation of the age of the technique, or as the author states, the technical modernity. The fundamental feature of this age is its irreversibility, i.e., the problems and solutions within it will always be technological. In the literature on the technical society or the information society, we find that the common elements in the discussions of the three authors—Paul Virilio, Zygmunt Bauman and Manuel Castells—address the question of time and space. Finally, our discussion follows the path of a critical debate between the Copenhagen School of International Security Studies in exploring an issue previously presented, i.e., the expansion of a technical society as stated by Heidegger, the contraction of time and speed as features of the information society and the dilution of borders, as discussed by Bauman. This theoretical approximation will be put in perspective *vis-à-vis* the capacity of analysis proposed by the Copenhagen School. To do so, the following two questions are fundamental:

a) How do we analyze the levels of conflict and the impact of the conflict on cyberspace?
b) How can we best comprehend the many levels involved in cyber conflict using the Copenhagen School as a theoretical starting point?

2 Martin Heidegger and the Question Concerning Technique: An Introduction to Modern Technique and Contingency Thinking

The discussion on the concept of contingency aims to understand the way in which one can analyze the modern technique, taking as a basic assumption the existence of a space of indeterminacy (which is itself technical modernity).

We consider the French philosopher and author of The Contingency of the Laws of Nature 1920, Boutroux, as one of the few authors who devoted himself to building a philosophy of contingency.

> If they were actually necessary, the laws of nature would signify the immutability and rigidity of death. If they are contingent, they dignify life and constitute points of support or bases which enable us constantly to rise towards a higher life (Boutroux 1920; vii).

On the other hand, Martin Heidegger presents the issue of *danger* and *salvation* as possible results of technical non-concealment. *Danger*, as presented, should be understood as the risk by which a man deeply involved in modern technique loses the possibility to access a more original condition. What is characteristic of the modern technique appears through the means by which it *requires* nature;

> The revealing that rules in modern technology is a challenging *[Herausfordern]*, which puts to nature the unreasonable demand that it supply energy that can be extracted and stored as such. But does this not hold true for the old windmill as well? No. Its sails do indeed turn in the wind; they are left entirely to the wind's blowing. But the windmill does not unlock energy from the air currents in order to store it (Heidegger 1977; 14).

Heidegger penetrates the question of technique and allows us to consider that the technique should not be thought of as simply leading our questioning in a single direction. One must not only ask about the technological instruments if one does not understand what is included in the principle that underlies the modern technique.

3 Reshaping Time and Space: Conceptual Dilemmas to International Relations Theory

Paul Virilio, Zygmunt Bauman and Manuel Castells show the breadth of their perceptions regarding the nature of the conception of territories, boundaries and borders in the twenty-first century. We present these perceptions as we seek to debate the present theoretical perceptions of space and time, real and virtual.

Speed is always pushed beyond what we once imagined to be the limit, whether it be in communications, transportation, labor, wars, food or even in the time that we spend on an operating table or a simple clinical examination. *Increasingly rapid.*

4 The Dromology of Paul Virilio and the Contraction of Time

Among the authors that we could bring to the discussion is Paul Virilio, who promotes a rather iconoclastic analysis of contemporary technique. Virilio speaks of a dromocratic society, that is, a society of speed, of dislocation, and of motion. He also speaks of an *esthétique de la disparition* and states that reality *disappears* before the impact of the technique, lives, and neighborhoods—everything that is in one moment, is not in the next.

Technical modernity offers this type of spectacle, such that the speed of the action and the high degree of the change that can be incurred upon the environment has no parallel in human history. In his study *Speed and Politics*, Virilio reveals certain characteristics of the emergence of a society based on speed and displacement. To do so, he expands beyond his dromology and discusses the ways by which Western society is structured under this assumption is to understand that the velocity and flows of information, people, etc., are a fundamental characteristic of modern Western societies.

Virilio, in his work *Information Bomb*, quotes Paul Morand and exposes the ambiguity of a film technique that is able to decompose a disaster in a series of gentle movements:

> Past, present and future—that old tripartite division of the time continuum—then cedes primacy to the immediacy of a tele-presence which is akin to a new type of relief. This is a relief not of the material thing, but of the event, in which the fourth dimension (that of time) suddenly substitutes for the third: the material volume loses its geometrical value as an 'effective presence' and yields to an audiovisual volume whose self-evident 'tele-presence' easily wins out over the nature of the fact (Virilio 2005; 118).

5 Time and Space in Zygmunt Bauman

In his article *Reconnaissance Frontier Wars of the Planetary-land* (2002), Zygmunt Bauman puts himself on the trail of thought over the fact, which, in a way, opens the twenty-first century. The attacks of 9/11 become significant as a landmark in the political as well as in the sociological analysis. This is the moment when the mainstream of these scientific fields are shaken by the violence of a new phenomenon, global terrorism.

Bauman understands this as the end of the Age of Space, an age that was to have its origin in the Chinese wall, medieval towers and bridges, Siegfried and Maginot lines and the Berlin Wall. It was a time when the territory implied to security, the boundary established the limits for identity and the recognition of foreign and territorial space meant power (Bauman 2002; 82).

From the moment the terrorist threat was planted within and among people, what seemed something apart from and something that was considered a matter of security emerges now as a matter of immediate survival. On the other hand, as the problem of insecurity cannot be resolved locally, the only possibility is the re-discovery of insecurity and the understanding that it can reach everyone, thus implying the need for global solutions (Bauman 2002; 82).

The type of knowledge involved in the composition of a modern technique is a more diffuse knowledge that is not directed toward a specific purpose, but rather, it produces side effects in a continuous way, i.e., as in a technological problem where more technology is necessary, a process that demonstrates the inevitability of modern technique. The modern technique inserts the possibility of distance between the actors, meaning that it is possible for one to reach—regardless of results—any individual without even *seeing his face.*

6 Manuel Castells and the Information Society: Beyond the Frontiers

Manuel Castells (1996) presents perhaps one of the major theoretical-methodological contributions to research on information society in his study *The Rise of a Network Society* where the presumption of territoriality gives the primacy to the concept of flows, shifting and breaking with the traditional notions of space and time.

The theoretical construction of Castells (2004) explores the debate over the network society; however, this concept cannot be fully developed without taking into account its definition of a specific culture of these societies:

> A network society is a society whose social structure is made of networks powered by microelectronics-based information and communication technologies. By social structure, I understand the organizational arrangements of humans in relations of production, consumption, reproduction, experience, and power expressed in meaningful communication coded by culture. A network is a set of interconnected nodes (Castells 2004; 3).

A culture related to a particular type of relationship between knowledge and its reproduction, which, through flows, disperses itself in the environment and focuses on the nodes of greater efficiency, thus generating different degrees of insertion and influence in the information system. The nodes act as checkpoints for this information flow, and progressively we will be able to understand, through Castells analysis, how global society organizes itself on the basis of these nodes in their political, social, economic and cultural contexts.

Castells (2007) analyzes an essential triad—power, communication and information—to understand the political relationships in the twenty-first century. In the network society, relations of power and counter-power unfold over this scenario whereby actors establish relations of power and the capacity of that power is established in terms of the actors' access to information and communication:

> Throughout history communication and information have been fundamental sources of power and counter-power, of domination and social change. This is because the fundamental battle being fought in society is the battle over the minds of the people. The way people think determines the fate of norms and values on which societies are constructed (Castells 2007; 239).

From this approach, and from that of a knowledge society and organized information in the form of a network, we propose a debate on ways and procedures by which the theory of international relations can attempt to comprehend this non-territorial world that is moving at high speed and a world where solidarities are no longer built on the basis of a territoriality aimed at security, but one that should seek, instead, non-territorial security.

7 Cybersecurity and International Relations Theory: Copenhagen School

Barry Buzan, Ole Waever and Jaap de Wilde (1998), in the debate within the international security studies and IR theory, are considered exponents of the Copenhagen School (Guzzini and Jung 2004; Stone 2009), which seeks, in a context of reorganization of the international system in the post-Cold War era, to enlarge and redefine the issues to be addressed within the realm of international security studies.

Positing that what makes an issue a matter of security is to be discursively positioned as an existential threat,[1] these authors affirm that security discourse has been used to legitimize extraordinary actions that extend beyond the existing normative scope.

The operationalization of this new framework for the analysis of issues among the emerging and diverse topics of a post-Cold War security agenda, occurs, by definition, in the units of security analysis whereby the referent object is the thing existentially threatened, the securitizing actor is the one that establishes the issue and states that the referent object is threatened and the functional actor is that which affects the dynamics of the sector analyzed.

8 Through a "New" Methodological Way: Securitization

The authors also outline a methodological division of security issues across sectors, namely, political and military—traditional in regard to international security studies—and economic, societal and environmental, each with specific units of security

[1] Briefly, for Buzan et al. (1998), demonstrating the influence of constructivist formulations in international relations, security would be a self-referential practice: the threat is not objective, but defined in an intersubjective process.

analysis to be observed. This addresses the new complex security agenda, its new themes and its new policies.

The framework of analysis shown by Buzan et al. (1998) translates into a vision in which international security is primarily a discursive matter, with the securitization[2] as a central concept under which may be subject, in theory, any public issue, or any issues conformed into three distinct categories, as a continuum, taking the state as referential:

1. Non-politicized: the State does not address the issue and there is no public debate.
2. Politicized: the theme is part of public policy, requiring government decisions on allocations.
3. Securitized: the extreme face of politicization when the issue is presented as an existential threat and when it demands emergency measures by the State.

The sectors of the theory of securitization would be, in terms of Buzan et al. (1998), the lenses by which the analyst observes issues, and accordingly, it is worth noting that lenses are foisted with the values and characteristics of each sector, that the nature of the threats and the units vary from sector to sector and that securitization can be institutional or *ad hoc* (Buzan et al. 1998: 27).

9 The Copenhagen School and Cybersecurity

While the theme of cyberspace is not specifically addressed by Buzan et al. (1998), it should be emphasized that Nissenbaum (2005), Hansen and Nissenbaum (2009) and Hart (2011), as well as other authors of international literature, apply to cybersecurity the theory developed by the Copenhagen School. This theory proposes that, given the importance acquired by the international security agenda, the adoption of a cyber-sector with its own units of security analysis and its own operating dynamics demonstrates that the literature also supports the application of the framework developed by the Copenhagen School to the issue of cybersecurity.[3]

The main contribution to the cybersecurity debate within the international security studies is offered in a paper written by Lene Hansen and Helen Nissenbaum (2009). These authors attempt to theorize, based on the ideas of the Copenhagen School, methods by which to analyze this subject. Three questions are addressed throughout the text: What are the threats and referent objects of the cyber-sector that distinguish it from other sectors? How can concrete instances of "cyber

[2] As the authors say, "*Thus, the exact definition and criteria of securitization is constituted by the intersubjective establishment of an existential threat with a saliency sufficient to have substantial political effects*" (Buzan et al., 1998: 25).

[3] A more detailed version of this topic is developed in Acácio (2011); Suarez et al (2011).

securitization" be analyzed? How can critical security studies take a "cyber talk" seriously?

The central argument of the authors is the impossibility of keeping cybersecurity embedded in sectors already theorized by the Copenhagen School given the importance that the issue of cybersecurity had been acquiring in the contemporary scenario of international security. Thus, it became incumbent upon new theorists to, in some way, update cybersecurity .

The authors compare the dynamics with the economic sector. The cyber -sector has been continuously interdependent and has had problems in defining geographical boundaries and competences, including the high degree of responsibility of the private sector. However, the potential for securitization of cyber-sector is higher than that of the economic sector.

There is a much stronger bond, however, between cyber-sector security and military security—military security and speed—because the link with this security, the authors note, is the fact that the backbone of the revolution in military affairs relies on digital technologies (Hansen and Nissenbaum 2009: 1162).

Nissenbaum and Hansen draw upon the ideas presented by Deibert (2002) in their discussion of referent objects, threats, policy options and world orders as well as what constitutes national security, state security, private security and network security (Deibert 2002; Hansen and Nissenbaum 2009, p. 1163).

10 Cybersecurity and a "New" Grammar for the Twenty-First Century

Based on previous insights, Hansen and Nissenbaum argue for a specific grammar regarding the cyber-sector, which we critique

> The Copenhagen School has argued that sectors are defined by the specific ways in which distinct "sub-forms" or grammars of securitization tie referent objects, threats, and securitizing actors together (Buzan et al. 1998: 27). This section delineates three security modalities that are specific to the cyber sector." (Hansen and Nissenbaum 2009; 1163)

1 *Hypersecuritization*, whose major premise is the theme the cyberspace presents an existential threat due to the possibility of damage caused by cyber attacks in the social, financial and military sectors and therefore, to the objects of reference of these respective sectors (Hansen and Nissenbaum 2009: 1164). The authors emphasize the similarity of the discourse on the possibility of catastrophic damage with the discourses in the environmental sector, in which the fate of the planet would be irreversibly damned if emergency measures were not taken by citizens and governments. At this point, the fundamental difference lies in the speed with which the cascading effects of a massive cyber-attack could hit people and states (Hansen and Nissenbaum 2009: 1164).

2 *Everyday Security Practice* suggests that this security grammar impacts the legitimacy of the state emergency measure and the acceptance of the emergency measure by the Audience because the speeches constantly mention aspects of

cybersecurity that affect the normal citizen, such as credit card fraud, e-mail hacking, etc. The objectives that the typical security Actors see in this language are to ensure the partnership of individuals to protect networks (using antivirus spywares, etc.) and to make the hypersecuritization of the cyber-sector more acceptable as individuals would then link the elements of catastrophic cyber-attacks to practices they observe in their daily lives (Hansen and Nissenbaum 2009: 1165).

Herein is a curious aspect of the discourses:

> The constitution of the digital as a dangerous space and the "ordinary" individual as an ambiguous partner and a potential threat is supported by medical metaphors like "viruses" and "infected computers" that underscore the need for "caution" and "protection." As in discourses of epidemics and contagion, cyber insecurities are generated by individuals who behave irresponsibly thus compromising the health of the whole(Hansen and Nissenbaum 2009; 1166).

Summarizing the argument:

> [...] Connecting everyday security practices with hyper cascading scenarios, it is this inadvertent or careless behavior within a networked system that move cyber security out of the realm of "corporate security" or "consumer trust" and into the modality of "proper" national % societal security. Moreover, there is a further link between hyper-securitizations and everyday practices in that the claim about the possibilities of disasters happening may be substantiated by the reference to individuals'[...] Linking back to the critical argument of securitization theory, namely that "security" provides governments with the discursive and political legitimacy to adopt radical measures, the question becomes at which point and how these strategies, and their harmonious constitution of state-society relations, can become contested (Hansen and Nissenbaum 2009; 1166).

3 *Technifications*—The idea of this third grammar, or language, according to Hansen and Nissenbaum, is that the environment of the hypothetical and speculative cybersecurity generates room for speeches from technical specialists whereby the knowledge necessary to understand certain technical issues is beyond the ability of a researcher on international security. Increasingly, what happens with respect to this grammar/language is the depoliticization of this issue on the state security agenda, thereby restricting the knowledge and understanding to the opinion of the experts in information security:

> [...] description of the invisible role of most security experts as they have transcended their specific scientific locations to speak to the broader public in a move that is both facilitated by and works to support cyber securitizations claimed by politicians and the media (Hansen and Nissenbaum 2009; 1167).

11 Sectors, Referent Objects and Cybersecurity

The idea is to create a sector specific to the issue of cyber threats and dynamic units of security analysis. Thus, the cybersecurity sector would connect referent objects, such as cyber networks and individuals, to the national or global security. The central purpose of Hansen and Nissenbaum is to define the three security grammars/languages in that security sector—hypersecuritization, daily practices and technifications—because they cannot be found in other sector dynamics presented by the Copenhagen School, albeit the inspiration and credit is appropriately given:

> The most significant lesson of bringing the Copenhagen School to cyber security may be to bring the political and normative implications of "speaking security" to the foreground. Cyber securitizations are particularly powerful precisely because they involve a double move out of the political realm: from the politicized to the securitized, and from the political to the technified, and it takes an inter-disciplinary effort to assess the implications of the move, and possibly to counter it (Hansen and Nissenbaum 2009; 1172).

Proposing the use of the units of security analysis, we argue that the referent object—that which is existentially threatened—would be the protection of critical infrastructures, critical information infrastructures and government websites. The securitizing actor—which places the issue of security by stating that the referent object is under threat—would be the State when it speaks before internal and external audiences about the possibility of cyber-attacks and the need to establish an agenda for such attacks within the State. The functional actor—which affects the dynamics of the sectors analyzed—in this case, would be the media performing the coverage of events, particularly with respect to cyber-attacks on government websites and large private companies.

The sectors would include, if not the separate cyber sector, a dominant military sector—in the case of analyzing state defense policies for cybersecurity—conjugated with dynamics from the political and economic sectors and the emergency rhetoric typically developed in the environmental sector.

The point made by the Copenhagen School and the critical security studies—and we corroborate it—is that the security discourse has served to legitimize actions within the policy because the term "security"—and the logic behind using it in political discourse—gives priority to the theme, thus resulting in its application on a security agenda. This premise regarding the power that the concept of security generates in the field of political practice is supported by Der Derian (1993), one of the first scholars on the topic, is quoted by Nissenbaum (2005):

> No other concept in international relations packs the metaphysical punch, nor commands the disciplinary power of 'security'. In its name peoples have alienated their fears, rights and powers to gods, emperors, and most recently, sovereign states, all to protect themselves from the vicissitudes of nature—as well as from other gods, emperors, and sovereign states. In its name weapons of mass destruction have been developed which transfigured national interest into a security dilemma based on a suicide pact. And, less often noted in IR, in its name billions have been made and millions killed while scientific knowledge has been furthered and intellectual dissent muted (Der Derian 1993; Nissenbaum 2005; 69).

12 Securitization in Modern Technique: The Real to the Virtual

Our analysis necessarily involves the concept of ambivalence, that is, an element that can be conditioned as an element of a certain political reality. In the case of its insertion in an information society, this element of analysis implies that the more a technological device in its various functions of organization and operation management (energy, transportation, financial, etc.) is inserted within the society, the higher the degree by which that same society will be able to build *security modes* that will take into account the political, social, and economic contexts and, in short, the degree of integration within a technological society. Thus, returning to Heidegger, Lomme Devriendt et al. (2011) explore the degree of integration regarding the information society in major cities around the globe, whereby the authors adopt the concept of Manuel Castells (1996) "new spatial logic". From Castells, Devriendt et al. analyze information flows and establish a ranking of these cities within the context of a global information society.

The analysis developed by Devriendt et al. shows the largest city in terms of information flow based on their the global environmental score (GSE), and find that this result is exceptionally close to the outcome of the global financial score according to the Cyber Security Defense Report. Accordingly, we have the United States of America, England, Germany, and France among the players with the greatest projections.

The ambivalence of technology insertion and a *raison d'etre* allow us to consider that the processes of integration in an information society accelerate the flow of information and knowledge, generate new territorialities, and imply a redefinition of the referent object as it loses its materiality and therefore demands a security apparatus that is highly adaptive and complex given the different political, social, economic and technological contexts in which it operates.

The question by which we can summarize our proposal for debate, which only indicates a path of research, is: How does the magnified securitization process of cyber security within the realm of technical societies produce a collateral effect? To increase the security of a highly integrated society in the logic of information flow, it is necessary to enhance the devices that allow such security. However, such devices are only possible by increasing the level of digital inclusion. Therefore, based on this logic, we are engaged in a process without return on cyber security, which allows no retractions thus opening a new logic to analyze the development of the international system.

References

Boutroux, E. (1920). *The contingency of the laws of nature*. New York: The Open Court Publishing Company.

Bauman, Z. (2002). Reconnaissance Wars of the Planetary Frontierland. *Theory, Culture and Society*, *19*(4): 81–90.

Acácio, I. (2011). Segurança cibernética: análise sobre a política de defesa Brasileira (2000–2011). Undergraduate Dissertation. (B.A. in International Relations/Strategic Studies), Universidade Federal Fluminense, Niterói.

Buzan, B., Waever, O., & Wilde, J. (1998). *Security:A new framework for analysis*. London: Lynne Rienner.

Castells, M. (2000). *The rise of the network society*. London: Blackwell Publishers.

Castells, M. (2004). *Network society—a cross-cultural perspective*. London: Edward Elgar Publishing Limited.

Castells, M. (2007). Communication, power and counter-power in the network society. *International Journal of Communication, 1*, 238–266.

Clarke, R., & Knake, R. (2010). *Cyber war: The next threat to national security and what to do about it.* New York: Harper Collins.

Deibert, R. (2002). Circuits of power: Security in the internet environment. In J. N. Rosenau & J. P. Singh (Eds.), *Information technologies and global politics: The changing scope of power and governance* (pp. 115–142). Albany: State University of New York.

Derian, J. D. (1993). The value of security: Hobbes, marx, nietzsche, and baudrillard. In D. Campbell & M. Dillon (Eds.), *The political subject of violence*. Manchester: Manchester University Press.

Devriendt, L., Boulton, A., Brunn, S., et al. (2011). Searching for cyberspace: The position of major cities in the information age. *Journal of Urban Technology, 18*(1), 73–92.

Dunn, M., Mauer, V.& Hensel, F. (2007). Power and security in the information age: Investigating the role of the state in cyberspace. Hampshire: Ashgate.

Dunn, M. & Brunner, E. (2007) Introduction: Information, power and security—an outline of debates and implications In M. Dunn, V. Mauer, & F. Hensel (Eds.), Power and security in the information age: Investigating the role of the state in cyberspace. Hampshire: Ashgate.

Dunn, M. (2007). Securing the information age: The challenges of complexity for critical infrastructure protection and IR theory. In J. Eriksson & G. Giacomello (Eds.), International relations and security in the digital age. London: Routledge.

Guzzini, S., & Jung, D. (2004). *Contemporary security analysis and copenhagen peace research.* London: Routledge.

Hansen, L. & Nissenbaum, H. (2009). Digital disaster, cyber security and the copenhagen school. International Studies Quarterly No. 53 (pp. 1555–1575).

Hart, Catherine. (2011). *Mobilizing the cyberspace race: the securitization of the internet and its implications for civil liberties*. Cyber-Surveillance in Everyday Life: An International Workshop.

Heidegger, M. (1977). The question concerning technology and other essays. (Trans:William Lovitt). New York: Harper and Row.

Hensel, F. (2007). Critical infrastructures: Vulnerabilities, threats, responses. CSS analysis in security policy, n. 16, v. 2. Zurich: Center for Security Studies (CSS).

Nissenbaum, H. (2005). Where computer security meets national security. *Ethics and Information Technology*, *7*(2), 61–73.

Stone, M. (2009). Security according to buzan: A comprehensive analysis. Security Discussion Papers Series, No. 1, Spring.

Suarez, M. (2012). *As Guerras de George W*. Appris, Curitiba: Bush e o Terrorismo no Século XXI. Ed.

Suarez, M., Acácio,I., Brancoli, F. & Monteiro, L. (2011). The limits and perspectives of securitization: Studies in the south american contemporary security context. In: ISSS/ISAC Annual Conference 2011. Irvine, Califórnia, USA.

Virilio, Paul. (2005). *The information bomb*. London: Verso.

Virilio, Paul. (2006). Speed and politics. Los Angeles: Semiotext (e).

Index

J.-F. Kremer and B. Müller (eds.), *Cyberspace and International Relations*,
DOI: 10.1007/978-3-642-37481-4, © Springer-Verlag Berlin Heidelberg 2014

Printed in the USA
CPSIA information can be obtained
at www.ICGtesting.com
LVHW010634171223
766672LV00004B/114

9 783642 374807